About the author

Stellan Vinthagen is Inaugural Endowed Chair in the
Study of Nonviolent Direct Action and Civil Resistance and professor of sociology at the University
of Massachusetts, Amherst. He is also a council
member of War Resisters' International, academic
adviser to the International Center on Nonviolent
Conflict (ICNC), co-founder of the Resistance
Studies Network (www.resistancestudies.org) and
editor of the *Journal of Resistance Studies*. Since
1980, he has been an educator, organiser and
activist and has participated in more than thirty
nonviolent civil disobedience actions, for which he
has served in total more than one year in prison.

A THEORY OF NONVIOLENT ACTION

HOW CIVIL RESISTANCE WORKS

Stellan Vinthagen

Zed Books
LONDON

A Theory of Nonviolent Action: How civil resistance works was first published in 2015 by Zed Books Ltd, The Foundry, 17 Oval Way, London SE11 5RR, UK

www.zedbooks.co.uk

Set in Monotype Plantin and FFKievit by Ewan Smith, London
Index: ed.emery@thefreeuniversity.net
Cover designed by www.stevenmarsden.com

A catalogue record for this book is available from the British Library

ISBN 978-1-78032-054-0 hb
ISBN 978-1-78032-515-6 pb
ISBN 978-1-78032-055-7 pdf
ISBN 978-1-78032-053-3 epub
ISBN 978-1-78032-507-1 mobi

CONTENTS

FIGURES AND TABLE

Figures

Table

ACKNOWLEDGEMENTS

Books are collective efforts. Although I am ultimately responsible for the existing text, many have made it possible. And for that I am grateful.

Over the years a lot of people have participated in classes, workshops, lectures and seminars where parts of this material have been presented and discussed. Students, activists and colleagues in several different countries – but mainly at the University of Gothenburg, and University of Massachusetts, Amherst – have contributed with suggestions, critique and questions. Simultaneously, my own practical experiences within movements – particularly the Plowshares, the global justice movement and World Social Forum, the Faslane 365, and the Freedom Flotilla to Gaza – as well as my extensive fieldwork and contact visits to amazing activists in the Global South have been formative. These conversations and practical experiments with nonviolent activism have been the laboratory that made the formulation of a new theoretical framework possible.

I want especially to thank the unique Nordic Nonviolence Study Seminar (Nornos) and our first decade of discussions together: Majken Jul Sörensen, Jörgen Johansen, Henrik Frykberg, Minoo Koefoed, Daniel Ritter, Mattias Linder, and Klaus Engell. The role of this seminar with experienced activists and researchers has been absolutely vital.

Furthermore, Ken Barlow at Zed Books showed an early belief in this project and encouraged me to complete it. It took some time and much effort to rewrite the text from the original Swedish manuscript of 500 pages (my PhD from 2005), and to get it translated with the help of James Garrabrant. This translation work received economic support from the International Center on Nonviolent

Conflict (ICNC). Thanks to an anonymous reviewer and the excellent work of the copyeditor, Judith Forshaw, the text took an important step forward. Finally, Kika Sroka-Miller and Ewan Smith helped out with the finishing stages of publication.

Lastly, I am grateful to my family, Li and Ninja, as well as to the communities where I live, the Eco-Village Krossekärr, Sweden, and the Pioneer Valley Cohousing, Amherst, USA.

Stellan Vinthagen
Amherst, September 2015

INTRODUCTION: THE PRACTICE OF NONVIOLENT ACTION

On 22 November 1999, solidarity activists made their way into the military training camp of Fort Benning in the USA. They entered in memory of the murder of six Jesuit priests, their housekeeper and her daughter, who, on this day ten years earlier, were killed by the military of El Salvador. For the occasion, the activists dressed in mourning and entered the camp carrying coffins and crosses. Names of people who had been killed or tortured by regimes in Latin America were written on the crosses. Some of the activists wore white death masks; others painted their faces blood-red. Among the activists were Hollywood star Martin Sheen, Catholic priest Daniel Berrigan, and a civil rights activist from Guatemala, Adiana Portillo-Bartow. During one weekend, 12,000 people of varying backgrounds and nationalities gathered to take part in a protest meeting against the US army's School of the Americas at Fort Benning; 4,408 of these people took the final step onto the grounds of the military training camp where officers from Latin America are educated in warfare and interrogation techniques. The purpose of the action was to shut down the facility by occupying it. By their persistent and peaceful presence, they hoped to disturb the business as usual of the camp.

Soon, the police arrested them. Through discussions and training, they had prepared themselves mentally for arrest. Each solidarity activist risked several months' imprisonment. Some were taken away singing. Some quarrelled with the police about obedience to a system that violates human rights. In accordance with the guidelines of the action, the activists did not use any violence against people when defending their occupation. Some sat down, others prayed, and some held one another's arms. They did not run away. They stood their ground, facing the strongest empire in world history – the USA – with their un-defended bodies. The action was public, advertised in advance to the authorities, and those arrested took complete personal responsibility for the 'offence' they committed. The following year another 3,000 activists were again arrested. It still goes on. This is one example of a special kind of resistance action, called *nonviolent action*, which is sometimes also called nonviolent resistance, nonviolent direct action, civil disobedience or civil resistance, among other terms – these are some of the sister concepts we will come back to. 'Civil disobedience' is a particular kind of nonviolent action in which the law is challenged, or even broken, in order to resist some kind of 'injustice'.

A nonviolent movement is understood here to be a movement where people in their action repertoire let their nonviolent means express their (nonviolent) goals. In a nonviolent movement, activ-ists contest 'violence', 'oppression' or 'injustice' while they them-selves avoid using such means. Nonviolent movements relate to a tradition formulated by Mohandas K. Gandhi, the person who created the concept of 'nonviolent resistance'. My interest lies in political nonviolent movements that make claims to contest a dominant or hegemonic power, and act within a society where organised violence and oppression are legitimised, normalised or accepted de facto by a vast population. In the anti-colonial liberation movement in India, nonviolent resistance was given both a practical and a theoretical content within a certain context and dynamic relations, which furthered the development and diffusion of the nonviolent repertoire.

This book aims to develop a conceptual framework and a new theoretical understanding of what 'nonviolence' is. It will do that by summarising and pointing out the weaknesses within previous research on nonviolence (Chapter 1), and by suggesting a new basic understanding of the concept, based on how nonviolent movements have applied it: as a combination of acting *against* violence and trying to do that *without* using violence themselves (Chapter 2). Chapters 3 to 7 then outline the proposed 'four-dimensional perspective' of nonviolence, while the final chapter brings the discussion and the whole set of sub-concepts together into a new theory of how we can understand this fascinating social phenomenon.

Throughout history, social movements have transformed systems at both national and global levels. The anti-slavery movement, the workers movement, the anti-apartheid movement and the freedom movements against the socialist dictatorships in Eastern Europe, to mention but a few, have extended beyond national borders and instigated real change.[1] In the current transition of globalisation, the forms taken by the state, society and the economy are changing fundamentally, creating new possibilities and increasing the mobilisation of movements. The last few decades have witnessed the fall of some forty dictatorships as a result of unarmed struggle, and, according to a study by Karatnycky and Ackerman (2005), the more nonviolent these movements were, the greater the degree of democratisation observed.[2] In their award-winning book *Why Civil Resistance Works* (2011), Chenoweth and Stephan show that even maximalist political goals are twice as likely to be achieved when nonviolent forms of struggle are used. Their results are based on comparing the last century's major political campaigns, including armed struggle. Nevertheless, much research remains to be done if we are to explain this relationship. The question is *how* civil resistance works, and that is what underpins this book.

The phenomenon of exercising nonviolence in a social movement, with the aim of achieving social change, is not an uncommon one.[3] Even so, nonviolence often goes unrecognised in academic research and mass media, and, when it does receive attention, its activities are often labelled as 'pacifistic' or lumped together with other traditions such as 'protests'. Its strategies, logics and repertoires are still unclear.

Both small- and large-scale nonviolent actions take place all over the world. Since the 1980s, the Brazilian Landless Workers' Movement (Movimento Sem Terra or MST) has carried out more than 2,000 peaceful land occupations. In the early 1990s in India, there was widespread nonviolent resistance against the impact of the structural adjustment programme: in December 1993, 5,000 farmers, students and unionists were arrested; in August 1994, 75,000 Indians nationwide were involved in peaceful actions and risked arrest.[4] In 1998, Germany recorded its largest police operation in the post-war period, to handle action against the transportation of the Castor nuclear waste containers. In April 2003, 7,500 people in the United States undertook 300 actions around the country to show their disagreement with the regime's illegal attack on Iraq.[5] Nonviolent movements have often preceded dramatic societal changes, the fall of dictatorships, peace agreements or radical democratisations.[6] But how do they do it?

There are numerous contemporary movements – from regional and national to transnational – that have not only followed but developed the nonviolence tradition. Among these are[7] the Civil Rights Movement in the USA in the 1950s, the anti-apartheid movement in South Africa, the anti-nuclear weapons movement in the 1960s, the environmental movement's occupations of con-

struction sites and the tree-huggers of the Indian Chipko movement, the first Palestinian Intifada's purchasing boycotts and
strikes against the occupational power of Israel, and the peace
camps at nuclear weapons bases across Western Europe during
the 1980s, when people set up camps at these bases and turned
political actions into daily life, as happened at the women's
peace camp at Greenham Common in England. Nonviolence
has also been used by the global justice movement, which took
part in peaceful resistance at top meetings of global regimes,
for example in Seattle in November 1999.[8]

For some movements, methods of nonviolence are a temporary *tactic*. For others they are a predominant *strategy*. And for
yet other movements they are even a *norm*, an ideology or a way
of life. Tactics are about winning a battle, strategy about winning the war. In tactical nonviolence, nonviolence characterises
an action or a campaign. During the World Trade Organization
blockade in Seattle, for example, very different groups united
under a *tactical* agreement on nonviolent guidelines for the
action at that particular time and in that location. At the end
of the 1980s, the so-called tree-hugger movement in Sweden's
Bohuslän Province attempted to prevent the construction of
the Scan Link motorway by, among other means, climbing into
trees that were to be cleared. As a result, nonviolence came to
characterise their entire campaign.[9] Originally, the predominant
strategy of Scandinavian social democracy, like the majority of
workers' movements before the First World War, consisted of
resistance by peaceful means, anti-militaristic ideology, and
an orientation towards negotiation. Likewise, nonviolent *norms*
were a distinguishing feature of the Indian anti-colonial movement.

Fighting war and oppression with peaceful and libertarian means

Nonviolent movements attempt to *fight war and oppression with peaceful and libertarian means*. These movements demonstrate the possibility of a peaceful social construction, even under difficult circumstances. Of course, this is complicated and requires the development of a practice of nonviolence founded on experience and systematic knowledge generation.

Research into nonviolence should describe both the possibilities and limitations of nonviolence. The aim of problematising nonviolence is to expedite peaceful liberation by contributing new theoretical and practical ways of handling its inherent problems. Hopefully, it can even lead to *critical movement repertoires* (new approaches, means of action, methods and strategies) through which actors can evaluate the social implications of their actions. New concepts for the various social aspects of nonviolence may help nonviolent activists implement them in practice. Consequently, theory and practice create a unity.

My aim is to develop sociological concepts for nonviolence by *using a sociological perspective to interpret and conceptually describe nonviolent moments in conflict situations (which are enacted in societies characterised by violence and oppression), in order to develop analytical tools and a critical movement repertoire* – and thereby further a combination of critical science and peaceful liberation struggle.

Polarisation between various meanings of nonviolence To begin with, we need to see how others have used the concept of 'nonviolence' and where any problems lie. Nonviolence is sometimes criticised for being reactionary, treasonous, a religious or moral involvement in political tactics, or a non-strategic pinioning of resistance movements' opportunities, which in turn serves only those in power.[10] Some even bluntly call it 'slave mentality',[11] 'sectarian'[12] or 'pathology'.[13] Stereotypes, as well as unsophisticated and stubborn theses about the pre-eminence of nonviolence, have complicated impartial efforts for peaceful liberation.[14] Much of the criticism against nonviolence is aimed at its partiality to absolute, universal, religious and moral arguments made by its proponents, not least among them Gandhi. Yet at times, nonviolence has been proclaimed to be the most effective solution for essentially all problems. It has even been justified based on the world's divine order or the moral goodness of individuals. Gandhi states: 'All miracles are due to the silent and effective working of invisible forces. Non-violence is the most invisible and the most effective.'[15] Unfortunately, Gandhi and other dedicated supporters of nonviolence sometimes serve as the greatest hindrance to getting more people to discover the phenomenon.

Nevertheless, pragmatism has guided practitioners of nonviolence through difficult situations in which struggle by military means was not a realistic option. Only afterwards did many react to its religious packaging. This reaction gained momentum in the 1960s and led to the development of an anti-religious and anti-moral 'technique approach' to nonviolent actions, as discussed in Chapter 1. The reaction to a one-sided interpretation then sparked a new bias: instead of moral or divine excellence, the universal effectiveness of nonviolence is suggested, and nonviolent action is seen as the instrument for every group that desires to fight a ruler.

This historical development has characterised nonviolence studies and divided the fields into two camps, with different groups' approaches to nonviolence being categorised as either a 'lifestyle' or a 'tactic'.[16] Lifestyle nonviolence is the activist's principal ethical or religious reasoning. It is characterised by their approach to life. In contrast, tactical – or, as the activists prefer to label themselves, 'technical' – nonviolence is the activist's effectiveness-orientation or anti-moral nonviolence, where furthering one's own goals is what counts most of all. This distinction can already be found in Gandhi, where it is called 'the nonviolence of the strong' and applied as a lifestyle with a belief in nonviolence, and where the 'nonviolence of the weak' is defined as a practical method in the sense that the result is the only thing that matters.[17]

Burrowes puts the 'pragmatic' and the 'principled' in contrast to each other.[18] The pragmatic seeks effectiveness, separates ends and means, views the interests of the conflicting parties as incompatible and aims to harm the opponent (without the use of violence). The principled chooses nonviolence for ethical reasons, views it as impossible to separate ends and means, sees conflicts as common problems and accepts the suffering that the opponent inflicts on the movement.

In many ways, these perspectives have reached a deadlock. However, I propose a third position that entails investigating the ramifications of the concept 'pragmatic'. I claim that nonviolence literature uses the concept incorrectly when it labels it 'amoral' or reduces it to being technically instrumental. This third position lies beyond the moral high priests of nonviolence and anti-moral strategy generals – it constitutes a *social pragmatism of nonviolence*.

Nonviolence as practical social knowledge In order to develop a sociological description of nonviolence, we must discard the polarisation overshadowing nonviolence studies. Polarisation is a simplification of the complexity of nonviolence. In fact, it is

an 'illusion'.[19] Gandhi understood that <u>nonviolence was a matter of combining strategy and morality</u>.[20] It is a combination, a
means of action that may be called 'principled pragmatism'.[21]
It derives from social beings integrating nonviolence into a
specific context. In the societal context, it involves groups in
action and it pertains to normative communities both carrying
out and subject to nonviolent actions. There are other aspects
of nonviolence that need be neither technical nor principled:
for example, aesthetic aspects that represent nonviolence as a
phenomenon that engages people.

My interpretation of nonviolence is characterised by a de-
emphasised perspective within nonviolence studies: nonviolence
as practical social knowledge or as *social pragmatism*. Here, social
pragmatism corresponds to *socially rooted practice*:[22] that is, a
practice meaningful in its consequences within a certain social
context.

My perspective rests on the assumption that humans can create their surroundings based on pre-existing materials. A *social
construction* of nonviolence requires a *practical knowledge*, both
to be possible and to be effective. In this regard, it demands
special knowledge. But instead of practical *technical* knowledge,
it concerns the practical *social* knowledge required to carry out a
specific kind of action, a nonviolent action in a particular context.

The dichotomous moral view that is the basis of the division
of nonviolence into lifestyle and tactics can be overcome with the
idea of nonviolence as social pragmatism. <u>Pragmatic nonviolence
has certain similarities with the two other types, but its morality
and techniques are socially rooted and based on practical knowledge of how groups function in their particular normative order</u>.
Nonviolence literature presents pragmatism as non-moral simply
because it stresses practical political consequences more than

moral systematics or a logically consequent theory. However, social pragmatism involves the practical consequences of action in *social* situations: what happens based on the actual experience of people, how people react and deal with each other's actions. Pragmatism does not assume that there are abstract principles or isolated techniques without a social context; rather, it assumes that the interaction occurs within a historically specific social order. Since every social group has a normative structure, even norms play a part in pragmatism. Thus, one can be a proponent of nonviolence if one perceives that this form of struggle is more effective for certain (long-term) goals in a certain (normative) social context.

Nonviolence is commonly motivated by externally imposed philosophical moral systems.[23] However, I use morality in another sense, one that affects social norms, sanctioned contexts and legitimate rules of action, as it refers to the development of moral representation among concrete, collective communities. Morality is relevant to how nonviolence works in each social group, precisely by virtue of existent and persistent notions of the approval or disapproval of actions. Thus, this type of socialised morality in groups, organisations, movements or societies cannot be disregarded when evaluating the possibilities of resistance. A resistance that does not consider the prevailing social morality will seem difficult to understand for those who are part of the moral community.

Therefore, moral nonviolence affects social dynamics and weighs heavily upon the social techniques and effectiveness of nonviolence. The classic dichotomy between lifestyle (moral principles) and tactics/techniques (effective principles) may mean that one overlooks the connection between (social) morality and (social) effectiveness.

I adopt the perspective that the sociality of nonviolence (non-violence embedded in social life) can be understood as a *social pragmatism* (normatively rooted in a community). Accordingly, in the chapters that follow I try to provide a conceptual description of how nonviolence is expressed socially.

Practical knowledge is a type of knowledge that cannot be completely captured theoretically, but must be acquired in order to be grasped. For instance, you can learn to ride a bicycle only by trying to do so. As practical social knowledge, nonviolence can be obtained only by carrying out nonviolent actions. The aim of my theoretical analysis is not to reproduce the knowledge itself – like a bicycle manual – but to describe the social practices that comprise the performance of nonviolence. I develop concepts and a theoretical perspective that allow for the systematic and critical study of the practice. Moreover, having concepts for various moments of action even helps further the practice itself.

The circumstances that we perhaps do not reflect on need to be delineated so that we can understand what enables nonviolent disobedience. Breaking the rules requires an understanding of the rule or norm that is broken – particularly if that breach is to retain creative space in locked situations, and to mobilise thousands of people: that is, if it is to be a nonviolent movement's civil disobedience.

The concept of nonviolence: a suggestion Nonviolence is commonly defined as an *action without violence*. The core lesson of the classic study of nonviolence, *The Politics of Nonviolent Action* by Gene Sharp (1973), is that nonviolence is a set of actions one performs or refuses to perform *without violence*.[24] I claim that this view of nonviolence does not correspond to the concept's historical use by nonviolent movements and its originator: Gandhi.[25]

Nonviolence is more than an action without violence. Similarly, everything that is done without violence does not constitute nonviolence.

In my preliminary definition (which will be expounded later), nonviolence consists of a combination of two factors: *without violence* and *against violence*.[26] Thus, nonviolence has two dimensions and its means of action combine both.

> Nonviolence = without violence + against violence
> Nonviolence – a two-sided phenomenon

For now, it will suffice to view *without violence* as not using violence oneself and *against violence* as counteracting the violence of others.

The point is that we need both of these definitions simultaneously in order to discuss nonviolence. An act does not become nonviolent simply because one does not use violence – walking, for example. Nor does an act become nonviolent simply because one fights against violence – for example, when armed UN soldiers patrol a border in order to observe a ceasefire agreement. However, a group of unarmed officers walking along the same border and attempting to prevent conflicts without violence can be said to be exercising nonviolence. It is precisely through fighting violence in such a way that one refrains from using violence that the act becomes nonviolent.

To act nonviolently is first and foremost not an act without violence. If this were the unique characteristic of nonviolence, then nonviolence would simply be attributed a non-property, to not act violently, which in itself is a non-action. This would be absurd. What makes an action interesting is that it is a specific way of acting, not that it occurs without a certain action.

Moreover, the category 'action without violence' is so broad that it becomes a trivial concept (and would include the liberation of British India, sleep, science and walks in the forest). This would be as petty and misguided as dividing colours into green and not green. As we will see, a nonviolent action occurs in relation to other parties and to the situation in which it is performed. It is not a special behaviour that can be conceptualised as distinct from the social context.

Let's take an example: the ordinary and overtly conventional act of growing vegetables. In itself it is neither a nonviolent action nor a political act. Growing vegetables is a normal, human subsistence activity performed throughout the world. Yet in a situation where a few own all the land and those without land starve, growing vegetables can become an act of resistance. An example is the reaction of the landless activists in Brazil's MST to one of the world's most unjust divisions of land. The landless people have formed groups that have forgone permission and taken up residence on land belonging to others. They have begun to cultivate the land and have refused to leave it, despite threatening exhortations from landowners, armed private militia, governments and police. Violent means are frequently used to drive out these landless occupants. As a result, a number of them do not dare repeat their act of resistance. Yet MST often succeeds in remobilising these landless activists and gathering new people who have no hope of obtaining a piece of land. When the land is reoccupied and new plastic tents are set up for the residents and the earth is tilled again, that is when you can say that the nonviolent struggle has, in fact, begun.

On average, one landless farmworker belonging to this national occupation movement is killed each week. Sometimes the police kill them, but for the most part it is the private landowners' militia who do so. Despite the landowning aristocracy controlling the majority of mass media, solidarity groups aiming to assist the land occupants arise both in cities and in the countryside, both in Brazil and internationally. So when academics, human rights activists and legal representatives act in solidarity with MST, they broaden the conflict and provide a supplementary array of methods. The result is the birth of a nonviolent movement. Thousands of people become engaged and different social groups get involved; various methods are applied and the struggle is upheld by a number of support structures and internal popular education, as well as by the generation of public opinion, meetings and the formation of special organisations.

If the landless occupants continue to be repressed, if they continue to return to their land each time they are arrested or driven off, if they continue to fight for their rights in the media, on the street, in squares, in fields and in the courtrooms, and if they continue to risk being killed or robbed of what little they own – then, in effect, all the components of a nonviolent struggle are in place and nonviolence has been realised. An action has been carried out and it has been repeated. Several different groups have formed an alliance and have succeeded in supporting each other to uphold their nonviolent action – despite violent repression.

The point is that any commonplace and conventional act can generally be transformed into a nonviolent act depending on its relation to the violence and oppression that prevail in a specific context.

The challenge to explain the social logic of nonviolence

Violence is exerted in various forms, both by and against individuals and collectives. In principle, nonviolence can be directed against all variations of violence. However, there are few nonviolent activists interested in, or even against, all forms of violence. Activists normally focus on a certain type of violence.

In this context, I emphasise the practitioner of violence that has demonstrably been the most important throughout history: the state. The state has a unique capacity for violence. It has a monopoly on violence and attempts to maintain the legitimacy of violence. The cases discussed below illustrate the state's direct exercise of violence through the police, the military or the assertion of repressive and oppressive structures. Yet sometimes a state acts via agents or in an alliance with non-governmental organisations: armed militia, guerrillas, mafias and other groups.

The violence exercised by the state or its allied groups is especially problematic since the capacity for violence is so extensive that it is sanctioned by the government's power structures. The violence is often embedded in militarism and is a component of a hegemonic power alliance, ensuring that large groups of people perceive the exercise of violence as justified. This makes nonviolent activism difficult. Although violence by individuals in political or private conflicts is also difficult to manage, state violence constitutes a comparatively overwhelming opponent. Nonviolence against the state's violence is a matter of undermining the exercise of violence. In the long term, it is a matter of undermining the capacity, hegemony and legitimacy that makes violence so powerful. Consequently, nonviolence involves resistance to violence. It is a direct attack and an attack against its structural basis of future attacks. For that reason, we can say that nonviolence depends on breaking the practice of the required accommodation of and obedience to violence. Nonviolence entails a moment of disobedience or a breach with the requirement of submission. The power maintained by violence becomes a power that nonviolence must undermine to attain success. The great challenge for the nonviolent struggle is not to stop the violence that is exercised at the moment, but to make the apparatus of violence so weak that it can be transformed into a new power structure in which the regime's exercise of violence is severely limited and subordinated into a true democracy and system of justice.

In relation to this, nonviolent actions can become a question of: 1) doing something without using violence despite the risk of being subjected to violence; or 2) refusing to use violence, despite the risk of being subjected to violence. Nonviolence is always related to violence and is a matter of doing or refusing to do a certain action in such a relationship. What one does or refuses to do involves a short-term or long-term undermining of violence. Like other actions, nonviolence is doing a specific thing or abstaining from doing a specific thing.

This means that nonviolence involves the risk of being subjected to reprisals from the very violence it is attempting to undermine. This also means that nonviolence continually transgresses expected behaviours and the conventional reactions of flight, submission or violent defence. To obey a power backed by violence (such as a dictatorship, the mafia, militarism or state power) is to counteract the struggle against violence. Anyone who refuses to obey laws, orders or rules as demanded by those in power is disobedient. One can also be called disobedient if the way one acts differs from what is expected, tolerated or prescribed by the prevailing power structure. Even in these cases, nonviolent activists risk reprisals. Subordinates are expected not to form alternative institutions, movements or other ways of living, or competing economic, cultural or political organisations. Representatives of power can ignore or ridicule such alternatives or, as Gandhi would have called them, 'constructive programmes'. But if these constructive alternatives grow to such a size that they challenge the legitimacy or effectiveness of the predominant power structure's own institutions, then they run a great risk of oppression. Constructive alternatives do not fundamentally differ from nonviolent disobedience, as nonviolence both creates alternatives to violence and undermines violence. Because nonviolence always stands in relation to violence (both as an alternative to and resistance against it), it entails an action that risks encountering violent repression.

A difficult challenging of norms Social interactions are regulated by action norms: that is, informal rules regulating accepted group behaviour. These action norms – sometimes formalised by law – are precisely what the nonviolent activists break. Like the violation of norms, decisions, rules or law, disobedience too derives from rules that govern normal, ordinary, intelligible, legal aspects of the social order. As soon as a form of disobedience defies a social order, it meets reactions from others, as recognised rules are generally not broken in a social community without there being consequences of some kind (control measures, internal conflict, punishment, reduced support, and so on). The movement as a whole, or an individual activist, risks being condemned or labelled corrupt, irresponsible, naïve, terroristic or treacherous, or disregarded in other ways as a participant in a legitimate process and community.[27] Another strategy of dismissal is to treat the movement as irrelevant and to approach it offhandedly or to ridicule it.[28] Slander and false accusations can also discredit the movement, as when the FBI spread rumours about Martin Luther King's 'affairs with women'.

Even if a movement has popular support, it periodically risks being disqualified by its opponents who have a stronger foothold in the existing order and therefore have a greater influence over the moderators of the public discourse.

Thus the inbuilt violation of norms prompts the socially problematic action repertoire of nonviolent disobedience. The action is not performed easily by the actor, and it is not necessarily understood by others, since – unlike established behaviour – it breaks sanctioned rules or goes against legitimate norms.

Choosing to be vulnerable Nonviolence is not just a problematic norm violation but also a form of risk taking. That is to say, resistance, whether violent or nonviolent, is a kind of risk taking. One can lose everything, even one's life. In this respect, the organised use of violence (war) and the relatively unknown nonviolence are similar. Both entail struggle, but the means and aims are fundamentally different. The nonviolent action repertoire presupposes the restraint of impulsive or violent self-defence skills acquired through military training. In cases where humans are violently attacked, violence is normally seen as justified. However, the culturally established behaviour of violence must be counteracted in order to facilitate nonviolent action. It requires a great deal of effort to maintain nonviolence and to make it intelligible.

In a sociological analysis of civil disobedience, Cohen and Arato (1994) describe the means of action as 'self-limiting radicalism', since the radical breach of the law is combined with a peaceable responsibility for the action before the reaction of the power structure. For instance, the activists who occupied the School of the Americas weren't deterred by the risk of arrest. Proud of their actions, they openly took responsibility for what they had done, despite the risk of considerable punishment. In other words, one may claim that nonviolence (not just nonviolent disobedience) entails taking a risk (through resistance) and at the same time making oneself vulnerable to violence (by depriving oneself of self-defence with violent means). A self-assumed risk where one does not try to protect oneself using violent defence, despite a serious risk to one's life and safety, is a behaviour that seemingly goes against the instinct of self-preservation. This vulnerable risk taking is an enigmatic characteristic of nonviolent resistance that must be elucidated.

Making new behaviour normal Individual nonviolent actions carried out by small groups of activists can be interpreted as odd examples, exceptions from the everyday political means of expression that can be (dis)regarded through comparison with deviant subcultures, peculiar psychological characteristics or extremist ideology. Yet how are we to understand recurring, collective actions that happen throughout various historical epochs, in different parts of the world, that pertain to different issues and against different kinds of social orders, and that are carried out by people belonging to social categories with widely differing interests? How can we understand nonviolent actions as a socially regular or *normalised behaviour*: that is, a socially legitimate, sanctioned and common behaviour in a society?

How is it possible that thousands of people persistently struggle for what they believe in without using violence, despite the fact that they subject themselves to violent repercussions? And how is it possible that people continue conducting illegal acts of resistance even when the most critical opponents in society do not resist? An encompassing culture of obedience is common, even in countries with strong nonviolent movements, for instance the USA and Brazil. Social critics in the USA do not normally openly break the state's laws; nor do those who view a breach of regulation as justified. Still, the nonviolent actions against the military training camp the School of the Americas continue, although fewer disobey today. So far, more than 10,000 activists have peacefully broken the law in opposition to the military's training camp. The disobedience is collective and regular, but nationally unusual and abnormal in a society where legalism and militarism are normalised. The majority of the landless peasants in Brazil do not dare occupy the large landowners' land due to the risk of being murdered by death squads. Nevertheless, more than 300,000 families have peacefully occupied land over the decades.

The nonviolent action challenge

When considered together, the three characteristics of nonviolent action – norm violation, vulnerability and normalisation – are a challenge to understand and explain. How are movements (in concrete social contexts) capable of constructing *nonviolent action that becomes regular and normalised, despite nonviolence being a puzzling action repertoire comprising vulnerable risk taking that breaks the expectations, normalcy and regularity of an established social order?*

It appears that the development of nonviolent action in a given context requires considerable experimental effort.[29] However, even when nonviolence activists eventually succeed in finding a specific and complete means of action that mobilises a movement, the nonviolent act is characterised by dominant cultures,[30] historical structures, and interactions with other actors involved in the conflict.[31] Thus the genuinely interesting scientific problem with nonviolent resistance is not the choice that people make to *not* use violence or to break the laws and norms, but how a social diversity develops, succeeds and upholds this complex and deviant alternative form of action.

Just like lawful protests or violent actions, nonviolent actions have their own strategies, techniques and unique logic. The organised use of violence – war – has changed dramatically throughout history. There are veritable rifts between the wooden club and the nuclear weapon, between the concentrated army on the battlefield and the key operations of special forces, between the trumpet signal and the high-tech information structure, between armies of farmers and professional soldiers. The violent power of war has become possible through a systematic com-bination of practical experience and theoretical research. The antithesis of war as a means in a conflict – organised nonviolent action – works in a similar way. The strategies of nonviolence are developed through experimentation with new practical ideas that then spread to other movements which adapt the forms to new contexts.[32]

In this book I develop a sociological perspective on how movements construct nonviolent actions. The first chapter is concerned with the main *social theories and concepts* used in studies of nonviolence: what distinguishes the theories and which concepts are used to describe the sociality of nonviolence.

Chapter 2 attempts to frame the concept of nonviolence by answering the question: how can we differentiate nonviolence historically as a movement's collective action and philosophi-cally as an idea structure? In this regard, my use of the con-cept of nonviolence is anchored in its application in historical movements. In line with my pragmatic orientation, this chapter discerns a specific historical and social phenomenon that com-bines practice and ideas. This lays a foundation for the following conceptual development and the subsequent discussion, which is an investigation of types of action.

Chapter 3 proceeds from the following question: which concepts are needed in order to describe the means of nonviolent action and their relation to rationality? First, I discuss how acts can be interpreted as being rational (motivated by reason) and meaningful (intelligible and possible to understand), in part as a form of 'communication' with the help of symbolic interaction.

The following chapters focus on the four types of action rationality that comprise the basis of a more detailed conceptual development. Chapter 4 concentrates on the issue of why concepts are needed in order to explore how we, through nonviolence, can handle competing truths and propositions in a conflict. Using Habermas's theory of communicative action, I discuss which concepts are required in order to describe the way in which the nonviolent struggle's action repertoire is oriented towards understanding and an attempt at consensus, thereby promoting Habermas's 'ideal speech situation'.

Chapter 5 discusses nonviolence based on the following question: which concepts are needed in order to describe how an individual, through nonviolence, can address *power relations* and oppression in a conflict?

Chapter 6 concentrates on elements of organised dehumanisation of the other. The chapter is based on an examination of the concepts required in order to describe how an individual, through nonviolence, can manage the group's hatred and images of the enemy in a conflict. The Gandhian point that self-suffering can break stereotypical representations or emotional distance between conflicting parties is reinterpreted with the help of Goffman's drama model. In this way, the analysis highlights 'utopian enactment' and puts suffering in parentheses.

Chapter 7 proceeds from the assumption that societies permeated by violence have a normative order and socialisation that permits violence, makes people prone to violence and normalises oppression. The possibility of a society with fundamentally less violence is predicated on another normative order and a new socialisation. The chapter makes note of previous discussions showing that nonviolence not only *breaks* norms but also *claims* norms. The chapter explores the concepts that are needed to describe how an individual can normalise nonviolence in a society characterised by violence and oppression.

Thus far, my argument has shown that nonviolence can be illustrated using four dimensions of rationality: communicative, strategic, dramaturgical and normative. This prompts the question of how to describe the unitary action repertoire's social integration. In the section ('Nonviolence as a social whole') that precedes the final chapter, I ask: how can we coordinate the values and actions of nonviolence within a social whole, a working *nonviolent society*?

In Chapter 8, I summarise the results of my investigation and discuss the internal relationships of the various concepts. This reveals how, ideally, it seems possible to combine elements in the repertoire of nonviolence in a productive way, but how internal opposition makes the ideal impossible to realise completely and permanently.

1 | NONVIOLENT ACTION STUDIES

Which main social theories and concepts are used to understand nonviolence? What separates these theories? Which concepts are useful in describing the sociality of nonviolence? We begin with Gandhi's perspective, as all theories of nonviolent disobedience refer back to him.

Gandhian nonviolence

During the famous Salt March, *Time Magazine* declared Gandhi 'Man of the Year', while Winston Churchill slighted him as a simple and 'half-naked fakir' who would be crushed. After he was murdered in 1948, Gandhi's image went through a reputational purification, turning him into the icon of India, peace and humanity.[1]

Although this book is largely based on Gandhi's understanding of nonviolence, it also encompasses decisive reinterpretations of that understanding. Gandhi highlighted the individual's spiritual capacity for coping with the trials of resistance. I highlight the collective and practical capabilities of the nonviolent movement based on its social dimensions. A broad sociological view necessitates a separation of nonviolence from its original contexts in order to recontextualise nonviolence in new social contexts. Gandhi developed his nonviolent repertoire of concepts, methods, strategies and organisational forms in racist South Africa and colonial India a century ago. Interaction with concrete opponents and specific issues was crucial to this. Notably, his nonviolence came about in relation to Hinduism.[2]

He did not present a complete package of nonviolence from the start. Instead, he experimented and sometimes, as he himself said, made mistakes of 'Himalayan proportions'. Consequently, Gandhi's nonviolence is treated as a touchstone and not as a book of answers.

Gandhi is commonly associated with peace in the sense of abstaining from using violence or not participating in war: that is, pacifism. However, Gandhi should be understood in terms of liberation. When it comes down to it, Gandhi prioritises the struggle for liberation above the principle of nonviolence. He thought that if one lacked the capability for nonviolence, or a belief or training in it, it might be right to use violence in extreme situations when fighting greater violence.[3] This stance distanced Gandhi from pacifism and as a result he is criticised for being inconsistent. Yet the case can be made that Gandhi was not necessarily inconsistent when he expressed this opinion in relation to concrete cases in which action was a duty but where those involved neither believed in nor had the ability to use nonviolence. Either way, it is clear that Gandhi inspired the long-term organisation of nonviolent capabilities, as awareness or will are insufficient in themselves.

Gandhi primarily developed a *philosophy of liberation* as well as a practical means of liberation: that is, nonviolence. This nonviolent action repertoire approaches oppression and violent methods in an unusual way, subsequently establishing a form of conflict transformation.[4] As we will see, nonviolence is a form of action that aims to manage all the dimensions of a conflict and to transform conflict into consensus. As such, associating Gandhi with peace misinterprets his revolutionary approach as well as his focus on resisting oppression and violence. In con-temporary India, for instance, Gandhi has been transformed into a representative of the establishment and raised to being 'Father of the Nation'. Everyone knows (or believes they know) who he is and they avow their respect for this 'holy soul' (Mahatma). Indian rupee banknotes are now adorned with Gandhi's well-known face – the face of a man who, when he was murdered, was living a life entirely without private property.

Gandhi derived his concept of nonviolence mainly from a Hindu perspective. If you want to understand Gandhi's philosophy as a whole, you must also consider its religious scope. On the other hand, this is necessary only if you are interested in his philosophy. That is, he can also be interpreted as a moral practitioner or a practical moralist:[5] 'I do not believe that the spiritual law [of nonviolence] works on a field of its own. On the contrary, it expresses itself only through the ordinary activities of life.'[6] Thus, nonviolence should be understood as being both spiritually and socially practical. Moreover, it is something that expresses itself through social activity, and, on these grounds, it is possible to interpret nonviolence purely in sociological terms.

Gandhi was complex. Within the liberation movement he was known to be a compromising strategist (sometimes too much so) and a down-to-earth politician. At the same time his influence in India has mostly relied on his role as India's spiritual leader. As the person responsible for the national movement's resistance campaigns, he was a hard-working speaker, letter writer and organiser who travelled extensively. He emphasised that a strong champion of nonviolence must believe in a divinity, yet Gandhi designated his close collaborator and atheist, G. Ramachandra Rao, as the foremost defender of nonviolence.[7] With these social and political underpinnings in mind, our focus moves to Gandhi's view on the sociality of nonviolence and its role as liberation from oppression and violence in social relations.

Satyagraha as idea and practice Gandhi's philosophy of nonviolence can be characterised as a theology of liberation, a philosophy of liberation or a philosophy of conflict transformation. Both
the philosopher Arne Næss and the sociologist Joan Bondurant
have tried to reconcile Gandhi's unsystematic and sometimes
contradictory views.[8] Based on both of these classics of nonviolence studies, we can glean the main characteristics of what
we can call *Gandhian nonviolence*.

Bondurant attempts to use the core elements of satyagraha
to summarise Gandhi's nonviolent perspective; this is also the
concept that Gandhi finds best captures the core of nonviolent
resistance. Satyagraha literally means 'to hold onto the truth'.
According to Bondurant, the three core elements in satyagraha
are truth (*satya*), nonviolence (*ahimsa*) and self-inflicted suffering
or asceticism (*tapasya*). The latter is not a matter of submission,
rather it is a demonstration of sincerity.[9] Nonviolence is, as we
shall see in the next chapter, a struggle against violence without
(using) violence. Thus, it is through nonviolence and suffering
that the discord resulting from conflict is transformed and truth
is attained. In line with Gandhi (and Bondurant), satyagraha is
what constitutes the starting point for the book's analysis of
nonviolence. Although the concept of 'nonviolence' is included as
one of the three elements of satyagraha, Gandhian nonviolence
must be understood as an integrated whole.

At the pinnacle of the Indian liberation struggle in 1930,
Gandhi, together with thousands of other activists, was jailed
once again. In his cell, he dedicated most of his time to spinning yarn, but writing letters was also part of his daily routine.
In one of the letters he writes:

> the path of ahimsa [i.e. nonviolence] ... may entail continuous
> suffering and the cultivating of end-less patience ... without

ahimsa it is not possible to seek and find Truth. Ahimsa and Truth are so intertwined that it is practically impossible to disentangle and separate them. They are like the two sides of a coin, or rather of a smooth unstamped metallic disc. Who can say which is the obverse and which is the reverse? Nevertheless, ahimsa is the means and Truth is the end. Means to be means must always be within our reach, and so ahimsa becomes our supreme duty and Truth becomes God for us. If we take care of the means, we are bound to reach the end sooner or later. If we resolve to do this, we shall have won the battle. Whatever difficulties we encounter, whatever apparent reverses we sustain, we should not lose faith but should ever repeat one *mantra*: 'Truth exists, it alone exists. It is the only God and there is but one way of realizing it; there is but one means and that is ahimsa. I will never give it up. May the God that is Truth, in whose name I have taken this pledge, give me the strength to keep it.'[10]

First, it should be said that truth (*satya*) is a central aspect of satyagraha (nonviolent struggle). For Gandhi, the true, or what is, is viewed as what is right, or perhaps even *what is right is what is*.[11] In other words, Gandhi is a realist. Of course, his realism is very different from Western political realism, which emphasises power relations and violence, not morality; however, like the Western tradition, he discusses and even explores that which is, the actual relations of reality. Even truth and God fuse together so that God becomes that which exists permanently: truth. This does not mean that God represents or accords with the truth or that truth is like God; rather 'Truth is God'.[12] If God is truth and not a being but a 'universal law',[13] then no major difference exists between Gandhi and a researcher looking for the truth, regardless of whether the latter views him- or herself as religious or an atheist. At its core, the constitution of reality and how reality should be are not different (such a 'difference' is precisely what denotes ethics in the Western tradition). According to both Gandhi and Hinduism, what is normally viewed as reality is an illusion or a false reality that we can see through.[14] Beyond that illusion of reality, there is no difference between that which really works in reality and that which should work – the effective and the morality. Gandhi can thus be viewed both as a realistic pragmatist and as an idealistic moralist.[15] Over time, and depending on the degree to which you follow the requirements of morality – or what is true or real – your actions will lead to success (that is, they will work practically).

Gandhi states that the justification of nonviolence lies in the fact that no one has certain knowledge of the truth, but all humans belong together and comprise a living unity.[16] If our knowledge about truth remains uncertain, it means that anyone can be right since they have an understanding that is a part of the total truth; for that reason, others must take an individual's understanding into consideration. To kill means to deny the possibility that the other person has something to teach us: if one day you realise that you were mistaken, the murdered person cannot be asked for forgiveness later. Since the truth itself is absolute but access to the truth is uncertain, a free inquiry into what is true is possible only if we do not kill each other during the search.[17] One should therefore assume one's own *relative* truth, one's inner voice or one's conscience, and hold true to it during the conflict, despite threats and the temptation to abandon it. At the same time, one must be open to being convinced by others' understanding of the truth; if not, one cannot attain a deeper understanding of the truth.[18] The search for *absolute* truth results in not using violence against others.

Second, nonviolence (*ahimsa*) is a central aspect of satyagraha. This is accompanied by the striving for non-egotistical 'self-realisation', or progress towards a life in service.[19] This self-realisation is not the same as the one that characterises modern individualism. Gandhi speaks of something that, according to Arne Næss, should rather be understood as a *collective self-realisation* whereby the individual ego dissolves and the oppression of any single human hinders the self-realisation of all others.[20] In this light, *himsa* (violence) should be understood as reducing the degree of self-realisation and *ahimsa* (nonviolence) as increasing it.[21] Thus, nonviolence is not only a negation of violence. To be passive – to *not* resist the violence or oppression that is exercised anywhere in the world against any one of us – was something that Gandhi viewed as a form of participation that in itself constituted the exercise of violence.[22] So the question of what constitutes violence or nonviolence is seen from a common (not an individual) perspective. Gandhi finds that 'exploitation' is the core of violence.[23] Importantly, exploitation is not only about economic profiteering, but also about profiteering as a whole, profiteering from a person's possibility of self-realisation as part of life or humanity.[24] In a strict sense, complete *ahimsa*, non-damage or self-realisation is probably impossible and thus a utopian ideal. It is hardly possible to stop all violence and oppression all the time. The essential criterion for being able to claim that an action is an expression of *ahimsa* is whether it is an *attempt* to further the possibility of self-realisation or an effort to fight *himsa*.[25] In practice, *ahimsa* is a question of trying to decrease, undermine or work against *himsa*, reducing it to the lowest possible level. In counteracting violence, unavoidable suffering arises.

Self-suffering or asceticism (*tapasya*) becomes a third central aspect of satyagraha: acting against power relations and using violence in conflicts lead to the suffering of the nonviolent actor, even if the intent is to avoid suffering.

The assumption is that you will suffer no matter what you do: if you accept oppression (which leads to the reduction of our common or mutual self-realisation) or resist, regardless of whether the resistance is conducted with violence or nonviolent struggle, suffering will result. It is a matter of how to reduce the total suffering (everyone's suffering) and how the unavoidable suffering can be used as a means in the struggle. A key strategy in violent struggle is to cause suffering for the other, as the other's increased losses are presumed to result in victory; in contrast, in the nonviolent struggle, a central concept is *accepting (the risk of) personal suffering*. The greater, collective suffering of oppression is something that one struggles against despite the risk of new suffering. According to Gandhi, the successful use of nonviolence in difficult conflicts is predicated on a lack of fear of personal consequences. Perhaps Gandhi demands more than is necessary. It is probably enough to handle the fear, to not let the fear control the action. Either way, nonviolent struggle sets up demands similar to those in military struggle. If you use nonviolence, it means that you are *prepared to die for what you believe in*. 'Non-violence in its dynamic condition means conscious suffering. It does not mean meek submission to the will of the evildoer, but it means the putting of one's soul against the will of the tyrant.'[26]

All things considered, satyagraha can be seen as the fight for truth and collective self-realisation through nonviolent resistance against falsity, violence and oppression, and a preparedness to endure the personal consequences of this fight and struggle.

What characterises satyagraha Nonviolent disobedience can be summarised using a number of concise rules and practical steps for concrete *satyagraha campaigns*.[27] The relationship between the means and goals of the struggle are decisive in understanding the Gandhian nonviolent liberation struggle. According to Bondurant, means and goals should be understood as being indivisible. *The means are 'the end in process and the ideal in the making'.*[28] In order to refine the means, Gandhi claimed that the movement needed to be well disciplined and not act contradictorily. Gandhi provided a number of rules of behaviour for the participants with the aim of creating a militaristic discipline: you should not foster any hate for your adversary; you should not retaliate when you are attacked nor resist arrest, but instead you should protect your adversary from attacks and insults, despite the risk of dying; you should act as an exemplary prisoner when imprisoned; and you should follow all orders given by the leaders of the satyagraha campaign – or leave the group if you are in disagreement with it.

The forms of resistance of civil disobedience and non-cooperation are, like 'constructive work', central means in a satyagraha campaign but are not satyagraha in themselves.[29] The means must be implemented in a particular way in order for them to be an expression of 'truth force'. Satyagraha requires more than just fighting without violence and maintaining one's own version of the truth. Bondurant says that what distinguishes satyagraha is the 'constructive programme', the gradual escalation and acceptance of the punishment.[30]

The *constructive programme* entails founding a new society and strengthening the self-respect of one's own group during the struggle. New, alternative institutions are built up in parallel to the resistance against the institutions being supplanted. Another common approach among resistance movements is to build a new society after the revolution. For Gandhi, this constructive work was the basis of resistance, a precondition for demolishing oppression. The constructive programme expresses Gandhi's utopia:

> Because the Constructive Programme represented Gandhi's positive means, it pre-figured his end-goal: the Sarvodaya society. Since the state is 'violence in a concentrated and organised form', Sarvodaya is a stateless society in which all political and legal authority have been abrogated, relations between people being governed only by moral authority. Structurally, it is 'a great society of small communities', each autonomous and self-governing but linked with others in a non-hierarchical network – part of an 'oceanic circle' ... Internally, each community is a participatory democracy, taking decisions by consensus, so that individual and collective self-government coincide.[31]

As such, the constructive programme should permeate every operation of resistance.[32] The constructive programme developed in the Indian liberation struggle was an ambitious practice that strengthened the power of both villages and poor Indians.[33] Before the national liberation movement commenced, Gandhi travelled widely throughout the countryside. His travels inspired the programme's design and led him to realise that most Indians lived in one of the hundreds of thousands of poor rural villages. He realised that these people were the bedrock of resistance.[34] The constructive programme encompassed a wide package of changes ranging from economic development of village co-ops to personal hygiene regulations. In building their own institutions – such as decentralised production facilities for their own

clothes through a local crafts industry and a parallel parliament
(the All-India Congress) – Indians tried to liberate themselves
from the economic and political dominance of the English.[35]
These steps undermined the British rhetoric that claimed that
Indians could not manage on their own. At the same time, it
became more difficult for the colonial power to effectively punish
the resistance. Once the resistance movement was well on its
way to establishing its own functioning political organisations,
economic co-ops, newspapers, social alliances and educational
systems, its internal resources could be used with increasing
effectiveness to support those who were punished when they
exercised resistance.

Second, satyagraha involves a nonviolent escalation: a progressive increase of nonviolent disobedience, not an escalation of
nonviolence to violence. This can be described as a 'horizontal
escalation': that is, an escalation through the involvement of
a growing number of people and a combination of nonviolent
methods.[36] The Ruckus Society, which played a central role in
the nonviolence training leading up to the 'Battle in Seattle'
that disrupted the World Trade Organization (WTO) meeting in
November 1999, described nonviolent direct action as a way 'to
raise the stakes in an ongoing struggle'.

The third part of satyagraha, *acceptance of the punishment*,
is more controversial and frequently misinterpreted. It is not
a question of fatalism, masochism, non-revolutionary politics,
reformism or religious mythology; rather, it is a method of managing disdain, hate and enemy images while furthering trust
between conflicting parties.[37]

Bondurant arranges the progressive escalation of satyagraha
campaigns into nine phases, which proceed from negotiation,
via agitation, ultimatum and boycott, to an increasing use of

non-cooperation and civil disobedience.[38] The final phase is founding a parallel rule. The model is not universal and the phases can arise non-sequentially. It is more a guideline for struggle – bound to and defined by each situation and conflict, in line with how Gandhi developed his action repertoire dynamically and contextually.[39] It is also likely that several steps must sometimes be applied simultaneously.[40]

Furthermore, negotiation remains a constant possibility if the other phases of resistance are sufficiently effective. Resistance essentially refers to an agreement stemming from dialogue – something that David Hardiman calls 'dialogic resistance'.[41]

Gandhi's system of norms and hypotheses Probably the best book about Gandhi's philosophy is the forgotten 1974 masterpiece by the Norwegian philosopher Arne Næss: *Gandhi and Group Conflict*. Based on a close reading of Gandhi's texts, Næss formulates a unique, coherent philosophical system for nonviolent disobedience (the entire system is summarised in the Appendix). The system's starting point is the rule of action or 'norm' N1: *'Act in group struggle and act, moreover, as an autonomous person in a way conducive to long-term, universal, maximal reduction of violence'.*[42] A theory of conflict arises from this norm and its logically connected hypotheses about how social conflicts work. The hypotheses are simultaneously assumptions about how the world, society and people work. According to this system, Gandhi could draw conclusions about which rules of action were most likely to reduce the level of violence, and, based on experiences from actual conflicts, adjustments could be made to the rules of action – and sometimes even to the underlying hypotheses about reality.

A number of hypotheses produce rules of action (norms) on

four interlinked levels. Each norm is a practical conclusion from a corresponding hypothesis. For example, the norm N3 arises from the hypothesis H3 that claims that: 'Short-term violence counteracts long-term universal reduction of violence.' If, after an extended period of experimentation in conflicts, it is shown that one of the hypotheses is incorrect, the corresponding norm will also fail. The overarching aim is violence reduction (axiom N1 above). How to achieve violence reduction is an empirical question: that is, a question about how we humans actually work. Therefore, we do not need to understand Gandhi's religious philosophy in order to understand his nonviolent liberation philosophy. God is not necessary, but faith in a nonviolent God or Truth eases one's preparedness to risk suffering when the struggle escalates.

These hypotheses provide a composite image of Gandhi's philosophy and the norms formed by a programme of action for nonviolent campaigns. They reveal his view on how the means of struggle characterise the possible result. They also show how a struggle against oppressive or violent systems, or social and organisational roles, can be combined with an attempt to create trust, friendship and cooperation between individuals. It is imperative to remember that every person has inherent value, fundamental rights and needs, even those who were the colonial system's willing henchmen. The representatives and decision makers of British rule, the East India Company's capitalists, the private in the military or his officer, the prison guard and other participants in colonialism were people too.

Næss's summary makes fascinating reading, precisely because of its systematic concentration of a very special form of struggle. As Næss also highlights the experimental and changing nature of struggle, Gandhi becomes relevant for us here and now. We are given the task of continuing the practical, political research and developing a form of resistance against violence and oppression, enabling peace by peaceful means and liberation by means of liberty.

The system of norms should be understood both as a moral call and as a theory of the truth function of conflicts. One should understand the rules as both a guide for how one ought to act morally as well as principles for effective success.

Theories of nonviolence

Gandhi coined the concept of nonviolent disobedience. Both theoretically and practically he developed the methodology for civil disobedience, yet a deluge of practical issues kept him from turning his world view into a coherent theory.[43] In fact, he doubted whether it was even possible.[44]

Authors have developed theories of nonviolence since the 1920s, and since the 1960s they have produced a significant body of literature about the subject.[45] Yet even today there is no delineated, unified scientific discipline of the subject. We lack a mutual way of discussing and using nonviolence. For that reason we must remain open to various descriptions in order to discover interesting studies.

The literature cites Clarence Marsh Case's *Nonviolent Coercion* (1923) as the first to attempt a scientific analysis of nonviolent action. Case proposes a functional typology of methods for social change, but his analysis is limited to the few cases known at that time. Richard Gregg's book *The Power of Non-Violence* (1935) made a strong entry in England, where Greggism dominated for a time.[46] He was the founder of a cross-disciplinary approach and a psychological perspective based on behaviourism, which was then popular. He makes connections to military research and claims that nonviolent war is similar to military war in several ways – above all in that it *demoralises* the opponent by weakening their resolve. This is achieved through the activist's refusal to retaliate even when under severe attack, thereby not providing any excuse or legitimation for the violence used.[47] Yet nonviolent warfare differs in that it also *re-moralises* the relationship between opponents.[48] When the nonviolent activist repeatedly tries to reach to the human person behind the violence, while resisting the oppression through peaceful disobedience, an opening for a human relationship is provided. Gregg presents the concept of *moral ju-jitsu*, which explains how violence backfires: by repeatedly contradicting the expected behaviour (to flee, fight back with violence or give up), the nonviolent activist creates a situation in which the violence used produces neither obedience nor retaliation, a situation that gives rise to imbalance and confusion, as well as openings for a changed relationship, according to Gregg. Gregg's analysis creatively bridges scientific theories and principles of nonviolence, resulting in new approaches and a new horizon of hypotheses.

Nonviolence research took off in the USA in the 1960s. Initially behaviourism, social psychology and system functionalism characterised the field of study. Then, during the 1970s, the research moved towards strategic resource theory concerning power and resistance, which has continued to exemplify perspectives up until the present day.[49]

A flourishing field of nonviolence studies Since the post-war era, nonviolence has been mentioned in social science from time to time, but only irregularly and only in certain aspects. When nonviolence is discussed at length, it is normally with respect to practical or ethical philosophy, a theory of rights, or national defence strategies. After 1973, Gene Sharp's analyses became almost as self-evident in the discourse on nonviolence as the ideas of Gandhi himself. With his paradigmatic influence, Gene Sharp has taken the decisive step towards a science of nonviolence.

The dominant technique approach Gene Sharp, 'the Machiavelli of nonviolence', is the creator of the dominant theory of non-violent actions and power.[50] Sharp believes that nonviolence can be a conscious choice if one learns the nonviolent technique approach and realises the inherent strength in organised and strategic resistance. His view of power and resistance is expressly technical. More than anyone else, he offers a smorgasbord of resistance opportunities for the nonviolent activist who is pre-pared to use this array of techniques.

Sharp defines *social power* as the ability to directly or indirectly control other people's behaviour.[51] This control is expressed in a power struggle between actors in which strategic measures modify their access to power resources. *Political power* is a form of social power affecting political issues and authority. It is used by those in power when exercising their will, as well as by those who obstruct those in power. Sharp's understanding of power is thus rather conventional. His unique contribution lies in his focus on consent and disobedience when wielding power – a view that stems from thinkers such as Gandhi and Hannah Arendt. Gandhi points out the strength of disobedience and Arendt speaks of power as a creative and collectively organised human ability to act. For Sharp, the obverse power of resistance is a strategic use of collective disobedience.

Sharp directs his criticism at the established 'monolith theory', which presupposes that humans depend on governments, that political power is massive and uniform, that power can indeed come from a few people, and that power is continual and self-perpetuating.[52] Sharp states that this is an incorrect and simplified view of power that dominates political theory and public understanding. It describes reality correctly only if both the opposition and the subjects of power believe in it and act as if it were true.[53] This myth of the unity of power has led to the absurd situation where a country of millions of people can be occupied simply by taking over its parliamentary building and imprisoning its government.

Moreover, Sharp claims that this simplistic view is the basis of the belief in political violence, and particularly in military combat. By killing those in power, taking over central positions and crushing others' organised capability for violence, power can be conquered like booty in war. Guerrilla warfare constitutes an exception: with its decentralised mobility it is more similar to the indirect strategy of nonviolent disobedience.[54]

In contrast to the monolith theory, Sharp asserts a pluralistic view of power, where the relationship between obedience/consent and disobedience/dissent plays a central role in the power struggle. According to Sharp, humans obey for many reasons, including habit, fear of punishment, a feeling of moral obligation, self-interest, identification with the dominant group, resignation or absence of self-confidence, and for resources. Sharp thinks that the subordinate group's obedience is a form of cooperation. Power is based on cooperation on the part of the subordinate and obedience is basically a choice.[55] Each power system is built on hierarchical chains of obedience by which a leader stands or falls according to whether the base of power obeys his or her words. Obedience is not automatic: it is an act, and therefore it is chosen. This choice gives the resistance new and unexpected possibilities to change power relations, possibilities that Sharp explores. You cannot force a group to do something if its members are not afraid of the punishment.[56] Disobedience is always possible, but the group's relationship to the punishment for its disobedience is what decides whether it dares to break the laws, orders and rules of those in power.

Bearing Sharp in mind, we can say that the key to successful resistance lies in finding ways to *change the relationship to punishment*.[57] For example, this can be done by means of nonviolence training, support groups, an accomplice voluntarily reporting a crime ('self-accusations'), alliances with established organisations, and collective disobedience similar to the Spanish conscientious objector movement MOC (Movimiento de Objeción de Conciencia) during the 1990s.[58] MOC formed one of Europe's strongest anti-militarist movements, changed the face of conscientious objection, which traditionally is an individual decision, transforming it into a collectively organised action, and finally made a conservative government end mandatory conscription in 1996.[59]

Violence is central in punishing disobedience. Arendt argues that power in its extreme form is characterised by everyone cooperating against a single individual and the extreme form of violence is essentially a matter of an individual action against the collective.[60] Thus, power is founded on cooperation between people while violence is an individual action. In this respect, Arendt and Sharp think alike, but Sharp argues in difference to Arendt, that violence can be both organised and rational as violence is potentially an effective instrument for collectives to achieve certain political goals.[61] Therefore, he argues that we need an alternative means of sanctioning, functional alternatives that makes violence unnecessary, and ideally ineffective.[62] Sharp builds on Arendt's argument about power as a political organisation, but highlights nonviolent sanctions as alternatives to violence in the struggle for power.[63]

Resistance, in the form of nonviolent action, is based on the understanding that governments depend on people, that power is complex, and that political power is vulnerable as it relies on the assumption that it can be controlled at its social origin.[64] It is through collective work that a society forms and changes its power. It is through the (re)production of economy, ideology, population and organisation that leaders sustain their power. Notably, the sustenance for a leader's power comes from the subordinate or cooperating population.

Sharp does not mention that regimes can manage without certain groups.[65] These groups are excluded yet still subordinate. Furthermore, the organisation of power does not depend on all groups, at least not to an equal extent. Essentially, this critique does not supplant the power theory as a whole. It means only that nonviolent disobedience must be organised among the groups that those in power de facto depend on.[66] For that reason, a strategic nonviolent campaign presupposes a concrete analysis of power.

Sharp sees the social sources of power as being authority, human resources, knowledge and skills, psychology and ideology factors, material resources and sanctions.[67] Power is entirely dependent on how much of these resources the ruling person has access to, which in turn depends on the degree of cooperation from the ruler's subordinates, both those against whom power is exercised and those who are allied to the ruling person. The crux of the matter is that all decisive *sources* of power lie outside the *position* of power. A competent ruler plays on the feelings and traditions of his or her subordinates and develops a charismatic personality, but that does not change the fact that the sources of power lie beyond the person in charge. Charisma is meaningful precisely because the person in power is dependent on human captivation and people's belief in him or her in order to gain access to power (the cooperation or obedience of others).[68]

Those in power do not create power but are *given* power by others who cooperate and support them. It is precisely the dependency relationship of those in power that reveals the leader's weakness and the opposition's possibilities, and the fact that subordination is a choice.

People who actively support or passively accept the conditions of those in power are therefore those who generate that power. Those in power are dependent on cooperation from a sufficient portion of their citizens in order to ensure economic security and a functioning administrative system. At the same time, those in power also rely on a large part of the population paying taxes and following the rules of the social system and not forming a collective resistance.

Consequently, it follows that the more extensive and detailed a leader's power and control, the more dependent he or she is on the cooperation of subordinates. In order to work, a complex, organised and highly technological society would seem to depend on the cooperation and obedience of large groups. This means that there are more options for nonviolent resistance in the late modern organisational society than there were previously, but it also means that those in power have access to more numerous and more coordinated forms of control.

Based on Sharp's theory of power, we can imagine how possibilities of resistance to power are created through the organised and strategic use of various disobedience techniques. Based on a perspective in which power is seen to stem from cooperation and obedience, we can understand the disobedience of nonviolent movements as a means of changing society and power. The historical research Sharp conducted comprises the empirical material for his analyses and provides us with a large number of examples showing how nonviolent disobedience can vary depending on society and situation,[69] even if Sharp himself does not relate techniques to socio-cultural factors to any great extent.

THE BASIC PROBLEM WITH THE TECHNIQUE APPROACH Sharp's theory is not free from objections. It could be said that it is problematically reductionist. It makes the meanings of other social dimensions invisible and disconnects the 'technique' from the social context.

One school of thought based on the technique approach was inaugurated in 1983 at the Albert Einstein Institution in Boston. This research has occurred in close cooperation with Harvard University, where Sharp's research became the model for a new generation of researchers of nonviolence who were interested in affecting the policies and military strategies of governments and generals.[70] A number of research projects within Sharp's paradigm have developed. For this technique paradigm, nonviolence is primarily the same as action methods.[71] Technique and strategy are conscious, rational plans of action that use methods to affect power relations and to put pressure on opponents. 'Just as bombs, artillery, tanks and infantry, properly deployed, can be successful, so too can methods of nonviolent struggle compel an opponent to "do our will".'[72] According to the technique approach, employers' lockouts, workers' strikes, states' boycotts of a dictatorship, the CIA's non-military operations in the same dictatorship – all of these things are examples of nonviolent action: methods that can be measured based on their ability to bring about a more or less effective (non-lethal)

NONVIOLENT ACTION STUDIES | 45

effect on other parties to a conflict.[73] Based on historical examples, in 1973 Sharp had already classified no fewer than 198 such behavioural techniques applied as nonviolent methods.[74]

Even propaganda and techniques from psychological operations conducted by the military are embraced:

> Psychological operations (PSYOPS) is the centrepiece of a well planned strategic nonviolent struggle. Its purpose is to influence attitudes and behaviors of target audiences, mainly through the use of propaganda. PSYOPS has proven its effectiveness time and time again, both in military campaigns and in nonviolent struggles, as a potent weapon to weaken, divide, neutralize and disintegrate an opponent's pillars of support.[75]

The former principal of the Albert Einstein Institution and retired US army officer Robert Helvey claims that nonviolent struggle can beneficially spread rumours, false information and 'black propaganda' to discredit the opponent.[76] Its effectiveness might decide the outcome of the power struggle.

Within the technique approach, nonviolent action essentially remains the same regardless of context. Universal methods are extracted from examples in antiquity and modernity as well as from radically different societies.[77] It is the *manifest behaviour* that defines various methods, not their interactive dynamics, processes or mechanisms.[78] The three main categories of nonviolent methods (protest, non-cooperation and intervention) can be interpreted as attempts to incite dismissive, subversive and symbolic effects.[79]

The technique behind these methods is mechanically technical rather than socially technical. By focusing on technique, researchers of the technique approach continually discover new forms of action, such as spreading underground newspapers (samizdat) and recording texts on cassette tapes (magnizidat) in communist countries. This results from their simplified view of the culture and social context underlying the technique. Thus blockades, gifts, kindness, strikes and similar actions are included in the universal category of nonviolent action. However, in reality these behaviours always arise socially and practically with the aim of stimulating nonviolent events in a specific social context. When these isolated behaviours are applied in completely different contexts, they might gain new meanings. The behaviours and strategic principles of the technique approach, which are compared with each other in systematic studies and quantitatively measured from their effects, disrupt Gandhi's context-based nonviolent action repertoire. This focus on technique is a kind of acultural behavioural technique – a radical variation on the popular behaviourism of its time, which accentuated causal relationships. As a result, the symbolic communication that designates human interaction – and that also includes meanings, cultural variation and the practical construction of social action – disappears.

In Sharp's view, it would appear that the citizens have the power in their hands. Whether they are aware of this and whether they have organised their ability to change the power relations is another question altogether. However, if power can mould their way of acting, feeling and thinking – as has been claimed since the cultural turn in social sciences in the 1970s – it becomes more difficult to organise resistance, as power is embodied in citizens and in their culture. Accordingly, even discourse about resistance may be characterised by power processes. In this respect, Sharp underestimates the ability of power to influence the conditions of resistance.

Despite this critique, I find that Sharp and the technique

approach have analysed an important dimension of nonviolence better than others. My main critique is that: 1) the technique happens in a social context; and 2) there are other dimensions to this. The meaning of this 'technical' power struggle changes when we consider all four dimensions of nonviolent action – as the rest of this book does at length.

Beyond the technique approach Since *movement studies* have barely touched on nonviolence, this study of collective non-violence borrows only limitedly from their research of collective protest actions and political movements (with the American Civil Rights Movement serving as a prime example). Doug McAdam and Sidney Tarrow (2000) broke relative silence within social movement theory with their article 'Nonviolence as contentious interaction'. In recent years, a certain interest in nonviolent actions has been noticed,[80] although, aside from a few exceptions, that interest still does not concentrate on nonviolence itself (i.e. nonviolence as a specific means of action) but rather on the mobilisation of movements and actions in general (where nonviolent movements sometimes provide illustrative examples). If this flourishing area of research began to take a serious interest in nonviolence, compelling and scientific discourses on nonviolence would follow.

> The strength of each theoretical perspective addresses the weakness of the other ... [Social movement theory is less strong] on identifying movement strategies and tactics that contribute to a recasting of the political context. On the other hand, the nonviolent action scholarship has focused on the trajectories of social movements rather than their origins, and has emphasized the role of agency, especially strategy, in promoting political change.[81]

In nonviolence studies, there are two additional, established interpretative perspectives that differ decisively from the dominant technique approach. One of them is *Gandhi studies.*

Gandhi studies centre on understanding what Gandhi meant, his philosophy as a whole, its significance for the life of modern man and for society, and the origin of this knowledge – simply put, understanding the phenomenon of Gandhi. Gandhi studies differ from nonviolence studies in that they investigate the hypotheses Gandhi and others proposed with the aim of understanding nonviolence. Accordingly, Gandhian perspectives on nonviolence interest me,[82] as I am not seeking a correct understanding of Gandhi's philosophy as a whole, but rather a correct understanding of certain aspects of Gandhi's philosophy pertaining to the social phenomenon of nonviolence.

Above all, *feminist nonviolence research* has inspired me because it considers nonviolence to be both morality and technique, and because it has replaced Gandhi's focus on suffering with supportive communities. Moreover, feminist variants of nonviolence research even critique nonviolent movements' (male) power production. In all these respects, its direction diverges from the technique approach.

The feminist nonviolent discourse Gandhi was radical for his time when he strove for women's participation in a traditionally male-dominated political culture.[83] Then, during the 1970s, a feminist criticism of Gandhi arose among women active in nonviolent movements; one of the forerunners was the journalist, feminist and anti-war activist Barbara Deming.[84] They criticised Gandhi for having had an essentialist view of sex and gender, expressed, for example, in his perception that women have a 'special' ability for nonviolence due to their 'purity'. In this regard he also reinforced patriarchal stereotypes.[85] Gandhi's ideas about the nonviolent activist's self-inflicted suffering and women's nonviolence were dismissed in order to empower oppressed groups in both separatist and communal opposition to the societal patriarchy and within the movement.[86]

The descriptive accounts of Pam McAllister and others have broken a silence and broadened knowledge about women's nonviolent disobedience throughout history.[87] In these accounts we find the seeds of yet another perspective on nonviolent actions.

Nonviolent feminism claims that nonviolence is '*both a principle and a technique*, a set of ideas about how life should be lived and a strategy for social change'.[88] This synthesises the positions that the literature normally describes as opposites: morality and technique.

Moreover, within the nonviolent movement, nonviolent feminism constitutes a radical critique of power structures in meetings, leader worship, authoritarian forms of organisation and, first and foremost, the 'importance of seeking out suffering'.[89] This sense of 'machismo' in the nonviolent movement is something they want to undermine.[90] 'Feminist nonviolence is the process/strategy/philosophy which makes sense of both my rage and my vision of the world I want to live in.'[91]

This perspective highlights Gandhi's thesis about the two sides of nonviolence, which in my interpretation is formulated in terms of *against violence* and *without violence*. Andrew Rigby interprets Barbara Deming's idea that nonviolence has 'two hands':

> The one involves an attempt to 'embrace' the opponent, the other entails an absolute rejection of the evil for which they are responsible. What gives that tension its dynamic and creative aspect ... is nonviolence itself; the refusal to inflict physical hurt upon the other in the process of struggle. Only

through nonviolence, it is believed, can compassion for one's opponent be held in dynamic tension with the anger at the evil for which they are responsible.[92]

Thus the most prominent feature of nonviolent disobedience becomes duplicity or complexity, a combination of resistance to and care for the opponent.[93] This duplicity expresses:

the unique ability of nonviolence to simultaneously accept and reject – to acknowledge and connect us with that which is valuable in a person at the same time as it resists and challenges that person's oppressive attitudes or behaviour.[94]

Feminist nonviolence accentuates the transformative power of the *communal support of small groups,* as opposed to individual courage or the quantity of the mass; the rightful place of wrath and all other feelings[95] in resistance, as opposed to the purity of an absence of violent thoughts and feelings that both Gandhi and King underscored; and the spontaneous initiative or decision, as opposed to technique dogmatism or discipline. Feminists sometimes describe the actions and corresponding emotional processes in different stages by first expressing wrath at the injustice, then sorrow at the victim's suffering, decisiveness to act and communal joy. In such a way, individual feelings are ritualised into shared experiences and expressed collectively. By means of 'ritual interaction' in small groups, emotions can be transformed and experiences of powerlessness converted into empowerment.[96] Even nonviolent feminism emphasises strategy and effectiveness, but based on the community's or individual's experience, the learning processes derived from actions, the context and the growth of self-confidence among movements, as well as their ability to exercise resistance.[97]

By underlining the social interaction in the nonviolent community, the perspective of nonviolent feminism helps override the dichotomy between technique and principled nonviolence. In part, I employ the duality of nonviolence (*against violence* and *without violence*); in part, I employ a view that sees the effectiveness of nonviolence as integrated within the social experiences and community of people (i.e. *social pragmatism*); and in part, I employ the power-critical relationship to nonviolence. As a result, my analysis can be understood as a sociological elaboration of the nonviolent feminist approach, in contrast to the technique approach and Gandhi studies.

The need to develop nonviolence studies

> Present understanding of nonviolent action still remains largely descriptive ... modes of communication and the creative, performative aspects of nonviolent conflict strategies have not been researched systematically.[98]

> Sharp's consent theory of power has been subject to critiques but no one has come up with an alternative theory of power that is more productive for activists.[99]

Nonviolence studies bear the signs of a young field: simplified descriptions and unsystematic approaches, inarticulate use of theory, imprecise assumptions and concepts and deficient open discussion (including weak knowledge of colleagues' work), as well as groundless assertions and spuriously optimistic plans.

One explanation for this is that it stems from two circumstances that this study tries to resolve: polarisation and confusion. Polarisation persists in relation to *defining what, in fact, constitutes the phenomenon being studied*. At the same time, researchers confound various dimensions of the phenomenon, in particular metaphysics, ontology and practical social knowledge.

Nonviolence studies need more *research developed through debate about applicable theory within the social sciences*. What is most necessary is a theoretical and conceptual development to capture the various dimensions of nonviolence – not just its strategic management of resources (the technique/defence approach) or ideological content (Gandhi studies). In order to describe nonviolence's practical interaction and symbolic communication between actors in various cultural contexts, we need new concepts that do not reduce action to a power strategy or theology and ethics.

Movements that illustrate the conceptual development

Having given an overview of the main existing research trends in the area of nonviolent action studies, and having argued for the need for theoretical and conceptual development, I now turn to those with the most sophisticated understanding of nonviolence – the nonviolent movements themselves – to illustrate the rest of the analysis in this book.

In developing a sociological perspective on nonviolence, it is fitting to stress its use in previously studied examples of nonviolent actions, thus demonstrating the concept's richness.[100] The nonviolent movements that recur in this analysis are presented below so that their distinct activities and situations can be understood. The actions discussed were mainly carried out by the Civil Rights Movement in the USA (1950s and 1960s), the Indian liberation struggle (from the 1920s to 1947), the British anti-nuclear weapons movements (1960s), the South African anti-apartheid movement (from the 1950s to the 1990s), the Brazilian landless workers' movement (from the 1980s to the present), the Palestinian liberation struggle during the first Intifada (from 1987 to the beginning of the 1990s) and the West German peace movement that was active during the Cold War (from the 1970s to the 1990s). In all these cases, thousands of people dedicated themselves to nonviolent civil disobedience but in different societal situations and historical epochs, under various social categories and with different degrees of success.

The Civil Rights Movement mobilised thousands of African-Americans in the USA to fight for equality in the struggle against the segregation laws introduced in the South with the support of the Supreme Court's 'separate but equal' doctrine. Those involved worked both legally and politically through several different national organisations. Attempts at legal reform had little effect for African-Americans in the South until the end of the 1950s, when nonviolent disobedience began to be carried out by a younger generation, notably including clergymen such as Martin Luther King Jr who spearheaded the movement.[101] First and foremost they held freedom marches and sit-ins in cafés and other places where they requested equal treatment, thus defying the rules of segregated institutions. In 1963, some 250,000 people marched to Washington, where King gave his world-famous 'I have a dream' speech. The following year King received the Nobel Peace Prize. The Civil Rights Movement's powerful mobilisation and success, not least in the mass media, led to the adoption of a number of important civil rights laws at the end of the 1960s. However, the movement lost much of its strength when King was murdered in 1968; the same tragic result affected the Indian movement when Gandhi was murdered in 1948. Soon after this, the Civil Rights Movement splintered. Groups that were ethnically and politically more radical fought – including with violence and separatism – for 'Black Power', but they did not succeed in mobilising much in the way of social change compared with the Civil Rights Movement.[102]

One of Asia's first anti-colonial struggles, the Indian liberation movement, began in 1919, although the Indian National Congress (INC) had existed since the end of the nineteenth century.[103] At first, the INC was 'a mouthpiece for Indians with Western schooling, who demanded constitutional, social and economic reforms'.[104] Then a few years after Gandhi had returned from his successful fight for the rights of East Indians in South Africa, the INC transformed into a national people's movement with revolutionary goals and a nonviolent strategy. Since India was a country with half a million villages, not just a few thousand intellectual city-dwellers, Gandhi intended to mobilise India's farmers into concrete campaigns linked to the national liberation movement.

Gandhi adopted religious concepts, national and traditional symbols, and the modern strategy of oppositional politics. Members of the movement used the traditional form of resistance, *hartal*, successfully. This approach combined strikes and boycotts during which the Indians simply stayed at home and refused to participate in production, consumption or other colonially organised social activities.

They carried out the first large non-cooperation campaign against the British colonial power in 1919–22.[105] As well as a series of lesser nonviolent campaigns, they also conducted two larger operations in 1930–32 (the Salt March) and 1940–42 (Quit India).[106] At times, up to 60,000 Indians were imprisoned concurrently for civil disobedience. Aside from various actions of resistance (such as refusing to accept awards, boycotting English textiles, blockades of shops and strikes), the Indian liberation movement also implemented a 'construction programme', which involved the construction of independent institutions in economics, education, justice, politics and other fields. Several constitutional negotiations were held with the British, but it was in 1947 that India received its formal independence; the price was the splitting of India and Pakistan, which led to the deaths of a million people. Gandhi was murdered in 1948 by a Hindu nationalist who, like many others, thought that Gandhi had been too lenient towards Muslims.

The movement of landless workers in Brazil, with its foremost organisation MST (Movimento dos Trabalhadores Rurais Sem Terra), or the Brazilian land workers' movement, is now arguably the largest nonviolent movement in the world. MST was formed during the 1980s and now mobilises about 1.5 million small-scale farmers and land workers who have no land with which they can sustain themselves. They have united in a struggle for democratic land reform that they encourage by means of the peaceful occupation of untilled land.[107] So far, they have completed 2,000 occupations and managed to distribute land to over 350,000 landless people. This is more than the government has succeeded in doing. During the movement's land occupations (*acampamentos*), people live in plastic tents for several years before the government might give them rights to the land. Like most historical nonviolent movements, this movement is nonviolent for pragmatic reasons. Although the land proprietors' paramilitary groups regularly murder the movement's activists (and certain individuals use their farming equipment or hunting weapons to defend themselves), MST has decided not to transform into an armed farmers' movement. It builds its nonviolent struggle on the historical experience of other farmers' movements that have been isolated and crushed precisely because they have taken up arms.[108] At the same time, the movement's choice of nonviolence does not only result from strategic considerations and military power relations; it is the product of a belief in peaceful methods of resistance and other fundamental principles.[109]

The Palestinian struggle for liberation during the first Intifada began in 1987 in the occupied territories at the initiative of those living on the West Bank and in Gaza: new groups, above all young adults, stood outside a Palestine Liberation Organisation (PLO) that at the time still accepted military struggle.[110] The Intifada (the term means 'shaking off') was based on 'the principle of the non-use of lethal weapons, and on a full escalation of the "campaign of civil disobedience"'.[111] The Intifada primarily used nonviolent methods, even if violence did occur in the resistance, or, if one prefers, the 'unarmed fight'. Participants constructed an underground university, established non-cooperation at all levels, and carried out boycotts, demonstrations, road blockades and strikes; they refused to pay taxes and declared their own state of emergency (during which everyone stayed at home).[112] The Palestinian popular committees organised the construction of alternative institutions in education, medical care, agriculture and other social services. When Israel banned the committees, the work continued through existing and accepted organisations such as the Scouts, their underlying aim being to give people support.[113] Nafez Assaily from the Palestinian Centre for the Study of Nonviolence discovered that Israel found this nonviolent struggle more difficult to handle than war. Israel had previously won wars within a few days, but it took several years to find a solution to this new approach. Eventually, in 1993, the solution became a peace process.[114] The Intifada was of great significance for strengthening the situation of women in Palestinian culture and for the generation of Israeli peace groups.[115]

In the UK in the early 1960s, there emerged a peace movement that used civil disobedience, demonstrations and protests against nuclear weapons. In 1960, the Campaign for Nuclear Disarmament (CND) brought about 80,000 people to London for its Aldermaston March. In the 1950s, the Direct Action Committee (DAC) introduced to Britain the idea of social change through the nonviolent actions of people's movements, but it never succeeded in mobilising itself, unlike the Committee of 100.[116] The world-renowned philosopher Bertrand Russell gathered 100 celebrities to sign the 'Act or Perish' appeal and a work group of competent activists, including some from DAC-organised actions. The ambition was to create 'waves' of 'mass resistance'.[117] The first blockade was carried out at the Ministry of Defence in Whitehall on 18 February 1961 when 5,000 attendees held a sit-down protest; in September, they were 12,000 in number.[118] After this explosive first wave, it proved difficult to mobilise that number of people again, although some large actions were conducted during the following years. A continued mobilisation of this British peace movement did not succeed, despite the fact that a wave of similar movements in the world led to the radical year of 1968.

The *nonviolent anti-apartheid movement* in South Africa arose out of the failure of both armed struggle against European colonisation during the seventeenth century and timid appeals to the overlords in an attempt to reach negotiations during the nineteenth century. After nearly forty years of protest, the African National Congress (ANC) changed its direction when the white regime formulated the apartheid policy in 1948. In a similar way to its Indian counterpart in the 1920s, the ANC transformed from a reformist organisation for an educated, urban elite into a revolutionary people's movement that mobilised the nation within a project of liberation. A national culture of resistance was created later and the blacks' accommodation and obedience were broken. From 1949 to 1961, the first wave of nonviolent disobedience was organised with strong traits of civil disobedience, demonstrations, strikes and boycotts.[119] The disobedience campaign in 1952 literally filled the regime's prisons and the activists refused to go home when they were offered freedom. Thus the regime was forced to appeal to the ANC to end its actions.[120] The resistance eventually led to extensive repression and the ANC was banned. After twenty years underground, another wave of nonviolence welled up in the 1980s (1983–94). This time it was international, with support actions, boycotts, economic aid and so on.[121] The collective disobedience that culminated in the Defiance Campaign in 1952 and the Mass Democratic Movement in 1989 is particularly interesting in this context.[122] Without a doubt, the ANC formed the basis of the resistance, but it was strongly influenced by ideas from a broader anti-apartheid movement and from activists in a number of groups that had stood outside the organisation at various times.[123]

The Graswurzelbewegung (the Grassroots Movement) and Kampagne Ziviler Ungehorsam (the civil disobedience campaign) were two nonviolence-oriented parts of a broader peace movement in West Germany. The Graswurzelbewegung is an anarcho-pacifist movement that is still active, with its roots in the anti-authoritarian student movement that arose in the mid-1960s.[124] 'The concept "Graswurzelrevolution" designates all groups and movements that want to radically change society from the bottom up, that is from the base and not some party or government organisation.'[125] Since 1972, it has cooperated internationally through a formal network – Graswurzelrevolution: Föderation Gewaltfreier Aktionsgruppen (FöGA); the network was open to all those active in the movement, as there was no formal membership.[126] During the 1970s, the Graswurzelbewegung initially focused on international anti-militaristic solidarity actions, and later against nuclear power. In the 1980s, they campaigned against nuclear weapons in West Germany. During the later period, the organisation's work was divided into several issues, for example asylum and refugee policies; in other words, the Graswurzelbewegung is simultaneously part of the peace, environmental, student and solidarity movements.[127]

Also active within the West German peace movement was the Campaign of Civil Disobedience until Disarmament (Kampagne Ziviler Ungehorsam bis zur Abrüstung),[128] organised by a handful of peace activists from a white, intellectual middle class. Inspired by Gandhi and Martin Luther King, the campaign's organisers wrote an open letter to the government, criticising the decision to allow nuclear arms to be sited in West Germany as of autumn 1983. The campaign publicised a list of names of people who promised to enact civil disobedience in the form of nonviolent blockades of nuclear arms transports and bases. In the letter, they offered negotiations for the disarmament of the medium-range nuclear missile, the Pershing II, stationed on US bases in the country. When the government reported that 'we do not negotiate with criminals', an extensive civil disobedience campaign was organised against the US Mutlangen nuclear weapons base outside Stuttgart. Nonviolence training was held throughout the country in order to prepare people for the risks of nonviolent struggle. In September 1987, 829 people from various social backgrounds had promised in newspaper adverts to carry out annual actions. In reality, many more than that participated: 3,000 people took part in just the spring manoeuvre blockade in 1987. Two houses were purchased next to the base and acted as a headquarters and the location of a permanent peace rally. For each event, the activists engaged in a blockade, each of them risking twenty days in jail. The actions became so extensive that a police station was set up on the base in order to handle all the activists. The area experienced an extremely high increase in criminality and finally the state government and the police offered to negotiate. Soon afterwards, the first agreement for nuclear disarmament was published (although mainly for other reasons): the so-called Intermediate-Range Nuclear Forces (INF) Treaty between the US and Soviet superpowers. It was precisely this middle-range nuclear weapon – the Pershing II cruise missile, as well as the Soviet SS20 – that the campaign had been directed at and that the agreement between the superpowers encompassed. In 1995, Germany's Federal Constitutional Court acquitted the activists and offered them damages.

2 | THE CONCEPT OF NONVIOLENCE

I have previously shown how my understanding of nonviolence has been developed based on the ways in which different historical movements have applied the idea and practice.[1] Without delving further into that contextual background here, this chapter conceptually defines what nonviolence entails from a social perspective, and thereby provides a foundation for my subsequent conceptual development of nonviolence.

Exploring the definition of 'nonviolence'

Initially, I suggested that *without violence* and *against violence* comprise the main dimensions of nonviolence. Practitioners of nonviolence see various forms of violence as immoral and undesirable and assert the necessity of a nonviolent way of life in the hope of establishing practices that counteract violence.

The varying meanings of nonviolence weigh heavily on the idea and its practice. As a practice, nonviolence encompasses persuading people that something of higher value transcends the brutality of violence. By merging this value with their practices, practitioners attempt to *embody* the former in a violent world. In doing so, they create a *social antipode to violence*, which undermines violence and oppression through resistance and competition stemming from nonviolent institutions and methods. Practitioners synchronously search for *something else* (a utopian belief, a hidden reality or a realistic possibility): for freedom from violence and oppression, 'God's kingdom', 'nonviolent revolution' or 'self-realisation'.[2]

Some describe the basic idea of the nonviolent movement in terms such as 'there is no way to peace, peace is the way', or, as the 'engaged Buddhist' Thich Nhat Hanh says, 'the practice is simply to embody peace during the walk'.[3] I find that the aim of the nonviolent movement can be summed up as *trying to apply the nonviolent future in the present as an alternative to and disobedience against current society's violence and oppression*.[4] As a result, nonviolence always engages with certain aspects of violence and cannot occur where violence does not exist.

When a movement expresses words and actions by means of *without violence* and *against violence*, we can then call it nonviolent, even if the movement itself uses other concepts.[5] In this way, we can identify the concept's social significance independently from its linguistic representation ('nonviolence' and 'violence', for example). In other words, identification would be an easy task if only those movements that used the correct term were counted as nonviolent movements. It would also be difficult to analyse the phenomenon of nonviolence, since the activists' heterogeneous claims would define nonviolence. For instance, there are those who say they practise 'nonviolence' yet they only advocate *without violence* and do not support acts of disobedience; these include the movement for Nonviolent Communication and the United Nation's (UN's) International Decade for a Culture of Peace and Non-Violence. Logically, their activities should be called something other than nonviolent.[6]

What is classified as *without violence* and *against violence* varies depending on which domain of violence and which domains of oppression are counted (see Figure 2.1) as well as which social domain the term refers to (see Figure 2.2).[7] In my interpretation, nonviolence is not decided by the agent's *intention* with the *action*, but instead by the action's properties: its expression and characteristics.

Without violence is a *nonviolent construction* (of the increasing ability to act without violence) and *against violence* is a *nonviolent resistance* (against the violence that arises despite the nonviolent construction).

Nonviolence = nonviolent construction + nonviolent resistance

The practice of nonviolence

 The concepts 'nonviolent construction' and 'nonviolent resistance' denote the social practice of nonviolence, while 'without violence' and 'against violence' are a purely analytical division of two dimensions of nonviolence. The practice of nonviolence is a combination of nonviolent construction and nonviolent resistance.

Nonviolent construction is the development, training and support of the individual or collective ability to act and live without violence. The level of ambition and the methods of nonviolent construction depend on one's view of violence and one's view on whether humans have a congenital ability to act without violence.

Nonviolent resistance – civil disobedience, for example – is the undermining, hindrance, obstruction or resolution of 'violence' or 'oppression' ('unjust' power relations), where the activists themselves attempt to avoid using violence or oppression.[8] The combination of struggle against violence and avoiding using violence oneself is incorporated into an ideological order that can vary in character. The content of nonviolent resistance can appear different depending on the strictness with which various actors view the constitution of 'violence' or 'oppression' (Figure 2.1).

Some activists, much like Gandhi, view thoughts and feelings as more or less violent, while others consider intentional killing as the only important criterion. For some, colonialism or the patriarchy constitute oppression, for others it is abortion or eating meat.

Those who view nonviolence as 'negative' (something that only says what it is *not*) have often questioned the concept.[9] However, the concept's ambiguity can be seen as a resource. Instead of this ambivalence preventing one from pinning it down, it allows 'something else' (other than 'violence'). The ambiguity forces one to question whether what one is doing is in line with the key values and ideas of nonviolence. To an extent, one avoids the power that is connected to the right to define it. The fight is still open, so to speak – the concept is not closed. A problem arises once one views the concept as 'non-action'; it then becomes neither nonviolent construction nor nonviolent resistance, but simply 'not using violence', something passive.

Both dimensions – *without violence* and *against violence* – derive from an antagonism between violence and its opposite. Non-violence 'always [has] an active, direct relation to violence. Non-violence is a confrontation, a negation.'[10] Thereby both *without violence* and *against violence* depend on the significance one gives to violence. Among the suggestions for the opposites of violence are 'peace', 'righteousness', 'justice', 'love', 'truth', 'freedom', 'basic needs', 'self-realisation' and 'kingdom of God'. Even the significance of the affiliated concept of nonviolence – *violence* – is thus allowed to remain ambivalent and open for discussion within nonviolent movements. Whether you see violence as force, renunciation of needs, injury, killing, evil, threat or something else, the two separate dimensions of nonviolence remain relevant. The concept of violence can be more or less inclusive within various movements.[11]

One's view on violence is a decisive characteristic that differentiates the types of nonviolent movement. In early Christian movements, the concept of 'evil' was used instead of violence – a concept that in many ways exceeded what we normally associate with violence: direct physical injury. The concept of evil is closer to Gandhi's use of the term 'violence': everything that reduces a person's possibility of self-realisation, where even thoughts and feelings can be violent.

Inspired by Gandhi, the peace researcher Johan Galtung has argued that violence is also 'structural' since certain social structures operate indirectly (by denying human 'potential') and have the same consequences as direct violence: injury and death.[12] Structural violence can be understood – and perhaps chiefly understood – as a kind of 'injustice' or 'oppression'; radical Christians in the USA in the nineteenth century would call it 'tyranny', i.e. a form of (unchristian) rule that harms the (Christian) people. For the New England Non-Resistance Society, 'slavery in itself [was] a form of violence'.[13] The practitioner of violence does not have to be aware of the consequences for others. In fact, it may be that the practitioner cannot be identified or the structures resulting in violent consequences were established with good intentions. As shown in Figure 2.1, the domains of violence can be more or less inclusive.[14] Similarly, even the domains of nonviolence can be more or less inclusive, depending on which definition of violence is seen as the most relevant.

Even when viewing violence in a narrow sense (as an irreversible physical injury caused by someone's conscious and forceful action against the will of the injured party), absolute nonviolence (without and against all violence) becomes an impossible task.

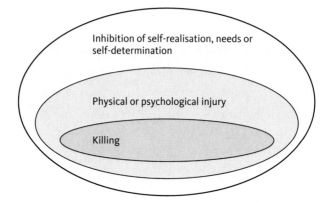

Inhibition of self-realisation, needs or self-determination

Physical or psychological injury

Killing

Note: The three concentric circles are only examples, as divisions can be made in several ways (see Galtung 1965). Normally, violence is designated as being closer to the centre and oppression (sometimes called evil, tyranny, structural violence, injustice or unjust power relations) as being closer to the periphery (cf. Young, *Att kasta tjejkast: Texter om feminism och rättvisa*, 2000).

2.1 The domains of violence and oppression

That is, if activists wish to respond nonviolently, as soon as someone attacks another individual or group, nonviolent movements should mobilise and effectively prevent the violence or protect that other. As there are over 6 billion humans on Earth, it is clearly impossible to fulfil this radical condition.[15] Thus neither *without violence* nor *against violence* can fully free itself from violence. This quandary makes inner contradictions relevant in each and every sense. It becomes possible to realise a minimal definition of *without violence* and *against violence*, in contrast to a maximal definition.

However, the two dimensions of nonviolence are intertwined conceptually. While the ability to create a community 'without violence' requires a simultaneous counteraction of all violence, the ability to act '*against violence*' ultimately and implicitly presupposes *'without violence'*, as the activists themselves need to avoid using violence: that is, if resistance is to mean resistance against 'violence' and not just against the violence of *others*. Otherwise, as soon as the activists used violence against violence, a new violence would arise, *regardless* of whether the violence they used could be claimed to make the world less violent in the long term. Thus, analytically speaking, *'against violence'* presupposes *'without violence'* in the same way as the freedom from violence in *'without violence'* presupposes the undermining of violence that is captured in the concept *'against violence'*. The concept of nonviolence is intrinsically strained. It has two convergent meanings, the consequences and common significance of which cannot be fully realised. Therefore, in practice, movements tend to stress one meaning at the cost of the other.

Without violence and *against violence* can move between particular and universal extremes depending on the extent of the *social domains*[16] – 'social domain' meaning the limiting criteria for and quantitative extent of the affected group (for example, a primary group, a religious group, a nation, a cultural community, or humanity). The smallest group is two people; the largest is humanity, or rather 'potential' humanity (including those who have not been born yet).

As a *particular* phenomenon, *without violence* is about how I, or my friends and I, live a life free from violence in which none of us exercise violence towards the others. The particular character of *against violence* involves the undermining of the violence that will occur within the group at some point, despite all attempts to avoid it. A problem for particular nonviolence is the difficulty of drawing a reasonable line between those who belong to this 'we' and those who do not. The *universal* characteristic of *without violence*, or *against violence*, relates to nonviolence affecting all of

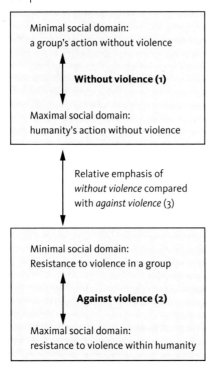

Minimal social domain:
a group's action without violence

Without violence (1)

Maximal social domain:
humanity's action without violence

Relative emphasis of
without violence compared
with *against violence* (3)

Minimal social domain:
Resistance to violence in a group

Against violence (2)

Maximal social domain:
resistance to violence within humanity

Note: The concept of
'nonviolence' includes three
tensions between extreme
poles; each of these stresses
a particular meaning among
several possibilities. Depending
on whether a minimal or a
maximal meaning is stressed
in (1) or (2), the 'social domain'
of nonviolence varies. In addition, the emphases on *without
violence* or *against violence* (3)
vary for different movements,
even if nonviolence, by definition, requires some degree of
combination of *without violence*
and *against violence*.

2.2 The varying meaning of
nonviolence

humanity. Thus, violence occurring in groups other than one's
own is just as important.[17]

The most *maximal meaning* of nonviolence is the one that
counts humanity as 'we', sees violence as 'inhibiting self-
realisation', and defines nonviolence as encompassing both
maximal *without violence* and *against violence*.[18] The most *minimal
meaning* of nonviolence sees 'we' as comprising only a primary
group (such as the family), counts only 'killing' as violence, and
treats nonviolence in practice as one-dimensional.[19] Between
these extremes, one can create several different combinations
with more or less broad meanings of 'we', 'violence' and 'nonviolence': for example, we as 'the nation', 'violence' as 'unlawful

injuries' and 'nonviolence' as a non-aggressive military 'defence' against the violent attacks of others on the nation.

The more minimal the meaning of 'we', 'violence' or 'nonviolence', the more movements will become nonviolent movements. In order to avoid ending up in a situation where everything is designated 'nonviolence', I include only those movements that view 'we' as at least both *their own group and other parties acting in a conflict* ('the enemy', 'opponents', 'third parties' and so on), define 'violence' as at least the causing of *permanent physical injury*, and consider nonviolence to at least *partially combine without violence and against violence*.[20] Movements with these characteristics are considered nonviolent movements. The nonviolent movements that are relevant can be thought to view 'we', 'violence' and 'nonviolence' in other ways, but the meanings of these terms should not be narrower than those given above. However, I do not claim that this delineation is the 'correct' one – definitions are tools, and useful for a purpose, and my purpose is to investigate a kind of 'nonviolence' that is more ambitious than the conventional type. I think that nonviolence loses its meaning when it becomes so inclusive as to denote all activity where killing is not permitted.[21]

The concept of nonviolence is a contradictory construction. The antagonism in movements between *without violence* and *against violence* manifests itself according to the relative emphasis actors place on the two sides of nonviolence (see (3) in Figure 2.2), the meaning given to 'violence' or 'oppression' (Figure 2.1), and the social domain of nonviolence (see (1) and (2) in Figure 2.2). We can see this when we perceive concepts through tensions and antipodes rather than as mutually exclusive categories.

In summary, we can identify the *domain of nonviolence* shown

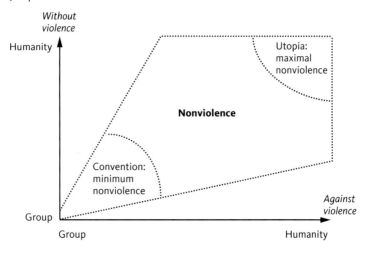

Note: The figure shows the domain of nonviolence as being separate from its minimal and maximal versions. The minimal version relates to the group only and is conventionally sanctioned in any social group. The maximal version encompasses the whole of humanity and is a utopian vision of something (im)possible. The horizontal axis approaches the maximal attempt at *against violence*; the vertical axis approaches the maximal attempt at *without violence*. Only what lies inside the dotted lines is 'nonviolence', since it combines an attempt to be *against violence* with acting *without violence*.

2.3 The domain of nonviolence

in Figure 2.3. Independent of the definitions of violence and oppression, nonviolence moves between *without violence* and *against violence* as well as between 'group' and 'humanity'. The nonviolence that is of interest here is what lies between its minimal and its maximal versions. Nonviolence can take the form of a social *convention*: the minimal nonviolence's normalising variant, which social groups apply internally. Nonviolence can also have a maximal version in the form of a described *utopia*: visionary, principled and ethical nonviolence that is expressed in literature, in the imagination, or practically and symbolically in social practice. Nonviolence here becomes a concept that binds reality within a group community (not using violence against each other) to a visionary ideal (freeing the world from violence).

The conceptual elements of the term 'nonviolence' are contradictory and challenging – philosophically and ideologically as well as practically and organisationally. The nonviolent movement thus comprises a social field in which the actors can *unite in abstaining from violence – in the forms of both without violence and against violence – but are not in agreement about what this abstinence means*. The problematic unity between the two dimensions of nonviolence means that different people, groups and movements can combine those dimensions in different ways but still be part of the same historical nonviolence movement. That is precisely what has occurred in the history of such movements.

Nonviolent resistance The two main concepts of nonviolence – nonviolent resistance and nonviolent construction – each have their own sub-concepts. Nonviolent resistance can take many forms; one of these is disobedience.

Disobedience is refusing to follow a legal or social rule or an authority's command. In its broader meaning, disobedience refers to nonconformist behaviour or a 'deviant behaviour'[22] – this could include choosing to not act, i.e. that one does *not* do what is expected.[23] Here, disobedience is discussed as a main form of resistance to power and structural violence – and thereby also to the ability to organise direct violence.

Civil disobedience is a specific form of disobedience and constitutes a supposed breach of the law, norms, order, regulations or other rules constructed by humans. It is carried out without (the threat of) violence towards others – at least not physical injury – and where at least a few actors take personal responsibility in public for their actions, since they do not view their actions as a (serious) crime, at least not in a moral sense.[24]

As an 'alleged crime' or challenge to the established 'right', civil disobedience involves the members of the affected social community giving serious consideration to their reasons for interpreting the act, at least initially, as being morally or legally criminal. Thus the authorities have at the very least a suspicion that a crime has been committed, while the activists have consciously taken that risk, with no certainty of the outcome. Defining civil disobedience purely as a crime in the legal sense and not, as here, as a social concept of something that *may be a crime* (with a risk of being convicted), one ends up in the peculiar position whereby actions that receive an acquittal in court (which sometimes happens) suddenly no longer constitute 'civil disobedience'. That would mean that the activists' successful actions – those where they convince others, even the courts, that the action was right – suddenly become something else.[25] This leads to a conceptual dilemma in which activists' successful civil disobedience cannot be *called* civil disobedience.

It is important to distinguish between disobedience against *legitimate* and *illegitimate* rules – that is, rules that have or do not have the support of the affected population. As a challenge of the legitimacy of rules, nonviolent disobedience against rules that are perceived as legitimate in a certain community will be more difficult to sustain or defend or for it to gain recognition. A common opinion is that norms are legitimate rules in a group while laws and other regulations are not necessarily legitimate. Yet the fact is that norms may also be illegitimate. Habermas claims that the legitimacy of norms presupposes that they can be questioned and examined (see Chapter 3).

Moreover, a breach of rules might also occur as a *consequence* of an action: that is to say, in cases where the infringement itself is not a goal, but arises as the activists try to achieve something else. An action group that blocks the WTO's conference building in Seattle is not necessarily against the USA's ordinance prohibiting sitting on a motorway.

Likewise, there is a difference between disobedience against a *single rule* and against a *regulatory regime*, as a crime against a rule can be supported by other rules while an infringement of a community's (legitimate) ordinance can hardly gain support from the relevant community (although it can be supported by other social communities with other regulatory regimes).

Nonviolent construction Nonviolent construction's 'politics of creative living' are central to nonviolence, but unfortunately they are often disregarded or developed in separate directions.[26] Nonviolent construction varies, like nonviolent resistance, depending on the context and other conditions. Several kinds of methods and activities can be discussed, but first three central concepts must be defined before moving on.

A *constructive programme* is a plan for the construction of social structures, institutions and practices that can replace those being fought against. The constructive programme expresses and builds upon a nonviolent goal. It comprises a coherent array of activities, methods, social institutions and organisations. Together, they create the preconditions for *without violence* and *against violence* by mobilising resources (knowledge, organisation, technique, people, money, and so on) and by promoting the self-esteem and dignity that empower subordinate people to resist injustice and oppression nonviolently. A fully fledged programme aims to integrate different groups of people and activities in a 'nonviolent society'.

Nonviolence training is the nonviolent movement's counterpart to military training, a time-limited and intensive preparation for nonviolent actions that focuses on certain special skills and knowledge to ease the social practice of nonviolence. Courses in nonviolence were organised by movements that developed in conjunction with the Civil Rights Movement, and then spread to other nonviolent movements. On such courses, dialogue, exercises and role playing help prepare people for actions, and they are trained to use meeting forms and dialogue-easing techniques and to handle power. The participants gain knowledge about nonviolence and how to organise and plan campaigns. The training is often thematic and suited to a group's current needs and can be carried out over a couple of hours or a few days, or it can last for months or even years. However, training longer than a week is still not common.

Nonviolent ways of life are activist experiments with new collective and individual ways of being.[27] A nonviolent way of life is about people representing their lives in a specific way based on strong values about the righteous life ('living witness'). This way of life is not private or a 'style', but a social phenomenon and part of the political means of expression in movements and, indeed, a typical part of late modernity ('life politics'). Following a Gandhian perspective, one can say that 'true *swaraj*' (true independence) is about 'counter[ing] our own "inner statehood" ... letting one's life become a "counter-friction" against the machinery of government'.[28] The ways of life of nonviolence are expressed in various terms such as simple living, voluntary simplicity, voluntary poverty, vows, vegetarianism, veganism, living community, intentional community, commune, co-op, peace camp and resistance community.[29]

The ambivalent assumptions of nonviolence

The general concept of nonviolence as we have examined it so far expresses an *ambivalence* within the concept itself. Thus, the solution to one problem gives rise to another problem.

One can analytically separate a number of opposing relationships that the collective actors must find ways to handle socially and that give nonviolence several *utopian ideals*. The utopian ideals provide something of value while being impossible to realise fully. They comprise the guiding aims providing a direction of improvement.

> In the nonviolent struggle, we must distinguish between the final goal which is a reconciled society of greater justice, flowering in liberty with all the transformations that spring from it, a task which is constantly set throughout human history – and the steps by which we realize it. Nonviolent commitment demands long and persevering combat: in fact, permanent commitment.[30]

The tension of this ambivalence reveals itself in several ways: firstly, in the attempt to *unite* what are basically disunited phenomena. The fight against violence is united with the construction of the capacity to live without using violence (uniting *without violence* and *against violence*). The struggle's *goal* (utopia or vision) is *united with its means* (the tools of the goal), and *morality* (what should be or is to be done) is *united with practice* (what is or what is done).[31] The attempt at union is expressed through 'good' examples of action as one hopes that they challenge and eventually change the other's violence and oppressive behaviour.

Despite bans, blacks and whites sat together in segregated cafés and diners and they demanded to be served on equal terms: they carried out a 'sit-in'.[32] By holding sit-ins, the Civil

Rights Movement tried to realise its goal of civil equality or non-discrimination and non-segregation in the USA. The goal was expressed with the concrete means of the action (sit-ins that, on a small scale, achieved non-segregated cafés by breaking segregation laws). '[You] will not only *advocate* your rights and the rights of others, but exercise them and take any consequences in a nonviolent manner.'[33] The attempt is beautiful, but an action cannot always realise the moral message. In practice, it is sometimes difficult to take the risks that morality demands, or to act as peacefully as the movement expects, for example when provocation and humiliation battered the courageous activists who went alone into white territory.[34] In Portsmouth, the activists reacted violently when they were attacked by whites who beat them with chains and hammers.[35] Similarly, the realisation of the action's goals can be difficult to demonstrate. The café that was to be made accessible to all in fact risked being changed into a space that few wanted to frequent, due to an irate mob driven by an insulted café owner and obstinate activists. Who can live up to the movement's practical representation of the vision of a future of equality and respect? But the *attempt* exists in the nonviolent action and is made visible to a greater or lesser extent through concrete practice.

At the same time, the inherent ambivalence of nonviolence is also shown through attempts to *differentiate* phenomena that are fundamentally quite likely to be impossible to differentiate. Nonviolent activists imagine that you can distinguish between the opponent as a *person* (the oppressor as individual and equal member of humanity) and the opponent's *actions or roles* (the oppression as a system of roles and institutions).[36] Their ambition is to show that, while directing the fight against those roles and behaviours that uphold the system of violence and oppression, all people (and in particular those who see themselves as enemies of the movement) still deserve care and respect. This differentiation between person and role expresses itself in breaking the power (of the oppression) and in facilitating dialogue (with the oppressors and others involved).[37]

The other difference enacted is the one between an *absolute truth* about reality (in an ontological sense) and the perspective or position of a *relative or particular truth* (in an epistemological sense). This difference applies in a fundamental sense when the nonviolent act strives for an increasingly wide consensus among a larger number of people.

The utopian ideals as a whole create a number of duplicitous assumptions. This duplicity is expressed in the action being contradictory or entailing demanding rules of engagement:[38] for example, activists should abstain from violent defence or revenge and should not exploit a weakness or a problem that has overcome the opponent[39] while also carrying out an effective resistance; activists should exercise civil disobedience and also obey what is morally correct while applying disciplined behaviour; activists should organise non-cooperation in certain contexts while developing cooperation projects with the opposition on what is agreed upon; activists should develop a constructive programme and even protect the opponent from injuries and show trust, despite risking their own safety or having previously been tricked.[40]

Each nonviolent group or movement *must*, in some way or another, manage to construct practical solutions to these dilemmas in order to unite *without violence* and *against violence*, goals and means, and morals and practice, and to differentiate between person and role, and 'Truth' and truth. The attempts to solve these problems also need to be developed in their specific contexts in order for the form of action to be socially meaningful and not absurdly contradictory. Attempts to handle these dilemmas are made understandable in representation and dialogue and together structure a nonviolent discourse.

Like their opponents, nonviolent activists fight for their cause, but unlike most social critics, they promote a consensus or a working agreement between different actors in the conflicts in which they participate. Sometimes it is a matter of breaking the existing power-saturated consensus or breaking the silence where the conflict is not recognised – even then, the aim is to build a genuine consensus by transforming the conflict. For Gandhi, it was a matter of arriving at an agreement with the opposition through confrontation, and of developing a common understanding. Since the nonviolent movement – based on our conceptual scheme – attempts to solve, transform and manage the conflicts in which one acts, takes into account all affected partners (not just dominating them out of self-interest), and is based on all of the conflict's aspects (not just its acute crisis), the contradiction should be interpreted as an *attempt to transform a conflict through consensus-oriented challenges to injustice, violence and untruths.* This attempt seems to create a fundamental ambivalence.

Thus, we have a reasonable explanation of in-built nonviolent opposition. However, *how* nonviolent movements actually handle this opposition creatively and dynamically so that consensus is furthered between the parties to a conflict is an entirely different empirical question. This interesting question lies beyond our area of conceptual examination.

The basic discursive structure of nonviolence My conceptual scaffolding characterises nonviolence using a specific discourse. Accordingly, *discourse* is a particular way of speaking about

Experiment with truth in social conflicts through:

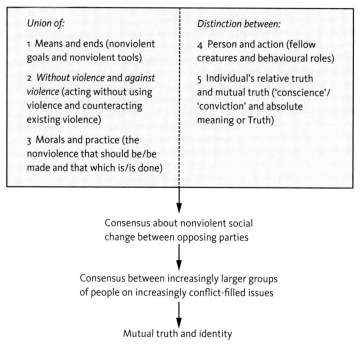

Union of:	Distinction between:
1 Means and ends (nonviolent goals and nonviolent tools)	4 Person and action (fellow creatures and behavioural roles)
2 *Without violence* and *against violence* (acting without using violence and counteracting existing violence)	5 Individual's relative truth and mutual truth ('conscience'/ 'conviction' and absolute meaning or Truth)
3 Morals and practice (the nonviolence that should be/be made and that which is/is done)	

Consensus about nonviolent social change between opposing parties

Consensus between increasingly larger groups of people on increasingly conflict-filled issues

Mutual truth and identity

2.4 Gandhi's utopian discursive structure of nonviolence

and understanding the world (or part of it) that perceives our speaking patterns as a form of active participation in creating and transforming our situation, identities and social relations.[41] Discourse encompasses *practical rules that conjoin speech and other actions*.[42] This is precisely what the nonviolent movement's utopian ideal does. With the help of the two preceding chapters, we can summarise the discursive structure of nonviolence that emanates from Gandhi in Figure 2.4.

Gandhi departs from the understanding that one can reach *satya* and unite in a collective self-realisation in the divine '*Brahman*' or '*atman*' that encompasses everyone. As we have seen,

Gandhi thinks that Truth and God are the same thing (*satya/ Brahman*). Reaching truth together (whether God, the cosmos or ultimate reality) brings about the end of ignorance and suffering and thus individual differences that cause conflict, as the ego and desire are dissolved; we are united in a common humanity (in liberation or '*moksha*' we become identical with *Brahman*).[43] And this common truth and identity can be reached by experimenting with truth in social conflicts.

We can travel far on the way to this utopian goal through consensus agreements and nonviolent social change. Yet the goal itself remains impossible: complete and mutual truth, in the sense of universal truth and an understanding of the ultimate reality.

The discourse expresses the ideal. Nonviolent action is always just an attempt to achieve this ideal. Whether the nonviolent discourse in a particular action contributes to mutual consensus – or, indeed, whether that is what the activists are striving for – or if, instead, it leads to a new power organisation of people's perceptions and behaviours (a 'truth regime' as Foucault calls it) is above all an empirical question, not a conceptual one.[44]

With this description of the discursive structure of nonviolence, a continued conceptual development is possible. We can state that nonviolence is a cohesive action repertoire – despite competing understandings of truth between the conflicting parties, indeed *thanks to* the disunity – since there is an assumption of an inherent communicative rationality in nonviolence. If this inherent rationality did not exist and was unable to manage the inherent contradictions of nonviolence, this form of action would instead need to be described as an exercise of power in the nonviolent activists' partisan interest, like the political influence of any other interest group.

Thus, the conceptual development itself leads me to state that *the inherent contradictions of nonviolence require a solution via some kind of immanent reason in the conflict's dynamics so that the unity can be made possible.* If not, nonviolence as an action repertoire does not work conceptually. In this respect, the first true challenge for conceptual development is to describe how nonviolence can express rationality, which is the focus of the next chapter.

3 | THE RATIONALITY OF NONVIOLENT ACTION

Which concepts are needed to describe nonviolent forms of action and their relation to *rationality*? This question raises the need to investigate how action types can be categorised and interpreted rationally. Based on a general sociological theory of action, I discuss how the interplay of actions can be interpreted. I then argue for a relevant typology of action for rational forms of nonviolent action. Finally, this leads to an argument on how to fruitfully interpret nonviolence as a consensus-oriented whole comprising four basic types of ambivalent interplay of actions. The main empirical cases used to illustrate the conceptual development of this chapter are the Civil Rights Movement in the USA in the 1950s and the West German Campaign of Civil Disobedience Until Disarmament of the mid-1980s.

As we previously saw, Gene Sharp understands nonviolent action as a goal-rational action that takes shape in strategy or technique.[1] By illustrating Habermas's typology of action with the help of a concrete example of civil disobedience, I argue that nonviolence can beneficially be interpreted as a kind of *multi-rational* action in conflicts, which should not be reduced to 'goal rationality'.

'An *action* can be understood as the realisation of a plan of action supported by the interpretation of a situation.'[2] Meaningful actions are studied here as 'conduct': situations in which actors are aware of each other's presence or potential presence and take each other into consideration when they act.[3]

The meaning of the actions is not limited to the meaning the actors themselves give them through their aims, attitudes, convictions or motives.[4] Actions carried out in social contexts are interpreted by those who are present in the communication of the situation and by others who are affected, where *social interpretations* influence the ways in which conflicting parties act in the context of nonviolent actions.[5]

The same form of action can have varying meanings and be rational from different perspectives – or, to be more precise, from different logics of rationality. For instance, activists preventing an operation by physically situating themselves as transport blockades is an action that prevents and expresses distance from something – not a form of action that points towards constructive possibilities for something else. Still, the blockade can be carried out as a creative activity. There are those in the German campaign who quite simply sat on the road and refused to move when the transport columns with nuclear weapons and service vehicles entered and left the nuclear weapons base. Notably, this action was conducted by retirees and former German soldiers who had taken part in the Second World War. Over ten days, 800 'senior activists' disrupted a manoeuvre in the forest, while others chose to use their professions as a blockade tool. Clothed in their white gowns, doctors and nurses closed the entrance to the base by holding their lectures with medical students on the roads. Priests preached to their congregations in front of the base's gates instead of in church. And former prisoners of concentration camps sat in rows clothed in their old uniforms. Others brought along their looms and wove cloth in the middle of the road. Yet others danced traditional dances. Another group tried to sell Christmas trees to the soldiers from a 'market square' right in front of the base's entrance. Each and every one of these actions – either a positive civil operation, a pleasurable activity or a reminder of a terrible historical genocide – was used as a tool that loaded the blockade with meaning. And this gave the blockade new meanings – it was no longer locked into only signifying a physical 'power struggle' between two parties.

The most powerful weapons humanity had ever created were blocked by seemingly powerless and everyday activities. 'Strength' in itself became symbolically restricted as frail pensioners pursued the nuclear arms soldiers by the hundreds during a forest manoeuvre and blocked roads and paths to such an extent that the military exercises had to be called off.

At the same time, each blockade gained a symbolic meaning by means of being part of a chain of blockades. The social groups' participation in the resistance to the nuclear weapons base created such a dynamic image that it was as if an entire society resisted. Blockades with 200 doctors and forty lawyers made it all the more difficult to disregard the activists or to view them as unemployed professional activists or flaky hippies. When nineteen judges sat on the road on 12 January 1987, it was clear evidence that blockades may be legal – perhaps it was the weapons that were illegal?

The blockade's 'negative' message of prevention gained a positive tone for its vision of the future – a demilitarised society of active social groups paralysing military dominance with steadfastness and humour, putting themselves in the way and asserting the value of their civil operations.

The German civil disobedience campaign organised blockades of the nuclear weapons base in Mutlangen as a single form of action that was repeated in the context of a single society. Still, its actions were accomplished thanks to their varying but concrete formulation and the participation of discrete groups in separate activities. Various types of blockades were carried out in the campaign by different social groups, giving rise to a variety of meanings.

The rational conditions of disobedience

Constructing institutions and ways of living without violence is neither particularly controversial nor difficult to justify. In liberal democracies it is normally legal to live without using violence, except when the state demands that individuals participate in its 'defence'. The resistance to violence, however, can be more controversial. A usual form of nonviolent resistance is thus civil disobedience. Disobedience as a category of action puts certain requirements or *necessary conditions of rationality* on the movement.

Disobedience, like any social act, presupposes a rationalisation or legitimisation that makes the act rational and justified, at least for those involved in the movement. This is *internal legitimisation*. As a result, to some degree disobedience must *tie into the participants' existing culture and experience*.[6] Disobedience must be comprehensible based on the conceivable world view or horizon of understanding of the movement's participants.

The Civil Rights Movement in the USA succeeded in mobilising thousands from the previously politically passive black groups in the southern states by tying into an already existing Christian culture among blacks. A peaceful will to fight segregation ensued from the unlikely combination of holy wrath (against the injustice of segregation) and Christian atonement (towards whites) that was preached by radical pastors in black congregations (cultural authorities). They mobilised symbols and myths from the Christianity that the slave owners had preached but gave them new meaning and put them in a new context.

Moreover, they eventually found a method that fitted this internal legitimisation: nonviolence.

As opposed to conventional social action, disobedience means a *breach of rules*. Conventional action is normalised in everyday life while disobedience is not. Since others will question the breach of rules, I find that disobedience, in contrast to everyday accommodation and obedience, requires an expressed and developed rationalisation. Thus, the choice of the rules you break or the choice of the form of disobedience cannot be arbitrary. The problem with or 'illegitimacy' of the rules as well as a suitable means of action therefore must be identified and made comprehensible. In its particular situation, the movement needs to show why a certain rule should be broken. This is because general disobedience against rules of all kinds, in all possible situations, will seem absurd (at least to others), and, if such a general disobedience spread, social order – regardless of content and form – would fall apart. Collective disobedience must be justified with some kind of special reason or argument. Without a *rationalisation for exception*, legitimisation of the breach of rules will not convince others.

If the action of disobedience is to lead to an extensive movement, new social groups or previously uninterested people must also be convinced of the meaningfulness of disobedience – that is, of its legitimacy. If movements also strive for social change and political results, then disobedience may appear completely irrational to the central groups and authorities supporting the existing order and its power elite. For that reason, an attempt to legitimise the action within its surroundings is required – a kind of 'consensus mobilisation'.[7] This means that the *external legitimisation requires a connection to the dominant society's norms, myths, ideologies and values.* The question is to what extent the movement must connect to the dominant societal structure in order to sufficiently legitimise itself, its actions and its goals. This connection must be made to some extent if the action is to be comprehensible.

The Civil Rights Movement connected to the dominant social discourse when it claimed that blacks had an equal role in the USA. By connecting its struggle against discrimination with the vision of pluralism, equality and national identity that had been the basis of the US constitution, the movement became difficult to dismiss. Many whites, above all in the northern states, could thus see the Civil Rights Movement as a part of their struggle against a USA that had lost its unique soul, as an attempt to regain the 'land of the free'.

An infringement of the norms or laws cannot be the only form of activity in the movement: activities that *support* disobedience are required. This is because disobedience must be asserted through various information channels and punished activists need support; otherwise it becomes more difficult to mobilise new participants. A parallel activity to disobedience exists and takes care of the aims that do not require a breach of the rules to be achieved. In practice, nonviolent resistance is not an isolated and single action but rather it attains meaning, in empirical contexts, through other connected, coherent actions throughout the whole of the movement. Nonviolent resistance cannot be carried out in an empty space: it is embedded – partly in nonviolent construction, and partly in the movement's other activities. Of course, this social integration of nonviolence can be more or less active in different movements. However, the necessary requirement for activities that support disobedience does not become less relevant because some movements fail to fulfil that requirement.

Goal-rational and value-rational actions

In this chapter, nonviolence as a whole should be understood as rational, as a complex form of action that is *communicative* and conducted *multi-rationally*, and that is also potentially *contradictory*.

Contradictions may arise because various types of nonviolent action are combined and different rational dimensions of the same action upheld. Contradiction is also understandable at a basic level as any attempt to achieve consensus between conflicting parties and simultaneously deal with several dimensions of a conflict will face problems.

But let's approach this step by step.

A nonviolent action is a form of social action. First of all, it is important to be clear that 'actions' are not necessarily clearly delineated events that drastically break with daily life. On the contrary, most actions are a continuous flow. They are waves of action sequences, and they sometimes break off from their current direction. Sometimes they are brought to people's attention and chosen consciously. If not, they continue in a more or less automatic flow of actions. An action does not have a concrete beginning or end – although we talk about them as if they did and analyse them as if they were clearly distinct units. At times, it is necessary to talk about 'big' and 'decisive' actions to put forward an argument, but this risks concealing how such actions are made possible. 'Big' actions – for example the landless farmers' occupation of land in the Brazilian countryside – merely consist of many 'smaller', everyday actions joined together.

A person carries out an action when what they do is intentional, and when it has a purpose, meaning or reason.[8] Actions are *practical conclusions that have been made based on intentions and beliefs*. For that reason, action and rationality are intertwined. But rationality is not a given, nor is it simple. The degree of rationality can be analysed, discussed and evaluated precisely because actions lay claim to rationality. For activists, their own actions appear meaningful and rational, but for new participants in the movement or outsiders that rationality might not be clear.

Let's look at how a civil disobedience action can be interpreted rationally.[9] Activists in the German disobedience campaign blockaded the nuclear weapons base in Mutlangen on 15 September 1986. The symphony orchestra Lebenslaute, comprising 120 musicians, placed itself in front of the base's two gates and played pieces by Bach, Beethoven, Mozart and Schubert as the campaign's first 'music-in' or 'Konzert blockade'. The police redefined the blockade as a 'demonstration' and the soldiers at the base were relieved of their duty. The police did not arrest anyone but stood by and listened to the concert. This meant that the symphony orchestra succeed in doing something that even the Soviet superpower found difficult: it paralysed the USA's nuclear weapons capabilities. Although it was clearly only at one place and for one day, the fact remains that the base was temporarily out of use due to Beethoven's music. When the orchestra that had played the whole day continued during the night, patience ran short. The police arrested the musicians and put them in holding cells.

The symphony orchestra's members displayed a mutual intention in their action. They wanted to 'block the passage in and out of the Mutlangen base during the concert'.[10] Their music was part of a 'life-affirming culture' that would pit itself against the 'death culture' that the base's war preparations were part of. They could not be reconciled. Of course, each and every person who participated also had their own reasons for taking part.

But despite the specific, concrete aims of each participant, one can ascertain a social significance in their symphonic blockade within the context of a number of directly related actions: for example, their press release and the statements given in police interrogations and subsequent trials. The action is *goal rational* to the extent that the participants had a result they wanted to achieve: to prevent the base's nuclear weapons-related operations. They tried to do this by temporarily closing the base, by showing that their conviction was so important that the risks would not deter them, and by arguing why this action was necessary and justified. By participating in a campaign together with others who carried out similar resistance, they hoped to create a sufficiently strong political force. In terms of goal rationality, the action was a tool for achieving the desired real events.

But the action was also loaded with a surplus of meaning – it was symbolic. As well as resulting in the complete shut-down of the base, it also pointed towards something beyond its immediate significance.[11] The action is a symbol for common people themselves doing something to prevent nuclear war.

A number of people perceive effective actions as non-symbolic, or, in other words, that symbolic actions are ineffective. But all actions can be understood as symbolic. Effective actions are symbolically loaded since they express the possibility of achieving results.[12] To the degree that civil disobedience is successful in achieving change – for example, stopping the planned export of weapons to a country – then disobedience becomes even more symbolically loaded precisely because it is a sign that disobedience brings about change.

Those actions normally classified as 'symbolic' are sometimes quite empty of meaning. If the symphony orchestra had played a peace concert in the city square, protesting against nuclear weapons, the symbolic message would not have been as strong. An orchestra in the square would symbolically have expressed something entirely different: namely, that we can stop nuclear weapons by playing music in a square. This would have involuntarily symbolised the peace movement's inability to stop nuclear weapons. Standing in front of the base, the orchestra symbolised the movement's inability to stop nuclear weapons every day – partly because they did not return day after day once they were let out of jail, and partly because other symphony orchestras did not blockade other bases at the same time – but it also symbolised the possibility of stopping operations on one base for one day. Therefore, the action also highlighted the possibility that *all* bases can be stopped on *all* days if people followed the orchestra's example. This 'symbolic effectiveness', which an action might express clearly and challengingly, depends on the harmony between the action's design and the interpreters' understanding, not on the actors' individual aims.

Equally, we can say that the action said something about *who* was involved: the activists, the police and the military *were attributed identities* according to how they treated each other. Identity arises out of social interactions where what matters is both your own self-image and others' definitions of who you are.[13] It expresses the difference between the individual or group and the others: we and them. Based on a social constructivist theory of identity, we can speak of reflexive identities that are created *through action* (performativity).[14] Identity construction is a struggle between perceptions. The police characterised the activists as 'criminals' but saw themselves as 'responsible keepers of the peace'. For some observers the activists were 'martyrs' sacrificed to a good cause; for others they were irritating 'troublemakers' preventing people from doing their legitimate

work. Identity is ascribed through both explicit designations and
the perceptions expressed in the action. Identities are therefore
not (permanently) given or self-assumed, but rather are common and impermanent, individually constructed self-images
that are sometimes disputed in the shape of conflict-loaded
relations. Activists do not decide meaning alone, since identities
are negotiated in interactions. Thus, the activists' credibility
lessens among their opponents if they act in a contradictory
fashion: for example, if they advocate equal and peaceful relations while also acting as if they were subordinate, morally
superior or prepared to use violence.

The orchestra's action can also be understood as *value
rational*.[15] The symphony orchestra managed only to stop the
activity at the base during one day. They could not count on
such a clear result in advance. Thus, it should also be reasonable
to interpret the blockade as value rational in the sense that the
result was not the only decisive one, but, for the participants
carrying out the action, it had *value in itself*. Whether the action
really could counteract the threat of nuclear arms, there was a
belief that it was of value. A 'planned genocide' would at least
not happen with their approval – 'not in my name', which is a
common slogan in nonviolent actions against nuclear weapons
in the USA. Regardless of what the participants actually believed
or wanted, we can say that the form of their action expressed
the message that it was of value in itself, whatever the result.
It is in this way that ordinary people's attempt to prevent the
nuclear arms threat becomes the value that the action expresses.

There is no reason to understand the same action as only
goal-rational influence, symbolic communication, identity construction or value rational. It is a combination of some sort. It
brings us to the question of whether we can even set a social

meaning – a mutual meaning – or if every act has different meanings depending on who evaluates it.

The social meanings of actions

The French philosopher Paul Ricoeur claims that actions should be interpreted in the same way as text:

> What should be understood in a text is first and foremost not the person speaking behind the text but what the text speaks about – *the text's* 'issue', that is to say the world that the text in some way develops *before* the text.[16]

Moreover, he claims that the text's intention is not the author's supposed intention, 'but what the text itself wants'. According to Ricoeur, hermeneutics has been damaged by being identified with the understanding of a psyche behind it. In the theory of action and subjectivist directions within hermeneutics, it is common for actions to be given their meaning based on the actor's attitudes, motives and psyche. What you are then trying to do is explain why a text was written as it was. If the explanation is convincing, you have involuntarily abolished the agent's addressing of other people, the attempt to communicate. A convincing explanation tends to disregard the communicative attempt. If, for example, we interpret a movement's demonstration against discrimination as an attempt to form a group identity, the question regarding discrimination tends to fade in importance. What is decisive is for us to understand the uniqueness of a movement's sociality; this, then, becomes our interpretation of what is said and done. The question of who says something is instead a question for the psychology of social movements. Naturally, the psychological study of social movements is both justified and interesting, but it is problematic if you mix the question of *who* says something with the question of *what* is said. The new social movement theory's use of the concept of 'collective identity' is in part an example of such a mixture.[17]

The meaningful action thus becomes objectified or fixed at the same moment that it is completed; in the same way, a discourse becomes fixed through writing, through it becoming text, and by escaping or leaving the agent, so to speak.[18] The meaningfulness does not depend on the nearness to the agent, but on the action's involvement in the social, its mutuality. When the action or the text is executed, there is no subject with a privileged right of interpretation, not even the actor. Of course, it is reasonable, if possible, to ask the actor what they want to attain, as those who acted can be expected to have convincing arguments or reasons. But no one has a 'copyright' on the action's significance – it is a mutual concern to be discussed. If the meaning were to be defined by the actor, each text or action would be only a time-specific document, a story among stories, a question of psychology or a function of a social position. The communication or social meaning would be abolished.

To understand the meaning of collective actions, we must make a number of important distinctions. We should distinguish between the *actor's intended* meaning for the action and the *action's* meaning. The action's meaning encompasses several dimensions that need to be interpreted as a whole: the context, effects, reactions of the affected and the intended meaning (if known), and here the *unintended meanings* are also meaningful for 'the reader' (potentially all people). Furthermore, we must also acknowledge that *meaningless* behaviour might exist – for instance, bodily movements based on physical reflexes that appear to be 'behaviour' but are not, or behaviour that is trivial with regard to a certain interest or context – although it will never be possible to make a definite judgement about what is indeed 'meaningless'. We should also note that there might be actions that are – for various reasons – meaningful for the actors, but that have nothing to do with the meaning of nonviolence. An *uninteresting meaning* – in the context of the aim of this book – is a meaning that is not of interest with regard to the nonviolent activity of social movements.

The hermeneutic perspective on nonviolent action means that we need to understand the action as a whole, when initially the important parts of that action may be unclear. Eventually the relevant social whole comes to the fore, which gives the action social meaning. Interpretation is carried out in an endless hermeneutic cycle of new interpretations. However, each interpretation is not as plausible as any other interpretation, since the validity of the interpretation relies on it being persuasively argued against alternative views. Even if you can make endless new interpretations, some are more convincing than others.

When activists from a local group of the German nonviolent movement Graswurzelbewegung blocked a transport of soldiers at Cologne's train station, they themselves (as individuals and as a group) had an intent behind their action. Once completed, an action is public and its meaning fixed; the action is like a manuscript that has gone to press and is fixed as a text. The fact that civilian train travellers were delayed was a predictable but unintentional significance. The conclusion is that, for the activists, preventing soldiers from travelling was more important than disrupting civil activities (regardless of whether the activists themselves were aware that they had made that their priority).

When the activists involved in the blockade handed out flyers and offered people coffee, dialogue and kindness grew out of their acts and the action became an interaction. When mass media later reported on the action, journalists bestowed it with further meanings. Long before the activists could regroup in the pub in Cologne's social centre after the police had released them, the action had 'left them' and a number of agents in society had interpreted it. The action lived its own social life. The activists showed that they were aware that the action's meaning was judged within its social context by making evaluations based on their own experiences and through the comments of other agents – for example, other activists, the media, soldiers, the police and travellers. The evaluation became an experience modifying both the design of forthcoming actions and their attempts to steer the (social) significance of those actions.

A nonviolent act of resistance has several relevant social meanings; our next step is to find out how this significance arises in the social sphere.

The construction of meanings A theory that can help us understand social interaction is *symbolic interactionism*. Symbolic interactionism sees interactions as a *social* creation built on *communication*. The founder, George Herbert Mead, distinguishes significant gestures that depend on their interpretation from non-significant gestures that occur automatically or from a reflex.[19] Interpretation bestows actions, ideas and objects with meaning. They become *symbols* expressing *another* action, idea or object beyond their immediate identity.[20] The genesis of a meaning creates the connection between at least two phenomena: objects and their reference to something else. Different meanings are in turn co-dependent and form a structure of meaning or symbols.

The underlying point of symbolic interactionism is that we act in accordance with the meaning or symbol that is connected to a particular stimulus, and not as a result of the stimulus itself; social psychology had previously argued authoritatively for the latter (as 'behaviourism'). Meaning is socially constructed and thereby to some degree general within its communicative community and context (a 'society'). However, this is not the case in an absolute sense, since every individual is a participant in the social process of interpretation, which is intersubjective and sometimes contested. Together, subjects give social meanings to themselves, others and the world – and also, of course, to nonviolence.

The structured communication of meaning Since the meaning of an action is created mutually through the understanding of others, in order to communicate you have to see things from those others' perspectives. This also means seeing yourself through the other, or making yourself an object.[21] An interaction means that individuals try to integrate their actions by accommodation and by interpreting meanings together. Joint actions of disobedience can be seen as creating a process of *interactive interpretation*. Stability in social interaction results from its history: each example of a mutual act is preceded by previous mutual acts, which means that interpretations, symbolic structures and meanings that have already been established socially continue to create institutions, such as marriage or nonviolence training. Accordingly, nonviolent actions cannot be as free as you would like them to be because every act of resistance necessarily builds on previously established meanings and experiences – and those meanings and experiences are based on collective understandings.

If we were to carefully interpret every single object in our daily life, we would be driven mad as we would be overloaded by the simplest things – like walking along a street. Interpretation is routinised, and routines repeat year after year until they become almost automatic. Sheldon Stryker, among others, took symbolic interaction in a more structure-oriented direction and claims that structure is a stable interaction or a regular pattern of action.[22] Existing power relations and culturally accepted meanings provide the actors with materials to choose from, defend and only partially renew. There are limited resources available for creating meaning, which makes reinterpretation difficult. In an analysis of nonviolent action, consideration must be given to the research that agents conduct into actions and to the interpretive structure that supports any understanding of nonviolence.

The mutually true meaning of nonviolence Symbolic interactionism presents a social life in which the meaning of symbols is endlessly communicated.[23] Not everything is of equal importance, but for all meaningful things there is a cooperation of understanding and struggle for understanding, a search for social knowledge in social life, where you are forced to search for a common understanding of the symbolism. If the meaning of symbols is decided socially in the interaction, then it must be possible to understand (*nonviolent*) *action's meaning* based on the theory of communicative rationality.

Habermas launched the concept of *communicative rationality* in the 1980s. This is a theory of discursive interaction that states how a truth or the morally correct is ascertained (discourse ethics).[24] Conversation is a communicative action in which a search for understanding (*verständigung*) and consensus (*einverständnis*) is built into the conditions of the interaction, in the very attempt to communicate.[25]

Habermas claims that there is a rationality built into spoken language and the 'life world' that people live through, and that this is fundamentally communicative.[26] This suggests that a theory of discourse can also be seen as a theory of democracy, truth and morals. Speaking to people – or carrying out 'speech acts' – is founded on us believing what we say (being honest), talking about something that affects us mutually (being inter-subjective), and letting the argument or reasons decide what is relevant (being interested in what is wrong or right).[27]

Communicative rationality with an orientation towards understanding differs from goal rationality with its focus on the project. The latter defines the so-called system – state or bureaucracy and the market. Communication depends on an agreement based on *convincing* one another, while goal rationality is technical and strategic in its search for the right instrument for already set goals – and is thereby connected to power, influence and *persuasion*.[28]

Based on discourse theory, Habermas and Karl-Otto Apel developed what they termed discourse ethics, which claims that what is ethically true is a consensus between all people after an endless conversation without the influence of power.[29] This endless conversation is the 'ideal speech situation', which is a utopia. The utopia helps us to search critically for ways to reduce the influence of power or to increase resistance to power.

We are not to believe that we can achieve this ideal speech situation. It is impossible. The ideal conversation serves as something to strive towards, a direction for communication. The ideal conversation thus becomes a measurement for critically judging the interpretations and agreements that arise in our social communication. Therefore, the action of nonviolence can be understood as being constructed from a social interaction in which action's de facto significance depends on the mutual interpretations prevalent in a situation, but where a more ideal

communication decides which ethical validity the nonviolent
act has (its de jure meaning).[30]

Types of nonviolent action

In order to describe nonviolence as a coherent action repertoire, we need a categorical system for possible relevant forms
of action. Based on a critique of Max Weber's classic social
action theory, Habermas has divided actions into four basic
types according to their orientation:[31] goal rational, normative,
dramaturgical and communicative. According to Habermas, an
action is a human activity that can be understood, that has
reasons or that claims something.[32] Each action has its own
rationality but different reasons. This means that actions should
be judged based on their own rationality.

These are ideal types, not empirical categories that can be
observed in a social interaction. An ideal type is constructed
theoretically and is a characteristic form that exaggeratedly represents a phenomenon and thus serves as a measurement for
evaluating and interpreting empirical cases.[33] The purpose of
a pure distinction is to clarify the separate logics and expressions that characterise actions and give us the analytical tools to
understand an everyday and complex action, which can follow all
rationalities simultaneously. One can even understand the ideal
types as dimensions of action that are analytically discernible
but in practice are interwoven aspects.[34]

For Sharp, nonviolent actions are about groups instrumentally
using effective forms of pressure to achieve their predetermined
goals. He does not exclude the possibility of persuading the
opponent in a conflict, but he relies on 'nonviolent force'.[35] In
those cases when nonviolence does not succeed – which, according to Sharp, is often the case – it is merely a matter of lacking

the right strategy. Nonviolence is about correctly assessing which social groups and resources those in power depend on most and how nonviolent resistance can be carried out most effectively.

Sharp's argument has convinced many, but it is an example of analytical reductionism that hides the multidimensional character of nonviolent struggle. Sharp reduces nonviolent actions to strategic actions in a way that makes resistance without violence and social change conceivable. However, they remain socially incomprehensible since the question of how nonviolence is constructed, maintained and made meaningful within a context is not answered socially, but abstractly and technically.

In contrast to Sharp's reductionism, I now illustrate a four-dimensional interpretation of a case of civil disobedience: normative, expressively dramaturgical, goal-rationally strategic and communicative. This is a case that Sharp himself analyses: the Civil Rights Movement's sit-ins.[36] The first collective sit-in action linked to the Civil Rights Movement occurred in 1942, planned by the nonviolent group Congress of Racial Equality (CORE).[37] CORE organised a rising and well-educated middle class of young people in the USA, both whites and blacks. They used nonviolence in an unusual non-religious and practical way, which made the form of action accessible to new social groups.[38] They were well prepared, they had a collection of rules for their 'Action Discipline' and seven concrete steps for struggle, and they discussed Gandhian nonviolence with reference to, for example, Gregg's *The Power of Non-Violence* (1935) and Shridharani's *War without Violence* (2003 [1939]).[39] After a few smaller actions, twenty-eight people went into Jack Spratt Coffee House in Chicago in groups of between two and four, in which one of them was black:

> With the discipline of peacefulness strictly observed, we
> occupied all available seating spaces at the counter and in

booths ... Waitresses looked at each other and shrugged. Then they looked at the woman in charge for a cue, but none was forthcoming ... Two whites, who were not obviously members of our group and were sitting some distance from each other at the counter, were served. One, a well-dressed, middle-aged woman, thanked the waitress when her food arrived, but sitting with hands in her lap, did not touch it. The other man, also older, promptly passed his food to the black beside him, who proceeded to eat it ... The woman in charge went to the lady who had been served and asked, 'Is your dinner all right, ma'am?'

'Oh, I'm sure it's just fine.'

'But you aren't eating it.'

'I know. You see, it wouldn't be very polite for me to begin eating before my friends also had been served.'[40]

Accordingly, the café staff were forced to try to solve the peculiar situation. They suggested that the black person should eat the food alone in the cellar. But the group's spokesperson refused. Then they suggested that they could clean up in the two other booths and serve them there, again sitting separately. When the group still refused, they were threatened with the final wild card: the police. James Farmer, who was one of the people who played a decisive role in transferring Gandhian nonviolence to the USA,[41] then said that he agreed and that it would be 'the appropriate thing' for the staff to do.

Within minutes, two of Chicago's finest walked in ... [O]ne of them asked, 'What did you call us for, lady? I don't see anybody disturbing the peace. What do you want us to do?'

'I want you to throw these people out, of course,' she replied.

'Lady, we can't do that. What're they doing wrong? You're open for business, aren't you? They're not trespassing ... You must either serve them or solve the problem yourself the best way you can.'

When the police left, the café's cook made the decision to serve everyone. The group then wrote a letter to the owner and thanked them for the change in their integration policy. When they checked a few weeks later, the change still held.[42]

This sit-in was just an early experiment with the method. It wasn't until the Civil Rights Movement blossomed that it became possible to mobilise a people's movement using sit-in actions, but by then, however, it was one of the most massive civil disobedience campaigns ever. The movement began with a spontaneous action when four youths from North Carolina Agricultural and Technical College sat down in a lunch restaurant in a shopping centre on 1 February 1960. When they sat in the section for 'whites only', they did not have to wait long for a reaction. One of the participants, Franklin McCain, described the incident as follows:

Once getting there ... we did make purchases of school sup-plies and took the patience and time to get receipts for our purchases, and Joseph and myself went over to the counter and asked to be served coffee and doughnuts. As anticipated, the reply was, 'I am sorry, we don't serve you here.' And of course we said, 'We just beg to disagree with you. We've in fact already been served' ... The attendant or waitress was a little bit dumbfounded, just didn't know what to say under circumstances like that. And we said, 'We wonder why you'd invite us in to serve us at one counter and deny service at another. If this is a private club or private concern, then we believe you ought to sell membership cards' ... That didn't go over too well, simply because I don't really think she understood what we were talking about, and for the second reason, she had no logical response to a statement like that ... At that point there was a policeman who had walked in off the street, who was pacing the aisle ... behind us, where we were seated, with his club in his hand, just sort of knocking it in his hand, and just looking mean and red and a little bit upset and a little bit disgusted. And you had the feeling that he didn't know what the hell to do. You had the feeling that this is the first time that this big bad man with the gun and the club has been pushed in a corner, and he's got absolutely no defense, and the thing that's killing him more than anything else – he doesn't know what he can or what he cannot do. He's defenseless. Usually his defense is offense, and we've provoked him, yes, but we haven't provoked him outwardly enough for him to resort to violence. And I think that is just killing him; you can see it all over him.[43]

This form of action spread like wildfire; already by April the new sit-in movement consisted of between 50,000 and 70,000 youths, of whom 3,600 were arrested by the police.[44] In Nashville, Tennessee, James Lawson – a student of Gandhian techniques and a priest – organised an effective campaign of sit-ins with role playing and training, strict discipline and advanced tactics, which became a model for many others.[45] The reactions of local whites to the sit-in actions varied. At a number of places the response was uncertain and eventually amiable.[46] At others, the activists were met with increasing anger and oppression:

Nonviolent black protesters were beaten and cut with razors and knives; hot cigarettes and cigars were burned into their arms and faces; they were spat upon and kicked to the floor; policemen locked them by the thousands into cramped, unsanitary jails.[47]

In the following sections, I interpret a form of action – sit-ins – and a movement's specific application of that form of action according to four different types of rationality. The discussion is supplemented with examples from other movements' nonviolent approaches in order to illustrate how a nonviolent activity can be categorised based on this action typology.

First rationality: normative action and morality Normative actions are practical actions regulated by a group's norms, institutions or principled morals, rather than by facts or instrumental calculations.[48] Norms are expressed in general 'ought to' statements and viewed as valid in communities of those affected. Above all, they relate to the non-formal and often unwritten rules of expected behaviour in various types of situations that each group needs to make in order to work together. In a norm-regulated action, the agent acts according to group norms.[49] The agent implicitly claims that the action is correct in its context and can give moral reasons if questioned. Acting normatively means belonging to a social community, qualifying oneself as a member by living by the community's rules. It is the type of action mainly highlighted by classics of social theory such as Durkheim and Parsons. Norms may also be formal and explicit. They are codified in etiquette, legislation, rituals, tradition and the lessons of moral authorities. They need not be formally expressed or taught, but are learned by participation in the group's culture and social activities, in an everyday and undramatic socialisation. Normativity is internalised in the socialisation and becomes the motives and habits of the people involved. All social groups and communities are connected through norms, but their normative worlds might look fundamentally different.

Acting normatively does not necessitate subordinating oneself to the dominant group opinion for all norms, even if that is how the literature has tended to describe it. Habermas points out that normativity is not evaluated only according to whether its motives and actions harmonise with the norm, but also if the existing norms in themselves value 'the generalisable interests of those affected and thus deserve recognition from those the norms refer to'.[50] Normative actions can even express disunity. An individual or group can claim that a norm should be interpreted in another way or simply should be abolished. Additionally, a community's subgroups (youth, for example) are allowed to develop partially different and even deviant norms. Furthermore, norms are never static. When society and the context change, norms must adapt and be given new meanings and practical applications. That is the conventional history of norm change.

'Normatively rational' means that one's action is explained in reference to what is valid in a specific situation. As long as there is a point of reference in the dominant system of norms, existing norms can be contradicted and changed. The breach of a norm is motivated by other ('superior') norms, or through reference to a common interest, questioning a certain norm's justification or its dominant interpretation. A group can never work without some kind of normative order, although that order can always be criticised. The unwritten norms in modern society have received competition from formal laws, which have the same basic function of giving rules to the community. A conflict between norm and law, or legitimacy and legality, can be expressed through a movement's nonviolent actions of disobedience.

NORMATIVE NONVIOLENT ACTION According to Gandhi, non-violent action can be described as an experimental normative system that focuses on claiming and testing the validity of non-violent norms. Interpreted as a form of normative action, you can say that the Civil Rights Movement's activists, through their sit-ins, follow or uphold certain norms and break or criticise others. In other words: *they simultaneously combine norm claiming and norm criticism.* The activists' sit-ins – peacefully putting themselves next to their fellow humans – follow basic norms and social rules. The activists can be said to be claiming norms that say that people who behave in the same way should be treated the same, that you should take responsibility for your actions and not harm other people (except in self-defence). At the same time, the activists break those norms that, in their view, are less desirable: for example, obeying the authorities and not creating fuss or conflict. The essential focus of the training, organisation and management of the Civil Rights Movement was on self-discipline and respectful behaviour towards whites despite provocation.[51] By not violating basic social norms, it was possible to gain understanding and even support from some whites. Despite, or due to, their breach with norms, the requirement for an adjustment to other norms was strengthened: for example, there was a need to display honesty.[52] This is reasonable because, by breaching norms, one puts oneself outside the community (or is excluded from it) and shows disloyalty to the group's basis and its rules for coexistence. The punishment is a ritual act that re-establishes the community and renews belonging.[53]

A sit-in is normatively problematic. By making their resistance public and taking personal responsibility for their actions, the activists were brought to justice. The court proceedings were an expression of the Civil Rights Movement's *examination* of and *challenge* to the dominant normative order. In the trials, the activists defended their disobedience based on basic norms in American society. 'Sit-ins were no rejection of the American Dream; they were the necessary although ambiguous steps taken towards its culmination.'[54] In addition, the law's codification of the order of norms was unclear, which meant that the civil rights activists sometimes had the court on their side.[55]

There is a contradiction in the normative orientation of the acts of disobedience. By not trying to run away from trials, a *combination of disobedience and obedience towards the order of norms* is dramatised. In part, the activists disapproved of the normative order's basic civil social contract (obedience to the state in exchange for the state's protection) by both carrying out and organising a violation of the law; in part, they admitted the normative order's legitimacy by making their violation of the law public and willingly submitting themselves to its scrutiny and verdict. The contradiction lay in the fact that an acceptance of the normative order's sanctions did not encompass obedience following the verdict; after having served their sentence and after their time in prison, the activists broke the norms again, and in the same way.

There is a difference between breaking a norm and refusing to obey the authority of the social order upon which all norms rest. Breaking norms is serious in itself, but defying the normative order's legitimate authority is a kind of social 'declaration of war', a revolutionary challenge to the dominant order. The Civil Rights Movement did not wage such a revolutionary struggle, but some nonviolent movements do. It is perhaps a unique property of nonviolent resistance that defying the normative order does not necessarily lead to complete expulsion. Certainly, norms are not broken without punishment ensuing; the simultaneous defiance and claiming of normativity of nonviolence impedes others' stereotyping of nonviolent activists. This is to say, nonviolence challenges the borders of acceptable behaviour with a normative disobedience.

Nonviolent resistance, as a normative action, becomes a repeated alternation between norm criticism and norm claiming, between obedience to and disobedience against the authority of the normative order.

Normative nonviolent acts do two things. First, they publicly and reflexively test (certain) norms via the contradictory combination of *norm breaching* and *norm claiming*. This makes a reconstruction of existing norms possible. In Chapter 1, I showed how Arne Næss summarised nonviolence in a cohesive system of norms, norms that are claimed in opposition to violence and oppression. According to Gandhi, *norm adaptation* is not a sufficient requirement for nonviolence. Gandhi goes a step further, arguing for the disciplined upholding of norms and standards. This is what could be called a radical *norm defence*: that is, a strict demand on the activists' active training in and upholding of certain (nonviolent) norms. Being prepared to die in defence of an enemy's legitimate needs or life is the ultimate consequence of Gandhi's nonviolent normative defence. In combination with disobedience and obedience to the normative order, the dominant order's legitimacy is undermined. Nonviolence opens up the possibility of new regulating norms within a reconstructed normative order, a nonviolent normativity.

Second rationality: expressive action and dramaturgy Actions that express something aesthetic or some meaning beyond what is done have a surplus of meaning and are said to be expressive. Following a dramaturgical perspective, the action is interpreted like a drama, which is a mutual work. When a person in the drama expresses something about themselves, they use 'self-representation'; this is a special, expressive type of action that, according to Habermas, is valid based on the subject's privileged experiences.[56] The agent then implicitly claims that the action is 'truthful' and honest because it is based on personal, exclusive experiences. This work refers to a subjective world, whereas normative actions refer to the social world. But the agent takes 'consideration [of] the observer [and] express[es] their experiences in a stylised way'.[57] Self-expressive actions are thus not private; rather, their rationality depends on the possibility of others recognising themselves, learning or understanding them – being convinced of the ego's sincere story about itself.

A drama cannot function alone: it requires a public, a public that views the action as believable, gives its impressions and is affected by the representation. Erving Goffman, the sociologist of everyday life, has developed a drama perspective that highlights how the aesthetic representation of our actions – where the decisive factor is not the 'content' but how we react and how we express ourselves – forms other impressions and perceptions about who we are ('impression management').[58] Impressions are formed through control techniques that affect and manage other people's interpretations ('façade', 'enframing', 'mannerism', 'expressive control', 'pace', 'caution' and so on). In the interaction of the drama, an exchange of respect and recognition occurs, but also a struggle through which we are allowed to deal with the established social interpretation.

When an agent's action fails to be credible in a social context (and they 'lose face'), they can use a number of techniques to appropriate the lost impression and to attempt to have 'another chance'. Those who fatally fail to manage their representations in a convincing way carry a 'stigma'. A stigmatised person is viewed not only as abnormal but also as less valuable and of lower status.[59] The risk of nonviolent activists being stigmatised is high, as breaking norms makes their representation less credible.

The drama can also be part of an honest attempt to become something one is not yet, to try out a new behaviour, to reinvent oneself and adopt a new role.[60] It is important to distinguish between human interaction in front of others being understood as drama, on the one hand, and humans sometimes being dramatically aware actors on the other. At one extreme is the naïve action in which the actor is occupied with their own action and does not see that the challenge is to maintain a believable performance. In that case, the benefits of alternative performances are not even considered. The drama happens without reflection but with a self-explanatory basis. One's own action is not doubted.

At the other extreme is the cynical action that is disguised and carried out strategically; in this, the actor sees him- or herself from the outside and consciously wants to achieve something specific with an action they know to be false (but whose falseness is skilfully hidden). However, the everyday action lies between these extremes, neither naïve nor cynical but sincere.[61]

There is a risk that cynicism surfaces in the politically strategic action. Apart from sincerely expressing who they are and what perspective they have, nonviolent movements are sometimes consciously theatrical.[62] For example, in the Graswurzelbewegung, the activists choreographed their own actions through role playing and rehearsals as well as devising certain actions when the activists dressed up.[63] Another example is the nonviolent blockades of the World Trade Organization (WTO) in 1999.[64] Activists dressed up as sea turtles and closed off all entries to the conference building for the world's most powerful economic regime so effectively that the entire conference collapsed. Not even the initial press conference or the closing document could be presented. The activists dramatised the environmental consequences of neoliberal policies. The turtles had been affected by fishing fleets since the WTO's rules had forbidden 'trade barriers' in the form of laws for special nets. Thus, the 'turtles' had enough and decided to stop the WTO. This dramatisation of the conflict was perfectly designed for CNN and other global news media – the problem caused by a complicated political and economic structure was illustrated dramatically.

With the drama perspective in mind, you could also say that activists in their nonviolent actions present a mutual identity, which provides others with a possible community to connect with. This is a perspective that is reasonable when trying to understand certain aspects of collective actions – *nonviolent performances and nonviolent identity construction*.

Expressive actions are expressed in nonviolent approaches, and above all in testing a new culture (to *bring utopias to life*) and preparing the *symbolic design* of actions in conflict situations through role playing (where the use of special clothes, materials and behaviours load the actions with meanings). Expressive activities say something about who participants are (when interpreted as identity narratives) and which meanings of the world are highlighted (as symbolic expressions, namings, definings or world narratives).

EXPRESSIVE NONVIOLENT ACTION If sit-in actions are interpreted as expressive actions, it can be said that they attempt to achieve three simultaneous processes. Nonviolent actions *dramatise 'injustice'* when they are subject to violence resulting from their action. The more violence that is used, the more brutal the segregation (and its defendants) appear. If the action (temporarily) realises what it set out to achieve – desegregation – then sit-ins also entail the activists *elucidating 'justice'*. Through the action, a vision of another possible world arises. Finally, the action is also an attempt to break up a categorical we–them dichotomy and aid a mutual *identification across conflict borders*.[65]

As long as no blacks entered the white areas of segregated institutions, the whites were not forced to experience the consequences of segregation. It was possible to live within a protected glass cage, to turn your gaze from the world outside. When blacks respectfully but without permission demanded to be served like everyone else, the conflict was dramatised. The drama increased when activists were arrested and imprisoned. For an outside observer, the situation appears to be a dramatic theatre performance. As the activists acted politely and were prepared to pay for the service, it was brought into the open that they were jailed only due to their skin colour and their practice of desegregation. When they returned to the cafés after having been released from jail and asked to be served again, the dramatisation of the conflict and the blacks' role as upstanding but calm equals were made more acute. At the same time, the white defendants of segregation became clearer in their role as oppressors. When non-segregated collective actions were carried out in parallel – the establishment of non-segregated cafés, blacks and whites cooperating in the Civil Rights Movement and so on – the alternatives became more obvious. It became easier for sympathetic whites to ally with the black-dominated Civil Rights Movement. As the actions were repeated and the conflict underscored dramatically, whites were drawn into the drama and eventually it became difficult for whites to avoid taking sides: either you were for or you were against segregation. The conflict was polarised.

The movement researcher Doug McAdam claims that the Civil Rights Movement, using 'innovatively strategic dramaturgy', consciously chose to act in Birmingham in 1963 because they could guarantee that their nonviolence would be met with brutality in that location.[66] In this breakthrough in their campaign, they could thus present a fight between a 'good' movement and a 'bad' system, which drew in the media and the audience – the American people. They failed a few years later because they were not able to re-create this ritualised confrontation, McAdam says. 'After 1965, civil rights forces came to resemble a movement in search of an enemy.'[67]

The point is that the Civil Rights Movement as a nonviolent movement sought out an enemy system, not individuals to identify as enemies. Moreover, they sought (which McAdam does not point out) to expressively present their opponents as human, as people who could be transformed or whom one could live with. Without this, the nonviolent strategy would be the same as terrorists' attempt to bait the system's underlying 'evil' and 'true' face. The Civil Rights Movement shows us how nonviolent movements go a step beyond traditional expressive rationality. The activists dramatically explore a just utopia by directly representing the future they hope for in their action, by showing kindness and respect, and by refraining from defending themselves with violence. Through the action the goal is realised – the segregated café is integrated, blacks and whites sit together, even if it happens only temporarily.

When the Civil Rights Movement began to grow in influence, traditional patterns of interaction between blacks and whites were broken, as were traditions that had established certain roles and had been incorporated as identities over time. In the new patterns of interaction, possibilities opened up for new roles and identities. The previously subordinate (and 'primitive') black citizen was transformed into a resistance fighter or an equal, and the stubborn segregationist became an aggressor. In this self-representation one can see the possibility of a self-esteem in line with not only 'black pride' or 'black power', but also anti-racist identities such as 'human' or 'citizen'.[68] Franklin McCain describes the process:

> If it is possible to know what it means to have your soul cleansed – I felt pretty clean at that time. I probably felt better on that day than I've ever felt in my life. Seems like a lot of feelings of guilt or what-have-you suddenly left me, and I felt as though I had gained my manhood, so to speak, and not only gained it, but had developed quite a lot of respect for it. Not Franklin McCain only as an individual, but I felt as though the manhood of a number of other black persons had been restored and had gotten some respect from just that one day.[69]

Martin Luther King thought that 'growth comes through struggle', that nonviolent actions work like a kind of therapy, a transformation from one character to another. He described the scene in Birmingham:

> hundreds, sometimes thousands, of Negroes [*sic*] who for the first time dared look back at a white man, eye to eye ... Bull Connor's men, their deadly hoses poised for action, stood facing the marchers. The marchers, many of them on their knees, stared back, unafraid and unmoving. Slowly the Negroes stood up and began to advance, Connor's men, as though hypnotized, fell back, their hoses sagging uselessly in their hands.[70]

Since the Civil Rights Movement's actions were mainly rights-oriented and not identity-oriented, and since the movement tried to include whites in the struggle, it was easier to win over sympathetic whites and make the issue into a common one.[71] The resistance was not primarily based on ethnic identity, which separated we–them in terms of black–white, but differed between those who were for or against equal rights; this was precisely what could make identification and inclusion possible across racial conflict boundaries. In this respect, nonviolence demonstrates that it is an attempt to create a potential community that embraces all parties in the conflict.[72]

Forming an identity is normally tied to pointing out a 'we' in relation to a 'them', especially in a conflict, and is thus a subjectivisation of oneself and an objectification of the other. This is unavoidable, and is often seen as a reason for enemy relations between groups. But according to symbolic interactionism, one cannot avoid objectifying oneself (i.e. the 'I' observes the 'me'), which means viewing oneself from the position of the other. Thus, communication between people enables us all, to some extent, to take on the 'other's' perspective and adapt our behaviour. No 'I' or 'we', no role and no person's identity can be formed without seeing oneself through another's eyes, imagining their world and how it looks and feels for our fellow humans. This means that the subsequent formation of a self-identity also leads to a relativisation of one's own identity. If one's identity were to be constructed only with reference to oneself, it would not only make communication impossible, but also make identity construction incomprehensible.[73] Therefore, we find ourselves in a constant and unavoidable empathy with each other, to the extent that we actually communicate; or, put more correctly, perspective-taking makes mutual meaning-giving possible. If the other's perspective is taken into account, it is always possible to make the appeal of nonviolence comprehensible to others. This appeal to a greater mutual empathy can succeed or fail, but the possibility of such an empathy exists as long as communication exists. Conflict and struggle are also forms of interaction, and as such they are also forms of communication.[74]

Expressive nonviolence means that you reveal justice and injustice (the 'good' and 'bad') in a representation of actions. And, simultaneously, roles and identities, the intrigue of drama, communication and possibilities for solutions are constructed and emphasised.

Third rationality: goal-rational action and strategy Goal-rational actions are carried out with the purpose of attaining a result and claiming validity based on facts about how the surrounding world works.[75] The action is rational in that it produces a desired result. Its degree of rationality can be judged and questioned based on how successfully the action tackles the surrounding world. An *instrumental action* is a causal and practical–technical goal rationality that deals with an objective world but without other goal-rational subjects, for example in material production and mechanical technique. *Strategic action* is a social goal rationality that is based on there being other goal-rational actors who must be considered in relation to specific goals and interests. The interaction is regulated by strategy if the actors' interests and maximal utility decide their actions, as is the case with a system of market and domination.[76] When strategic action is translated into language, 'linguistic communication [becomes] one means among others', with the goal of achieving success.[77]

STRATEGIC NONVIOLENT ACTION The sit-in actions were goal
rational in a fundamental sense: using means to achieve a
goal based on how reality really works. In preparation to nonviolent actions, data is collected and the situation evaluated, with
the aim of basing strategies and requirements on an informed
view of reality.[78] In the Civil Rights Movement, a 'social inven-
tory' was used in which facts about social groups and relations
were documented.[79] If one interprets a sit-in as an open strategic
action, one can, like Sharp, claim that civil rights activists tried
to undermine the preconditions of the oppressor (the segregation and discrimination of blacks) by refusing to give those in
positions of power access to power resources. One of the central
sources of power is people's obedience to the law, another is
economy. If a large enough number of blacks intervened in
the segregated establishments despite the fact that they would
be imprisoned, then the costs to society of upholding segregation might eventually be considered too great. Police presence,
arrests, trials and imprisonment indirectly created economic
costs for society. In addition, groups of whites connected to
the campaigns and common economic boycotts were organised
at the establishments.[80] Other kinds of costs arose as well. An
increase in militant activity against segregation in the southern
states was reported during the sit-in campaign.[81] In a strategic
action, you count the available choices of action based on your
opponent's way of thinking and on your and other actors' priori-
ties. The peaceful action of the civil rights activists made the
whites in the segregated south stand in shame each time they
conducted their assaults on the activists. Liberals in the north
criticised segregation, and an alliance with President Kennedy
was established in 1963. The court verdicts also made the segregated southern states retreat since the federal laws did not

support segregation. A political and moral cost arose when the segregationists lost prestige, legitimacy and alliances.

There are several examples of how violent repression created political backlash effects (what Gene Sharp calls 'political ju-jitsu') that worked for the benefit of the sit-in movement. A few hours after a bomb exploded in the home of a lawyer who was defending activists in Nashville, 2,500 demonstrators gathered and marched to the mayor.[82] The attention this brought and the agitation it caused in many camps in the city made the event a breakthrough for desegregation in Nashville – the opposite of the bomber's intention.

There is a point at which those in power feel compelled to negotiate with activists in order to achieve an agreement and prevent a continued increase in disobedience.[83] A redistribution of power resources can occur through calculated moves in a strategic play of different interests. The important thing is to use the fact that the exercise of power, to some extent, depends on the majority of whites and blacks accepting the social order, at least in their practical, daily actions. If enough people or enough important groups refuse to follow that order, the self-interest of the elite can force them to compromise with the resistance before it becomes all-encompassing and the system fails.

In strategic nonviolence, one takes into consideration the opponent's and other actors' varying interests and makes use of these to the greatest extent possible by playing them against each other and affecting their cost–benefit calculations. In other words, one increases the costs of the current policy and increases the benefits of the desired changes.

Fourth rationality: communicative action and dialogue Communicative action is organised via the dialogue's mutual interpretative work.[84] A communicative rationality or concerted rationality develops through an argument that seeks to reach an understanding: that is, an argument in which various reasons are weighed against each other and filtered by mutual reflection.[85] In its 'weak' variant, communicative action is oriented towards an understanding; in its 'strong' version, it is oriented towards an agreement. A person's 'speech act' is met with another person's 'speech act', creating a dialogue. Dialogue is the primary example of this approach, but the other aspects of coordinated action, which relies on previous communication, also constitute communicative action. Dialogue engages participants in a social situation: it arises in relation to a theme that actualises a segment of their life world. The dialogue is an understanding-oriented activity in which actors seek an agreement on the definition of their action situation. Based on a previously established understanding, or on an understanding that is received during the dialogue, they forge a plan of action with the aim of managing their situation.[86]

In practice, dialogue is exercised in social situations where traits of power disrupt the orientation towards an understanding. Habermas finds that communicative actions are the foundation on which other actions are able to build the possibility of making themselves understood, rational and valid. All actions presuppose language as a medium for their rationality, but non-communicative actions apply language based on only a limited subject. Language is the medium of influence based on personal interest (strategic), the mediation of cultural values and pre-existing consensus (normative), an understanding of self-representation (dramaturgical), or the representation of objective facts (instrumental). Sometimes the subject is limited to a type of action that is so powerful that a 'general medium' can make the dialogue completely unnecessary within a particular system: for example, economic action through money in the market system. However, it is only through communicative action that the validity or rationality of all of these dimensions of actions can be proved.

A communicative action has three requirements to be valid in relation to three separate 'worlds': speaking means laying claim to what is true (in the objective world), following the normative context (in the social world) and the statement is honestly meant (in the subjective world).[87] These mutual understandings that are created in dialogues make various forms of action coordination possible.[88] If the orientation towards understanding does not lead to disruption, it leads to mutual agreement, the validity of which is recognised by all parties and open to criticism, and thus the agreement is binding for all the participants. Such a mutual agreement differs from influence.[89] 'Influence' does not occur through mutual reflection of the reasons for plausibility of arguments, but rather is an effect caused by the actors' perceptions, decisions or actions through means such as money or power.

COMMUNICATIVE NONVIOLENT ACTION Communication does not occur only through dialogue. Symbolic communication is like a text, an imprint of a story. If one interprets nonviolent actions as a form of *symbolic communication*, one can say that they are *nonverbal enactments of arguments or symbolic messages in a process of understanding that relates to the way in which the involved parties should coexist*. The action brings together people, arguments, mutual understanding and conflict. It can break a previous silence and bring a hidden conflict out into the open, thereby helping to create a theme for discussion. The action's meanings arise from people's dialogues and possibilities of mutual interpretation, and are not limited to private motives, the actors' consciousness or the perspectives of individuals (even in cases where these become the subject of the dialogue). Through the Civil Rights Movement's sit-ins, something was said in a societal discussion about segregation and human rights. Regardless of how the actors or observers in the concrete situation understood the action's symbolic language, we can now assume that the Civil Rights Movement communicated a message to those who wanted to interpret it, either then or today. The actions 'speak' to us still, in a message about our equality as people and the possibility of being disobedient.

Given that the sit-ins occurred nonviolently and an open, personal responsibility existed before, during and after the resistance, the activists were able to engage others in dialogue about their action: waiters and waitresses, café visitors, neighbours, colleagues, politicians, the police, prosecutors, judges, prison guards, journalists, prisoners, businessmen, union activists and others.

One can interpret the symbolic meaning of the action – and of the dialogues carried out in parallel – as part of a communication process that was oriented towards understanding. The Civil Rights Movement's disobedience can be understood as *resistance to the power traits that disrupt the possibility of understanding or consensus*.[90] In a true dialogue, the dialogue partners have the freedom to agree or to counter-argue (to say yes or no to an argument, suggestion or claim by providing reasons). A strategic rationality in nonviolent resistance can contribute to democratic conversations between conflicting parties.[91] Through the strategic action, the nonviolent movement can *force its opponent to enter into dialogue* about a solution to the conflict. This occurs by the resistance creating an *interest* in listening, as in workplace negotiations or strikes. We can therefore see how a goal-rational action that temporarily disrupts power relations can facilitate the possibility of communication.

Communication can be articulated in other ways. Symbolic thinking is strongly developed in parts of the nonviolent movement. The brothers Dan and Phil Berrigan and a movement of Catholic nonviolent activists in the USA – which is largely based on the Christian resistance collectives the Catholic Worker Movement and the Plowshares Movement – are not developing a strategy of influence and try not to cause particular effects in political questions but rather have developed a perspective that appropriates nonviolent direct action as a *witness to truth*.[92]

The proponents of testimony and truth distance themselves from actions directed at 'effectiveness'. This may make it appear that they are against the triumph of nonviolence, which is not true. Their reasoning can be understood as follows: a focus on effectiveness makes the movement apparently effective, while in reality it is part of the problem; however, a focus on truth makes it effective in a true, nonviolent and meaningful sense.

One of the proponents of the perspective is Jim Douglass, the activist who dedicated his life to fighting the 'White Train' that transports nuclear arms equipment to Trident submarines at the Bangor base in the USA. He illustrated his reasoning in a criticism of a blockade of the train in July 1984:

> It was the spirit of what we were doing. I know now that what we had within us ... was the spirit of wanting a victory – the victory of stopping the train ... We wanted victory, even at the expense of compromising the nonviolent means we had chosen ... Some of us were willing to risk the lives of others to gain the victory of stopping the train. In seeking victory, I believe we lost truth ... I believe the nonviolent spirit of love

and truth can stop the White Train. But if we ever struggle again for a victory on the tracks, the train will keep on going. It will go faster. We will become part of it. And the train will kill us all.[93]

Non-verbal actions can be understood as contradicting dialogue's understanding-oriented basic approach: one actor might disrupt the dialogue by interfering in a situation without ensuring that there is an understanding or an agreement with others, or they might express frustration at a culture of silence. But if their action is combined with a desire for dialogue, it has the potential to strengthen the conversation by becoming a source of (provocative) material for discussion. When the activists blocked the train transporting arms to soldiers in a war zone, they not only broke the law but also made it clear what they thought about a political question. The action thus becomes an invitation to discuss the issue, the law, an individual's rights, and their action against something they believe is wrong in society.

Ricoeur believes that a text or an act differs from a dialogue and should be understood as a monologue or a fixed speech. But if an action is understood as part of a dialogue, it can then strengthen that dialogue, in the same way that a newspaper article or a new book becomes material for discussion. This happens each time the fixed speech is actualised in a subject, even if this happens long after the action has taken place. Despite the argument that a dialogue and a non-verbal action exist on different levels, they can still strengthen each other by means of the symbolic and interpretive charge the action has. But communication can be improved only on condition that acts of disobedience are integrated within a process of dialogue.

Accordingly, nonviolence involves acting symbolically and communicatively, yet the changes that are to be achieved are carried out concretely and practically. When the civil rights activists conducted their sit-ins, they achieved their goal – integration – by breaking the regulations that sanctioned segregation. Afterwards, thousands of people broke the law and segregation became difficult to uphold in practice. Eventually café owners, restaurateurs, politicians and the police had to try to reach an agreement with the activists. This was due to a practical problem, as the actions led to a moral and political discussion in the media and among the public – in particular on a national level, since agitated northerners criticised segregation.

Even if the movement's resistance made it impossible to ignore the criticism and forced the issue onto the agenda, it was not just the purely physical action in segregated establishments that brought about the end of segregation. If the defenders of segregation had been prepared to pay the price economically and politically and had isolated themselves from the north and the rest of the world, they could have continued for a length of time. The sit-ins also illustrate how the nonviolent movement's escalation occurs on such a limited scale that it *can* achieve dialogue with the opposition and *must* enter into dialogue in order to reach a permanent solution. This could be called civil disobedience's combination of *coercion into dialogue and freedom through agreement*. The opposition is forced to listen to what the nonviolent activists have to say but is not forced to accept a predetermined solution. Instead, the solution is based on the arguments and good reasons that emerge in a dialogue – in this case by convincing Congress and the President, which led to new federal regulations. In this respect there are two elements to this process: the coercion that creates the dialogue *situation* and the freedom that upholds the *understanding or agreement* that results from the dialogue.

Nonviolent resistance interrupts false dialogues and the power of silence; at the same time, dialogues are a necessary part of communicative nonviolent resistance. Without conversations, there is no possibility of a mutual truth, justice or agreement.

Logically, then, you can say that it becomes *mandatory that the act of disobedience is not sufficient in itself*. It cannot be truly effective if it leads to the desired result by itself, as other citizens would then be ignored. If the act is so strategically successful that you do not need a dialogue to manage the conflict, then it is disconnected from communication. Sharp rightly emphasises the strategic dimension of civil disobedience. However, the problem is that every line of reasoning that reduces nonviolence to merely a strategy also abolishes dialogue.

Nonviolence as consensus rationality?

Based on the discussion of nonviolence's strategic, normative, expressive and communicative dimensions, it is reasonable to assume that nonviolence is a *multi-rational conflict activity*. Nonviolence can conceptually be described as rational based on several kinds of rationality. But since nonviolence comprises *one* action repertoire that combines various acts, the question is whether the action itself could be defined as rational. Of course, according to Habermas, no conflict exists between the different (ideal) types of action; however, it is reasonable to assume that some conflict arises between different principles and how to apply and integrate them. Even if the types of nonviolent action can be combined in varying creative entities, each combination requires a *rational coordination of differing rationalities*, and I claim that this coordination is *consensus rational*.

One plausible interpretation of Habermas views communicative rationality as being dominant, to some extent, over the other forms of rationality. Of course, each rationality has its own place, its relational world, and in that sense they are equivalent. But, on a sociological and political level, Habermas's project is a struggle to strengthen and develop democracy. His criticism of modern society is that the political economy's strategic and instrumental rationality ('system') dominates the communications of civil society. An operative distribution should prevail between the rationalities, a kind of functional cooperation. However, we have to account for the fact that, as a principle, conflict rules. How that conflict between rationalities is negotiated is important. Habermas would never suggest that we resolve tensions between the rationalities with a strategic plan, an instrumental calculation, a normative tradition or an individual's expressive rationality. There is only one rationality with the capacity to negotiate between different claims: democratic dialogue and its institutionalising communicative rationality should decide. After all, communicative rationality is about the collective assessment of different claims, and the (supposedly) free resolution of such tensions into (temporary) agreements and understandings. Thus, it is reasonable to argue that, in the end, democratic dialogue should resolve the tensions, contradictions and problems between the rationalities that are practised.

Social action is based on communicative action – and the conditions of mutual understanding inherent in communicative action make interactions between other actions possible.[94] Through speech acts, people agree on how to coordinate plans of action. In this, there is a basic similarity between Habermas and Gandhi. In Habermas, the rational types of action are coordinated by communicative rationality (mutual rationality); in a corresponding manner, in Gandhi the mutually recognised truth (*satya*) is a superior goal in the nonviolent struggle. Thus, according to a Habermasian perspective, one must conceptually describe nonviolent movements as multi-rationally *consensus-oriented*. This, however, does not mean that nonviolence avoids conflict – quite the contrary.

In the following four chapters I explore the concepts that are necessary in order to look at types of nonviolent action from a consensus perspective. The logic of the following chapters is founded upon the starting point that the main goal of nonviolence is a mutual truth attained through nonviolence (satyagraha), and that *the types of action can be understood as rational ways of dealing with anything that hinders the search for mutual truth*. The goal of the nonviolent struggle is that all parties involved in a conflict reach consensus, both in a rational agreement and in a social arrangement that all can accept (both cognitively and emotionally). Through his 'experiments' with the truth in social conflicts, Gandhi tried to provide a method for reaching that point together, in the most effective way. A nonviolent conflict transformation furthers the conditions of a genuine dialogue. But in highly divisive conflicts, it is often not enough for one party to try to show goodwill. For that reason, nonviolent conflict management needs to try to *counteract the hurdles* in the path of dialogue and agreement.

This enables us to overcome a central weakness in Habermas's consensus theory. The widely spread perception that he does not consider power relations in communication is not true. Many readers miss the fact that Habermas distinguishes between a utopian or an *ideal* dialogue on the one hand, and an *empirical* dialogue on the other. Habermas states that ideology and manipulation create 'distortion', that the political economy 'colonises' the communicative institutions in civil society, and that systematic restrictions for communication are common and comprise a 'structural violence'.[95] However, he does not help us counteract that distortion, colonialism and violence. Habermas simply has no interest in how to *practically* reach communicative agreements in *violent and oppressive conflicts*, which was Gandhi's focus.[96] Simone Chambers asks how sufficient communicative interests and competencies can be developed:

> Habermas does not deny that discourse requires an interest in mutual understanding, but he never deals fully with the possibility that citizens might generally lack such an *interest* or not possess the *competencies* to pursue such an interest. In a world where negotiation, instrumental trade-offs, and strategic bargaining are the most common routes to reaching collective 'agreement' and resolving disputes, it is plausible that the most serious barrier to [communicative] discourse can be found in the conversational *habits* that citizens have become used to.[97]

What we have to ask ourselves is whether nonviolence can be described as communicative and consensus-oriented even in violent conflicts. Social contexts in which discursive incompetence and insufficient interest in agreement characterise the interaction create a central problem for both Habermas's theory of communicative rationality and Gandhi's claim that truth can be developed through nonviolence in conflicts. Consensus requires not only formal norms for agreement and the right to participate, but also the actual right to be heard, the right that one's argument and interests have a practical importance in a mutual evaluation.

In order to consider these hurdles to consensus seriously, I choose to discuss the practice of nonviolence in social conflicts where all of Habermas's criteria of dialogue collapse, a situation that could be called a *dystopian dialogue situation* (or the *worst-case scenario of dialogue*). For that reason, we will start from those conflicts in which the participants' claims for their own dogmas have replaced a mutual orientation towards understanding. Those conflicts in which power techniques structure the dialogue and decide what arguments can be approved, or conflicts where the power techniques of disciplined discourses form the subjects that are discussed. Those conflicts in which 'the other' is not seen as an equal dialogue partner, and not even as a person, but as a crafty enemy or simply as an uneducated monster. And finally, those conflicts in which violence excludes nonviolent participants and threatens the critical voice that does not conform to the claims of power. The question is how nonviolence and its communicative rationality are to approach consensus between conflicting partners or dialogue partners under such conditions.

The types of hurdle that nonviolence is assumed to manage are as follows:

- *The communicative rationality of nonviolence is prevented by various truth claims, disagreement and dogmatism.* Because everyone has a limited capacity to speak about what is mutually true and correct, and it is both possible and necessary to act or to take a stance, the group's knowledge differences can be a hurdle (i.e. different views of what is valid knowledge). This makes understanding each other's perceptions and perspectives difficult. This can be expressed in anti-intellectualism, indoctrination, fundamentalism or an authoritarian mission for its own truths. This hurdle is best handled with *dialogue facilitation* (Chapter 4).
- *Power, injustice or oppression are obstacles to the strategic rationality of nonviolence.* Existing obedience relationships can result in unequal positions in a structure, where one part wins if

the situation remains as it is. For example, this can take the form of classes or genders having different status, or as the separate rights of different generations or ethnic groups' differing privileges. This hurdle is dealt with using *power breaking* (Chapter 5).

- *Hatred, stereotypes or enemy images are obstacles to the expressive rationality of nonviolence.* In this case, people socialise in different groups that are kept separate structurally, and so the cultural, social and psychological distance maintained between them can form emotional hurdles. For example, this can take the form of distrust, lies, prejudice, manipulation, contempt, insensitivity for the suffering of others, indifference and sadism. This hurdle is overcome with a *utopian enactment* (Chapter 6).

- *The legitimised and socialised use of violence is an obstacle to the normative rationality of nonviolence.* Since people are injured psychologically or physically, they are prevented from participating fully in the dialogue. This takes the form, for instance, of mobbing, maiming, murder or war. In a society where violence and injuring others are sanctioned, (some) violence is normal. This hurdle is handled using the *normative regulation* of nonviolence (Chapter 7).

Thus, in such social conflicts, our description of nonviolence as a consensual–rational phenomenon is put to the test. Based on the previous discussion, we now move on to a Habermasian perspective of nonviolence that is oriented towards understanding and involves consensus (nonviolence as *consensus rationality*). In part, this will establish the basis for a continued conceptual development by exploring the context (Habermas's communicative theory and thus the rationality of nonviolence) for a critical (non-empirical) test: the *dystopia of dialogue*.

4 | NONVIOLENT 'DIALOGUE FACILITATION'

In essence, the various action types of nonviolence seek to reach a truth that unites people (satyagraha). The question is: how can this succeed when our opinions differ so much, especially in conflicts riddled with violence and oppression? Which preconditions ensure reflexive and truth-oriented dialogue in situations where so much is at stake, where absolute demands, violence, threats and the denial of needs are the reality of the conflict?

This chapter discusses the concepts necessary to describe how nonviolence can be used to handle competing *truth claims* in a conflict. This competition affects how nonviolence activists manage both varying positions on the same issue and varying grounds for the legitimacy of truth claims.

If activists want to follow the logic of nonviolence, then communication, understanding and agreements not only characterise how activists relate to each other, but they also concern (to the highest degree) how they deal with their differences in conflicts. This chapter's communicative interpretation of nonviolence is illustrated with the help of *dialogue facilitation* internal to movements and in movements' external relationships with other parties in conflicts. Internally, the dialogue orientation takes quite idealistic forms. In this chapter, we will also see how nonviolent movements develop forms of 'consensus' and 'alternative meeting techniques' (which are advanced techniques for meetings, dialogues, discussions and managing differing perceptions) where the focus is equal participation and democratisation. As we shall see, the dialogue orientation of nonviolence presents itself in quite a different way in external relationships.

First, I discuss the relationship of nonviolence to truth and communication in order to explore how this is enacted internally in movements, and then in external relationships in conflicts characterised by domination and dogmatism.

A common truth

A wrong does not become right because it has been going on for a long time. But matters can be set right not by means of the sword but by persuasion. If [some] are in the wrong, they must be shown their mistake. They should be won over by persuasion.[1]

The predominant truth-seeking of nonviolent struggle is not only a matter of *how* activists enact their truth, but whether they provide convincing arguments or *reasons* for the movement's claims and demands.[2] The rational reasons must be so convincing that they can get the conflicting parties to find common truths.

In contrast to Sharp, I am of the opinion that nonviolence should be understood as both truth-seeking and a strategic power struggle.[3] For Gandhi, searching for the truth comprises the core of nonviolent struggle.[4] Juergensmeyer finds that Gandhian conflict solutions also entail fighting for *the whole truth*, not just one's own cause, and that each person has a part of the truth.[5] It is a matter of finding convincing principles that are promoted, regardless of which party stands for what, and of the nonviolent struggle *simultaneously fighting for all the principles that appear justified*, and even supporting the 'opponent's' opinion when they have a point.

As we have seen, Gandhi's concept of nonviolent struggle,

satyagraha, means the 'truth force', or holding on to (*graha*) the truth (*satya*).[6] Thus dialogue and negotiations lie at the centre of nonviolence.[7] In an unusual analysis that connects Gandhi and Habermas, the American political scientist Stephen Chilton finds that:

> Satyagraha is nonviolent, but this nonviolence is not just physical but also psychological, refraining from causing psychological damage to the other or using psychological pressure (guilt, shame, fear) to gain one's end. And even more, Satyagraha rejects moral violence, meaning the appeal to any force other than, in Habermas' famous formulation, the 'unforced force of the better argument'. Such moral violence would thus include rhetorical tricks and sophistry … [Satyagraha is] characterized by a firm holding to one's understanding of the truth, a simultaneous consciousness of one's fallibility and the need for others' perspectives, a consequent care for the other, and a respect for law insofar – but only insofar – as it embodies our underlying communicative relationship with the other.[8]

In pre-independent India, the Dalits – that is, the 'repressed' or 'broken' (or 'untouchables') – were victims of everyday violence, systemic dehumanisation and injustice (and they still are, despite 'untouchability' being illegal). In 1924, Dalits started a struggle for the right to use a road that led to the higher castes' temple in Vykom that exemplified both the nonviolent '*graha*' and its focus on '*satya*'.[9] Even if researchers debate the accuracy of some of the details in this story, it is instructive and serves as an illustration of the Gandhian nonviolent approach.[10] Gandhi instructed the activists to hold a vigil in front of the police's road block, which was put in place to prevent these 'untouchables' from 'dirtying' the holy place with their presence. For weeks and months on end, the 'untouchables' stood there in their vigil before the barrier. 'During the rainy season the road was flooded, and the protesters kept their vigil standing in water up to their shoulders as the police patrolled the barricade in small boats.'[11] After sixteen months, the authorities gave up and changed their policy. But that was not enough. The activists stayed on the road even though no barrier impeded them. They waited for the higher castes to become *convinced* and for the government to decide that they had the *right* to use the road.[12] Thus, they did not expect anything less than a change in their opponents' denigrating view and their permission to use the road. Such a transformation through conviction did happen, claims Gandhi, although research has shown that it is more likely that change occurred through an accommodation due to the pressure of the resistance. In any case, in the end the 'untouchables' began to use the road.

The criteria for the utopian truth-seeking of nonviolence, which Arne Næss expresses in a set of action norms and hypotheses about nonviolence (see the Appendix), have several basic similarities with the criteria for the 'ideal speech situation' (see the list of dialogue-facilitation methods below).[13] Both are forms of laying down truth or justice.[14] Both seek a theoretical basis and a practical method of consensus among divided people.

According to Habermas, an *understanding orientation* is inherent in interpersonal dialogue, in communication itself. A dialogue consists of speech acts between at least two people, a communicative action. A dialogue's understanding orientation takes effect no matter what the participants' aims are, as long as they participate in the dialogue. A quarrel becomes a quarrel precisely in lieu of a frustrating search for understanding. Even individual words are impossible to use without a fundamental and sufficiently mutual background of understanding that teaches us what words mean in our specific language community. But this background of understanding has been created through conversations in previous generations and, in fact, has been thematised, questioned and re-created continually through dialogue.

Habermas emphasises that such understandings can be warped, temporarily or systematically, through various features of power. Dialogue is unavoidably built on an orientation towards understanding but at the same time the dialogue in no way guarantees that an understanding will be reached. Dialogue only opens up the possibility of understanding.

Communicative rationality is a *mutual reason that arises through dialogue*. It stands in opposition to the antagonism of the concept of the philosopher or the rational subject being alone in their room and coming to realise what is true or correct. Reason's smallest unit is the argument between two people, not a sovereign subject's philosophical reflections. A statement's validity about morality or truth emerges from the dialogue's reflexive and common examination of rational reasons.

With the aim of discussing at length how nonviolence's communicative rationality can be described as a practical application of Habermas's dialogue criteria, I have tried to put together the most concrete criteria possible based on Habermas's theory of communication. This list describes the various criteria that together comprise the conditions for an ideal speech situation. One should note that the compilation and formulations are not direct quotations but rather an interpretation of Habermas.[15] The criteria are universally valid but may prove to be incorrect through convincing argument – that is, communicative rationality.[16]

- Something *is claimed pertaining to a theme* (something is said to be valid in the social or the objective world) and relevant *reasons or grounds* for that claim can be given if someone questions it ('truth', 'rightness' or 'truthfulness' are claimed).[17]

- Statements are *honest* (they mean what they say) and are treated as such ('mutual trust').

- *Power* does not affect the participant's statements or the understanding of what is claimed (and nor does it 'disturb' the dialogue in other ways).

- There is unlimited *time* (to ask each other for clarifications and for a full discussion).

- All relevant *information* is available or made public.

- All *those affected* are included and participate equally; they present their own statements and question those of others ('universality').[18]

- Everyone's statements are *acknowledged* equally by all as relevant claims ('reciprocity').

- Each and every person is prepared to change their standpoint if the arguments presented are *convincing*, but only as a result of the force of those *arguments* ('reversibility', 'yes or no position', *'Bindungseffekt'*).

The dialogue criteria are not conventions but *inescapable presuppositions.*[19] They cannot be avoided. According to Habermas, as soon as you enter an argument, even when arguing that certain criteria do not apply, your critique is built on the conditions of those criteria.

> Habermas' basic premise is the following: first that each and every one who puts demands on holding an argumentative conversation must accept its rules, and second that these rules imply the basic premise of discourse ethics. A person

who tries to argue *against* the rules, for example by arguing for the legitimacy of using force in an argumentative dialogue, commits a performative contradiction. ['A performative contradiction – as opposed to traditional logical contradiction – is a contradiction between the very fact that one says something and the content of what is said (e.g. the claim "I do not exist").'] The person(s) in question thus cannot rightly claim that they have shown the validity of their statement through argumentation.[20]

The ideal dialogue should thus be interpreted as unrestricted communication between people. If the communication is not restricted, the rationality of the understanding orientation is given free rein. Habermas finds that an ideal dialogue is a plausible basis for elucidating what is true or right. *Ideally*, honest statements about what is valid are made in an unlimited dialogue between all those affected, in which all relevant facts and arguments are known, without power disturbing the conversation.[21] The ideal brings out the inherent character of an orientation towards understanding and the possibility of consensus.

Naturally, an unlimited dialogue between all those affected and where power has no influence cannot be fully realised. For that very reason, the ideal dialogue should be understood as immanent in a desirable *utopia*, a guiding rule for how we, through a radicalised democracy, can come closer to the ideal state and for what we can plausibly view as true. It exists, but only as a precondition of communication and as a potentiality. Its reality, however, is always compromised by greater or lesser restrictions of some kind.

Likewise, absolute nonviolence cannot possibly be fully realised, which is something that Gandhi often pointed out.[22] Despite the impossibility of achieving full realisation, there is the possibility of going part of the way towards it, of using the ideal dialogue situation and maximal nonviolence as guiding aims.

Habermas finds that the argument is central to truth and justice. Habermas's theory of communicative rationality's ideal dialogue further develops Kant's classic 'categorical imperative',[23] where the validity of every norm is laid down through 'a principle of universalisation':

> *All* affected can accept the consequences and the side effects its *general* observance can be anticipated to have for the satisfaction of *everyone's* interests (and these consequences are preferred to those of known alternative possibilities for regulation).[24]

The principle states that a norm does not serve universal legitimacy if it does not 'limit *all* to accept the perspectives of *all others* in the balance of interests'.[25] The premise of universalisation is the fundamental *rule of argumentation* that applies regardless of culture or epoch, and out of which Habermas provides procedures for a communicative rationality.[26] Habermas does not define a universal morality but a universalising method in order to reach a contextually anchored morality ('procedural ethic').[27] Habermas thus breaks with Kant on one decisive point. Kant's philosophy of consciousness involves the content of morality being established in a rational individual's isolated reflection, while Habermas's theory of communication provides only *procedural principles* for interactive conversation, which is the only source that can provide morality's substantial content.[28] Only practical conversations between real people in real contexts can establish what is just. No one person can do this. Correspondingly, moral principles can be criticised and their justness can be questioned.

The dialogue about moral justness is steered by the universal rule, and therefore by the ideal criteria.

When we question a statement, we presuppose that there are reasons to justify the statement, reasons that can be contradicted with other reasons. An argument's openness to critique or examination points to the possibility of a reasonable debate. For both Habermas and Gandhi, communicative rationality is a partial description of how communication is and how it should be. Gandhi thinks that nonviolence and love are a 'law' that applies to all of our reality. Habermas believes that an attempt to reach an agreement is inherent in dialogue, as long as the participants mean what they say (that the statements are honestly stated).[29]

Even if agreement cannot be achieved, decisions or understanding can be facilitated through dialogue. Mutual *decisions* (consensus) need not depend on people being in agreement with regard to their opinions.[30] That is a common misunderstanding. Consensus can sometimes be an expression of compromises that are so extensive that no one is truly satisfied. In a consensus-oriented form of decision making with the right of veto, situations can arise where all those involved are in disagreement and unhappy with a suggested resolution. However, the suggestion can still be accepted (by consensus) as long as no one lays down a veto (thus blocking the possibility of making a decision in order to allow for more argumentation). Such a mutual decision can grow out of an insight about what is the best thing to do in the prevailing conditions of disagreement. In addition, the weaker variety of consensus, communicative *understanding*, does not mean agreement at all, but only understanding.[31]

A struggle against whatever prevents the search for truth is required in order to realise the understanding orientation of the use of language: namely violence, manipulation, censorship of facts or arguments, exclusion, belittlement, and lack of time and power. Gandhi found that even emotional blocks posed obstacles to dialogue.[32] Both Gandhi and Habermas strive to find out how individual morals can be transformed into a collective morality or common interests.[33] They both seek a *democratisation* of the administrative and economic instrumentalism and colonialism of liberal democracy – what Gandhi calls 'nominal democracy' – a democratisation that entails an integration of politics and morals.[34]

> It is to avoid this vicious circle of violence and exploitation that Gandhi made an inversion of the Hobbes-to-Lenin approach to political theorizing ... Gandhi's action project of satyagraha has the twin objectives of enabling humanity to realize its potential for rationality and goodness, and thereby securing a moral or democratically legitimate social order.[35]

Gandhi's ideal democracy has several names: '*purna swaraj*' (complete self-rule), 'integral democracy', '*ramarajya*' (the people's sovereignty based on pure moral authority) and '*sarvodaya*' (a social order that promotes the welfare of all).[36] 'Real *swaraj* will come not by the acquisition of authority by a few but by the acquisition of the capacity by all to resist authority when it is abused.'[37] Anil Karn describes nonviolence as a 'war against non-democracy' and a striving for moral, social, economic, political, international and global democracy.[38]

The similarity is primarily shown in the ways in which Gandhi and Habermas see mutual truth as a predominant goal and in the fact that they both seek methods and structures that minimise the obstacles to understanding.[39]

Gandhi highlights the personal experience of truth, not just the mutually understood rational argument about such experiences. One's own experience (physical and emotional, as well as 'spiritual') is important for one's will and engagement and is a guideline for the struggle, a continuation of the attempt to understand the truth. However, actions cannot be motivated by motives: they require factual arguments.[40] Thus, even if an insight into the truth requires a high spiritual (or mental) state, that experience or insight is an insufficient argument for truth – when all is said and done, its validity rests on a free agreement between affected parties, as it does for Habermas. What is required is a mutual dialogue and an agreement reached through the argument's convincing power.

Both Gandhi and Habermas navigate between extremes – on one side, universalism, objectivity or absolutism, and on the other particularism, subjectivism or relativism – and end up with a kind of *common truth* (which is intersubjectively valid). Here, we see that Gandhi in the early twentieth century coincides with the knowledge claims of contemporary sociology, which show that even (natural and social) science's knowledge about what is true depends on theoretical paradigms, world views and discursive power fields, and that objective knowledge independent of time, place and person is fundamentally suspect, or quite simply implausible.

Gandhi, unlike postmodernism, claims that there exists an absolute truth (even if we have only fragmentary access to it). Like Habermas, Gandhi claims that a valid truth is reached mutually, through our transcendence of both the truth of objectivity (which disregards human subjectivity) and the truth of subjectivism (which disregards the common conviction).

One of Gandhi's main reasons for nonviolence was the insight that he, like others, could not be completely certain of what was really true.[41] The act of killing denies alternative truths, and proclaims an impossible monopoly of Truth. The truth of which we are mutually convinced becomes the only plausible alternative. The truth is the end and nonviolence the means, or, more correctly *(the nonviolent) truth is the end and (the true) nonviolence the means*. All people, even those who torment others, belong to a whole.

Satyagraha should be understood as a form of struggle in which everyone's needs are in focus and where there is a distinction between the opponent's role and personality.[42] Based on a struggle against the role and a dialogue with the person, you can try to reach a common truth that takes into consideration the needs of all. The parties' different truths dissolve in a process where agreements bridge the antagonism of the conflict.[43] In order to more easily reach an agreement, compromises are desirable, but only if they do not relate to fundamental principles. Gandhi was known to have changed his views at several points in his life – he thought this was positive and highlighted it as an experimental openness in the search for truth.

Seen according to Gandhi's perspective, you can say that the opponent in a conflict is in fact a blessing and an invaluable part of the experiment with truth. Without a free and nonviolent agreement with the opponent, there is no possibility of coming closer to a greater understanding of the truth. Without agreement, nearing the truth is impossible.

We can complement Gandhi with Habermas and say that killing another person means that the ideal dialogue is rendered impossible, all those affected cannot participate in the dialogue, and the communicative rationality cannot be realised in full.[44] When a human dies, a specific version of the limited truth or part of the argument in the dialogue about the truth disappears. Force, power and violence are on a utopian level, not means that are part of the Gandhian search for truth or the Habermasian communicative rationality.

The idea of 'dialogue facilitation'

If a common truth is to be the goal of nonviolence, dialogue must be furthered during the resistance struggle. In particular, the dialogue between parties to a conflict must be supported precisely because the parties disagree about what is plausible, correct or true. If those who are in disagreement can agree to something, then it is possible that, for them, their agreements are closer to a 'truth'.[45] But bringing people together in a dialogue is not enough, even if they listen to each other and have enough time to do so. To the maximum extent possible, you have to make sure that everyone affected is included, that they are heard, and that decisions or judgements are not formed due to the influence of power, whoever or whatever created that power. Resisting power in a dialogue means counteracting exclusion, suppression, manipulation and undemocratic control. Resistance is required whereby you attempt to open the dialogue and counteract new forms of power. This means that the nonviolent movement needs conflict management to further dialogue at the same time as it fights power and violence without using violence or power itself (while movements will differ in their view on how problematic different forms of 'violence' or 'power' are).

In the ideal speech situation, people are equal participants and listen mutually to each other's arguments. But in real speech situations, power is present. Sometimes power is a decisive obstacle to the dialogue's understanding. It can occur in a clear way or a hidden way. In many cases there is a systematic distortion that makes understanding a chimera. A number of problems arise, ranging from a dominant interruption of others' arguments, threatening body language and authoritarian orders to manipulative friendship coteries and slander, among other things.

Therefore, it makes sense in nonviolent movements for there to be an awareness, in large part inspired by feminism, of the problematic roles and oppression that arise in meetings. Lists of concrete behaviours can be found in nonviolence handbooks and role-playing training is used to transform and counteract them.[46] In this feminist tradition, the nonviolent movement has tried to find methods to work against oppression and to liberate interpersonal dialogue since the 1970s. These dialogue-disruptive behaviours are similar to the 'master suppression techniques' that the Norwegian feminist Berit Ås has shown to be used especially against women: invisibilising, ridiculing, withholding information, the double bind ('damned if you do and damned if you don't'), blame and shame.[47] The feminists at the Empowerment Network at Stockholm University (ENSU) have developed counter-strategies and 'validation techniques' in order to be able to confront master suppression techniques and change the social climate.[48]

The nonviolence trainers Hildegard Goss-Mayr and Jean Goss have formalised a 'nonviolent dialogue' with five steps:[49]

1 Discover the truth of the adversary.
2 See how we have failed to recognize another's truth.
3 Discover and recognize our own responsibility in this conflict, even if it is only passivity and silent complicity.
4 Presentation of injustice. Tell the other person about the evil that he/she has done, and the reason why we are trying to dialogue.
5 Produce concrete proposals.

Understood in this way, a nonviolent dialogue would be the

opposite of rhetoric and methods of influence.[50] An understanding of and openness to the opponent's arguments are
emphasised rather than skilful presentation of the arguments
of one's own side.

Dialogue facilitation through alternative meeting structures within the movement

However, facilitation of dialogue also means that you can
use methods to create the conditions for dialogue by counteracting what prevents it – among other things, the influence
of power. The current of feminist nonviolence has developed
new participant- and dialogue-oriented organisational forms for
nonviolent actions. For feminist nonviolent activists, organising
oneself 'equally' or 'anti-authoritarianly' is part of nonviolence.
Traditional meeting structures in which men dominated dialogue and decisions were replaced in the 1970s by an *alternative
meeting technique* that encouraged participation and *consensus
decision making*.[51] Since then, these forms of organisation and
decision making have had a strong influence on new generations
of activists in nonviolent movements. Training handbooks from
nonviolent movements from different parts of the world offer
several similar methods.[52]

Dialogue facilitation entails counteracting the influence of
power and improving the possibility of equal participation,
honest assertions, careful listening and a search for truth and
understanding through dialogue. Methods and forms of communication are central for dialogue facilitation and to create
new dialogue-furthering institutions.

The methods counteract the eventuality of the dialogue being
disrupted by power or misunderstanding.[53] Facilitating dialogue
occurs through structuring dialogue situations in such a way

that you maximise equal participation and minimise the risk of misunderstanding. For instance, in dialogue facilitation, a participant's silence is not perceived as an approval of a statement; instead, all opinions are checked off in a 'round'. In the round, everyone can talk in turn without others interrupting, except to ask for clarification. Rules and roles are established in order to encourage the shy speakers and to limit the dominant ones. Power in a normal dialogue can arise in the form of time dominance (speaking more than and at the cost of others), a powerful tone of voice, or the use of authority signals, threats or other master suppression techniques, such as ridicule. In the traditions of the nonviolent movement and the feminist movement, a division of responsibilities, both for the group's community and its activity, as well as the rotation of these roles of responsibility are central for dialogue facilitation.[54] Dialogue meetings normally involve 'facilitators' (who in essence correspond to a chairman), with perhaps a 'co-facilitator' helping out, a 'timekeeper' (who ensures the reasonable allocation of time between subjects and participants), a 'vibes-watcher' (who notes feelings, relationships and group energy as required), secretaries and 'process observers' or 'oppression observers' (who note and intervene in unequal gender patterns and other unreasonable power relations).[55] The various roles take primary responsibility for various aspects of the group's activity, make the participants aware of the dynamics in the group, and decide what is to be done about any problems that arise. The roles relieve pressure on the affected individual's or group's responsibility for anything that disturbs the effectiveness of the group's actions or its sense of togetherness.

In nonviolent movements, not only are the responsibility roles of the meeting structured, the meeting itself and the form of decision making used also have their own structure.[56] The group uses a so-called alternative meeting technique with agendas and methods, and structures the dialogues with the aim of improving the possibilities of agreement, understanding, community and effectiveness. For example, it uses 'personal sharing' so that everyone knows what has happened in everyone's private life and that might affect the dialogue. This enables the possibility of adjusting the meeting according to the participants. Here, for instance, the participants speak about times when they have slept poorly and therefore why they are inattentive.

Also included in the agenda is an 'evaluation' of the meeting, the aim of which is to reflect on how the group's decision was reached – in other words, the dialogue's process and not just its result, which normally occurs in other ways (for example, through a discussion about activity reports and special evaluation meetings).[57] Nonviolent activists reflect on the ways in which something can be improved in order to reach an understanding or effectiveness. Principled decisions are made through agreement while the details are delegated. 'Consensus' is applied, and, as this is a form of decision, each participant has the right of veto and can block the decision if they feel principled resistance to it. This does not mean that everyone has to think in the same way, only that a decision cannot be made if anyone is against it for reasons of principle. If a veto is not acceptable – due, for example, to an acute need to make a decision or because of conflicts about principles – there are various ways out of the impasse.[58] The training handbooks provide methods for how to handle each difficulty that could arise.

Examples of dialogue-facilitation methods (discourse methodology) These methods aim to facilitate understanding in accordance with dialogue. Often, alternative meeting techniques are used together with a selection of traditional techniques (such as meeting protocols). The list below does not claim to be exhaustive. These techniques that promote dialogue directly are combined with nonviolence training exercises in which methods to counteract oppression are developed through role play (see Chapter 7).

- *Small groups* (discussions in small groups of approximately three to ten people so that egalitarian participation is made possible) and *workshops* (several groups offering different subjects at the same time and from which the participants choose according to their interests).
- *Round* (everyone gets the chance to express themselves in turn and without being interrupted). Both suggestion and decision rounds exist.
- *Allocation and rotation* of responsibility roles (for example, facilitator, timekeeper, vibes-watcher and oppression-observer).
- *Personal sharing* (a round in which everyone briefly reports on their private life and how they feel).[59]
- *Buzz groups* (a quick discussion with between two and four people sitting next to each other).[60]
- *Consensus decision making* (with the right of veto for individuals or groups) and *groups of representatives* (coordination groups or 'aquariums') if the decision affects several groups.[61]
- *Active listening* (a formalised method of listening).[62]
- *Paraphrasing* (the listener reiterates what is said in their own words).[63]
- *Brainstorm* (ideas and suggestions are written down without discussion).
- *Cross-groups*[64] (a schedule of group combinations and times

that enables many people to take part in the discussions at different times and in a variety of different small groups) and *work groups* (the decentralisation of work tasks into small groups).

- *Evaluation* (of the dialogue quality and process).

The dialogue facilitation methods listed above can be interpreted as an illustration of how to create an ideal dialogue situation to the extent that it is possible to do so. In discussing nonviolent activists at Seneca Peace Camp, Simone Chambers states:

> The similarities between this view [see Women's Encampment for a Future of Peace & Justice 1983] of consensus formation and Habermas's are striking: the conditions of practical discourse are designed precisely to guarantee that all participants have the right to speak and be heard.[65]

But in contrast to Habermas, who 'often talks in terms of non-interference as opposed to positive requirements', nonviolence activists create methods, attitudes and learning processes that are designed to help people handle power problems and misunderstandings that arise in practical dialogue.[66] They complement Habermas's discourse ethics with a *discourse methodology*.

In nonviolence manuals, participants in consensus processes are encouraged to facilitate decision making by taking personal 'responsibility' and expressing their views, by showing 'self-discipline' in using vetoes and 'respect' for the views of others, by striving for 'cooperation', and, when disagreement arises, by 'fighting' for change, learning and agreement without using 'put-downs'.[67]

Both dialogue facilitation and power breaking involve people, using various methods, temporarily trying to steer the communication or stop the interaction with the aim of strengthening that communication. Every facilitation technique and action method that is not understanding-oriented is itself a 'veto' that intervenes in the so-called free and 'normal' interaction, and stops or transforms the requirements for dialogue or other social interaction. The aim is to increase the options available for understanding. In a round, for example, the dominant party is limited so that they are not able to discuss what others say until everyone has been given their chance to speak. When the vibes-watcher interrupts a free discussion in order to check what those who haven't said anything have to say, domination is again stopped. Thus, it is not surprising that dominant speakers or those in power in society often view nonviolent methods as 'silly', 'extreme', 'oppressive' or 'criminal'. The methods employed are forms of resistance and are often used with the aim of preventing the dominant party's 'free' use of power.

Dialogue facilitation through power breaking in external conflicts

It is a common misunderstanding that nonviolence means attempting to convince or reach an understanding with individuals in power. Gandhi has encouraged this understanding by claiming that 'perfect' nonviolence can even convert people such as Hitler. In this, I find that Gandhi becomes something of a literal fundamentalist. Few activists have, in practice, been inspired to adopt approaches as ambitious as this. Nonviolence does not need to be interpreted so absolutely. The communicative orientation of nonviolence does not mean that all the world's individuals have to be in agreement. That is, and will remain, a utopia. An alternative interpretation of nonviolence is that its communication can never be viewed as being isolated from the power relations within which the participants communicate.

In contrast to the idea that it is possible to convert or reach an agreement with everyone, I wish to claim that activists must combine power breaking and dialogue facilitation if they are to avoid reducing the complex action repertoire of nonviolence simply to utopianism and naivety. A central point in nonviolence is that the resistance's power breaking opens up possibilities for dialogue. In relationships where dialogue does not work (at the moment), activists need to carry out resistance for the dialogue to become meaningful. For that reason, communication needs to be adapted according to the various power traits of those involved. In a nonviolent movement's external relationships with various types of counterparts, groups or onlookers, its communication needs to take the prevailing power relations into account. In principle, this means that the *dialogue* is directed at external groups that find themselves in a position of subordination, while *negotiations* are held with those who are in intermediate positions or who are in power. 'Negotiation', in contrast to dialogue, is a more pragmatic trading of costs and benefits and a distribution of resources between the parties to a conflict, for example between trade unions and employers. In difficult conflicts, characterised by violence, oppression and enemy images, the level at which communication is possible is pushed downward within the hierarchy. Then, the nonviolent activists' contact with those in power is reduced to merely signing any treaties that result from dialogue or negotiation with middle-level and bottom-level actors in a society. In less violent or hostile conflicts a dialogue might be possible with middle-level actors, and if the nonviolent resistance is pushing the regime towards the brink of revolution, a dialogue might even be possible with factions at the highest level. It is all a matter of empirical and contextual circumstances, outside the scope of this conceptual analysis. The point here is to make a connection between the *type of communication* (dialogue or negotiation) and the *type of group* in a society that is structured according to unequal power relations (the top level, middle level and bottom level of a hierarchy).[68]

In his classic text – *Letter from a Birmingham Jail* – Martin Luther King Jr develops the connection between resistance and dialogue orientation. The letter was an open answer to several priests who criticised the movement and King for their drastic methods. The critics suggested that King should instead try negotiating with his opponents:

> You are quite right in calling for negotiation. Indeed, this is the very purpose of direct action. Nonviolent direct action seeks to create such a crisis and foster such a tension that a community which has constantly refused to negotiate is *forced to confront the issue*. It seeks so to *dramatize the issue* that it can no longer be ignored ... a type of *constructive, nonviolent tension* which is necessary for growth ... We bring it out in the open, where it can be seen and dealt with. Like a boil that can never be cured so long as it is covered up but must be opened with all its ugliness to the natural medicines of air and light, injustice must be exposed, with all the tension its exposure creates, to the light of human conscience and the air of national opinion before it can be cured.[69]

When the disobedience campaign in Mutlangen began, the organisers – who were inspired by King – sent an open letter to the government in which they stated: 'We are determined to continue these blockades until we are convinced of your willingness to negotiate.'[70] The government then responded that they did not negotiate with criminals. That was in spring 1984. In 1987, they changed their tune. By then, over 100 individuals had been imprisoned and the campaign had mobilised thousands of activists in regular blockades in which even lawyers participated, and, after 2,000 convictions, a local judge had begun acquitting activists. Pending cases swamped the justice system. A legal, moral and political crisis seemed imminent. One of the participants, Uwe Painke from Tübingen, describes how the resistance and dialogue fitted together:

> it was a very interesting experiment towards the dialogue with our opponents that would have eventually to turn into disarmament negotiations between a government and its own citizens. Our 'bargaining chip' was the immense trouble we caused to the Pershing II nuclear troops and thereby to the whole Nato military strategy in Central Europe.[71]

Escalation is central to nonviolence: escalation of both the construction of new and parallel institutions through nonviolence and the undermining of existing institutions by nonviolent resistance. One should understand the escalation of nonviolent struggle as a part of *both* dialogue orientation and power breaking. The dialogue should be tested before resistance is instigated. Dialogue with opposing factions can be possible even in a situation of oppression at certain moments (depending on external crises and on political and economic market conditions). Serious preparation is necessary, according to Gandhi. The dialogue's argument must build on methodical factual research into the situation.[72] During the sugar cane workers' struggle for better working conditions, Gandhi and his collaborators carried out thousands of interviews with the workers in order to really know what their conditions were like before any discussion with their employer began.

The goal of non-cooperation is 'to reduce interaction to the level at which the dominant group will be obliged to negotiate'.[73] According to both Gandhi and Habermas, dialogue requires that all parties listen to each other and take each other's arguments into serious consideration, based on those arguments' merits and not on power interests or tactical games. When power prevents dialogue, it becomes necessary to intensify one's resistance until one's opponent listens again and is willing to enter into a dialogue – in the same way as unions force employers to the negotiation table through strikes.[74] The combination of functional resistance (the strike that affects profits) and a willingness to negotiate together with a readiness to compromise explain why some union movements in Western Europe have had such enormous success historically. According to Gandhi, when dialogue works, you cannot continue to increase your resistance, for then there is a risk that the struggle will develop into a way for you to force your own limited truth onto your opponent. In summary, it can be said that power breaking achieved by resistance is a precondition for dialogue and that dialogue is part of the goal of resistance.

One of the most significant examples of a nonviolent movement that achieved dialogue in a conflict characterised by violence and oppression is the anti-apartheid movement in South Africa. Apartheid was one of the more brutal oppression systems and founded on the white's dehumanising view of the other; in this, it had many similarities with Nazism in Germany. Through the anti-apartheid movement's escalation and its primarily nonviolent struggle during the 1980s, negotiations became possible – first by secret dialogues and later in open constitutional negotiations

involving more actors, which resulted in the first general and
free election 1994. What is remarkable about this context is that
the ANC chose – despite its devastatingly overwhelming election
victory – to govern together with its former enemies in a coalition
government. This made it possible for the Truth and Reconciliation Commission to work in a historically unique way. The
principle was: 'Amnesty in exchange for truth.'[75] The underlying
belief was that the truth about apartheid must be revealed but
that punishment of all guilty parties would lead to catastrophe,
quite simply because so many had been involved. A principle was
assumed that was contrary to usual trials: if you told everything
about all the crimes you had committed, you had the possibility
of obtaining an amnesty. However, what was *not* said could later
lead to trial and imprisonment. Unlike in a criminal case, truth
became a means of self-preservation. Even if the truth did not
create a general sense of forgiveness and reconciliation, it still
undermined enemy images.[76] And it led to the country avoiding
civil war and turned it into a liberal democracy within a few years.

What gives someone the right to limit the actions of another?   In
the claims of both dialogue and power breaking, there is, however, one conflict. Regardless of whether its intentions are good,
resistance risks becoming a threat or a force, and therefore it
risks undermining the conditions of dialogue. For example, a
struggle's initial campaign demands can be perceived as a threat
or lead to the sort of humiliation of your opponent that you are
trying to avoid. Gandhi tries to deal with this problem in several
ways. And because of this risk, compromises, constructive programmes, cooperation with one's opponent (when possible) and
avoiding exploiting others' weaknesses should all be emphasised
(see the Appendix).

The opponent's weakness should not be exploited as doing so would mean risking that agreements were forced through.[77] But it is not always easy to decide when one's actions are exploitative and when there is a (justified) resistance. Gandhi thought that you should not take advantage of problems that arise in other conflicts or situations. For example, Gandhi chose to temporarily interrupt the South African Indians' struggle for their rights when the regime was suddenly faced with another problem: a large strike.[78] Several of Gandhi's collaborators disagreed. They thought that the situation was the right one to exploit to strengthen the struggle, since the regime found itself in a weak position. For Gandhi, however, this was the right moment to show that the struggle was not primarily about defeating the regime, but about winning it over to their own cause.

Does nonviolent resistance mean that nonviolent movements 'force' a mutual agreement? If the mutual truth is essential to liberation and if each individual can encompass only a limited amount of knowledge about that truth, then coercion in conflict management becomes problematic.[79] In this case, a group would force its version of the truth onto another group and any statements about 'mutual truth' would be no more than rhetoric. For Gandhi, the goal was for both parties to develop through the conflict, not for one party to force a change of opinion or will.[80] If the opponent has no other choice remaining, satyagraha is no longer achieved.[81] Gandhi's principle about not exploiting weaknesses in the opponent's position is unique for a resistance strategy and shows his interest in preserving the relationship with the opponent. Agreement – not victory – is the goal. In the same way as the agreement in itself goes beyond the conflicting perceptions, it also forms part of the nonviolent attempt to transform the relationship. The agreement aims not only to reach knowledge about truth, but also to attain social integration. Gandhi's position becomes more complex when he combines this desire for an integrated agreement or mutual truth with a realistic evaluation of power relations as something that hinders those very agreements. For that reason, it is logical that resistance is necessary in order for dialogue to be possible. Before the Salt March in 1930, he wrote to Lord Irwin, the British government's representative in New Delhi (the Viceroy).[82] In the letter he expressed this characteristic duplicity of resistance and dialogue. He rejects the idea of beginning with a conference between the parties if India's independence is not on the agenda:

> The proposed Conference is certainly not the remedy. It is not a matter of carrying conviction by argument. The matter resolves itself into one of matching forces. Conviction or no conviction, Great Britain would defend her Indian commerce and interests by all the forces at her command. India must consequently evolve force enough to free herself from that embrace of death.

Thus it is the resistance struggle that should decide, not arguments. But he continues by formulating his own ambition to *convince* or 'convert' the British people, not force them:

> I know that in embarking on nonviolence I shall be running what might fairly be termed a mad risk. But the victories of truth have never been won without risks, often of the gravest character. Conversion of a nation that has consciously or unconsciously preyed upon another, far more numerous, far more ancient and no less cultured than itself, is worth any amount of risk. I have deliberately used the word 'conversion'. For my ambition is no less than to convert the British people through nonviolence, and thus make them see the wrong they

have done to India. I do not seek to harm your people. I want to serve them even as I want to serve my own. I believe that I have always served them. I served them up to 1919 blindly. But when my eyes were opened and I conceived non-cooperation, the object still was to serve them. I employed the same weapon that I have in all humility successfully used against the dearest members of my family.

Thus, *even resistance expresses the will to convince*, even the will to serve the British people. And that leads him to the conclusion that a conference is desirable after all:

The plan through civil disobedience will be to combat such evils [e.g. the salt tax] as I have sampled out. If we want to sever the British connection it is because of such evils. When they are removed the path becomes easy. Then the way to friendly negotiation will be open. If the British commerce with India is purified of greed, you will have no difficulty in recognizing our independence. I respectfully invite you then to pave the way for immediate removal of those evils, and *thus open a way for a real conference between equals, interested only in promoting the common good of mankind through voluntary fellowship and in arranging terms of mutual help and commerce equally suited to both* (italics added).

The point is that negotiations are meaningful only if there is equality and effective cooperation and the situation created is created through resistance. Here, the connection between Gandhi and Habermas is stretched to its extreme. Habermas's 'ideal speech situation' presupposes Gandhi's 'nonviolent resistance' in order to be meaningful in a world characterised by power and violence. Without resistance, dialogue only *appears* to be dialogue, as it is a new power technique and part of the political economic dominance. On the other hand, resistance becomes a liberation process only when the future relationships of all those involved are allowed to be decided in an understanding-oriented dialogue. Without equal negotiations, oppression is merely transformed into a new oppression. Resistance is therefore the means to make dialogue meaningful and possible in relationships formed by domination and violence.

Sharp thinks that nonviolence's mechanisms of change are comprised of four forms: conversion, accommodation, disintegration and *nonviolent coercion*.[83] This special type of force occurs if the opponent is deprived of their possibility of exercising power and (organised) violence.[84] When a sufficiently large group of people no longer obey the people in power who are affected by their obedience, despite the activists being punished, those in power have to accommodate the group, whether they want to or not. The basis for the exercise of power – obedience – has been taken away. Thus, the 'force' consists of a reduction in the type of possible acts that a regime can employ.

Sharp distinguishes between forcing someone to do something particular and reducing someone's alternative forms of action. I make a corresponding distinction but based on variants of consensus. In terms of the consensus that arises through interaction aided by the nonviolent movement's process of conflict transformation, several levels are possible simultaneously: *de facto consensus* (accommodation, acceptance, adjustment and obedience), *de jure consensus* (contract, compromise and agreement) and *utopian consensus* (conversion and conviction).[85] The difference between a consensus that is imposed and one reached by free will is essential and useful, but the moral dilemma for the nonviolent activists is still not resolved. What gives someone the right to limit the actions of another?

Næss writes that there is not necessarily any force inherent in Gandhi's conflict theory.[86] You have to differentiate between how your opponent is forced to address changed *situations* in social relationships and how your opponent's *perception* is changed. Simply because your opponent's will or perception changes in connection to coerced changes in social relationships does not mean that the changed will or perception is a *result* of the coercion, according to Næss. On the other hand, you can talk about an element of coercion in the nonviolent struggle in the sense that you *force your opponent to experience and listen to certain specific things*. However, if a person, through new experiences and knowledge, changes their evaluation or understanding, we do not normally say that they were forced to do so. In any case, Gandhi suggests, if some degree of force is involved in changing perceptions in a nonviolent struggle, you should then work at liberating yourself from it.

Nonviolent conflict transformation strives for a common conviction and agreement. However, a certain force is clearly exercised when others are coerced into creating new relationships or conditions and in reducing the number of actions available to one's opponents. It seems necessary for movements to try to minimise the risk of coercing others into changing their perceptions or agreeing to contracts in the struggle.

How all dimensions matter for dialogue facilitation

As we will see later in the book, the different dimensions of nonviolence all contribute to making a meaningful dialogue possible. Dialogue facilitation is both one of several methods within the nonviolent repertoire and the central type of rationality that coordinates the other rationalities. The prevailing orientation towards dialogue in nonviolence is noted in several ways in a movement's approaches. Dialogue requires the nonviolent movement to be acknowledged as a (potentially) serious dialogue partner. Dialogue is impossible if images of the enemy show them as inferior or treacherous. For that reason, in order for dialogue to work, trust must be promoted with the help of utopian enactment in parallel to dialogue facilitation.[87]

Activists are not believable within a dialogue with the opponent if they cannot show that they know what they are talking about. For that reason, the movement's own research is essential for any critique of the prevalent relationships, in the same way as its own structuring of alternative institutions and systems is essential for its credibility as a constructive, practical actor. When German anti-nuclear activists stopped activities at a nuclear power plant in Whyl, they were able to do so partly because there were so many occupants present that the police had to withdraw, and partly because so many remained – they created a village on the site that was maintained for over a year.[88] They created, among other things, the people's university 'WhylerWald' and cultivated the land communally. Credibility, however, is not the only reason for creating alternative social structures.

The movement needs to 'prefigure' the possibility of a new society and to build a resource base and autonomy. If nonviolent activists' organisations are too dependent on the regime they oppose, they cannot develop enough force to have an impact based on their convictions on treaties with opponents in a conflict. The movement therefore needs to develop 'microcosms of a new social order' with the help of parallel economic, political and cultural institutions: for example, a parallel legislative parliament and the movement's own administrative government.[89] The Swedish workers' movement's Folksriksdag, where a parallel democratic form was created before the breakthrough of democracy, is an example of how a fight for voting rights can both reveal and create alternatives in a struggle against an oppressive regime.[90]

In addition, the movement needs to have legitimacy and a social basis among those groups that are affected by the oppressive system, as well as a common democratic process that can articulate demands. Without this, any communication will be directed only at elite groups rather than addressing the actual people in power, the subordinates. For example, the anti-apartheid movement's demands were formulated as early as 25–26 June 1955 in 'the people's congress', a true demonstration of what democracy means. And it occurred not in a clandestine place, but at the heart of the dictatorship: Johannesburg. The closing declaration – 'The Freedom Charter' – was based on a long-term dialogue process that 'literally involved millions of South Africans' who sent in suggestions from conferences, meetings in people's houses, association meetings and study circles, despite extensive persecution from the regime.[91] This parallel national constitution was unanimously approved by 3,000 delegates, despite the police arresting people during the debate. 'It was perhaps the first true representative meeting in the union's history,' stated Chief Luthuli.[92] It legitimised the ANC as the representative of the people through the whole anti-apartheid struggle.

Power breaking allows a movement to promote a self-preserving interest in dialogue among power elites. Resistance can occur through a gradual escalation from protests and isolated actions to widespread non-cooperation and oppression-preventative interventions. One can claim that the combination of the international boycott of South Africa and the mass defiance campaign at the end of the 1980s – and their escalation – forced the apartheid regime to enter into dialogue with the ANC in the 1990s.[93]

Another outstanding example is the important role of the Scandinavian unions in creating the welfare state. Employers did not need to listen to the solitary worker who was not connected to a union as this person could easily be replaced and had no economic power. To a large degree, it was through workers joining organised unions that extensive strikes could force agreements with those who owned the capital. The longer the strikes continued, the less the owners profited from their factories, thereby increasing their incentive to reach a negotiated agreement. Resistance is what enables a (more) equal dialogue, and the possibilities of nonviolent resistance are the focus of the next chapter.

5 | NONVIOLENT 'POWER BREAKING'[1]

If the state is to exist, the dominated must obey the authority claimed by the powers that be.[2]

Parliaments have no power or even existence independently of the people ... Imagine a whole people unwilling to conform to the laws of the legislature, and prepared to suffer the consequences of non-compliance! ... No police or military coercion can bend the resolute will of a people who are out for suffering to the uttermost.[3]

Power relations that either prevent certain people from airing their views or ignore majority decisions are decisive impediments to the growth of mutual truth through dialogue. There are elites, people in power, the proprietor classes and other high-status groups that, because of their positions in society, have an interest in maintaining existing conditions. How can you reach an agreement with people whose social status or position of power stops them from being interested in listening or even wanting to listen? When privileges are threatened, arguments can be perceived as being quite ineffectual. Nonviolent resistance is an attempt to tackle the problem of the lack of interest in dialogue shown by those in the dominant positions of power.

Nonviolence, in the sense of *against violence*, involves effective resistance against the power structures and social institutions that make violence possible and that are connected to the power perspective formulated by Gandhi, in which obedience and disobedience play central roles. As we saw in previous chapters,

Gene Sharp is the main innovator with regard to this perspective.[4] In this chapter, I criticise and attempt to explain the fundamental thesis of Sharp's theory of power and nonviolence with the help of Foucault's power theory. Unlike Habermas, Foucault develops a detailed theory relating to the production of power.

The main arguments in this chapter are quite simple, even if the reasoning becomes theoretically complex. Gandhi claims, and shows in practice, that power regimes depend utterly on the population's cooperation or obedience. As a result of an extensive and organised movement of non-cooperation and civil disobedience, economic production may stagnate, bureaucracies stall, trains stop, prisons become overcrowded, and cultural dominance rupture and drive society to the brink of chaos. In some cases, increased repression can lead to increased resistance and protest. Gandhi's systematic development of the potential of popular resistance was a source of inspiration for Sharp when he wrote the nearly 1,000-page, three-volume work *The Politics of Nonviolent Action* (1973). Sharp was a forerunner in a field of critical power research that showed how, in practice, power rested on a diverse social basis rather than on any governmental decision or leader's charisma. Sharp criticised the period's dominant view of power and showed how modern society depends on the citizen's cooperation. However, the nonviolence research that was inspired by Sharp (and others) was not linked to the decisive theoretical change in direction that occurred in the field of power research in the social sciences during the following decades. Existing research on nonviolent movements focuses on resistance to centralised state power.[5] While nonviolence researchers continued the debates of the 1970s about the polarisation between elite perspectives and pluralism, power research in the late modern period moved towards an increasingly nuanced analysis that showed how power is produced in everyday habits, friendships, family, ideologies, feelings, stories, city planning and perceptions of conscience, and even in our way of communicating about things and thinking about reality. This has led to the current situation in which it is no longer convincing to argue that there is a strategic struggle between the people's democratic freedom fighters and the regime's power interests. Every political conflict, even between a violent dictator and a nonviolent people's movement, is much more complex and contradictory than Sharp's perspective suggests. And this means that Sharp's basic power perspective needs to be compared with and developed from a theoretical confrontation with the more recent power research's fundamental ideas. That is the purpose of this chapter. In this context, it is interesting to note that such an advance in Sharp's power theory brings us back to aspects of Gandhi's thinking that Sharp chose to disregard – things such as morality, emotions, the constructive programme and personal development.

In this chapter, I compare a number of late modern theories of power that contradict the simplified analyses of nonviolent 'consent theory'. The key power theory of the French philosopher and historian Michel Foucault also needs modification. The power-producing rules of both behavioural schemata (techniques) and patterns of speech acts (discourse) need to be actively and constantly *applied* in order for them to dominate, even when the applications themselves are moulded by power. The application of rules involves the de facto cooperation of the actor, irrespective of free will or knowledge. An actor, by definition, is acting and *making* a choice – and a 'rule' is not an actor. Even if power is everywhere, it is not everything. Power is not total.

Accordingly, my conclusion is that power is *participatory*

subordination, and resistance is not, as is often assumed, simply another form of domination, albeit one that fights power ('counter-power'), but the *undermining of subordination* ('anti-power').[6] Resistance is concerned with breaking up power relations in which humans are made into 'tools' for external interests or 'servants' in oppressive hierarchies. The use of disobedience and non-cooperation by nonviolent movements thus attacks the very foundations of power.

Let us now go through the argument step by step. I start by clarifying what 'power as consent' means, and then begin a necessary theoretical development with the help of Foucault, arguably still the most influential power researcher in the social sciences.

Power as consent

Concepts such as 'coercion' and 'dominance' imply the existence of a force from 'above' in a hierarchy and are usually understood as 'power'.[7] Sometimes violence or war are also seen as power. The nonviolent tradition, however, does not treat coercion, dominance or violence as characteristics of the social phenomenon of 'power'. Nonviolent activists, as I will argue, view power as a form of cooperative *subordination* ('obedience'). Power does not primarily emanate from above – on the contrary, it originates from below, through subordinate behaviour. Strictly speaking, power 'over' someone does not exist; it is an illusion produced by normalised subordination. Basically, subordination is seen as being accepted (de facto) by its subordinates, even when it is accepted involuntarily in the form of obedience, since all obedience (like all human acts) implies choice.[8] 'Therefore, *all government is based upon consent*.'[9] 'Power as consent' seems to be a common perception held by various nonviolent movements, at least implicitly.[10] Power relations are created by subordination, which is expressed as obedience and through voluntary or involuntary cooperation.

Gene Sharp, 'the foremost writer in the world today on the subject of non-violent action', essentially claims that 'people in society may be divided into rulers and subjects; the power of rulers derives from consent by the subjects; non-violent action is a process of withdrawing consent'.[11] Sharp provides historical examples and illustrates the effective use of hundreds of forms of action, and he defines *social power* as the ability to control the behaviour of others, directly or indirectly, by managing groups of people whose actions affect other groups of people.[12] This is expressed in the strategic struggle between actors in different 'loci of power'. Political power is social power relating to political questions. Political power is about the authority and influence leaders can use to enforce their will upon others, and, on the other hand, the means people use to influence those in positions of power. What is unique about Sharp's contribution is the way in which he develops theories from Hannah Arendt and Gandhi. Gandhi stresses the force of disobedience in power relations,[13] and Arendt claims that: 'The extreme form of power is All against One, the extreme form of violence is One against All.'[14] As Arendt sees it, power is built on some form of organised cooperation between people, while violence is basically an act by an individual. Sharp argues that violence is not only an expression of irrational wrath, but also a working method to attain certain political goals.[15] Violence, not power, is the moral problem and is what could and should be abolished.[16] Sharp agrees with Arendt's reasoning that power is a creative human ability to act collectively and consensually, but he emphasises nonviolent sanction techniques as alternatives to violence in the transformation of power and cooperation.[17] For Sharp, as for Gandhi, the counter-power of resistance becomes a form of *non-cooperation* with power systems.

As we have seen previously, Sharp's starting point, when refer-ring to the dominant understanding of power at the time, is a criticism of what he calls the established 'monolith theory'. This can be summarised as people being dependent on government, and it assumes that political power is massive and uniform, that power really can emanate from leaders, and that power is an entity.[18] This is an oversimplified theory of power or a popular perspective that nevertheless can describe reality accurately if, and only if, both the opposition and the general public within an existing power structure are made to believe in it and therefore act *as if* it were true.[19] The normalised monolith perspective is explaining why everyone, both citizens and rebels, focus their claims and attempts on revolutions on the government buildings and the parliament, as if power inhabited these spaces. Further-more, the monolith theory is the basis of a belief in political violence, especially in military struggle and war. By physically capturing the 'place' of power, one gains power, as if the 'place' were something that could generate power within itself.

Resistance, however, in the form of nonviolent action, assumes that governments are dependent on people and that power is manifold and vulnerable, because the control of power sources depends on many groups.[20] Nonviolent resistance is based on the idea that *political power is most easily controlled at its origin.*[21] The ruler's power 'depend[s] *intimately* upon the obedience and cooperation [of] the subjects'.[22] It is from the (re)production of the economy, social institutions, ideology and the population that the leaders' power derives its nourishment. That nourish-ment comes from the subordinated inhabitants, who may choose to disobey. 'Obedience is at the heart of political power.'[23]

Sharp differentiates the social roots of power as authority, human resources, knowledge and ability, psychological and ideological factors, material resources and sanctions.[24] The strength of power depends completely on how much of these various resources the power-holder can access, and this ultimately depends on the degree of cooperation shown by the subordinates. The main point is that all sources of power lie *outside* the formal executor of power (a leader or government). Using his charismatic personality, a skilful leader plays on the feelings and traditions of the subordinates, but this does not change the fact that the sources of power lie outside him.[25] Charisma is especially important because a power-holder gains access to power through the enthusiasm of his people. The only judges who decide on what behaviour counts as 'charismatic' are the people themselves.

The power-holder himself does not create power; instead, it is given to him by others in their daily cooperation and support.[26] The necessary act of choice by the subordinate, the leader's weakness and the possibilities of resistance are all manifested in the power-holder's position of dependency.

The sort of cooperation that generates power consists of active support, passive acceptance, or unwilling obedience to demands or rules imposed by the power-holder. The person in power depends directly on cooperation from a significant section of citizens to maintain the economic and administrative system and the sanctions that support it. He is clearly dependent on the vast majority of the population paying their taxes, following the rules of society and not putting up collective resistance. When only 0.01 per cent of the Indian population ended up in prison, it became a political and practical problem for the British colonial system. Some 60,000 people in jail and scandals relating to brutal violence forced the Empire to make concessions and engage in negotiations.

While power's dependency on its subordinates might be fundamental, Sharp pays no attention to the fact that there are groups that the power-holder can do without, groups that are excluded but still subordinated.[27] At the same time, one group of leaders may be allied to other power systems, thus compensating for a lack of internal power with external support, for example through an international finance agreement. But this kind of critique does not undermine the theory as such. It only indicates that the nonviolent struggle must influence or be organised within the very groups on which power de facto depends.[28] Therefore, a strategic struggle needs to be based on a relevant analysis of the power being targeted, which will vary according to context.

Sharp argues that power systems are built on hierarchies, or chains of *obedience* where leaders stand or fall according to the level of *cooperation* within the power pyramid. According to Sharp, people are obedient for many reasons – habit, fear of punishment, sense of duty, secondary advantages, psychological identification with the leading group, acceptance or lack of confidence and resources, among others. For the purpose of this analysis, it is sufficient to accept that people do subordinate themselves in their behaviour, whatever the reasons.

Sharp claims that even unwilling obedience is a choice.[29] Obedience is not automatic since there is always a choice; resistance is an option. Sharp considers the subordinate's *obedience a kind of voluntary cooperation*, even when violence is used as a threat. This gives resistance new and unthought-of possibilities for changing power relations – and Sharp regards it as his task to investigate these possibilities.

Violence is a central part of the punishment for rule-breakers, and it is assumed that it will make people obedient even when they do not want to be. Key groups such as the police and the military support political and financial elites through the threat of organised violence. Since one cannot force anyone to do something unless they fear the punishment,[30] it suggests that the key to successful resistance lies in finding ways of changing people's relationship to punishment or to the other harmful consequences of disobedience. Accordingly, Gandhi stresses fearlessness and voluntary acceptance of suffering as central to nonviolent resistance. How this ability is fostered then becomes the difficult problem to be solved. For Gandhi, this is through spiritual purification; for Sharp, through informed and disciplined strategy; for feminist nonviolent activists, through the empowerment of communities of support ('affinity groups').[31]

From Sharp's consent theory of power, we can anticipate that the possibilities for resisting power are created through the organised and strategic use of different techniques of disobedience. Sharp maps a trajectory for nonviolent resistance and indicates a number of basic techniques and dynamics based on historical research. Many examples of the ways in which nonviolent resistance can be expressed in different societies and situations are given.[32] Since power depends on cooperation, resistance becomes possible as *non*-cooperation, and the disobedience of nonviolent action becomes a means for achieving change in society. Organised nonviolent resistance in the form of disobedience can be powerful as a type of action that challenges the very foundations of power – that is, if this concept of power is correct.

Using Sharp's theory, one can maintain – in an analytical sense – that the citizens or people in a society have the power in their own hands. However, this may be true yet still be impossible in real life. Whether the citizens are aware of this and able to change the relations of power is a completely different question. The capacity of resistance depends, according to Sharp, on knowledge and strategic understanding. I maintain, however, that the citizens' capacity for resistance depends, in a profound sense, on whether or not power has the ability to shape people. If power is able to shape our ways of thinking, behaving and acting, resistance becomes much harder, as that power is incorporated within us as individuals and in our culture. In that case, even thinking and talking about resistance may be marked by the features of power. The problem is that Sharp simplifies the ability of power to influence the conditions of resistance.

For Sharp, nonviolence is something people choose consciously in order to correct an unjust situation, once they have learned the techniques of nonviolence and realised the strength of organised and strategic resistance. It is all a matter of using cognitive knowledge and strategic thinking in applying the effective techniques of nonviolent struggle. His view of both power and resistance is pragmatic and technical. Certainly, Sharp's perspective is a profitable one and he develops our understanding of nonviolence beyond earlier, mostly religious, ethical and personality-based interpretations;[33] however, it is also rather one-dimensional,[34] becoming a kind of anti-thesis of idealism and spiritual pacifism. With a simplified concept of power comes a simplified concept of resistance.

Sharp is presented as the foremost interpreter of this concept of power as it is understood today, even by critics. In my view, though, a nonviolent movement expresses a more nuanced understanding of power, and thus adopts a more realistic application of resistance.[35] Sharp's theory is a reaction to the simplified theories of his time (such as classic realism), and is merely one step on a path that was developed independently and in a much more sophisticated way by others.[36] Such power theories are not incorporated within the later Sharpian 'technique approach',[37] nor by researchers slightly critical of this approach.[38]

Although Sharp's reasoning assumes the existence of a conscious and free will, not formed by power,[39] I assert that the autonomous mind is not necessary for the survival of the basic theory. The power theory is ultimately built on the *fact* that subordination is created or changing, not on how this is done.[40] Even if power does shape people's consciousness and actions, I claim that this perspective remains valid: power arises from the *participation* of the subordinate. In fact, Sharp asks for research to be conducted into how the will of a person is formed by institutions and how it could be liberated,[41] indicating the need to incorporate such an understanding into the consent theory.

Power as productive discipline In a sense, Sharp and Foucault complement each other. Using the metaphor of 'war', both investigate strategies and techniques to describe political struggles. A slight difference is that Sharp emphasises resistance, and Foucault power. Still, the theoretical differences are considerable. It is true that they are unanimous in their opinion that power is unstable, changeable and spreading, but Sharp perceives power as a zero-sum game:[42] there is a certain amount of power to share and fight over. When one group gains power, another group loses power. Foucault, on the other hand, thinks that power can increase in one place without decreasing somewhere else. Sharp's concept of power is characterised by the Anglo-Saxon philosophy of the subject: individuals with a free will try to govern others against their will. Coming from a European continental tradition, Foucault is more interested in how different techniques of power form our consciousness and actions. Power does not only *prohibit* – using laws that you can annul through substantial disobedience – but also *produces* society and is partly *incorporated* in people's minds, language and behaviour. Foucault understands power as unstable and dynamic, yet constantly reproduced.

Different behaviour-forming techniques and discourses re-construct social life irrespective of what the participants want or do not want. Power is 'not built up out of "wills" (individual or collective), nor ... derivable from interests',[43] 'neither given, nor exchanged, nor recovered, but rather exercised ... in action'[44] within 'an unequal and relatively stable relation of forces'.[45] Power is about how actions, independent of the actor's intentions, can structure the space of other actions.[46] According to Foucault, power is a productive act of dominance. The acting individual does not control the activity; rather, it is the activity that controls the individual and forms their personality. A set of techniques dominates those who exercise these techniques, irrespective of whether they are 'leaders' or 'subordinates'. The individual does not exercise power; power expresses itself *through* the individual.[47]

Foucault actually maintains the opposite view to Sharp. The nonviolent activist cannot be outside power, make a decision to resist, and then act against that power. Resistance does exist as a possibility, but the strands of power have infiltrated the think-ing, language, methods and culture of the nonviolent activist. To Sharp, the struggle for power goes on between participants, while, to Foucault, the struggle creates the participants. Since these standpoints do not seem to be mutually exclusive, the question is whether this necessarily leads to the eradication of the nonviolent understanding of power as subordination.

It is important that we do not get power and the techniques of power mixed up. With Foucault, power has a tendency to appear as a virtual force without individuals or actors.[48] This is probably not a correct understanding of Foucault, but some of his followers tend to abolish the actor and the making of choices, making the jagged intentions and consciousness of individuals solidify into pure power.[49] This creates a risk that power is mythologised as *self-acting* techniques and discursive structures. Power techniques (of behaviour) or discourses (of speaking) have to be applied and then followed by other people, otherwise they will not be effective in creating power. Techniques and discourses are social performances, not performative objects. When we moderate our behaviour to fit a routine or scheme of techniques, we become part of the shaping of power. It does not matter (for power production) if this happens to be what we want to do or if we do it without thinking. Power will be at work anyway, if our action produces subordination.

Foucault has wrongly been criticised for reducing everything to power.[50] But knowledge, truth, discourse and resistance are not the same as power. If they were, there would be no need to talk about the ways in which power forms these other phenomena. Despite everything, there are, according to Foucault, 'no relations of power without resistance ... [and it] exists all the more by being in the same place as the power'.[51] After all, spaces free from power always exist somewhere. The choice, will, desire, decision or personality of the actor is not completely determined by power. If it were, people would not act: they and their behaviour would be simply 'power effects'. Foucault talks about 'plebs', 'a feature in the social body, in classes, groups and individuals themselves which in some sense escapes relations of power'.[52] It is not a social entity but a plebeian *quality* or *aspect* of different entities. This plebeian quality evades power by existing on its borders or beneath it, and, interestingly enough, by disengagement, by *not* resisting. When unmanageable resistance is stabilised after some time, the risk of power creeping into and configuring the resistance arises. Then resistance may become normalised, disciplined, and shaped by power. I maintain that this plebeian quality of evading power opens up possibilities of resistance that involve more than just counter-power, but Foucault does not help us to understand the resistance that confronts power. Even though Foucault claims that resistance is where power is, plebeian avoidance or resistance is not explored, since power itself is what interests Foucault.[53] While no person or group can exist outside power relations, they cannot exist totally within power either.

Power as subordination The scientific discourse on power is preoccupied with the argument about different *aspects* of power, often with exclusive theories citing one or other form of power as the ultimate one.[54] This leads to conceptual inflation, which makes it difficult to identify what is *characteristic* about either the power phenomenon or anything that is not power. Some authors, such as Foucault, are completely focused on *how* power works, what techniques are used and how forms of power manifest themselves in different ways. In fact, Foucault consciously avoids the question of what is the common factor of 'power'.[55] An understanding of what constitutes power cannot be based on certain individual expressions of power. From Sharp, we have seen that, within the nonviolent tradition, power is coupled with cooperation or obedience. Foucault uses the term 'subjugation', which implies someone who has been defeated by overwhelming force, or even 'manufactured'.[56] My central concept continues to be 'subordination', which implies participation by the subordinate:

> As doers separated from our own doing [through power], we
> re-create our own subordination. As workers we produce the

capital that subordinates us. As university teachers, we play an active part in the identification of society, in the transformation of doing into being.[57]

The social phenomenon of 'power' is characterised by *one actor who subordinates him- or herself, partly or entirely, by relinquishing the practical responsibility or intention of their own behaviour*.[58] The actor behaves like a 'non-actor', as an instrument to be used. The crucial point is that a transfer of behavioural control happens through the actor *relinquishing* control, whether they want to or not, consciously or not. What matters is the existence of obedience or, rather, the active and participatory transfer of responsibility, which produces subordination, *the de facto behaviour*, no matter what motive, reason or cause underlies the act of subordination.

Subordination is essentially an activity that is expressed in relationships and interactions. It does not have to be a *person* to whom the actor is subordinate – whatever we obey is what we let rule our activities. It can be a person, a group or an imagined nation, but equally it may be an idea, a principle, a place, a machine, an ideology, a tradition, a god, or a part of nature. The person who gives up control over their actions does not have to feel forced to do so and may not even be aware of the power that they are giving away. Subordination may, for example, take the form of an obvious yet unquestioned way of structuring our lives according to the 'laws' of a watch chained to the wrist. Or subordination may mean a subconscious obedience to a dead yet internalised and 'active' father.

Subordination may even be like glue, something that sticks when you try to rub it out, refusing to go away, like the situation of poor Brian in the Monty Python film *Life of Brian*. Brian, who is mistakenly believed to be the Messiah, succeeds in fleeing from his fans through the labyrinthine streets of Jerusalem. He wakes up the next morning in his house, startled by hundreds of his devotees waiting outside and shouting: 'Show us the Messiah! The Messiah! The Messiah!' He greets them with 'Good Morning' and they reply in chorus: 'A blessing! A blessing!' Frustrated, he shouts: 'Look. You've got it all wrong. You don't need to follow me. You don't need to follow anybody! You've got to think for yourselves. You're all individuals!' With one voice they all answer: 'Yes, we're all individuals! ... Tell us more!'[59]

In this way, power becomes a very special form of relationship – a subject's inferior positioning in relation to socialised objects, or a social interaction in which someone repeatedly subordinates him- or herself, thus giving someone else the power to master the subordinated individual. This signifies that power is only a possibility: it is something we can do, or that we can stop doing. Subordination is not a state. To subordinate yourself is an action. It also indicates that power is reproduced through repeated subordination. Power may be produced every day as a routine, reluctant and slow, or with growing intensity and willingness. It can always change.

Manifestations of subordination Now, let us see if it is possible to connect 'power as subordination' (the modified consent theory) with other power concepts. The first obvious counterview is power as superiority or dominance. Power expresses itself as *superiority* in relationships only if we view its results or effects while we exclude its production. Then, an illusion of permanence is created. That kind of power order may be understood simply as a *stable process of subordination* where those who are subordinated continually give away their independence or their actions. This creates a state that looks like superiority or dominance when really it is not – and this could be revealed by disobedience at any moment.

Sometimes stability will be expressed as *legally regulated authority* or mutual *contracts*.[60] It stands to reason that there are certain situations in which some subordination is both democratically decided and morally desirable, and is something for which we ought to strive. It is quite possible for people to prefer one sort of subordination to another and to knowingly choose to limit their freedom of action. If that is so, power can assume a more stable form.[61]

Power as subordination implies that the phenomenon of 'power' should not be confused with its *symbols*, such as weapons, social positions, elite or expert status, money or personal charisma. Still, the connection is not completely irrelevant. Power symbols can work as *tools* for power reproduction in certain cases. In situations where stable, unconscious and uncriticised states of power exist, it may appear *as if* the will of elites, money or certain possessions were a powerful force in itself, or as if power were a property that could be owned and claimed. However, this is not the case, as any withdrawal of subordination would demonstrate.

The liberal society's parliamentary buildings or a corporation's board of directors are commonly treated as a powerful force. As if, by *social magic*, the 'men of power' can subordinate millions of people and make them change their behaviour. In its apparent stability, power is *materialised as social facts*. A forceful symbolism of power emanates from such a situation. Those sitting in the 'house of power' have power because that is how they are treated. Therefore, a 'power-holder' is not a myth: as the actual receiver of people's subordination, the mythological 'power position' is embodied in a genuine power-holder. Properties, personal traits and social positions are forms of power if (and only if) they promote regular subordinate behaviour. The creation of subordination in a society is facilitated if certain behaviours are connected to advantages (money, appreciation, social positions and so on) while other behaviour is threatened by sanctions of various kinds. Even more crucial is the nurturing of *perceptions* that power and subordination are desirable.

Subordination always transfers the intention, coordination or direction of action from the actors themselves to somewhere external to them, but it may manifest itself in many ways. Power shows itself as a structured or regular social activity, which creates certain (but shifting) *centred places or positions* in which the coordination of action takes place. Subordination can occur temporarily, consciously, and according to or against the *will* of a subordinate person. Subordination can be unconscious and, through *incorporated* patterns of behaviour, it may appear to be eternal.

Acquired behaviour can be in the form of mental schemes of thinking, which direct our thoughts and our perception of the world.[62] Acquired behaviour can also petrify into semi-automatic physical routines and thereby become a part of our body, a 'habitus', or a disposition to certain subordinated positions within hierarchical social fields.[63] The French anthropologist Pierre Bourdieu demonstrates how we develop behavioural patterns that are conditioned by our member groups' relative power positions. Habitus is about how we, when we grow up in a certain economic and cultural social class, half-consciously adopt embodied forms of behaviour, which, through regular repetition, become part of our personal style and taste. We submit to certain group-specific patterns of behaviour that structure our will and way of thinking, even though we do not make an original or conscious decision to subordinate ourselves.

It is like playing football. If you are good, you know the game well enough to give others some guidelines. However, the exceptionally good player knows how and when to do the unexpected, to break the guidelines in order to master the game. Only through practical training do you get a feeling for the game and learn the various practical schemas of playing. These cannot be taught in a classroom and no books can explain how to practise them. We *know behavioural patterns with our bodies*, through the internalised memory of earlier behaviour. The knowledge is *embodied*. In this way, human beings are formed by their socialisation into a family, a class, a culture, a (football) team or a group with its specific patterns of behaviour, emotional styles of expression, implicit concepts of the world, and dispositions structured according to its social field of possible positions. This internalising of our history and position in society becomes part of us, making it difficult for us to perceive and act outside that pattern.[64] As power lives within the subordinated body, resistance becomes harder. It is like the 'iron cage' (of bureaucracy) that made Max Weber pessimistic about human rationality, but now it encompasses any kind of social and practical knowledge, becoming the 'matrix' in which we live and perceive life.

Power has many facets and there is a changing pattern of *powers*: each individual relationship can be a power relation in which there is a continuous *struggle*.[65] The power and its accompanying struggle look very different in different contexts. The struggle can take place as an observable fight in an arena,[66] or as an only partly visible competition between people with different symbolic capital to invest in order to act in a legitimate way within a specific social field.[67]

Even the opposite of a struggle – *non-acting* – can be a form of subordination, when power makes us avoid certain acts or prevents open conflicts from arising.[68] In these situations, it is more difficult to determine whether power is really at work. Every action, by definition, obliges you – at least temporarily – to eliminate other possible actions. In every moment, there is more than one possible action. One action is chosen in a particular instance, but next time another may be.

Despite the many manifestations of power, I stand my ground. The power-holder is a power-holder only for as long as subordinated people keep reproducing their power. The more people refuse, the less power is given to a leader, a technique, money or a position. If the groups that give a leader access to the sources of power refuse to obey, the leader loses his power. The better a group can withstand the sanctions of a leader and reject his temptations, the less power he has over the group. The very existence of incitements – 'the carrot and the stick' – implies that power is dependent on a certain level of cooperation from those who are subjugated.

It is a fact that there are almost always people who, despite everything, choose to resist by not subordinating themselves. The dependence of power is highlighted by the fact that dictatorships react with massive sanctions and retaliation against even small numbers of people who resist them. Still, it is a common belief that non-cooperation works only within a liberal democracy. Perhaps the power-holders are more aware than their subordinates of their vulnerability and dependence on massive cooperation from the inhabitants who provide their power with its strength.

But when oppressed people realise this and are given the means to stop cooperating, then those in power no longer stay safe in their positions. In a society of minority rule, this is more visible. As early as 1920, Gandhi claimed that India would be able to liberate itself as soon as its people realised the injustice and fragility of a vast country being colonised by a few thousand colonisers.[69] The British Empire would not be able to build all the prisons required to control millions of Indians on the day they decided to disobey the regime and follow their own 'laws': that is, the decisions made by the parallel government, the All-India Congress Committee, that had been constituted by the Indian liberation movement. Furthermore, the Empire would not profit from keeping its colony if the administration and economy collapsed. After a few decades, Gandhi's revolutionary ideas were victorious. India became independent through a struggle in the form of massive non-cooperation and civil disobedience, despite repeated massacres, brutality, mass-imprisonment and torture.

At the other end of the spectrum – where power is normalised and accepted, not seen as colonial occupation or oppression but as natural or even as a holy blessing – subordination is less visible. As power seems able to exist even when actors act mainly in their own interests, consciously and of their own free will, the importance of power can be difficult to discern. Power simply exists if you can establish that the actor abandons their individual and practical responsibility for their actions. It is harder, though, to establish the significance of a particular power relationship, since this depends on whose interest we emphasise and the importance we give to it. A typical example of responsibility being renounced is that of the worker who acts through a union to improve working conditions, but lets the professional union leaders decide what should be improved. Another example is the citizen who obeys the laws of a society, even when some laws are seen as unjust, in order to be able to lead a quiet life. The questions of whether a specific kind of subordination is morally problematic or not, and of how a judgement is arrived at (by the individual or by a deliberative democracy that includes everyone concerned), are difficult political issues that we will not develop here. What matters is to identify subordination when it does exist. If we do not see power – in all its variety – we will not be able to resist it.

From consent to cooperative subordination After reviewing several different concepts of power, I claim that what characterises the phenomenon of power is an abandoning of initiative: the displacement of practical responsibility for one's behaviour. As we have seen, this can occur completely or partially, consciously, semi-consciously or unconsciously. Cooperation is what makes power so special. Analytically, power can neither be taken nor owned; it can only be given away and then only temporarily, while subordination continues. A social interplay, with all its everyday differences, fluctuations, conflicts and misunderstandings, is amalgamated in *one united intention* and the actor is *transformed into a tool* for others to use. In its pure form, power is an interaction in which *many people act as one, as if they had been reduced to one body and one brain.* This is why power becomes so powerful and attractive, particularly to the subordinated. Through subordination, we become part of a whole, a community of people. In real life, though, we find many hybrids where resistance and the struggle for power coexist, and where different power relationships overlap, some stable and others in constant flux.

Even if subordination is the factor that distinguishes power, its *techniques* and the ways in which it manifests itself seem to be unlimited. Humanity has developed vast cultural variations, which have facilitated subordination throughout history. Physical discipline, rhetoric, separation into categories, exclusion, isolation, surveillance, standardisation, training, examination of knowledge and punishment are just a few examples.[70] Over the course of history, men in power, scientists, priests, missionaries, psychiatrists, sports trainers, teachers, military officers and factory bosses have developed sophisticated knowledge and specialised systems for making people subordinate.

We make a mistake if we assume that any person in power has independent control or even conscious knowledge of the full potential of these techniques. Many power techniques have been consciously developed for the purpose of keeping and extending power. But, throughout history, the consequences of new techniques have not been controllable or even imaginable. The medieval monasteries were not intended to serve as the models of discipline for modern society, but, in fact, they did.[71] The extensive power exercised in society today hardly results from one single conspiracy by the elite; rather, it is an unintentional mix of consequences emanating from various competing conspiracies among elite factions, and from the liberal reforms of earlier authoritarian societies and brutal regimes. Foucault shows how several disciplinary techniques – such as Jeremy Bentham's Panopticon prison structure – have been developed with the intention of humanising the royal excesses of brutality.[72]

The critique expounded by liberal reformists against the public and brutal punishment of criminals in the Middle Ages has given us the advanced techniques of control, discipline and normatively guided behaviour modification that are now routine in prisons, factories, hospitals, schools, military barracks and asylums. The divergent, disobedient or 'abnormal' are no longer exposed to violent pain. Instead, there is a whole science of behaviour control in 'total institutions': that is, in isolated social complexes where all parts of the individual's life are formed.[73] Interestingly, efforts to reduce the brutal punishment of the state have resulted in an increased production of power through the *development of sophisticated and hidden forms of subordination.* Perhaps surprisingly, this new repertoire of power techniques opens up new possibilities for resistance: for example, the undermining of established definitions and symbols of power through humour.[74] Every new power technique can be regarded as a tool for new forms of resistance to contest, reverse, 'misplace', mimic, 'misunderstand' or deconstruct.

This does not appear to be a new phase of power, but an additional repertoire. The option of brutal violence still exists if all else fails, and, as we see from state behaviour in modern wars, the tools of medieval-style brutality have increased.[75]

The most sophisticated exercise of power uses techniques and discourses that regulate the will, one's opinion and the perception of one's interests. By *establishing the idea that the order of power is right, natural, eternal, holy, good, invincible or advantageous to people*, subordinates can be made to consider obedience a duty, a necessity, intelligent or a sign of maturity. These connections between truth, knowledge, law and power are at the centre of Foucault's critical investigations of power.[76] In this way, knowledge becomes a matter of regulating and moulding techniques, where a world of ideas is created that will preserve or develop power. Through power-structured discourses – 'truth regimes' – ideas, particular interests and practices are interlinked. The power knowledge within these discourses is effective because it does not need a conspirator who governs in the background. It is enough that these techniques are disseminated through history and in social organisations by those who, for various reasons, see a pragmatic use for them. Networks of power threads without a single, stable centre pierce the social body. Physical violence hurts – it is noticeable and visible – while power can be like radioactive radiation: odourless, tasteless and invisible.

It would be a misconception to understand power as voluntary or legitimate only because it depends on a crucial level of cooperation by, or choice of, the subordinated. This cooperation in power relations is considered a *distortion* of the ideal form of cooperation, participation and understanding for which the nonviolent movement strives.[77] Manipulation, brutality, dependency, discrimination, ideology, isolation, threats, poverty and the ordinariness created by traditions mean that the subordinate's participation grows out of a tangle of lies, denials, shame, temptations and limitations. Even a concentration camp or death row has its dull everyday routine and familiarity that are experienced by those whose life takes place there and that turn unthinkable acts into normal ones. Furthermore, we live in an existential insufficiency where it is hard for us – even under suitable conditions – to fulfil moral demands or to live our lives in the way we would like to.

Power as a 'relinquishing of responsibility' involves practical responsibility, initiative, decision, and control of our own activity. Ethical responsibility is something different. It would be naïve to claim that participants should blame themselves when things start to go wrong. Rather, personal blame should relate to the person who profits from the relationship, not to the one being exploited. The fact that the subordinated participate signifies that there is hope of resistance against the abuse of power. Any ethical judgement must consider how subordination is created – usually by a combination of threats and temptations, but mainly through a lifelong moulding process – and what it is reasonable for a human being to accomplish in a certain situation or position. Such an ethical judgement is beyond the scope of this investigation. What concerns us here is an understanding of systems of subordination and the potential for resistance.

I maintain that it seems reasonable to claim that, even when subordination is the result of a non-mutual and exploitative interaction, it depends on some form of participation by the subordinated. A distorted participation occurs when the meaning, orientation or content of the activity is replaced in such a manner that participation works *against* the vital interests of the subordinated, sometimes even with self-destructive consequences. It is surely in the interests of the slave to obtain food and protection from their work, although slavery is not in their interests. When behaviour is distorted, the activity is no longer controlled by the actor in the specific situation, but by the more or less stable interests that lie outside the actor.

Power exists only as long as it is reproduced, as long as subordinates continue to transfer practical responsibility for their actions. The *possibility* of regaining control over our actions is never renounced completely. Action can be reclaimed even if it may entail a process of 'unlearning' and the reforming of old patterns of behaviour, which may take time and collective struggle to be effective. Accordingly, power, in a profound sense, is about *activities* and *relationships* – habits, roles, structures, speech and interpretations – and not about its manifestations in the form of power symbols (such as the American Express Gold credit card or an FBI identity card).

Even if transfers within interactions, by definition, lead to a centralisation of power through the transfer of responsibility from one actor to another, the power centres are temporary and numerous. The centre of an interaction shifts depending on changes in that interaction. Since every micro-interaction may express a subordinate relationship, power is not a stable

entity. Instead, it is multi-centred, complex, unstable and contradictory.

Coercion, violence and power Generally, a society's established
social order, long-standing traditions, socialisation of new generations, status hierarchies, financial facilitation and legitimating
ideologies are all that is required to make most people in a
society subordinate themselves. Subordination under an existing political system may take place through devoted support,
unreflective habit or reluctant acceptance. Within such a social
order, the need for coercion and violence arises only to control
those smaller groups that resist, or the ones that misuse the
social system. In any society, there is normally a large group of
people who give their passionate support to uphold the power
system. These people consider subordination not only morally
correct or necessary, but a duty and part of the natural order of
things. They may even rejoice in the 'blessing' of being chosen
to subordinate themselves to the superior power, and thereby
they contribute to the growth of power.

Coercion may facilitate people's subordination, but it does
not necessarily do so, as power in everyday situations, as we
have seen, emanates from an undramatic and naturalised practice in which subordination comes into existence almost as an
automatic behaviour.

In socialisation, we go through *act-intermediating institutions*
right from childhood. These are social institutions in which we
learn to transfer responsibility for our actions to acknowledged
principles or authorities.[78] This learning starts in the family and
with friends. Through socialisation in a society where power is
normalised, the transference of responsibility is gradually shaped
into something natural and self-evident – even something that

is morally desirable – in work, politics, the family and everyday life. Power-oriented aspects of religions, mythologies and ideologies are central elements in the distortion of our understanding of how power is produced. This results in the tragic situation in which the very people who provide the foundation for the strength of the power order believe themselves to be powerless and are unable to see from where the powerful derive their power.

In extreme situations, when we become acutely aware of the choice between obeying and disobeying, it may be too late to refuse. The amount of power accumulated by sluggishly changeable habits and stabilised socio-material structures may simply be overwhelming. Then participation in a power relation is experienced as coercion. While the decision to act is still our own, it does not feel as if any choice exists. Yet, as long as we act, and subordination is surely an activity, disobedience is possible, despite the experience of 'coercion'.

Coercion can also be real – or *effective* coercion. Strictly speaking, the use of *physical enforcement* is not a social interaction and therefore is not a power relationship.[79] In situations when people are carried away, tied up, hurt or killed, no active participation whatsoever is necessary. The result is independent of the people victimised. That is what makes force so effective. When this occurs, it is more of a physical energy development of force, with quantifiable causes and effects. Causation, not choice, determines what happens.

When the effect of enforcement hurts people, it is usually called 'violence'.[80] While the *ability* to use violence is often coupled with power, as it is the result of many people's organised subordination in the production of weapons and wars, violence is not power in itself. Even if violence can accompany power in certain situations, violence and power are analytically separate, at least if we refer to the conventional form of (direct) violence (and not 'structural violence'). The difference is that an act of violence depends only on the decision of the violent actor. Power, on the other hand, depends on the active approval of the subordinate, in the form of subordinating acts; this is how power gains its effect. Even the reluctant and practical cooperation of spirited intellectuals critical of the existing power order is necessary; without it, power does not exist in that relationship. The more they criticise and protest while in everyday life they (practically) obey the system, the more they (involuntarily) construct the democratic appearance of that society, hence legitimising power.[81]

Power may draw more or less strength, depending on the level of subordination and energy people invest. The more de facto recognition power obtains from concerned participants, the more effective power becomes. *Power is something we give or are offered*. Violence, on the other hand, does not demand the active participation of the person being hurt; this, then, is also a characteristic feature that makes an act 'violent'. *Violence assumes somebody's autocratic exercise against someone else*. Either you exercise violence or you are affected by it.

Power and violence are therefore separate social phenomena and may either enforce or obstruct each other. Violence can be used as a threat, as a compelling reason for subordination, towards those who otherwise do not obey or bend to the ordinary techniques of behavioural manufacture.[82] Under circumstances and in places where power reigns without competition, no violence is needed. However, if conditions are reversed, violence may be helpful. In an analytical sense, power is absent when violence exists. Simply put, the most extreme result of violence – the killing of a human being – is something that ensures that there will never again be subordination within that relationship. Killing results in an absolute absence of power. In fact, violence is a sign of the (current) *failure* of power.

However, power may benefit from the effects of violence on people, by using violence as a *threat*. The threat of pain or damage may promote subordination, and sometimes that threat has to be made real by the demonstrative use of violence. This means killing the right number of people in order to make *others* subordinate themselves. If one kills too many, the ground on which power is built literally disappears. Thus, *the threat of violence is a possible mainstay of power, not power in itself.* Accordingly, different advanced techniques of organised violence (in war, state security, or the police force) may be used to support the order of power in widely disparate societies – liberal as well as fascist or socialist.

Neither the threat of violence nor its use automatically produces power. When resistance confronts violence, this demonstrates the *possibility* of not submitting to its compelling force. Resistance may also arise under regimes of extreme violence, as in the Nazi concentration camps, where there were regular uprisings.[83]

Even if resistance is not exercised at a particular moment, a choice always exists.[84] In this context, the important thing is that, even when faced with the brutal threat of violence, people do have a choice, being 'condemned to freedom'. They can choose to obey, or they can choose to resist no matter what, and thereby refuse to subordinate themselves. Power seen as subordination – giving away responsibility in social interactions – anticipates the fact that the subordinated person has the *capacity to act.* Otherwise, subordination would be impossible, at least in an analytical sense. Power as seen by the nonviolent movement suggests that people are never completely powerless or dominated, that the subordinated always have the capacity to resist, even if this may not always be effective or preferable.

In a practical and political sense, it becomes a more difficult question to judge the realistic level of a person's capacity in specific life situations. Then we need to consider practical knowledge, emotional support, and resource building. Unfortunately, this text needs to limit itself to the fundamental theoretical possibility of resistance to subordination.

Since *power is a special case of interaction*, interaction is not power in itself. Interaction or cooperation may equally be based on dialogue and on mutual and equal agreements, which power does not affect in any crucial way. The same is true for socialisation, which, in a power system, contains central elements of power reproduction without being power itself. Socialisation may simply be based on purely intimate contacts, dialogue, and the continuous and conclusive freedom to choose. It is not necessarily based on subordination. In order to judge if and to what extent power is present, we have to undertake an investigation of an actual example of these social activities. Bitter experience, though, shows us that power is both common and devastating in real life. The piercing pervasiveness or capillary character of power implies that power can make its way into anything anywhere, into the most unlikely places, at the most unlikely times. When even the language or the culture of speech we use to talk scientifically about power is infected by techniques of power, it gets complicated, to say the least, to know what's what and to find a way to resist.

Identifying resistance

Like Sharp, I have argued that you can understand power as a form of obedience or active subordination, where cooperation from the subordinate is crucial. Unlike Sharp, I have adopted more sophisticated concepts, especially Foucault's, by saying that power is many faceted and an obvious element in social activity, and therefore it is also a silent and often hidden shaper of people. Accordingly, not even the will, body and mind of the resistance fighter is free from power.

Opposing the common interpretation of Foucault, I have argued that it is possible to combine incorporated techniques of power with 'power as subordination', therefore with choice and active cooperation. I also claim that Foucault's techniques of dominance *anticipate* the cooperative subordination of individuals; if not, such techniques would not be able to dominate us. As behavioural schemata or patterns of speech acts, their rules need to be applied in order to dominate. The always present possibility of refusal – a silent 'no', the unwillingness to 'understand' orders or a passionate expression of destructive rage against the status quo – is an existential and unavoidable part of being a human being and an actor.[85]

Power creates the subject – the normal person or disobedient activist – but is not the sole designer. If the individual were conditioned completely, we would be talking about 'effective force' and not power, and the individual would cease to be an active being. Choice would disappear and the human being would simply become a victim, a result of history, and nothing else. The theoretical idea of 'total power' does not seem reasonable when we see how power – despite its developments, dissemination and organisation of new techniques throughout history – is still met with resistance in some form. It is as unreasonable as the idea of 'freedom from power'. Power seems to be an obvious aspect of all social life as we know it. The notion of a social life 'free from power' originated in our wished-for utopias and visionary dreams, which are loaded with an understandable and necessary but unrealistic longing for freedom, which in turn paves the way for the reappearance of resistance. Even if the questioning of power leads to a practice that creates new power forms, that very questioning shows that power is not absolute. However, this is true only if power and resistance are different things, which I claim that they can be.

Foucault shows us how the techniques of power work and points out that resistance is always present where power exists – but he does not help us to understand 'how it is possible, what it is for, or why it merits our support'.[86] Resistance is not merely a power struggle or a counter-power;[87] it is also a phenomenon that differs from power. Even if powers disperse globally into all social phenomena, resistance must analytically be something else. We would otherwise not be talking of resistance, but merely of another kind of power technique, or 'power'.

It is reasonable to conclude that violence may also be used in *resistance* to power. Through a resistance movement, the state's apparatus of violence may be destroyed and thus also the threat of violence which supports that power. But since subordination does not arise through effective coercion, but through the subservient person's own subordination, *violence seems neither necessary nor central for resistance*. Still, it may compensate for a weak mobilisation of individuals. For the purposes of this text, it is enough to note the analytical difference between the *goal* of resisting power and the *tool* of violence, which clearly may be used to further resistance but which is only one of several possible tools. Nonviolence is another possibility. For Gandhi, nonviolence is a struggle against both violence and power, in an attempt to reach reconciliation and truth.[88] This discussion indicates that such resistance attacks the foundations of power.

If power is supported by the threat of violence, it seems necessary for the success of a resistance movement that the struggle continues *despite* opponents' or power-holders' threat, or use, of violence. If not, nonviolent resistance would have to be abandoned every time activists became victims of violence, and therefore such 'nonviolence' would not be effective against repression.

We may say that our ability to determine when people subordinate themselves and where power exists does not mean that we have found something to help us explain a specific social phenomenon or situation. It does not even mean that we have found something that is undemocratic or immoral. All people let some other interests or persons determine their actions at times. Letting the needs of children and the sick become more important than your own private interests – hence subordinating yourself to their vulnerability – may even be *what is moral*.

Sometimes power is trivial and negligible. At other times even occasional actions and apparently inconsequential power relations are crucial to the understanding of what has happened and why.

A central expression of power is the very shaping of our ideas of how power and resistance are made possible. Power has an existence of its own by the virtue of our experiences and ideas about what power really is. The people who are simultaneously the objects and subjects of power have perceptions of what power is. Powerlessness benefits – as does autocratism – from its own legitimating ideologies. When actions take place as if power existed, then power has a social existence by virtue of its consequences. Resistance becomes hard to imagine and may even *be made unrealistic* if power is understood as a 'monolith' – some manifest dominance emanating from a place far away

– or as a 'total power' that exists within personalities, societies, alternatives, oppositions and struggles.

If instead we understand power as subordination, in line with the nonviolent movement, then it has some interesting consequences for how we understand resistance. Resistance becomes the attempt to hinder or break relations in which human beings are made into tools for others or are used as servants in a hierarchy. Resistance may be directed towards the structure, process, relations or techniques of subordination. Thus, *'resistance' is about the undermining of subordination*.

On a utopian level, the project of the nonviolent movement is about *dissolving* subordination, creating space for a new social order that all involved have agreed on freely – a global deliberative democracy. But, in practice, nonviolent resistance is about hindering the present system of subordination, a system that certain mobilised activists consider to be wrong.

Foucault has shown that power may form several different global and local strategies.[89] Therefore, the specific obstruction of subordination needs to be formed according to the power being fought and the specific case, context and situation.

A typology of resistance Counteracting subordination through nonviolent resistance may happen in diverse ways. The literature proposes different categorisations of *nonviolent techniques*.[90] Resistance can entail *communicative and discursive attempts* with the help of, for example, appeals, witnessing, reinterpretation, information, good counter-arguments, symbolic contradictions or the resolution of emotional blocks. The power order's discourse comprises a way of speaking that is guided by rules and preserves power – a truth regime. If the truth regime is undermined, counter-discourses can arise. Opponents, those who are

Ruling class [margin annotation]

in a submissive position and temporarily neutral parties can all perhaps be brought to change their perceptions and actions in the power relation with the help of dialogues and negotiations. As a form of resistance, this is about expressing contradictory views and breaking the structure of the propaganda, discourse and ideology of those in power.

However, in conflicts characterised by power, disobedience through discourse or dialogue are probably not enough. What is needed is the creation of a competing and alternative pattern of relationships and interactions, via the formation of *parallel cultural, economic or political institutions*. Here, we create the social leeway needed for a new order. The social integration of a new society and the creation of an alternative to the oppressive institutions that the movement attempts to overthrow recall Gandhi's constructive programme. This new society does not arise from the ashes of the old but is developed during the resistance struggle, both to credibly show the preferred new order and also to create the resources required to make the necessary progress possible.[91]

As we have seen, nonviolence entails a *non-cooperation with the role* that the opponent plays as part of an oppressive social structure, and a simultaneous *cooperation with the opponent as a human being* and part of a human community.[92] The nonviolent activists should both protect the opponent's legitimate needs and come to the rescue when the opponent's personal safety is threatened. As there is something you already agree on, you should aim for a cooperative project with your opponent. This promotes emotional bonding and constructive societal change, at the same time as enemy images and the opponent's power base are weakened. This approach aims to strengthen the nonviolent aspects of society and to provide a basis for cooperation between conflicting parties. This constructive work can also lead to new alliances benefiting from the change in approach. The creation of competing institutions that replace those opposed by the nonviolent movement is supplemented with the strengthening of existing institutions that are *not* part of what is being fought. There are many examples of this among nonviolent movements. Together with hundreds of other Indians, Gandhi voluntarily enlisted in a British medical corps during the Boer War. During the West German nonviolent movement's blockades of the nuclear arms base in Mutlangen, it was viewed as an important part of the struggle to invite soldiers to dinner in the activists' homes or to drink beer together in the local pub. The peace activists and the soldiers had different aims, but they could still meet together over something genuinely human: food and drink. In this respect, the opponent is seen as a human being despite the conflict situation and is assumed to share at least some values and desires with members of the nonviolent movement. But non-cooperation with the opponents' oppressive activities and roles as the oppressor are central to nonviolence and can be expressed in, for instance, refusing orders, striking or boycotting. If they cooperate with their opponent, the activists risk being manipulated. Loyalty can develop through practical labour; however, the opponent also risks being led into new loyalties. The combination of cooperation and non-cooperation with an opponent is an expression of the contradictory approach that characterises the nonviolent movement.

When power is domineering, part of one's resistance may involve *removing oneself* from it by establishing geographical or social 'free' zones. Extricating oneself from power relations can be perceived as the opposite of 'resistance', but that is not necessarily true. By detaching oneself from any aspect of the dominant power, *space* is created for action, thought and initiative, while, at the same time, an *absence* occurs for those in power.[93] Sometimes simply removing oneself, fleeing or 'not expressing one's resistance' to a hegemony is necessary for the success of a subordinate group,[94] or it may be a precondition in order for power not to dominate.[95] A resistance group such as the Indian liberation movement's ashrams or an eco-village in the forest may work like a free zone for a social experiment with alternative lifestyles and institutions. The creation of free zones for 'critical communities' is a central aspect of the movements' ability to mobilise and creatively renew their repertoires.[96]

Even if many individuals are convinced and refuse to subordinate themselves, there might be an effective group of people who continue to subordinate themselves and thereby stabilise power. In such cases, an alternative solution could be to undertake actions that directly *impede* the power system's processes: this could be through action forms such as organised roadblocks, sabotage or civil disobedience.

It is also conceivable that humour, self-irony or other *playful methods* reverse preconceptions, meanings, prejudices or habitual perspectives. One example occurred in Sweden in the 1970s when homosexuals fought the law's definition of homosexuality as an illness by calling in sick to the Swedish Social Insurance Agency.[97] 'Hi, I feel a little homosexual today and unfortunately I can't go to work.' Another was when Norwegian conscientious objectors decided to break *into* prison to protest against a comrade being jailed.[98] When they refused to leave the prison unless their comrade was also released, the police had to carry them out in front of the media's flashing cameras. In both of these actions, the order, discourse and methods of power were de-dramatised. The Swedish homosexual activists transformed a stigmatising label of sickness into ridicule of the state, as the state naturally could not give sick pay to homosexuals just because they were homosexual. The Norwegian conscientious objectors made the prison sentence meaningless, for what sentence could a court impose on the activists who broke in? – hardly time in jail.

Furthermore, one can view the provocative activist group Out-Rage! and its action to highlight British society's prejudice against homosexuals as undermining power relations that depend on fear, avoidance and the desire for a 'quiet life'.[99] During the 1990s, for example, the group held a 'kiss-in' where hundreds of gays and lesbians openly showed their love. A group of people dressed up for the occasion also carried out 'The Exorcism of Lambeth Palace' in the area in front of the Archbishop of Canterbury's residence. The 'exorcists' commemorated the Christian church's persecution of homosexuals throughout history and tried, by means of rituals and prayers, to forgive the Christians and drive out the 'demon of homophobia' from the English church. Similarly, Queer Nation in the USA fought against oppression by 'outing' famous people who did not publicly stand up for their homosexuality. The organisation also instigated an offensive in which members claimed their right to be different ('We're here, we're queer, get used to it', 'Queer in your face', 'Bash back'), which was in stark contrast to the traditionally careful, petition-ing and shame-ridden style of protests.[100] In the wake of Queer Nation's manifesto in 1990, a number of offensive action groups were established, such as the civil disobedience group ACT UP.

To summarise, six basic nonviolent methods should be con-sidered:[101]

1   *Counter-discourse*: Communicating with well-supported counter-arguments and counter-images (discursive strategies)

that disrupt power's truth regime and can convince isolated individuals (for example, fact finding, symbolism, countering enemy images by counter-behaviour).

2 *Competition:* Creating alternative and competing nonviolent institutions (in cultural, political and economic areas, for example).

3 *Non-cooperation* with the system's roles or functions (including boycotts) combined with cooperation with people who focus on legitimate and mutual needs (such as relief work during a natural catastrophe).

4 *Withdrawal*: Removing oneself from destructive power relations (for example, flight and the creation of free zones).

5 *Hindrance*: Stopping or preventing the processes of oppressive power systems (blockades, occupations, interventions, and so on).

6 *Dramatising* injustices or communities with humour (for example, self-irony, redefinition and shock).

These nonviolent methods of resistance can together create the space needed for mobilisation and alliances (via communication and cooperation), alternative social systems (constructive work, free zones and competition), the removal of support for and participation in the existing system (refusal and avoidance), and making existing systems' processes difficult, or impossible, to carry out (impeding). Together, the methods can, in the best case scenario, lead to dialogue and negotiation with various power groups, which can enable a new and more acceptable social order. The power groups need to comprise not only elite factions or political leaders; in this power and resistance perspective, it is equally important to negotiate with those who subordinate themselves (salary earners and the police, for example) as it is to negotiate with 'those in power'. After all, it is the former who uphold the power.

The combination of focused cooperation and non-cooperation with one's opponents is a central aspect of nonviolent resistance. Despite this combination creating an unusual contradictoriness, it still appears reasonable. Each society requires some form of order to work, and an effective boycott or refusal to cooperate risks leading to the social order breaking down. The creation of new forms of order, along with the avoidance of existing institutions, can counteract this risk of breakdown.

If power can be seen as subordination, nonviolent movements are, in principle, well suited to resisting that power. I argue that nonviolent movements, instead of changing society by trying to *take power*, try to *dissolve* power according to their utopian values: to transform an oppressive and exploitative structure of subordination into a voluntary and equal cooperation built on argument, open conflicts and mutual truth. Through this utopian ambition, they can, in practice, achieve a *transformation* of the prevailing power structures and a decrease in oppression.

6 | NONVIOLENT 'UTOPIAN ENACTMENT'

As the anti-colonial guerrilla war in Algeria raged, Frantz Fanon worked as a psychologist and published *The Wretched of the Earth* – often called the 'Bible of the Third World' – which inspired a generation of anti-colonial freedom fighters around the world.[1] In the foreword, the French philosopher Jean-Paul Sartre argues that a slave can become human only by murdering his or her owner.[2] Through violent rebellion, the dehumanised slave becomes an equal with the slave owner. Sartre's point is that the distorted master–slave relationship dehumanises the slave, disabling any attempt at humanistic solutions. Humane relationships presuppose that a person is taken seriously as a human being, that their arguments, desires and needs are viewed as valid. A slave demanding equality through argument would appear as preposterous as a four-year-old demanding equal treatment with adults, or perhaps an animal formulating a plea. As a liberty-oriented nonviolent activist, I have felt both inspired and provoked by Sartre's reasoning. I am, however, convinced that he is wrong on one decisive issue. It is not *violence* that makes the slave an equal. It is the rebellion's *resistance*, the decision to definitively stop subordinating oneself, to say no whatever the consequences. If the master–slave relationship is dehumanising, it is by breaking the inhumane relationship that slaves become human beings in the opinion of both themselves and their oppressors, not through violence. In the previous chapter, I argued that subordination is a relationship in which a human being becomes a tool for someone else, but that this can be changed by resistance. Like Sartre, I find that there is always the choice of saying no. Unlike Sartre, I believe that there are effective forms of resistance other than violence, especially if we aim for the liberation of subordinate collectives, not just individuals. But, like violence, nonviolent resistance sometimes carries incredible personal risks.

I have set out conceptual frameworks that highlight how nonviolence seeks a common truth (Chapter 4) and undermines oppressive power relations (Chapter 5). If these two strategies work well, they obstruct the organised exercise of violence and dissolve oppression, thus normalising nonviolence throughout society. However, even the nonviolent movements that have 'won' have involved only a fraction of the population in nonviolence. Even during the Indian mass mobilisation for liberation, participation was limited. And at Gandhi's funeral, liberated India's government violated his nonviolent utopia by letting Indian soldiers fire a salute. Step by step, the government abandoned nonviolence. Eventually, the military even acquired nuclear weapons.

The threat of violence and oppression's violation of human value persist during and after the nonviolent struggle. Certain groups continue to discriminate, hate and kill, despite the peaceful behaviour of the nonviolent movement.[3] It is also well known that conflicts bring about polarisation and escalation.[4] If a conflict group has weapons and wants to exercise violence, it can do so – especially if it is acting on behalf of the state (which, by definition, has a monopoly on the legitimate use of violence). As stated in Chapter 5, violence does not require the assistance of those affected – violence is a decision made by one side. The struggle against violence requires something more than dialogue facilitation and power breaking.

The desire to harm, kill or exercise violence is fuelled by enemy images, fear, hate or other psychological, political or cultural forces. It becomes more acute when cultural authorities, government agencies or the state authorise these emotions.

This chapter focuses on the concepts needed to describe the ways in which nonviolence is used to tackle hate and enemy images of groups during a conflict. Essentially, emotions play a role in both the exercise of violence and the transformation of conflicts, and, subsequently, in the possibility of promoting consensus between parties: 'each emotion motivates and organizes perception, cognition, and actions (behaviour) in particular ways'.[5] My discussion of nonviolence is based on the problem of dehumanising stereotypes and enemy images in conflicts that are characterised by power and violence, where 'the other' (the nonviolent activist) is seen as non-human and dismissed as part of a civilised, negotiated solution.[6] In rebelling, the slave risks suffering: enemy images do not disappear simply because the slave revolts (with or without violence). Gandhi and many of his successors have pointed out that rational arguments are insufficient against hate and that suffering can be a way of reducing the emotional distance between conflicting parties.

> If you want something really important to be done, you must not merely satisfy the reason, you must move the heart also. The appeal of reason is more to the head, but the penetration of the heart comes from suffering. It opens up the inner understanding.[7]

Affecting 'the heart' means going beyond a cognitively rational argument and getting people to understand emotionally. The key to this emotional understanding is, according to Gandhi, suffering.

In contrast to Gandhi's theory of suffering, I, with the help of Erving Goffman's drama model, discuss nonviolence as a risk-filled utopian enactment.[8] Goffman is one of Habermas's theoretical inspirations, but using Goffman directly, instead of using Habermas's own reasoning, helps us in confronting a fundamental objection against Habermas's theory of communication: namely, the problem of arguments being *disqualified* because the people making them are not perceived to be worth listening to (for instance, they are viewed as 'savages' or 'primitive'). The problem is decisive. Dialogues collapse if the participants do not mutually recognise each other as equals or at least as competent partners in the dialogue. A political problem arises not because the *arguments* are dismissed, but because the *person(s)* expressing them are.

This kind of utopian enactment – or 'as if' action – is somewhat similar to what is discussed in social movement literature as 'prefigurative politics' (or 'horizontalism', among other terms):[9] that is, activists experiment within their movements with the creation of a new society and act in a 'utopian' way. However, 'utopian enactment' and 'as if' actions are different to prefiguration in several important ways. They are about acting in a way that looks towards the future *within and in confrontation with a violent conflict*, where the high risk of violent repercussions is taken into account. Utopian enactment is *focused on an individual's relationship to the other*, the opponent, and it attempts to counter prevailing images, emotional predispositions and attitudes towards the activists by acting in a way that is the *opposite* of the expected behaviour. At the same time, it embodies an attractive, *shared* possibility of living together in respect and mutuality, in the hope of opening up new relationships with the other. As will become clear during the discussion below, 'prefigurative politics' is more relevant for the next chapter, the theme of which is the creation of a new and nonviolent society.

'Utopian' is a concept I have used repeatedly without providing a more detailed conceptual discussion, but that discussion is now necessary. I use the concept both in the general sense, as a 'future-oriented action', and in the modern sense of people themselves creating a new society. I am, however, not using it in the traditional and negative sense of 'idealistic' or 'unrealistic', something that preferably should be called *utopianism*. I also use it with special reference to the nonviolent movement, in the sense of 'making the future the present' by 'constructing situations'; this is similar to the concept adopted by Situationists in Paris in the 1950s and 1960s.[10] The modern kind of utopia is rooted in a spatially oriented literary form (for example, Thomas More's book *Utopia* from 1516) and a religious conception of the coming 'thousand-year kingdom' (millennialism) that describes a 'movement in time'.[11] One of the predecessors of the nonviolent movement, Gerrard Winstanley and the 'Diggers' in seventeenth-century England, formulated one of the earliest utopian texts. In 'The law of freedom in a platform' (1652), Winstanley proposes the establishment of a 'commonwealth', which was later created as local 'commons'. Nineteenth-century thinking on utopias is characterised by the Enlightenment's 'emancipatory discourse' and the perception that society can be *improved*.[12] Gandhi viewed absolute nonviolence as both practically impossible to realise fully and a meaningful ideal lending direction to the struggle.[13]

In today's nonviolent movements, the organised development of alternative institutions and practices and 'visionary exercises' are part of the trainings.[14] The belief is that a societal analysis of problems and a vision of what you want to achieve can help you develop a strategy of nonviolent struggle.[15] Using this strategy, you can then plan and carry out actions.

The problem of suffering

We shall match your capacity to inflict suffering by our capacity to endure suffering. We will meet your physical force with soul force. Do to us what you will and we will still love you. We cannot in all good conscience obey your unjust laws and abide by the unjust system, because noncooperation with evil is as much a moral obligation as is cooperation with good, and so throw us in jail and we will still love you. Bomb our homes and threaten our children, and, as difficult as it is, we will still love you. Send your hooded perpetrators of violence into our communities at the midnight hour and drag us out on some wayside road and leave us half dead as you beat us, and we will still love you ... Be assured that we'll wear you down by our capacity to suffer, and one day we will win our freedom. We will not only win freedom for ourselves, we will so appeal to your heart and conscience that we will win you in the process and our victory will be a double victory. (Martin Luther King)[16]

Martin Luther King's view of the political, transformative power of suffering did not come from just his Christianity but also from Gandhi. According to Gandhi, it is necessary for participants in a nonviolent struggle to be disciplined so the coordination and dynamics work.[17] In order to set the power of truth free in the nonviolent struggle, activists must show their truth-seeking honesty by being prepared to lose all ('fearlessness') – their property, their friends, their body – everything except their 'honour', which is the only thing they can retain with certainty.[18] Gandhi finds that the activists' readiness to suffer for their cause and endure the opponent's punishments leads to a softening of the opponent's 'heart', conscience or sympathy. This dynamic arises from the 'voluntary suffering' (or 'self-suffering'), which, as we previously stated, is a central part of the nonviolent struggle.

Voluntary suffering is not about helpless suffering; rather, it is an accepted, goal-oriented, intentional, persevering and publicly exposed suffering.[19] It is not a suffering derived from seeing oneself as worthless or as a powerless victim, but a suffering that results from one's belief in one's own integrity and in something of higher value.

Gandhi's approach was unconventional in the sense that he found that suffering had a value as a liberator of *the other* – the oppressor's heart, sympathy or conscience.[20] Satyagraha as a 'love force' and the endless love towards our fellow humans were, for Gandhi, equal to the endless ability to endure suffering for the truth or for the life of our fellow human beings. Gandhi claims that satyagraha, nonviolence and civil disobedience are only new names for the ancient 'law of self-suffering'.[21] The only real limitation of the application of nonviolence lies in the individual activist's 'strength to suffer'.[22]

Gandhi does not mean that suffering in itself is powerful. Rather that suffering is powerful if it stems from a conviction about the truth.[23] The reason why Gandhi is often misinterpreted may depend on the fact that he occasionally made statements such as activists should 'find joy in suffering'[24] or '[p]ain to a *Satyagrahi* is the same as pleasure',[25] which can sound like praise for suffering itself. This has led some to explain this reasoning with reference to his personality, childhood or Hinduism, rather than seeing it as a socially oriented, practical struggle of liberation.[26] However, my opinion is that the conversion of 'the heart' should be understood as an attempt to *resolve the emotional blocks or social distance between conflicting parties*.[27] Voluntary suffering can bring about empathy, sympathy, perspective or trust, depending on how the suffering is handled.[28]

In nonviolence literature, voluntary suffering is generally viewed as a creative force that incites people and societies to change.[29] Naturally, no one claims that suffering creates sympathy for the activists, regardless of the issue being discussed. Rather, they find that, due to the focus on the issue and the activists' perception of what is just and true, suffering becomes a truth-bearing power.[30] The existing literature sees voluntary suffering as functional for several reasons: it demonstrates a spirit of generosity; it is a kind of training in self-control; it saves human lives; it shows love, sincerity and support for the opponent's needs; and it protects the lives of others if the nonviolent activist makes a mistake.[31]

In the 1930s, Gregg made one of the first attempts to interpret nonviolent struggle according to the theories of social psychology. It is not the design of the action *before an audience* ('a performance') that he focuses on, but the individual energy, feelings, initiative and morality of the struggling people. He mentions the audience only as it amplifies the dynamic, and he stops at the primary unit of analysis for any interaction: two people. Gregg disregards socialised role playing in the interaction of groups; he therefore misses the significance of how our personalities emerge from childhood as a result of others intimately viewing our behaviour, emotions and morals. We are socialised by seeing other people and being seen, and this seeing is of crucial importance for how we understand the role of suffering in nonviolence and conflicts.

Nonviolent feminism (and other sources) criticises the emphasis on suffering in nonviolent action studies.[32] The focus on suffering highlights individual strength and martyrdom, something that can be tied into a patriarchal assertion of a man's power over others and his feelings. Instead of suffering, feminists affirm how nonviolent struggle can create 'empowerment', a process of self-trust and the ability to use one's own capacities as an individual and as a group. Like Gandhi, they see power not as a personal attribute but as something created within a relationship. By changing relationships – private or political – you can exercise power (in the sense of liberating the ability to act) and avoid becoming either the oppressed or the oppressor. This takes place through the dual approach of nonviolent struggle:

> to acknowledge and connect us with that which is valuable
> in a person at the same time as it resists and challenges that
> person's oppressive attitudes or behaviour.[33]

Nonviolent feminism helps us see how disobedience can be made possible in the face of our fear, imperfection, habits of obedience and internalisation of the socialisation of norms. However, empowerment, or group capacity through solidarity, does not mean that suffering disappears. Like nonviolent feminists, I find that nonviolence means accepting the risk of suffering. The risk of suffering arises as an unavoidable consequence of engaging in a struggle and refusing to injure the opponent.

Thus, the controversial question remains: what social function and role does suffering have in our nonviolent struggle? It is important to understand that suffering is not unique to violence. We can state that it is not only religious believers or nonviolent activists who are prepared to endure suffering for something they value. Soldiers are prepared to risk their lives for their duty and nation. Parents are prepared to endure suffering to protect their children. And activists of various kinds are prepared to suffer for their ideological conviction that there can be a better future for coming generations. Common to all these different examples is the fact that people believe that suffering derives from a duty, a responsibility to others or something you need to accept in order to reach your desired aim. However, nonviolent struggle differs on one key point. Through nonviolent resistance, you face the risk of suffering with your eyes open, *without trying to defend yourself or escape*. You can say that nonviolent movements define themselves by using (the risk of) suffering as a *means* in the struggle.

Risk-filled utopian enactment

Gandhi's thesis about the political role of suffering in the liberation struggle was developed in specific social contexts – segregated South Africa and colonial India – characterised by racism and ethnic superiority and inferiority, as well as by ideologies that allowed special treatment of, and power over, certain people who were represented as being of lesser value. For that reason, it was necessary for a liberation struggle to clearly show the humanity, civility and egalitarianism of the subalterns. If the goal was a society with good relations between all people, then military struggle was excluded. One way of making the liberation activists' humanity clear is to show a kind of courage that differs from the courage displayed by the militarised people in power – the courage to die for one's belief in an egalitarian society.

> The Negro's [*sic*] method of nonviolent direct action is not only suitable as a remedy for injustice; its very nature is such that it challenges the myth of inferiority. Even the most reluctant are forced to recognize that no inferior people could

choose and successfully pursue a course involving such extensive sacrifice, bravery, and skill. (Martin Luther King, 1963)[34]

My interpretation of nonviolence is that activists use the risk of suffering in order to undermine enemy images, emotional blocking and hate. It is a way of stimulating the growth of a minimal and *necessary confidence* between conflicting parties.[35] Yet suffering is not the central social factor in the dynamic. Instead, this lies in the *redefinition* of actions, roles and situations generated by violence. What makes this redefinition a power in itself is that it is *materialised in concrete actions* carried out in a situation in which the nonviolent activists *risk* suffering. Suffering has a meaning in that it constitutes an indicator of the activists' sincerity and dedication. By taking action because of a vision, despite the risk of suffering, nonviolent activists are considered to be serious parties in a conflict. They cease to be 'non-people', 'God's enemies', 'treacherous', 'rats', 'cockroaches', 'dirty', 'barbarians', 'idiots' or 'animals'. Nonviolence undermines violence by combining practical redefinition and the risk of suffering, which is achieved by *rehumanising* enemy images.

Shaping nonviolent behaviour In modern nonviolent actions, Gandhi's lofty demands on activists have been replaced by relatively practical *nonviolent guidelines*. These action guidelines secure a sufficient level of necessary nonviolent discipline, including in heterogeneous groups that unite around nonviolent methods for purely tactical reasons.[36] The guidelines have become fewer over the years and the requirements have decreased.[37] The National Lesbian and Gay March on Washington used a typical set of guidelines:

For the purpose of building trust and a common foundation

for safety, participants in the Supreme Court Action are asked to agree to the following:

1. Our attitude will be one of openness and respect for all people we encounter.

2. We will not engage in physical violence, even in the face of hostility.

3. We will seek to express our feelings of anger, frustration, and pain without verbally abusing any individual.

4. We will not bring or use drugs or alcohol other than for medical purposes.

5. We will not carry any weapons.

6. We will not run, intentionally destroy property*, or in any other way promote panic or endanger the wellbeing of any person participating in, or in the vicinity of, the action.

All participants in the action are expected to participate in a Non-Violence Training Session and be organized in affinity groups.

*While property destruction is not necessarily, or in all cases, a violent act, it can create a dangerous situation if carried out in the midst of a large group of people.[38]

Even if today's nonviolent guidelines do not impose Gandhi's exacting demands on nonviolent action, they express a *humanity despite the violence and oppression expected from the opponent.* The will to uphold applicable guidelines is often strong. It is common to use 'affinity groups', work groups, 'peacekeepers' (the movement's own guards)[39] and nonviolence training in order to maintain the nonviolent character of the action.[40] With the help of *affinity groups* – where the participants are divided into small groups – you can create safety, support and flexibility. This enables you to carry out confrontational actions with many participants.

What was powerful about nonviolent actions, like those carried out by the Indian liberation struggle, was not that activists suffered for a truth but that the actions expressed an *appealing utopianness* in which both parties were socio-culturally anchored. Despite being met with contempt, threats and violence, the activists acted *as if* their opponent was an equal, a friend, and this had an impact on people.

The goal was mutual equality, and the thought that the ends and means characterise each other was so prominent that the activists acted (on their own behalf) as if the goal had already been reached.[41] What I call a *nonviolent 'as if' action in a situation of risk is a way of applying the goal in the present, despite the risk of suffering*. Through 'as if' actions, two simultaneous processes occur in the utopian enactment: on the one hand, *exposing injustice* or something shameful (through the violent repression of nonviolent people); on the other, *exposing justice* or something desirable (through the utopian behaviour of the nonviolent movement). Since the Indian liberation activists wanted to establish a future relationship with the British characterised by equality, freedom and respect, the more violence or hate the British expressed, the more the activists acted with a peaceful discipline. The 'as if' action gains power by contradicting enemy images and stereotypes.[42]

The dynamic assumes that the majority of people want to live in a world that embodies equality, freedom and respect. Nonviolence *presupposes a belief in the human potential* to abstain from violence and oppression. For some, this belief is based on religion, but it can equally well be secular. This trust in people is not about them being 'truly' good and wanting to do well, but that change is possible.[43] Nonviolence is built on the belief that good will is *always* there, at least as a *possibility*.[44]

A desire cannot be realised easily. There are many obstacles. People may not see any realistic possibility of living according to a desired vision as long as there are threatening people, or as long as society accepts or even encourages people's potential for spite, exploitation or the desire to dominate. It may also be the case that people have encountered so much pain in life that they have given up. There are several individual psychological and culturally collective obstacles that the nonviolent struggle needs to overcome. By acting with greater care and respect as they encounter greater contempt or violence, the nonviolent activists try to convince even the most 'cold-hearted' opponents. The activists need to show that the 'enemy' – which is how their opponent sees them – will not injure them, not even if the opponent lays down their weapons, protective gear and tools of control.[45]

However, other forces counteract the promotion of equality and there is much that can disrupt the activists' goal. There are relationships not based on power relations, and therefore not affected by non-cooperation. A social and emotional distance between conflicting parties can obstruct understanding.[46] Decisive social differences between the parties (concerning class, culture, ethnicity or gender), might generate alienation, enemy images, prejudice and quite simply the readiness to kill, especially if they are combined with ideological representations of some groups' inferiority and real differences of privilege.[47]

By distancing oneself from violence through nonviolence, one attempts to bridge the emotional barriers of social distance. This attempt leads to the activists risking suffering, but suffering itself does not generate any decisive sympathy. In fact, this is rather self-evident: if it were not the case, mass murder, concentration camps and war would not be possible. Instead, what appears to be decisive is *why* the activists suffer, in what situations, and what they do when punished.[48] *Choosing* to risk suffering (in a situation in which you can avoid it) is fundamentally different to merely falling victim to suffering. Voluntary suffering means that the price of suffering is seen as acceptable in order to achieve something of higher value. The difficulty in a conflict loaded with enemy images is to get one party to understand the other as a fellow human being with human value and also to view suffering as a human problem.[49] The underlying belief is that the oppressor's potential for brotherly or sisterly feelings is released when they *recognise themselves* in the other's suffering. In order to achieve this, the nonviolent struggle uses *utopian presentations in risk situations*; this is where activists illustrate a common attractive vision (utopia) despite the danger of punishment or provocation hanging over them.[50] The prevailing and mutual suspicion in conflicts makes friendly gestures non-convincing. Something else is needed to make the friendliness so clear that it cannot be regarded as a trick, idiocy or cowardice. When such an act comes at a cost to the person carrying it out, then it becomes difficult to reject or dismiss as dishonest.[51]

Let's take an example of the social dynamic of utopian risk management. During the United States' era of segregation, activists carried out a nonviolent invasion of beaches reserved for whites ('wade-ins').[52] The wade-ins inspired a local civil rights movement in Mississippi in May 1959.[53] With nine other blacks, Gilbert Mason went to Biloxi Beach, a forbidden part of the enormous coastline. There is a double dynamic when a black, nonviolent activist is punished for having gone onto a 'whites-only' beach, happily singing, wearing a swimming costume, carrying a packed lunch and accompanied by family and friends: the act is both risk-filled and utopian. When the activists are manhandled and put into jail, the brutality of those in power is exposed at the same time as the activists' good intentions are made clear. Not only are civil rights champions imprisoned, they are imprisoned because they tried to socialise with people of another skin colour on the beach on a nice, warm summer's day.

Oppression becomes all the more grotesque and the vision of community all the more appealing when violence is exercised against constructive nonviolent activists who neither defend themselves (with violence) nor give up. The more violence that occurs and the clearer the utopian symbolism, the more difficult it becomes to uphold the legitimacy of power. The violent oppression in the southern states and the Civil Rights Movement's peaceful demands for liberal political rights stood in sharp contrast to each other. In this respect, it is possible that an emotional distance is converted into a common desire for reconciliation – at least a sufficient level of trust and respect can be established, enabling negotiations for change.

According to Sharp, a participant in a nonviolent struggle can endure suffering without having religious beliefs if they understand that the *technique's functions require* that they do not flee or submit to the desire for revenge.[54] Sharp talks about the dynamic in the nonviolent activists' suffering as *political ju-jitsu*. The consequent nonviolence shows the use of violence in the worst possible light and undermines the legitimacy of violence, and thus the position of those in power. The effect of violence rebounds on the perpetrator, as in ju-jitsu, where the power of the attack becomes the force of defence.[55] Those who exercise violence's pure strength are turned against themselves because the activists do not give the violence legitimacy, and this leads to lost support and reduced power resources. Sharp claims that a regime or a person in power must at least legitimise their violent actions before the potential and existing groups who support their power.[56] For moral or pragmatic reasons, non-violent activists refuse to seek revenge or use violent defence, even when this may seem reasonable. This creates a moral and political pressure on those in power: alliances are disrupted, neutral parties take sides, and insecurity spreads among those who have given their support to the order of power. Previously indifferent parties and groups suffering under the exercise of violence are also affected. The more violence a regime applies to a challenging movement that resists without violence, the more the regime discredits itself.[57]

Undermining the legitimacy of power is only part of the non-violent dynamic. Nonviolence as ju-jitsu is not only about *without violence* but also *against violence*, in this case as a form of utopian enactment – a confrontation where violence is pitted against an attractive possibility of something else. When the nonviolent movement's actions expose the brutality of the opponent and the appealing utopia of community, certain possibilities arise. *If the emotional distance is overcome, while the opponent's power base and political legitimacy are undermined, a readiness or a will for understanding and negotiation can be set free in the opposing parties.*

Emotional blackmail If activists perceive their own truth as the Truth, seek short-sighted success and see suffering as a key to victory, there is a risk that a confusion between suffering and truth will characterise the struggle. By using their voluntary suffering, activists can create such strong emotional reactions that they manage to get others to subordinate themselves to their demands. In such actions, there is a risk that *emotional blackmail* will arise. Most people are affected badly by others' suffering, especially if they are in some way made responsible. During the Vietnam War, there were activists who, in their resistance to the war, committed suicide by setting themselves on fire in public places ('self-immolation').[58] Today, over 100 Tibetans have used self-immolation as protest against the Chinese occupation. Gandhi diligently fasted to enlighten his own nonviolent activists, his family and other Indian groups in cases where he thought they were oppressive and where he wanted to change their behaviour.[59] His fasts were often indefinite, which meant that they entailed an obvious risk to his life. One can legitimately point out that fasting has a different meaning in Indian culture, where Gandhi's fasts were interpreted as his penance for his own and others' moral mistakes ('fasting for purification').[60] But, based on other good reasons, a fast to the death can be perceived as essentially the same thing as a hunger strike and thus an attempt at blackmail, at least in the West.[61] This is the way most hunger strikes are applied by prisoners. Prisoners fall into this blackmailing most probably due to their lack of normal political rights and freedoms, which makes it hard to articulate claims or protest against injustices in any other way. But others also apply this sort of pressure through suffering. In 1999, an British animal rights activist fasted for so long that he came close to a life-threatening coma. His fast was linked to concrete demands made in relation to the British government's animal protection policy. In all likelihood, politically motivated fasting can even be depicted as a moral problem in India, at least the indefinite version, something that Gandhi himself noted.[62] A creative nonviolent resistance uses a number of different possibilities for exposing the type of painful suffering – what Erik Eriksson calls 'demonstrative self-suffering' – that enables an audience to react. And when that suffering becomes so intrusive that those who are made morally responsible cannot ignore it, then concessions are forced from them.[63]

Nonviolent activists who want to creatively use the risk of suffering in their struggle also need to try to avoid their suffering becoming a new obstacle for empathy, trust and emotional bridge building. Therefore, they have to avoid making their struggle into blackmail.

Our mutual role playing If this risk-filled utopian enactment perspective on nonviolent activism has been reasonable so far, then a sociological analysis of nonviolent struggle should assume that the (risk of) suffering is tied into the actions of resistance carried out by activists in order to convince others of a desirable goal (utopia) and with the desire to reach a common agreement with the opponent in a conflict (Truth). The challenge is to describe this management of (the risk of) suffering *sociologically*.

Gandhi distinguished between a person and a person's (violent) action, and this is the key to a sociological understanding of violence. You can say that nonviolent struggle *distinguishes its opponent as a person and as a role player* in such a way that you support and respect the person while fighting the role. It is a matter of 'hating the sin, not the sinner'.[64] Robert Burrowes finds that Gandhi's nonviolent approach is about meeting the needs of all people:

> [A] method of struggle that satisfies three conditions: It must destroy need-denying structures, create need-satisfying structures, and respect the needs of the conflicting parties during the struggle itself.[65]

The opponent in a conflict has a genuine and legitimate need for community, meaningfulness, nutrition and security, for example. There will always be situations in which nonviolent activists can and should support their opponents as human beings.

This positive confirmation of the legitimate needs of everyone and the division of human roles warrants an interpretation of the nonviolent struggle as a blend of *personal support and role resistance* in one and the same relationship.

Effective communication requires mutual understanding: that is, the interaction has to express the same meanings for all parties involved. Communication collapses if the parties cannot find at least one possible mutual definition of the situation: who we are and what we are doing here. This requirement is used by nonviolent activists to disrupt fixed roles in conflicts.

In their interactions, people *take each other into consideration.*[66] This seemingly simple statement means that the actors are aware of each other, make judgements, identify with the other, and try to work out what the other is going to do. This evaluation does not occur only at the beginning of the interaction but *through the whole process*. Each person must take the other into consideration and count on their opponent doing the same. However, they also have to be aware that they are both *taking the other into consideration.*[67] This leads to something more than a simple sum of actions, where one action is adjusted as a result of another, and so on. Rather, it is a union or a *transaction* of actions – a weaving together, as can happen in a creative stream of dialogue. This transaction is built up within the situation and constructed during the ongoing action in a fluid process of development.

Nonviolence uses the demand for improvisation inherent in personal commitment that is necessary in the formation of roles.[68] At the same time, nonviolence uses the social pressure to adapt to existing norms. In order to understand how this can happen, you can, like Goffman, interpret social interaction based on a theatre metaphor.[69] Each person simultaneously plays several social roles (mother, teacher, military officer in the reserves, widow, and so on) by acting in front of several separate audiences (children, students, soldiers or relatives). Sometimes this structural division does not work and so a conflict of roles arises and 'correct' behaviour must be improvised (for example, when a child becomes a peace activist). In relation to each audience, the social space is divided into a front-stage and a backstage region. Playing one's role and the performance occur in the front stage, as on a theatre stage,[70] whereas backstage, beyond the audience's gaze, the act can be entirely different: jokes about the audience, repetition of difficult parts before the performance, or, after the public performance, an intense outburst over the team's poor effort on stage – this is similar to what occurs behind the theatre stage in life. In the backstage, internal meetings of the movement, nonviolent activists prepare their performance. They discuss what action is suitable, both before and after their performance on the stage of conflict.

According to this perspective, a conflict can be translated into a theatre performance with a stage's structure and props (the context of the conflict), an audience's interpretation (groups that are not directly involved) and a cast of fixed roles (the actors' pattern of action) that coordinate in a performance of the dramaturgical script (conflict situation, conflict theme and the configuration of the conflicting parties). The social interplay of roles works if the different actors maintain a somewhat similar definition of 'what we are doing here'. The common definition is what holds the play together, which is necessary in a conflict.

Behind the disunity there is an implicit agreement about the existence of disunity. To a certain extent, it is obvious from the start – in a theatre thanks to the director, and in society because of the established traditions of previous generations. A definition is being held up if it is re-created and modified commonly in each new play or social interaction. Adherence to a *common definition* is a fundamental rule if a social encounter is to work.[71] The play's coordination thus requires the different actors to act according to a commonly constructed definition of the situation, behavioural patterns, conflict subjects and configuration. Only then is uninterrupted social interaction possible. Also, the performance should be convincing for the audience in order to become socially accepted. How, when and where the play is performed is also regulated, but in different ways in different normative communities. Each believable performance requires an approved connection to the role, a suitable capacity to play the role with skill and an engagement that corresponds to the audience's expectation.[72] One could say that the audience's interpretation is the only societal court in this context: it sovereignly decides what is acceptable.

People become individuals, Goffman states, by publicly claiming what or who they are and then trying to act as if they really have the qualities they claim to have.[73] The nonviolent activist's problem is that they meet actors and an audience who are sceptical at best and directly hostile at worst. This situation results from nonviolent activists reacting against previously established norms and threatening a society's concept of justice. It becomes necessary to undergo a test to show that you are not 'just playing a role' but are really who you say you are – a kind of *authenticity test*. There is nothing unusual about this: the audience always has a latent suspicion resulting from its self-reflexive awareness of inner qualities *being represented* in expressive behaviour, which makes people understand that qualities can be misrepresented. The nonviolent activist's problem of convincing the audience (and other actors) is simply the normal problem of social trust, but to an unusually high degree and with greater risks. The civil rights activists who carried out sit-ins at segregated cafés had to put up with threats, beatings and ridicule without retaliating or leaving their seats.[74]

In order to develop sociological concepts for the ways in which nonviolence handles suffering, we first need to understand nonviolent movements in terms of drama, a drama between protagonists and antagonists in a competition to win the right to manage the audience's interpretation of fairness and power relations.[75] Managing the interpretation occurs through the formulation of a script when the action is being prepared, and then improvisation during the action and adjusting afterwards in the evaluation process. The drama of the action arises in a planned intervention in the public space, which is remade as a stage and where other actors are attributed roles. The drama's gallery of characters is central, especially those that might be called (with a bit of hyperbole) 'perpetrators', 'victims' and 'saviours'. A convincing performance requires the movement's activists to apply a dramaturgical loyalty, discipline and adaptation to other actors' actions.[76] The movement risks being branded (or stigmatised) as having less value, or as being irresponsible, naïve or treacherous. For that reason, the movement continually needs to counteract this risk. The audience's interpretation of the drama is an encompassing process that always affects the play and that depends on all the actors. New interpretations of norms, situations and roles are the goal of and the driving force behind the movement's actions in the public sphere. By first trying to get the public – and other involved actors – to see the situation as unjust and as a common concern, and by illustrating the solutions, the movement hopes to contribute to social change. Through our actions towards our surroundings, based on our interpretations, a convincing new interpretation can stimulate a change in behaviour. The movement's directed dramatisation of politics ('framing') highlights not only injustice or the problem but also those responsible and justice or the solution. The movement then becomes the key to making the solution feasible.[77]

> Nonviolent action is performative, not in the sense of actors in a play, who enact an external reality ... but as actors constituting this reality in the moment of performing.[78]

In a conflict-ridden interaction, nonviolent actions construct new interpretations while established perceptions are picked apart.[79]

A duel between two logics of drama Within sociology, the concept of a social 'role' is fundamental, particularly within the symbolic interactionism of Goffman. Roles are proscribed action performances in institutional settings or other rule-based contexts, and they are seen as expectations of certain behaviour by others within the social environment. Whether people identify with their roles or not is a different and separate issue. Irrespective of that, people continuously experience a social pressure to conform to expected performances. Roles are formed in relation to common norms and must fit together. In a heteronormative society, a mother stands in relation to a child and a father (as a role configuration). An 'oppressor' relates to oppression. The slave's role is a precondition for the slave owner's existence. If a role changes, a number of accompanying roles must be changed. According to Goffman's drama perspective, people exercise a number of control techniques that aim to manage the impression they have on the audience.[80] Among other things, you exercise expressive control of inconsistent feelings and behaviours that risk disturbing the performance of the role: for example, your facial expressions, clothing, body language and tone of voice should be controlled in order to suit your performance. People even have a tendency to idealise their role before the audience. Doubt and difficulties are hidden or denied in the performance, but not backstage.

A *conventional role discipline and an idealisation are strengthened* in a nonviolent movement – through conscious strategy and internal training – *and make a utopian 'as if' action possible.*[81] Nonviolent activists break their expected role behaviour in the conflict through their constructed combination of disobedience (against apparently unjust rules) and peaceful behaviour. An amicable rebel suddenly gets up on stage. A kind of 'nonviolent social strain' creates the possibility of transforming an oppressive role structure.[82]

In *Handbook for Nonviolent Action* (1989), the War Resisters' League gives advice to nonviolent activists who end up in violent situations.[83] The starting point is that a goal is 'reasonable', that you believe yourself to be 'fair', and that you can communicate that to your opponent. The rest is a matter of discipline. You should move slowly; speak about what you are going to do; not say anything threatening, critical or aggressive; state the obvious ('you're hurting my arm'); break expectations without seem-ing threatening and 'create a new scenario for the opponent'; appeal to the opponent's 'better side' and 'decency'; resist as powerfully as you can without increasing the opponent's wrath;

and then encourage the opponent to speak calmly while you listen, not criticise. These rules can vary in different nonviolent handbooks, but they tend to be similar and the point is always that the nonviolent activists are trying to take the initiative, to act as if the two sides were equal friends.[84] The aim is to break the oppressive drama by *doing the unexpected*: to not go along with things, to not fulfil the role of victim or assailant, to smile before an attack, to look into your opponent's eyes and put out your hand in greeting, or to do something unexpected – ask for directions to a tourist attraction, or suddenly fall onto the floor in a violent epileptic attack.[85]

In Roxby, Australia in 1984, the police stood in line guarding a uranium mine. In front of them stood a corresponding line of activists:

> Emotions of anger and fear were running high [when a] Maori activist calmly strolled down the space between the two lines, playing his guitar and singing. The group moved back, confused by this action by a third party. Then followed an acrobat, flinging himself down the line in a series of somersaults and flips ... no violence ensued that day.[86]

The unexpected is not created only through the way in which activists react. *Who* reacts is sometimes decisive. On 24 February 1988, the police, accompanied by police dogs, cleared a road blockade of 150 activists without forewarning. This was during the tree-huggers' struggle against the planned motorway in Sweden's Bohuslän Province.[87] People were shocked and several injured, but the police chief calmly stated that they had completed their task. The problem was simply that one of the anonymous activists was Erol Coleman, a policeman and environmental activist. The police had battered a colleague. The border between 'activist'

and 'police' had become hazy and the debate about police violence gained new meaning. In another tree-hugger action, the
police calmly and routinely arrested activists who sat in the trees
trying to prevent deforestation. When they were going to be
arrested, one of the activists remained in a tree with a sleeping
bag and provisions; the police discovered that he was one of their
colleagues, Lars-Eric Persson, a commissioned officer in charge
of the Uddevalla police station. A police officer had occupied
the tree and now the police had to arrest him. Expected roles
had been broken. Similarly, a media sensation was created in
West Germany when a judge at the district court in Schwäbisch
Gmünd was to sentence another judge who had helped blockade
nuclear weapons transports. When 500 judges then published
an announcement in the newspaper and expressed their support
for the action, the confusion of roles became acute. On whose
side did the law truly stand?

An unexpected breach with an established drama may also
occur through new groups entering the situation, through nonviolent intervention. As early as 1966, the British organisation
Non-Violent Action in Vietnam tried to stop the bombings by
arranging for hundreds of volunteers from the Western world to
protect threatened villages in North Vietnam by their physical
presence at the bomb targets.[88] But the intervention was a fatal
failure because of its poor organisation, support and training,
among other reasons. The results were somewhat better when
the Vietnamese themselves organised self-help villages and engaged Buddhists in rebuilding bombed villages each time they
were bombed, despite members being murdered and deported.[89]
They confronted the war by walking through the hail of bullets
between fighting parties and by setting themselves alight with
petrol on the streets of Saigon.[90] Similar interventions in war

dramas have occurred on many other occasions. The resistance to the USA's illegal war and occupation of Iraq grew thanks to the activism of an unexpected group – the survivors of the terror attack on 11 September 2001 and the relatives of those who died.[91] Such interventions can be well or badly organised, but they disrupt the predictable logic of the violent defence and attack between stereotyped enemy groups that a war pulls people into.

A powerful method is to *redefine the situation*. In Australia, Anzac Day is an annual holiday when people mourn Australian soldiers who have died in war. In Canberra, in 1980, when the military conducted their yearly parade through the city in memory of their fallen comrades, a number of women followed along. The signs they carried showed that they were mourning the women raped by soldiers during war.[92] The women were arrested but the following year more women were there, doing the same thing.

Initially, such nonviolent 'as if' actions create *social chaos* when preconceived ideas about a situation and people's roles are disrupted.[93] The confusion arises since the expected role behaviour upon which the coordination of social interaction rests is broken. Other people are shaken in their understanding of what they are doing and normal social interaction becomes impossible. The script of the drama makes the roles dependent on each other. It is like theatre. Playing *Hamlet* is not possible when the expected lines and behaviours are not forthcoming.

During the week before Christmas 1974, people in Copenhagen saw several unusual sights: a '*julemandshær*' (an army of Father Christmases) of 100 activists dressed up as Father Christmas marched in military formation along the city centre's roads.[94] At the front of this *julemandshær* rolled a 6 metre tall, traditional 'Christmas goose' and a Father Christmas in command, carrying a red flag. Before they even got a glimpse of the strangest army ever to invade Copenhagen, the surprised city-dwellers heard both the military boots of the Father Christmases in a rhythmically steady march and their peculiar Christmas carols. After they had entertained the old and ill at Nørre Hospital with songs and small Christmas gifts, they marched onwards to a porcelain factory where half of the workers were to be sacked. Father Christmas Thiel explained to the foremen that they had a great plan for a new and useful form of production that the factory could implement so that no one would have to become unemployed. After some negotiations, they were able to meet the workers in the dining hall. There, the workers offered them beer, the Father Christmases sang and everyone danced together for an hour before the police came. After the Father Christmas army was brutally thrown out of the factory, they marched to the labour court. Waiting there was a crane together with the pneumatic drills and sledge hammers they had rented. On the crane, they hung a banner with the words: 'Klassedomstol – Knus den' ('Class court – crush it'). From the top of the crane, Father Christmas Skousen read a speech written by Ole Krarup, a professor of law, about the injustice of the labour court. In the confusion created by a sudden smoke bomb, the *julemandshær* attacked the court building with their sledge hammers and began tearing the building down. Again, the Father Christmases were arrested. On Sunday 22 December they again marched through the streets of Copenhagen. This time they went into the popular store Magasin. On the year's most hectic shopping day they began handing out books from the store's bookstore counter. The Father Christmases wished a Merry Christmas to all and happy customers accepted the free books. But, after a while, a warning message was sent over the speaker system and the police were summoned.

After an 'as if' act leads to chaos, there are various attempts from those surrounding the chaos (other actors or the audience) to get the dissidents to fall back into old habits. People try to repair the definition of the situation and the drama. If the dissidents do not give up immediately due to social pressure, a test of strength ensues. The test of strength is a *social adjustment struggle* that pulls in two directions: either the dissidents are returned to their established roles or all the actors improvise a new drama together, one that is different enough to work.

The sit-ins of the Civil Rights Movement transformed the American South in a similar way. 'At first annoyed, then angered, then confused, white Southerners in scores of places came fairly rapidly to a grasp of the rightness of the protest.'[95] The decisive pressure to adapt results from the lack of alternatives. The people's interplay in everyday social situations must continue in some way; if not, society does not work. However, it is probably more common for dissidents to yield to the stark pressure of established patterns, an impatient audience and a larger group of actors.

The organisation of an individual dramatic intervention is therefore not the most difficult task for the movement. It is *maintaining* continuous nonviolent resistance over a longer struggle that is key to dramaturgical success. This is about a *collective*'s maintaining of the utopian action. Isolated nonviolent actions will be disregarded as individual deviations from an established stereotype – even if the stereotype is always, to some degree, undermined.[96]

What made the struggle of the inhabitants of Kynnefjäll in Bohuslän Province in Sweden so special was not that they left their homes in April 1980 to stop machines from entering the government's programme area for radioactive waste,[97] nor that they were so unified in the local community. It was that they decided to truly protect their environment, unlike those who say they will without meaning it. They continued the occupation even when the machines were pulled out, and they demanded a written promise from the government that the nuclear waste would not be stored in their district. Beginning in 1980, the mountain was watched around the clock. A guard's cabin provided warmth on winter nights, its electricity generated by wind power. After twenty years, the inhabitants of Kynnefjäll got their promise from the Swedish government: a letter from the Minister of the Environment, Kjell Larsson, who wrote that the highland was no longer of interest as a final storage place. On 7 February 2000, they finally stopped guarding their mountain.[98]

The new role behaviour ('as if' action) undermines an established understanding, which leads to the possibility of a new pre-understanding – a common drama with new roles. If the new, nonviolent role behaviour is upheld and cannot be dismissed (that is, it is extensive enough to disrupt the normal order), other actors are forced to choose between adapting their roles or physically removing the drama saboteurs. The original role of the characters, the scenography and the script can be adapted to take account of the change *if* the new behaviour is both understandable and regular: that is, predictable. A *mutual improvisation* becomes possible if there is trust in the new pattern of action. As the breaching of roles does not happen at random but according to a new kind of pattern, there is at least the possibility of other actors taking part. A social action is like a theatre piece; it is impossible to perform if others fail to act according to comprehensible behavioural patterns that can be melded together. People must act within a certain framework according to each other's expectations if they are to perform together. This does not mean that stereotypes are needed for social interaction, only that the improvisation must have a theme and follow certain limits and that the action is recognisable and understandable.[99]

But the 'as if' action only creates this possibility and mobilises a facilitating power (a *social pressure to adapt*). The social pressure to conform to the old norms, drama and roles will be strong. 'The many cognitive and motivational processes that underlie stereotype development and maintenance make them highly resistant to change'[100] – even more so if the opponents experience strong emotions or threats. A theatre director can exchange a new, nonviolent role with one that is like the old one: this is what happens when the nonviolent activist is jailed or killed and people return to their obedience.

This is when the movement's ability to resume its dramatic intervention – again and again, if necessary – is decisive in whether or not trust in the new behavioural pattern can emerge.[101] If activists continue to break their expected roles with respect, openness and nonviolence, despite punishments and provocations, a new pattern of interaction can seem almost believable even to opponents and suspicious parties. For conflict transformation to succeed, it is also important that the other actors do not feel threatened and that a 'value alliance' can be made.[102]

If activists can go through the trials of suffering without giving up their dramatic intervention, the distrust and hate of the enemy image can be transformed, giving rise instead to a collective *expectation* of the new behaviour. Also, some kind of *mutual understanding* is required for interactions to work at all. This combination of *expectation* and *understanding* can be understood as the socially effective 'invisible force' of nonviolence that Gandhi discussed. In this dramaturgical interpretation of nonviolent struggle, suffering becomes a *test of authenticity* for the new drama of equality.

An inclusive identification

> We must make [the opponent] feel that in us he has a friend and we should try to reach his heart by rendering him humanitarian service whenever possible. In fact, it is the acid test of non-violence that [in] a non-violent conflict ... the enemies are converted into friends.[103]

Using dramatic interventions, nonviolent struggle tries to undermine the polarisation of conflicts between stable identities: the difference between friend and enemy. I call this process the *inclusive identification* of nonviolence.[104] Utopian enactment creates a possibility of identifying with someone who was previously one's enemy, opponent or the other. The nonviolent movement can be said to strive for an identification that *includes people on different sides in a conflict*.

Identities are unstable, discontinuous and open to change, depending on context and situation – whether heterogeneous, ambivalent or simply diversified.[105] But in conflicts they are presented as stable; it is a typical trait of conflicts that identities are fixed and polarised. Nonviolent activists try to upset this apparent stability in order to ease identification. Such identification is about our ability to identify with others without adopting a new (fixed) identity, to construct a bridge between groups without changing our own belonging. People involved in conflicts where nonviolent actions are carried out represent both themselves and others; they create identities in the sense of *subject positioning*. In our narratives, the positioning of a subject is formed by weaving it into a context of time, space and

NONVIOLENT 'UTOPIAN ENACTMENT' | **239**

relationships so that a 'narrative identity' is created. Through nonviolent positions, narratives and actions, conflict-generating identities are destabilised.

As a consequence of Gandhi's radical interpretation of Hinduism, nonviolence was viewed as the means by which Indians and the British could be freed from the illusion of separation, a way to make them see how they were all part of the same humanity and part of the same body and soul: *Brahman*, Truth or God. Identification thereby becomes a resistance to existing differences between people and identities, and at the same time an approach towards a universal community, an indivisible identity. Like the interactionist George Herbert Mead, nonviolent activists assume that there is a fundamental dependence: that it is not possible 'to experience an I without The Other'.[106]

But the nonviolent struggle's transgression of identity borders need not be, despite Gandhi's view, the only means by which community and unity come about. Another possibility – and perhaps just as meaningful for the peaceful transformation of a conflict – is that *nonviolence breaks up solid identities*, destabilises them and offers new non-essential hybrid and flexible identities, thus undermining the conflict's polarisation of opposing parties. Inclusive identification can relate reflexively to collective identity, as has been argued by today's post-structural and feministic researchers. A radical interpretation would be that the identity destabilisation of nonviolence is a kind of *anti-identity*.[107] But, in this case, this is only one side of the identity-handling element of nonviolence; the activists also try to bridge the gap between the experienced identities.

For example, it is clear that the majority of blacks and whites during the confrontations between the African National Congress (ANC) and the apartheid regime in the 1950s saw the two sides as 'we' and 'them' in a classic sense: on the one side there was an extensive movement of (mostly) blacks against the apartheid policy; on the other were (only) whites chosen to be part of the apartheid government. But if we jump ahead in history, an opposing image appears. After the first free general election in 1994, the ANC won a majority with a large margin, but instead of using support from the rest of the world and from the South African legislation to govern sovereignly, President Nelson Mandela invited people to form a coalition government where previous enemies cooperated (from both black and white organisations). The civil war that was expected did not occur and a 'rainbow nation' of peoples was launched. Today, there is a widespread, common identity as South Africans (of black, white, coloured or Asian origin). Between the 1950s and the 1990s, there was, in other words, a political resistance process that was generally peaceful and that gave space to inclusive identification. It was also important, for example, that the ANC decided early on to allow white members (unlike the Pan Africanist Congress (PAC), among others), and that the decision to give all ethnic groups the same rights was stated in the ANC's basic declaration, the Freedom Charter, as early as the 1950s. It is hardly a coincidence that South Africa gave the world an example of a (relatively) successful process of reconciliation. This dramatic transformation from an institutionalised racist system into something with universal rights for everyone is a valid change created fundamentally through unarmed civil society resistance, although I do not suggest that South Africa is a non-racist society today, which it clearly is not.

Neither victim nor enemy: transforming suffering I have argued that nonviolent action can be understood as part of a *drama* where the conflicting parties' role legitimacy is decided by the audience's assessment of their performance. If the nonviolent movement intervenes in an understandable and stable way in the drama, its breach of expected role behaviours can increase the audience's confidence in the new role pattern and can even work as a social 'force'. This drama is a social interaction in which all actors construct the dynamic together and where the audience also plays a decisive role.

When power and violence rule, it can be critical that there are many people who together undermine obedience and fear. In the South African struggle against apartheid, there was a breakthrough during the Defiance Campaign in 1952 when 6,000 activists were involved in acts of civil disobedience:

> But the fear of going to gaol had lost its sting. 'No amount of police presence could dampen the enthusiasm with which the down-trodden masses supported the defiance campaign,' says Yusuf Cachalia. 'In the past, when a white kicked a black or sacked him for no reason, he lifted his hat, lowered his eyes and said, "Ja, dankie baas." What he felt in his heart was something quite different. The defiance campaign gave him the courage to say, "Now I'm going to look you straight in the eye. I'm not going to look down and doff my hat. I'm going to face you." It gave blacks the opportunity to manifest their dignity.'[108]

The two role patterns – the logic of violence and the logic of nonviolence – do not link up with each other: the definitions are contradictory and it is as if two incompatible situations exist at the same time. The perpetrator expects that the victim will be paralysed with fear, try to run away or retaliate. Nothing else is appropriate for the violent situation, script and roles that conventionally have been provided. When something else altogether happens, the game is disrupted and there is a moment of chaos. When the burgeoning anti-apartheid movement's activists no longer showed fear but looked their rulers in the eye, the logic of violence was broken. One who calmly refuses and dares to face the person with the monopoly on violence breaks the power of that violence – they break the expected pattern. The actors may experience this as if time were literally frozen for a few seconds. The confusion that arises because of the unexpected behaviour might be enough for the situation to *become* different. However, the nonviolent activist cannot count on this happening.

The grasp of pre-understanding and habitual thinking can be strong. The perpetrator has, through socialisation, been trained to understand what this type of situation is and what the other is. In deep conflicts between groups, it is normal for the socio-cultural process in some way or other to dehumanise members of the other social group through their presentation.[109] By using a tendentious selection of experiences and stories in combination with a little truth and some lies, you learn to see the other as a demon, a traitor, dirty or sick, as someone with less value. A radical racist ideology of violence such as Nazism conventionally uses systematic dehumanisation of the other. 'Nazism views the stranger as bacteria or as excrement, that is to say as living waste products.'[110] By constructing enemy images, people are prepared for violent action, actions that are not allowed against members of one's own group. Moreover, there are authorities and structures (such as culture and the economy) that uphold discrimination and exclusion based on conventional definitions of the situation and the Other. In this way, the perpetrator is constantly reminded by their surroundings what 'really' is the case and who the other 'really' is: a dangerous enemy who is inferior to me and to those I love, one who deserves to be sacrificed for truth, morals and order.

Cultural dominance creates experiences of being treated as inferior and of the oppressed feeling powerless, while the oppressor obtains a self-evident sense of righteousness through their exercise of power. A 'double consciousness' arises among the oppressed through 'simultaneously being defined by two separate cultures: in part the other's dominant culture, in part one's own ... the paradoxical experience of being invisible while simultaneously being positioned as different'.[111] Thus the struggle is also a struggle for a sense of self, dignity and identity, something the Black Consciousness Movement understood when they proclaimed: 'Black is beautiful!'

Certainly, in order to handle behaviour in conflicts that are deeply rooted in the culture, in people or between groups where existential interests are at stake, more than just unexpected and creative role interventions are needed. A person's honest intent cannot be made believable for suspicious parties in any way other than by showing sincerity in one's actions.[112] For the nonviolent activist, there is no alternative other than to stubbornly *resume* the intervention and creatively *explicate* the offer of mutual friendship and one's utopian enactment of justness. This is exactly where Gandhi's emphasis on suffering comes in. He expresses it in an extreme way, suggesting that it is necessary to learn the art of dying in order to be able to apply nonviolent resistance.[113] I would rather say that a nonviolent activist, like a soldier in war, must be prepared to *risk* their life. The difference is that in nonviolent struggle the activist who is killed does not *make a great enough impression on the other* (rationally or emotionally, for example), whereas in war the soldier who is killed is the one who fails to be *the first to injure the other suffi-ciently enough* (physically, economically, technologically, and so on). Both the activist and the soldier are, as a result, prepared to die for something valuable, but the difference is that the activist is not prepared to kill for their beliefs.

For the process that enables violent action, the creation of psychological and cultural distance between people and the presentation of the other as a dangerous stranger are central.[114] If you succeed in reducing this distance, the difficulties of exer-cising violence increase. Social distance makes human suffering an anonymous, hidden mass suffering. The nonviolent move-ment's challenge is to *make suffering visible and to do it person-ally – to humanise the sufferer*. This process is the opposite to the dehumanisation employed by war. The social psychological distance is broken by people meeting and recognising themselves in the other.[115] When a *human like me* suffers, there arises the pos-sibility of empathy or sympathy, the heart softens.[116] If empathy develops in the 'prototypical' representative of the enemy, then the interaction can transform the stereotypical representation of the whole group. And with increased empathy, the risk of violence also decreases.[117] But it is not certain that recognition will lead to positive emotional reactions:

> sympathy is a consequence of either cognitive processes (e.g. perspective taking) or an optimal level of emphatic arousal – one that is strong enough to orient the empathizer toward the other person, but is not so strong that it is aversive [and creates personal distress].[118]

Suffering can awaken both sympathy and aversion due to strong feelings. For the perpetrator, a solution can be to avoid contact. As the opponent meets nonviolent activists in confrontations, it is difficult to avoid seeing suffering. But contempt can also be fostered by those instances in which you recognise sides of yourself you want to repress or you look down upon or despise, or quite simply when you cannot do anything about the situation.

One reason for the perpetrator's contempt for the victim might be the victim's display of obedience.[119] This submission becomes a kind of confirmation of the subordination, 'weakness' and lower value of the other. That combatants in the heat of war can, despite everything, show respect or even admiration for the enemy's violent strength is a well-known fact. Strength is often respected. The nonviolent struggle is a force, yet an entirely different kind of force. For Gandhi, it relates to individual mental strength and religious belief. For nonviolent feminists, it is about a group's strength, its cohesion and solidary support for each other's vulnerability. For every nonviolent movement, it involves putting up with suffering because of a conviction about something of a higher value.

Sometimes groups are seen as being of less value just because they have 'lost' or 'failed' socially, economically or militarily – regardless of the reason why.[120] What can culturally be seen as 'weakness' can thus promote contempt. An already subordinate culture's nonviolent struggle therefore risks being faced with contempt when it suffers, as suffering in itself can be seen as a sign of weakness and lesser value. Subordination of groups can be legitimised through representations of their lower worth and poor qualities (for example, racism first appeared as a European ideology during Europe's colonisation of the world). My conclusion is that what plays a decisive role is *how* the nonviolent activist suffers and *why*. And the view of the perpetrator is key.

We can imagine two main forms of approaches to suffering:

that we suffer with a kind of pride and stubborn refusal to give up; or that we suffer with doubt and a resigned appeal for mercy. The first form of suffering tends to show the opponent a kind of strength while the second shows weakness. Perhaps that is why Gandhi said that one should 'find joy' in suffering. As mentioned earlier, such statements have led previous interpreters to claim a 'masochistic' trait of nonviolence.[121] But that is not an interpretation that looks at the whole of Gandhi's nonviolent conflict approach. Happiness does not come from the experience of suffering; rather, happiness is the result of the true or utopian act that is realised *despite* suffering and whose true message becomes credible for others *through* the suffering endured for the cause. It is an action that gains poetic beauty because it puts itself above the painful experience and breaks the dynamic of violence. Joyous behaviour becomes a powerful contradiction to the anticipated role behaviour. Joy suits neither the victim nor the enemy, but a joyous and creative action during suffering is an ideal that can be realised only in exceptional cases by a nonviolent movement. The more extreme the suffering, the more extreme the joy, and the more extreme Gandhi's expectation that activists should 'find joy'. In this respect we must abandon Gandhi's stress on the nonviolence of strong individuals and his implicit contempt for weakness.[122] Instead, we need to explore how the social and nonviolent dynamic can become strong enough to overcome the cruelty of suffering and joylessness.

For the dynamic to work, the minimal requirement is an ability *to avoid both the role as a victim and the role as an enemy.* As long as the nonviolent activist succeeds in avoiding these conditioned pitfalls and creatively expresses something else, the right conditions exist for a nonviolent enactment.

Even if neither empathy (for equals) nor sympathy (for the weak) ensues, the utopian action and readiness to suffer can work. It is sufficient that a *minimal amount of trust* is present: that is, enough trust for the other's argument to be taken seriously and considered valid in conversation about right and wrong and at least to be the basis of an agreement. This does not mean that an agreement will necessarily be reached, only that it is possible. 'Minimal trust' does not mean that the activists must succeed in being viewed as equals or friends. However, they have to succeed in *preventing their disqualification*, being taken seriously as competent dialogue partners, being recognised as people who can create a readiness in the opponent to listen seriously to the activists. Trust is also needed for another reason. Agreements with previous enemies are risky, especially if the oppression has caused extensive suffering over a long period of time. The desire to seek revenge on previous oppressors when the chance is offered is reasonable. Therefore, there is a deadlock among those currently in power: the difficulty of maintaining the existing order must be weighed against the risk of civil war or extensive revenge if a new order of power is allowed (for example, a new dictatorship – something that we have seen occur in a number of former colonies). For every act of violence that those in power have carried out, it is unfortunately more difficult to stop oppression, to imagine an equal relationship and democracy, including for those in power. The spiral of violent destruction thus affects both sides, albeit in very different ways.

The nonviolent activist must work against both their counterpart's disparaging representations of the activist's inferiority (as 'non-human' and a victim) and representations of the activist's future desire and capacity for revenge (as the 'treacherous and cruel' enemy).

Suffering sometimes becomes unavoidable since you have to try to carry out nonviolent 'as if' actions *even – or especially – if* you are subject to violence and oppression, and therefore to suffering. It is when oppression is at its worst that the need for resistance is greatest. And resistance is conducted against both the opponent's power base and violence-generating enemy images. At the same time, the utopian enactment becomes strongest when violence is carried out, since the contrast between oppression and utopia is strengthened (the *contrast effect*). The activist then risks something and their sincerity (that they really want to be an equal friend, not a new oppressor) is put to the test. Here, it becomes clear whether an agreement is a goal or an imposition of one's own views onto the opponent. In violent conflicts characterised by enemy images and hate, it is not really about which perception is just: what is important is to achieve the necessary first step to enable all parties to see that everyone's current perception is understandable and is not an implausible position. Understanding each other is the beginning of transformation.

Gandhi finds that nonviolence works badly if you use nonviolent resistance only because you do not have access to weapons, or you do not dare use them. If you willingly refrain from using the possibilities (however great or small) you have to injure others, then sincerity becomes so much more convincing. A situation in which you have the ability to (and, from a conventional perspective, should) defend yourself by injuring your opponent is precisely the type of situation where you have a chance to show that you do not want to do so.[123] If activists, despite provocations and assaults, do not try to injure the other, their sincerity finally becomes such a convincing power that it is difficult for opponents to defend themselves against it.[124]

In sum, you can say that nonviolent actions that occur 'as if' friendship, peace and justness already existed, and *despite* the suffering that nonviolent activists are subject to, comprise a *utopian enactment*. This enactment contrasts with the oppression of violence and is the nonviolent resistance's attempt in a social drama to win *the audience's active support and the opponent's sufficient trust*, both rationally and emotionally. The conclusion is that we, through the drama perspective, can see how nonviolent resistance makes suffering a *means of communication* in the struggle against suffering.

The utopian enactment of nonviolence

My conceptual description of nonviolence's handling of suffering is based on social psychological drama theory and a reinterpretation of Gandhi's emphasis on suffering's central role. Gandhi's view is that suffering is fundamental, rather than a *background risk*, and that it makes action that appeals to a utopia *credible* even for those who are suspicious or hostile. Utopian enactment is a difficult task in itself; it is perhaps an impossible requirement in the opposing movement's fight against a dehumanised view of people, discrimination, violence and oppression. Gandhi's instructions for the nonviolent struggle are often utopian and seem unrealistic. At the same time, I believe that it is possible to understand this utopian perspective as political realism, as it may be the only thing that works in a reality characterised by systematic violence and oppression. In any case, it is the only possibility if you want to undermine the system of domination, not just exchange one dominant class for another. The fact that you cannot do something fully is no argument against doing it to the extent you can. It is possible to conceptually describe nonviolence as a plausible strategy and a coherent action repertoire for genuine liberation.[125] But this presupposes that you understand utopia as an inspiring possibility that guides your effort, not something that you can expect to accomplish fully.

Voluntary suffering is acceptable if you hold something to be so valuable or true that suffering is seen as a price worth paying. In order for this truth to be convincing even for others, the *argument or reason for the truth must be revealed through the nonviolent action and must be more convincing* than existing arguments against it.[126] Let's call this *argumentation enactment*. It is not enough for the truth to convince the activists, and especially not if it exists only in the activists' consciousness. The truth needs to become a living action, *socially materialised*, convincing by virtue of its visible existence. It is not enough for it to be described with words, as words do not bite the opponent who looks down upon their enemy or who fears deceit. Voluntary suffering becomes a necessity when reasonable arguments do not work. The point is to try to *convince through action* in conflict arenas where the activists are not recognised as equal partners in dialogue or members of a society.

Suffering must be presented as meaningful, worthy of admiration and understandable to the opponent, otherwise it risks strengthening existing contempt. Someone who exercises violence needs to feel contempt (or other emotions of dehumanisation of the other) in order to defend their own behaviour. When the activist challenges the power system and openly breaks laws despite the imminent danger of being punished, frustration awakens in the opposing soldiers, police and guards. But an incomprehensible voluntary suffering risks transforming the activist into a lunatic or a fanatic.

If the activist's actions cannot be understood, or, more precisely, if the action can be misinterpreted (with the help of propaganda, slander and censorship), the activist will come across as mad, someone who 'should blame themselves'. In such cases, the nonviolent action becomes a provocation made by an idiot who exposes himself to suffering because of his preposterous ideology. Consequently, the incomprehensible suffering can be dismissed as something that does not have anything to do with our community.

The nonviolent struggle must try to make sure that it is difficult to misinterpret. If at all possible, the opponents of the nonviolent movement will misrepresent the struggle. I suggest that the three following stages are decisive in making unavoidable suffering into a functional part of nonviolent resistance against enemy images and hate:

1   A desirable ideal or conviction of the truth enacted in *clear and mutually attractive practical* action (action 'as if' the utopian ideal already existed). The enactment is formed as a contradiction to existing prejudices and enemy images, through arguments for the utopia, and is attractive to different parties (this is the *argumentation enactment*).

2   A *risk-filled situation* does not prevent the enactment; on the contrary, the enactment then becomes clearer and more credible. (This involves a *test of authenticity*. If repression is used, a *contrast effect* is created when activists attempt to *convince through action*.) ⟶ *will people accept the risk*

3   The enactment is *repeated* (by other activists if the first were jailed or killed) for as long as the enemy image remains intact and the movement's people and arguments are not taken seriously in dialogue or negotiation (that is, 'to hold onto the truth', satyagraha). *repeated action until dialogue is reached*

The nonviolent activist must be prepared to endure violence, contempt and suffering in their attempt to engage the opponent with the hope of realising a utopian desire for equal friendship. In the struggle against extensive suffering – regardless of who suffers – activists put themselves at risk of their own, temporary suffering. The goal is to minimise the total suffering in the long run. They unite their refusal to injure people with their disobedience against every requirement to participate in an oppressive situation. The respect for the other as a person is combined with a lack of respect towards the (oppressing) roles and systems that the other attempts to uphold. In parallel to their resistance, the activist is constructive and attempts to create alternatives, possibilities for cooperation and mutual agreements with the opponent. The key is this double force: to resist and to embrace simultaneously.

The practised behaviour then shows that the activist is not, for instance, someone who is barbaric, violent, weak, dirty, unreliable, petty, stupid or evil, as the propaganda claims.[127] This form of conflict transformation is a *consequent contradiction*, an action that is the opposite of what is expected, which attempts to establish a new expectation. Instead of acting in expected ways, the nonviolent activist acts in a utopian way, 'as if' the future, violence-free state had already been achieved. This builds upon a presumption that most people would prefer to live in equality and friendship, with the precondition that the obstacles to this could be removed, and that you practically, emotionally and rationally received support and inspiration on order to live in this way. This method is based on *departing from the opponent's enemy image in a creative action to maximally and consequently express humanity through contradictions*. The malicious portrait of the nonviolent activist shows them as treacherous and unintelligent, so the movement must show honesty and intelligence through a practical, clear act, and in an unquestionable way. The satyagraha struggle aims to convince and inspire the opponent to believe that equal friendship is possible and desirable, since the basic axiom is a consequence of humanity's (potential) togetherness (see the Appendix).[128]

This form of conflict transformation is a critique of the idealistic rationalism that believes that arguments decide a dialogue regardless of the power, violence or social distance that can disrupt communication. This critical rationalism of nonviolence claims that a basic precondition for the dialogue's rationale is that the parties take each other's words seriously. If the conflicting parties do not emotionally perceive each other as truthful, their statements will not be taken as sincere. Thus, the communicative rationality will collapse. Nonviolent conflict transformation therefore means that you manage emotional blockages (enemy images) at the same time as you claim the truth through your arguments, promote a normative community based on nonviolence, and nonviolently fight power relations between the parties.

Previous studies have not highlighted the capability of nonviolence to simultaneously *reveal both injustice and justice* by trying (through their utopian enactment via 'as if' actions) to apply the nonviolent future in the present, *precisely where this is most difficult, near violence and oppression.*[129] By this, I mean that revealing an injustice works much more powerfully if the action simultaneously manages to reveal the possibility of a utopia. The *contrast* in the performance of the unjust and the just is dramaturgically genial and not a provocation of a brutal opponent, as some have suggested.

The strength of the nonviolent struggle in conflict transformation comes from its *double approach of both careful respect and immovable resistance.* The struggle takes into consideration every person's infinite value while simultaneously opposing every act of oppression, regardless of which group or side in the conflict the person belongs to. The line drawn between the person and the act leads to a dialectical approach and creates a very special dynamic. Based on the struggle against one of several systems of oppression, the patriarchy, Pam McAllister formulates this view as follows:

> nonviolence is the merging of our uncompromising rage at the patriarchy's brutal destructiveness with a refusal to adopt its ways – a refusal to give in to despair or hate or to let men off the hook by making them the 'Other' as they have made those they fear 'Others'. Together, these seemingly contradictory impulses (to rage against yet refuse to destroy) combine to create 'strength' worthy of nothing less than revolution – true revolution, not just a shuffle of death-wielding power.[130]

To refuse to act violently

+

To stand up relentlessly against the opressor

7 | NONVIOLENT 'NORMATIVE REGULATION'

We live in a world with a 'hegemonic discourse on violence' that depicts nonviolence as unrealistic and 'unthinkable'.[1] Societies produce unreflective habits of obedience that are sometimes disastrous and lead to genocide and extensive violations of human rights.[2] In particular, societies characterised by oppression, social injustice and militarism transform absurd social conditions into something normal, natural, self-evident or imposed by divine power. As we saw in Chapter 5 on power breaking, this requires the production of consent and obedience so that unjust power relations can remain in place.

An extensive investment is made to train people (almost exclusively men) in organised violence (through military conscription or in professional armies). This military education is both a practical training of skill and a normalisation of the use of violence. Aside from formal education in the techniques of violence and oppression, there exists an informal training whose importance we easily underestimate. In a society characterised by oppression, socialisation normalises that oppression: it legitimises oppression and makes it self-evident ('natural'). One example is the gender power hierarchy. In a patriarchal society, men are socialised to perceive dominance over women as natural and legitimate. During their normal upbringing, men are also taught something that has an even greater impact: the practical ability to dominate – in other words, patriarchal behaviour is internalised and becomes part of a person's identity. When oppression lasts for generations, it becomes such a strong, self-evident thing that it can even be difficult to recognise it as 'oppression'.

Nonviolent movements are in opposition to societies that have organised and normalised violence and oppression. As we have seen, this is partly a matter of prevention and intervention (nonviolent resistance). But if nonviolence is to become a true alternative, it must proceed in a way that corresponds to the hegemonic society that normalises violence. It must normalise nonviolence, at least within its own social community.

Gandhi's version of nonviolent normalisation was called a 'constructive programme', and was summarised in a short text in 1945 following a long period of practical experimentation with *swaraj* (self-rule). The constructive programme was developed with the aim that it would comprise another part of the resistance struggle, as a kind of realisation of India's and the population's 'complete self-rule' (*Purna Swaraj*) during the struggle, from the local village level and into all of society's institutions.[3] The programme itself, with its total of eighteen constructive projects, was 'only illustrative' and was adapted to the prevailing Indian context. The supporting idea was that nonviolence consisted of both demolishing resistance and edifying construction.

> Those who think that the major reforms will come after the advent of Swaraj are deceiving themselves as to the elementary working of non-violent Swaraj. It will not drop from heaven all of a sudden one fine morning. But it has to be built up brick by brick by corporate self-effort.[4]

The home production of Indian clothes using the world-famous spinning wheel – which became an emblem for the free nation's flag – was, through its practical orientation and far-reaching popularity, a symbol of 'the unity of Indian humanity, of its economic freedom and equality ... [the] decentralization of the production and distribution of the necessaries of life'.[5] The emphasis on the constructive programme was so strong that Gandhi even claimed that civil disobedience was not 'absolutely necessary' for liberation if 'the whole nation's' cooperation in the constructive programme could be guaranteed.[6]

Gandhi's point is that constructive work and resistance are tied together: 'before, after, as well as *during* satyagraha campaigns'.[7] The two main functions of the constructive programme were that it:

> generated the moral strength and grassroots leadership required for nonviolent direct action and helped convert the drama created by nonviolent direct action into concrete community development.[8]

The Civil Rights Movement's 'Freedom Summer' in Mississippi in 1964 has commonly been interpreted as a departure from nonviolent resistance, as pure 'social' work and something 'non-Gandhian'.[9] But in the movement's voter registration programme, social services in the form of 'community centres' and support lectures at 'freedom schools', initiated by the student leader Robert Moses, we see precisely the sort of constructive work that makes the resistance of a people's movement possible.[10] Through a radical reform programme, Moses inspired the 1960s new left in the USA to make 'participatory democracy' a central value.[11]

The German nonviolence researcher Theodor Ebert is fundamentally a supporter of the technique approach, but, unlike Sharp, he emphasises the constructive side of nonviolence.[12] Ebert sees the escalation of the nonviolent struggle involving both its sides: *subversion* and *construction*.[13]

Subversive *protests* against societal injustices are matched by constructive *functional demonstrations* for positive things that can replace what is unjust. When resistance and construction escalate to the next level, *legal non-cooperation* (boycotts, for example) and *legal role innovation* are required. Role innovation means that the activists experiment and develop new knowledge and skills for the future nonviolent society, with the help of new behaviours and institutions such as nonviolence training and self-help organisations. The third step in the escalation of non-violence entails combining *civil disobedience* and *civil usurpation*.[14]

> [The activists] act as if the new social system, which corresponds to the demands placed by the activists, already exists and takes over, without regard to the hitherto dominant persons, the positions and the corresponding roles that they strive to achieve. This means that the high point of the escalation includes, in the minds of the opposing parties, a conception of a conflict between two social systems, the dominant system and the rebel's system.[15]

Self-organisation leads to the creation of a 'free space' for the constructive development of a new social system. The most radical version of civil usurpation involves the movement 'form[ing] its own legislative, executive and judicial institutions' that replace the dominant system's institutions as a 'parallel government', a 'parallel public administration', a 'parallel administration of justice', and possibly also revolutionary legislative organs. Through a 'replacement committee', those new institutions can be filled with new competent people if the dominant system liquidates the competing leaders.[16] The nonviolent movement's ability to develop techniques for civil usurpation is, according to Ebert, the key to successful resistance.[17]

Theodor Ebert's 'subversion' here corresponds to my use

of *nonviolent resistance*, while 'construction' corresponds to *nonviolent construction*. Like Ebert, I find that the constructive dimension of nonviolence is decisive; however, in contrast to his emphasis on 'civil usurpation', I find that nonviolent construction has a rationality that transcends its function as part of a power struggle. For Gandhi, loyalty to the collective and humanity come before everything else. Thus, in order to be able to exercise resistance, you should first be a loyal, law-abiding citizen and a constant friend before you choose an opponent. The construction of nonviolence's social institutions is not only about effectiveness and the construction of an alternative and parallel system. The construction of nonviolent relationships has value in itself because it is the ultimate aim of the struggle. With the help of this 'other side' of nonviolent resistance, movements try to *socialise and normalise nonviolence in a community*, even in conflicts.[18] The ultimate aim is to make nonviolence legitimate and applicable in a practical way throughout society, but the activists, if they fail to overthrow the hegemonic social order, still have the satisfaction of creating their own social community, which can then try to spread nonviolence to others.

We have previously stated that it is possible to describe nonviolence as being rational in several ways simultaneously. But even if nonviolence is reasonable, it is not necessarily viewed as *justified*. In order to make nonviolence normative, people have to see nonviolence as a guiding principle for how they ought to live and act. Perhaps a pioneering generation can achieve this once they have built up the nonviolent community, but what about new participants? And what about children born into the nonviolent community? How is the normative view of nonviolence diffused in a society, and from one generation to another? In Næss's systematisation of Gandhi's philosophy, we see how nonviolence can be said to impose a number of normative rules for the action of activists – some of them certainly unconventional and strict. In fact, some are difficult to understand – for example, that you should be prepared to risk your own life to protect 'the enemy'. In addition, nonviolent resistance entails breaking society's normative rules according to certain deviant rules of action that are normatively established in the nonviolent movement. And, finally, in order to rationally break free from a norm, you must *claim* another norm or norm interpretation – or at least you must do so if you are going to act socially and not just privately sabotage an order. A continual claiming and practising of norms can create a new norm community within the movement, or, if the movement is successful, within a changed society surrounding the movement. A normative order does not need to be organised harmoniously, although the social order's values and principles must coincide to some extent. The question is therefore how a movement can persuade participants and members of society to follow its specific set of nonviolent rules.

This chapter focuses on the ways in which nonviolent construction can create an ability in society to act without violence. Here, I study which concepts are required to describe the *normalisation* of nonviolence in a society that is characterised by violence and oppression. I discuss these activities within social movements in connection to the concepts 'nonviolent construction', 'normalisation' and 'normative regulation', although they also correspond well to the term 'prefiguration', which is commonly used within social movement literature. In Maeckelbergh's definition of prefiguration as 'the conflation of movement means and ends, [the] enactment of the ultimate values of an ideal society within the very means of struggle for that society', we recognise a similarity with what nonviolent activists are doing.[19] The same can be said of Van de Sande, who claims that 'the means applied are deemed to embody or "mirror" the ends one strives to realise' as 'experimental and experiential practice'.[20] Springer connects prefiguration to the active attempt to create a new society in the 'shell of the old', and to the hallmark of anarchist tactics – direct action. He sees this not as a 'grand gesture of defiance, but ... instead the prefiguration of alternative worlds', and argues that such a prefiguration 'is to be "worked out" in its living, breathing process of its participants, not through the predeterminism of (hierarchical) planning'.[21] Still, the literature on prefiguration does not tend to relate to a particular social theory (Habermas's, for example), or to Gandhi and nonviolent movements.[22] And, more importantly, prefiguration is part of what nonviolent movements do, but here it is not the main activity of concern: normalisation and normativity are. Therefore, this discussion will view the prefigurative politics of nonviolent movements as expressions of normative rationality.

Nonviolent construction is illustrated in part through the movement's *nonviolence training* – sometimes called 'preparation for nonviolence' or 'experiential' or 'participatory' training – and in part through the institutionalisation of a *nonviolent society*. For Gandhi, the constructive programme constituted the 'training' for actions. The training of individuals and the construction of a new society were not treated as two separate activities, which is the typical approach today.

> Civil Disobedience, mass or individual, is an aid to construc-
> tive effort and is a full substitute for armed revolt. Training is
> necessary as well for civil disobedience as for armed revolt.
> Only the ways are different ... For civil disobedience [training]
> means the Constructive Programme.[23]

'Nonviolent discourses': training in new norm behaviour

Up until the 1950s, people prepared for nonviolence through disciplined life rules, constructive work and spiritual 'purification' through fasting, meditation, prayer and serving the poor.[24] The training was part of an ascetic tradition of 'preparing oneself', similar to the '*paraskeuaz*' that the Greek Stoics applied: 'practices by which one can acquire, assimilate, and transform truth into a permanent action ... [as] a process of becoming more subjective'.[25] Gandhi emphasised constructive social work and a structured and practical life of service in a village collective as preparation.[26] The ashram 'institution was founded partly to train leaders'.[27]

However, it was the Muslim nonviolent activists from northwestern India, Khudai Khidmatgar (God's servants), who used training in a modern sense.[28] They were recognised as adopting nonviolence in a more disciplined way than other groups within the anti-colonial movement and they organised themselves like soldiers, which, traditionally, these Pashtuns also were. They wore red uniforms, were divided by rank and title, and were even organised in traditional military units (company, brigade and so on). They lived according to daily routines, practised running exercises, and were drilled at special training camps. They were known for their fearlessness and strict discipline, and they unsettled the British to a great degree. As a result, at times they were repressed extensively: at one point, 12,000 were imprisoned simultaneously and some were even tortured. But the number of recruits increased, and by 1938 they had over 100,000 members.[29]

The form of education in nonviolence that characterises today's nonviolent movements began in the North American Civil Rights Movement.[30] Among other things, training with 'hassle lines' was introduced. This involved role playing in which the Civil Rights Movement activists took part in activities that were similar to running a gauntlet: they tried to resist a white crowd's provocations and taunts, an exercise that is still taught on courses. From the Civil Rights Movement's initiative with role playing and the small group forms of the Women's Movement in the 1970s, a tradition of *reflection, skill training and support in groups* has developed.

This type of education is an essential part of the movements' internal normative organisation of nonviolent practice. By using a coordinated and disciplined *nonviolence discourse*, they try to create a *normative regulation, a new legitimate social order.*[31]

It is common for nonviolent courses to undertake practical group exercises, employing peaceful ways of communally handling various problematic situations and reflecting on the principles and strategies of nonviolence. The course leaders' task is to present a well-thought-out schedule, conflict-loaded situations, exercises, possible methods, experiences and principles, as well as problems that small groups can discuss. The underlying idea is that the course leaders create the conditions for learning and the participants themselves arrive at (their own) answers through practical experimentation: '[The trainers] aid the group, including themselves, in a search for truth.'[32] This means that the course leaders do not need to be the most experienced activists: that is not why they lead the courses. Their pedagogy is the most important element. Courses in nonviolence do not use classroom lectures as the ideal format; rather, they employ *mutual training exercises in small groups*, experimentation and reflection. We therefore see how Gandhi's famed 'experiment with the truth' has developed into a form of training.

One classic training handbook suggests training tools that

are specially constructed to 'shake us out of stereotypic roles in which we have functioned for a long time'.[33] The training affects not only the formation of traditional political roles and their methods, but also daily life and languages as well. In this 'training for social change', you seek to convey new actions, techniques, speech forms, feelings and ways of thinking. The challenge is to break old habits and structures and form new habits and structures. The educational methods used in non-violent action training – role playing, practical exercises, games and conversation – can be interpreted as a collective attempt to achieve *a reformation of embodied patterns of action and a mutual reflection about this reformation*. Acts are evaluated, utopias constructed, existing action practices are broken down and new practices are taught and disciplined.

Nonviolence training occurs through voluntary participation, over a limited period of time, and usually in temporary small groups. As in other structured social contexts, the participants take on roles based on the expectations that people express together. The roles are continually adjusted during the training. One can claim that, in role theory, innovation, flexibility and ingenuity are all required to some degree in all interactions due to the lack of consensus, incomplete instructions, role conflicts and the impossibility of fulfilling the requirements associated with roles.[34] Role actions thus require *continuous correction*; participants have to adjust their role behaviour during the course and sometimes act inconsistently in order to manage conflicting demands.

The French sociologist Pierre Bourdieu developed a materialistic and cultural theory of how we develop habits and roles, how we are socialised and learn behaviours, and how power relations permeate this process. With the help of Bourdieu's 'habitus' theory, we can interpret what nonviolent activists are trying to do with their training.

Habitus: the embodiment of practice

Pierre Bourdieu argues that 'habitus', or embodied practices, are formed by relative power positions in society and are created through practical exercise, not through rational or theoretical teaching or formal schooling.[35] Practical knowledge resides in the body's movements and the patterns of the consciousness and has only a partially conscious character. Habitus is comprised of dispositions that decide our action and should, according to Bourdieu, be viewed as a form of 'socialised subjectivity' – an embodiment of social dominance relationships that is difficult to change.[36] Habitus is a concept that positions itself 'in the interstices' between subject and structure, or between 'practices' and structure. Habitus is related to habit, but it is more than a routine. It is an 'embodied' or 'internalised' habit, one that has become part of who we are.

A habitus is always connected to a *social field* of relationships and to a struggle between actors, for example in the political or the literary field.[37] Habitus corresponds to positions found in the various hierarchies within a given field. A position corresponds to the individual's disposition (i.e. the habitus); this means that a disposition is a practical incorporation of the field's power order as articulated in a position in that field. At the same time, being active in the field also means letting the field be part of you. A habitus is activated within a field and one person can acquire several types of habitus that are relevant to their various social fields.

Specific practices are embodied as dispositions. They can only partially be made into the subject of theoretical description or be changed by being made conscious. Embodiment means that the body can be constructed from lived experiences. Thoughts, theories, analyses, feelings, habits and skills – which all are practices – are trained through repetition and refinement. They materialise in posture, patterns of movement, psychosomatic reactions, tone of voice, mimicry, energy, muscle strength, mobility and so on. Bourdieu's framework gives rise to the question of how participants' existing *obedience habits* (as some nonviolence handbooks call them) are thought to be reformed in an educational situation and turned into a new *disobedience habit*.

The principles behind practices are not conscious or constant rules, but are implicitly 'practical schemes'.[38] Practices are neither complete, coherent or incoherent; they are continuously reconstructed and improvised and are historical. Through the 'practical mind', a person creates a certain personal 'style' or 'taste', which is connected to their social position. A practice is difficult to imitate and should rather be understood as an art form that can be taught only through practice.[39] This practice gives us access to the special '*pre-logical logic of practice*', which is organised along oppositional lines and according to economic logic – the maximisation of material and symbolic gains.[40]

Habitus and the logic of practice are closely tied together. Habitus is produced by:

> The conditionings associated with a particular class of conditions of existence [and are] systems of durable, transportable dispositions, structured structures predisposed to function as structuring structures, that is, as principles which generate and organize practices and representations.[41]

We are talking here about productive dispositions for action, an incorporated creative pattern of behaviour. Habitus is not controlled by an actor's conscious goals, but it can be mastered without an individual's – even the actor's – underlying organisation or purpose. However, it is sometimes possible for habitus to coincide with the actor's own strategic calculations.

The actions of movements, according to Bourdieu's view, require a practical competence that is taught through its specific practices. The only way to learn nonviolent action is by carrying out nonviolent action.

An individual's early experience of economic and social conditions – as well as of the ways of life that result from such conditions for one's primary group (normally the family) – characterises the habitus the individual lives with for the rest of their life. Habitus structures one's perception and understanding of subsequent experiences in accordance with previous experiences. The thoughts that lie behind or beyond the structural principles become quite simply 'unthinkable'. Habitus is a product of history and produces history through the behaviour schemes that history generates. This internalisation of external relations creates a person's dispositions, which in turn form that person's will and motivation, in a non-mechanical way. A whole repertoire of thoughts, perceptions and action can be created in a relatively free and creative sense, thanks to our practical ability (habitus) – but only the repertoire that habitus enables.[42] *The individual constantly reconstructs their habitus, and that reconstruction is carried out with the help of the material that constitutes the habitus.* Habitus, the embodied history, should not be understood as old relationships governing new ones, but as a relationship between what was and what is. Ruptures become both possible and necessary through the tensions that exist between previous experiences and present conditions. By embodying history, which is what we do when we create our habitus, history becomes second nature – a part of us – and thus history is transformed into forgotten history. The so-called unconscious is simply forgotten history, something that history itself produces.[43]

In other words, the practice of collective action is captured in its history. Previous collective actions decide which actions are possible and conceivable today. The historian-sociologist Charles Tilly, who studied centuries of oppositional movements, claims from his macro perspective that there is a corresponding imprint of history on resistance. He finds that a movement's action 'repertoires' occur in certain historical frames and relate to the processes of change occurring in society.[44] Movements create discourses, organisations and types of action based on their historically situated experience of discourses, organisations and types of action. Within the existing repertoire or framework, activists can give their opposition a personal expression. Activists are creative innovators but work from an existing toolbox.

Habitus can be understood in several ways. It can be an incorporated power relationship, the way in which social structures 'come to life' and take effect through our bodies and our minds. Habitus can be an actor's 'structuring' of structures,[45] the way in which the actor maintains and modifies their life's structure. Habitus is the 'glue' that binds us to societal structures by encouraging us to reproduce our previous experience. Since we are born into an already existing system of structures, the structures precede the individual. Thus we are formed, unconsciously and continuously, by the structures, frames and regulations. We become the structures, or, more correctly, *the structures become us*. We do not have a completely conscious or full control over the structures; but because they work through us – that is, they exist only within and between us as a community – we have the possibility to change them. We can, at least in the long term, transform (certain) structures with the help of (other) structures and practical modifications over time.

Like Foucault, Bourdieu is not an author who discusses at great length how power relations are transformed through the conscious intervention of actors. On the contrary, movements are criticised as vain attempts.[46] Apparently, the possibility of an actor independently deciding on change is non-existent. According to Bourdieu, it is not the actors who make relative autonomy within current structures possible, but habitus itself: or, in other words, the active presence of all the past, *through* the actor in the present. Change takes shape through the 'intentionless invention of regulated improvisation'.[47] Habitus is never an exact copy of our previous power relations; it is filtered through our constant cooperation. Even the *actor's will is decided by habitus, 'the non-chosen principle behind all choices'.*[48] However, there always remains a choice,[49] but a choice that is always limited by the constituted process resulting from the history of prior choices.[50] Each choice is an experience that leaves an imprint on the person, an imprint that cannot be undone and that decides future decisions through its formation of motivation, knowledge and personality.

The very ability to act is dependent upon and enabled by the actor's habitus – as an existing 'hereditary ability' to act.[51] In turn, habitus is formed by the actor's relationship with the objective conditions that prevail, with what is possible or, in other words, with power. This acquired ability takes shape as a selective perception that tends to confirm or intensify itself rather than transform itself. Habitus is quite simply the reason why people who are oppressed do not rise up in situations where modified objective conditions make it possible, or why people 'cut their coats according to their cloth'. Habitus tends to make the likely

outcome a reality, but in a non-mechanical way.[52] Without a bodily transformation or a reconstructed social practice, collective
action or liberation is not possible. The entire situation is a catch
22: without changed structures, no changed habitus – without
changed habitus, no changed structures. Change is possible,
however, but the individual is unable to change him- or herself.[53]
Bourdieu should be read as if *collective change were possible over
time through mutual reflection, construction of a new social field and
practical training*.[54] And therefore nonviolent groups' skills training, utopian communities and alternative organisations appear
in their true light as possible ways out – attempts at liberation
from the internalised shape of power within the activist.

Nonviolence courses as ways of modifying habitus

New patterns of behaviour are not created or mediated in
a simple way in a new educational situation. Sometimes they
are acquired through a great effort of thought and sometimes
through involuntary imitation, but above all through practice,
repetition and variation ('training'). 'Being able to choose is
integral to having acquired the dispositions towards certain
actions, so being innovative is integral with the discipline of
having trained thoroughly in an art.'[55] The child's struggle to
learn to walk becomes, in time, a self-evident act of walking, a
nearly involuntary 'sleepwalking'.

A practice's scheme can certainly be summarised in generally
held guidelines, but when those guidelines become the cause
of action and not the reverse, the practice will cease to work.

Bourdieu intimates the possibility of change through 'reflexive
analysis' and 'self-work', or quite simply by 'pit[ting] one disposition against another'.[56] But this must occur under fortuitous
social conditions that strengthen the possibility of change. The

combination of critical reflection and the construction of new social fields opens up the possibility of a change in habitus.

Practices involve our conscious participation, at least in part, as they are not automatic. Practices need the actor to *continuously adjust* their practice. However, we are unable to change embodied practices merely by being given new information or explanations.[57] The process of making people conscious that has stood at the centre of attempts at liberation since the Enlightenment – not least in the nonviolent movement's feminist 'consciousness-raising groups' – seem to have obvious limitations when viewed in this way.[58] Habits, like petrified and incorporated symbolic constructions, are practices that cannot be changed simply by rediscovering the stored meaning of habit. Regular practices change during their practice, through action, by behavioural rules being broken, in small adjustments and the repetition of new action sequences during training, through the establishment of new habits.[59]

If this train of thought is correct, a *habitus modification* should be possible through a combination of self-critical reflection and creative practice of new actions under favourable conditions (social support for the new habit, for example, until it becomes internalised as habitus).

There is disagreement about the degree to which habitus is mutable through the conscious intervention of people.[60] I assume that liberation from internalised behavioural patterns requires a critical interpretation of the problem with current habits, suggestions about the direction for new patterns of behaviour, and concrete and repeated practice of new behavioural patterns, through which old habits are broken down and new ones built up.

To avoid the new habits of disobedience becoming asocial

and meaningless, however, there is a need for communal self-reflection on the behavioural changes.

Habitus modification is achieved in nonviolence courses through the dissolution of behavioural patterns and social experimentation.[61] Modification occurs through the repeated use of *brainstorming, games* and *role playing*. In brainstorming, one tries to stimulate the imagination by limiting all criticism of suggestions made through the association of ideas. New ideas are given the opportunity to surface and to transcend ingrained mental structures. Whether those ideas are realistic or worth following up is something you decide in a subsequent discussion. Games have a similar function in disrupting the ingrained activity patterns of both body and mind and in allowing participants to be open to change.[62] Through role playing, new behavioural patterns are tried out and practised in conflict situations, and, in evaluating the role play, you try to discover the value of new ways of acting. You could say that habitus is made into an object for reflexive and systematic examination.

When viewed through habitus, the nonviolent movement's ambition to unite ends and means becomes easier to understand. A radical democratic organisation such as the Graswurzel-revolution tries to adopt a higher degree of internal democracy than we perceive as characterising the German liberal society it opposes.[63] Through independent groups, consensus, alternative meeting techniques, arbitration and so on, a greater degree of participation in decision making is practised than is the case with majority voting. To have an effect in the organisation, the means must be applied and the goals practised. 'Prefigurative politics' makes the movement into a training camp that socialises members for a new society. The activists' practical experience and their exercises within the organisation become a way of modifying their own habitus. Conflicts within the organisation between ends and means become conflicts between the habitus the activists have acquired in the current society and the habitus the organisation strives to refine as part of the future society. Activities undertaken by a radical democratic organisation can thus be interpreted as a form of habitus modification towards an increased ability to practise democracy.[64]

Nonviolence training as normative regulation

A social community does not work without some kind of normative order. In a nonviolent movement's resistance to (certain) societal norms, a normative order of nonviolence is established within the movement together with (other) socially sanctioned rules of behaviour. Here, the activists are given the choice of forming a new normative order that upholds their power, or one that values democratic participation, equality and critical reflection, or a combination of the two. The nonviolent community's norms are established (for the participants) as justified behavioural rules through the experience of its prefigurative politics and movement culture. This establishment of norms occurs in the movements' training activities, among other places. I call the activity a *normative regulation*.

A normative regulation requires a set of behavioural rules to be established as an ideal for the community's participants and as something worth striving for, as values that are legitimate or valid morally and ethically, or as rules that you otherwise wish to follow and try to make others follow. These norms are linked to sanctions of various kinds, whereby the person who breaks them has to face the consequences. Even if a nonviolent community tries to apply less violent sanctions, they might still feel violent to those affected. This covers everything from obvious punishments to barely detectable dislike, from brutal exclusion from the community to minuscule changes in the possibility of someone obtaining a reward, or perhaps a wall of silence or a lack of response. However, infringements of the norms are registered and are important.

This means that a normative regulation requires rules that are taught practically and ideals that can be made into the participants' ideals. A normative regulation can occur as an *effect* of the way in which a social team works or as a regulating *goal*. Training is a suitable form of normative regulation. By definition, training is a certain temporary activity in a radical context where a systematic resocialisation becomes possible.[65]

A key training method is the use of *simulations*. Here, problematic situations are enacted in which activists are challenged to act differently, through games and exercises using roles, conflicts and solutions. Role playing or other simulations work as tools with at least four different purposes:[66]

1 A *resocialisation*, where previously socialised roles are broken down and unlearned. This is made possible through a mix of social reality and acting or imagination, in order to facilitate socialisation in new habits and roles.
2 Learning new *practical skills* through exercises.
3 A *social reflexivity*, where an understanding of others, of oneself, and of social interplay and roles is thematised and questioned.
4 An *empathy construction*, where conceptions about 'the other' are acted out in engaged situations and intensive games. Participants constantly dress themselves in and change roles in the game, playing parts including those of their opponents, for example as a police officer or soldier.

Habitus training and the nonviolent field

The regulation of new norms requires a simultaneous modification of people's dispositions and the positions of the social field. If nonviolence training is to work, a creative *habitus modification* should occur during the training that is integrated within a new *field of nonviolence*. It is by taking on the social field's various positions that the training becomes meaningful and the skills practised can be applied in daily life. Training, like any other form of socialisation, creates the *dispositions* that correspond to the field's *positions*. As a result of new nonviolent institutions being built within the movement, there is a need for activists to have the requisite skills. For this reason, training without a social context risks becoming meaningless. From a perspective informed by Bourdieu, we can say that a training session without fields is just as ineffective as a field without training. In conventional socialisation, there is a social field in which humans are formed through a combination of informal socialisation and formal training, for example the academic field. Here, as in other fields, positions must be taught and transformed into dispositions; if not, 'students', 'researchers' and 'administrators' would not be able to interact within academia.

One solution is to weave together action and training, as occurred in the Congress of Racial Equality (CORE), which shaped nonviolence training in the USA: 'After theory and role playing training CORE members would go and test their ideas in the community, then come together and evaluate.'[67] In an integrated way, their training was a driving factor in creating campaigns and their action was part of their training: 'action as training' and 'training as action'.[68]

In one of the few power-critical reflections about nonviolence training that I have found, Charles Walker thinks that there was a tense struggle between organisers and trainers: indeed, the tension was so strong that it bordered on cultivating enemy images. The organisers felt that the trainers saw training as a 'substitute for action', while the trainers felt that they were treated like 'the cooks: have the meal ready on time; don't tell us how to run the project and we won't tell you how to cook the potatoes'.[69] Walker saw a solution through the integration of institutionalised training and movement strategy, since nonviolence sometimes needs to be stable and predictable, and sometimes creative and spontaneous.

The dilemma of nonviolence training is that it normally comprises a short, intense training session of a disobedience habitus that does not have any social roots or belonging. That is a serious problem, since a habitus (or disposition) is always related to a social field (and corresponding positions). The training provides only a short-lived experience of how another subjectivity and behaviour could be possible; however, that new possibility is not sustained. Activists are dominated by an obedience habitus that is bound to the hegemonic field: that is, the social structures that the participants come from and go back to after the (weekend) training session. The participants normally have few possibilities of attending longer courses or, after the training, of being able to participate in a social context where their new skills are welcomed and stimulated. Thus, there is habitus training without an accompanying social field.

A nonviolent resocialisation requires, in other words, nonviolence training embedded in a field of nonviolence. For that reason, Gandhi found that nonviolence training required training in new practices in a nonviolent context, an ashram. The creation of nonviolent institutions and societal structures, which continuously sustain and stimulate habitus modification, makes nonviolent normalisation more likely. In nonviolent movements, an effective normative regulation should expect that any work required for the social construction of 'parallel institutions' has the precondition of replacing the hegemonic society's institutions.

We therefore come to a point in the discussion when it becomes necessary to look at the way in which nonviolent construction builds this new social field: a *nonviolent society*.

Nonviolence as a social whole: the nonviolent society

The action types of nonviolence have been discussed separately in the previous chapters with the aim of providing space to develop one new concept at a time. Nonviolence comprises dialogue facilitation, power breaking, normative regulation and utopian enactment, but above all it is a way of acting, a form of action, not four separate ones. The ideal types are purely rational dimensions of nonviolent action; they are not four different actions or separate alternatives that can be carried out in practice. The overarching aim of nonviolence means that the different types of action are woven together.

This concluding section shows how making the four separate elements into a whole is built on a development of the normative activity. Here, with the help of empirical examples, I will illustrate how the values and behaviour of nonviolence can be institutionalised and coordinated to form a social whole, which is simultaneously a meaningful and working whole – or, in Bourdieu's terms, a field of nonviolence of conjoined relations of dispositions and positions.

Gandhi places high demands on an individual's ability to both avoid and fight the use of violence (*without violence* and *against violence*) in cases where striving for *perfection* is seen as necessary. Gandhi thinks that the effectiveness of nonviolence is created by the high level of perfection adopted in carrying out nonviolence, and that a single person could stop a war if that person were nonviolent enough.[70] At the same time, perfection is not a precondition for nonviolent struggle, nor, in fact, is it even possible.[71] Gandhi points out that the stronger you are in your conviction, ability and experience of nonviolent struggle, the more powerfully you can act – or, more correctly, the more powerfully the truth can have an effect with you as its channel. Perfection is a constant striving that never ends; however, anyone can begin using the technique and can become better through practice.[72] Perfection is often discussed from an individual and spiritual perspective, but here we shall look at *perfection from a collective and practical perspective*. The point of departure is fundamental to sociology: above all, it is possible for the individual to fundamentally alter their way of living and character when the social community is radically changed in such a way that it facilitates the change that is occurring in the individual.

By emphasising his struggle against violence, Gandhi differs from pacifism and the peace churches of Christianity.[73] Interestingly enough, Gandhi found that nonviolence's strength increased in proportion to the person's ability to use violence.[74] It is through the wish to *not* injure others, despite the possibility of doing so, that nonviolence gains its strength, not through an inability to use violence. It is by showing respect for one's opponent as a person during the action that one's respect becomes convincing.

Both *without violence* and *against violence* require a certain capacity to act with skill, the resources with which to act, knowledge and a practical ability for nonviolence. The constructive programme that Gandhi advocated could be understood as *the creation of the individual and collective ability to live and carry out nonviolence*.[75] *Without violence* presupposes a number of abilities and resources – personal as well as social – that are cemented or institutionalised in order to work under stress and in risk-filled situations. After those moments in which nonviolent campaigns collapsed into violent riots, Gandhi retreated to life in the village collectives – ashrams – that he had created together with his most loyal companions. Life in the focused social existence of the village community encompassed daily training to foster or discipline nonviolence. What could be interpreted as a period of reticent existence in the countryside actually entailed intense preparations to build a core troop of dedicated *satyagrahis* who could organise the mass campaigns that followed.[76] The most famous disobedience campaign – the Salt March and its extensive disobedience to a selection of unjust laws – arose after a longer period at the ashram. Characteristically, the march began from Gandhi's own ashram, with a core of eighty-one devoted nonviolent activists.[77]

The re-creation of individuals' behavioural patterns and society's institutions involves long-term practical work in which learned or simply embodied habits are broken down and built up in a new *nonviolent resocialisation*. Previously, we have seen how nonviolence training is one element in the process of re-socialisation. In this context, we will see how resocialisation in turn is part of the process of constructing a society. For Gandhi, the goal was a 'nonviolent revolution' that would create a new society concerned with the welfare of all.[78] One example is the North American nonviolent organisation Movement for a New Society, which, through its focus on alternative forms of meeting, behaviour and work, was an inspiration for the development of more participation-oriented nonviolence during the 1970s. Nonviolence resocialisation means constructing the preconditions for nonviolent approaches to life, ways of life and institutions, both those that through their radical *without violence* orientation comprise new ways of living together and solving conflicts and those that generate self-assurance, knowledge and the resources for nonviolence activity.[79] This resocialisation of nonviolence work has the effect of facilitating peace and easing resistance.

> My present ambition is certainly to make of Sevagram [Gandhi's ashram] an ideal village. I know that the work is as difficult as to make of India an ideal country. But while it is possible for one man to fulfil his ambition with respect to a single village some day, one man's lifetime is too short to overtake the whole of India. But if one man can produce one ideal village, he will have provided a pattern not only for the whole country, but perhaps for the whole world. More than this a seeker may not aspire after.[80]

As I have previously indicated, Gandhi did not limit himself to developing methods of resistance that could liberate British India from colonialism. He strove for liberation from below, where both distinct individuals and India's social groups could liberate themselves from all forms of violence and oppression. The ambition was to revolutionise the society at its base, or, as his devotee 'JP' called it in the 1970s, 'Total Revolution'. According to the anthropologist Richard Fox,[81] Gandhi's utopian vision consists of a concrete societal-revolutionary project with nine parts: *progress for all* (*sarvodaya*); a *simple life* in which the individual's desires are subordinated to societal needs; *self-control* at all levels (*swaraj*); *serving one's neighbour* and the local first of all (*swadeshi*); *spiritual resistance* against injustices and dominance (*satyagraha* and *ahimsa*); *mutual agreements* between workers and company owners ('trusteeship'); *self-sufficiency* of basic goods ('bread labour'); *local autonomy* (the self-rule of the villages or *panchayat* raj); and *organised anarchy* (oceanic circles and *ram-rajya*). In other words, the nonviolent campaign comprised, for Gandhi, a societal construction project, one in which participants simultaneously tear down the oppressive institutions that exist and build up nonviolent institutions that replace them. In this way, true liberation and independence (from colonial regimes) require a societal reconstruction.

If nonviolence is conducted by groups that fail to find a context that supports their activity, then the movement risks becoming temporary, socially limited and vulnerable. One extreme is the small group of similar friends who carry out isolated actions that neither challenge nor mobilise others. The other extreme would be a nonviolent movement that is so powerful that it succeeds in transforming society completely – carrying out a nonviolent revolution – not just in a national society but in all the violence-permeated systems of dominance that characterise the societies of the world. In the latter case, we would be talking about a global nonviolent movement. Neither of these extremes is particularly interesting – the first because it is too private; the second because it is too utopian and distant. We need flexible concepts that describe variations in the ways in which groups succeed in forming their own social contexts of nonviolence.

In the nonviolence movement, people speak of 'creating community'.[82] When the French Gandhians started ashrams in Europe, the movement was called La Communauté de l'Arche.[83] The Civil Rights Movement's Southern Christian Leadership Conference and Martin Luther King spoke of *the beloved community* and stated that their goal was:

> [a] genuine intergroup and interpersonal living, *integration.*
> Only through nonviolence can reconciliation and the creation
> of the beloved community be effected.[84]

The concept of 'community' has the advantage that it can be used to describe both a local community and a society, regardless of size. The only researchers I have found who suggest that nonviolent movements can be seen as fundamental to society are Swee-Hin Toh and Virginia Floresca-Cawagas in their article 'Institutionalization of nonviolence'. On the other hand, this argument is clearly present within nonviolence movements.

When the nonviolence-oriented liberation theologian Frances O'Gorman speaks about the Christian base communities – Base Ecclesial Communities – it is as 'seeds of a new society': 'The [power] pyramid can be moved by resistance and organization of a new society.'[85] A society is a community that does not only dedicate itself to a concrete task (as does an organisation) nor is based exclusively on kinship (like a family). The societal concept can describe various types and sizes of social contexts: local society, internet society, national society, artist society or the global society. But the concept can also express various degrees of coordination or complexity: for example, the society may be (dys)functional or (non-)differentiated. Conventionally speaking, 'society' refers to a nation-state context. But a society need not be of a certain size or complexity in order to be a society. The society's number of members or degree of complexity perhaps decides whether it can face the challenges of other existing hegemonic societal forms.

In contrast to Sharp's technique approach that emphasises the effectiveness of universal methods since they conform to strategic principles, I strive towards a conceptual development that helps us understand nonviolence historically and culturally contextualise its movement repertoire.[86] In this perspective, nonviolent actions are constructed not from universal systems of ideas or strategy theories but based on a complex and dynamic social interaction where the situation, context and people's concrete experiences decide.[87] The basic idea is that the social construction of a group's habits within a working institutional system and a meaningful integration of nonviolence are required in order to uphold the struggle for nonviolence, even in the long run and under pressure.

Habermas perceives society's integration as a dual process that combines rationalities:

> Whilst the goal-oriented aspect of social action is relevant for the material reproduction of the lifeworld, the understanding aspect is important for the lifeworld's symbolic reproduction.[88]

Societies coalesce in two ways according to Habermas: partly through social integration of the understanding orientation of communicative actions; and partly through the systematic integration of goal-oriented activities. A nonviolent society coalesces in part socio-culturally (through ideas, values and meanings of actions being integrated with each other) and in part as a social system (by means of the behaviour's regularity, conditions and consequences coalescing). In this respect, the interpretation of nonviolence as an integrated society relates to the way in which nonviolence can be socially regulated in meaningful, sustained institutions and integrated into functional social systems. In other words, societal integration demands that all four types of action discussed thus far are coordinated both meaningfully and effectually.

The most dedicated nonviolence activists of the Indian liberation movement lived together in a collective life in the villages. They combined the movement's need for an action tradition with ashrams: monastery-like religious communities (based on Hinduism, Buddhism and Islam). Through practical work, discipline, daily routines, serving others according to certain principles, meditation, prayer, and communal actions and movement organisation, the nonviolence values were internalised and established a capability for nonviolent struggle.[89]

In recent movements, beginning with the Civil Rights Movement, various forms of temporary communities such as 'collectives' or 'nonviolence training centres' have replaced the role that ashrams once had.[90] As we have seen, nonviolence training consists of intensively coaching the behaviours that nonviolence requires and imparts useful knowledge.

The construction of a nonviolent culture of resistance is not simple. In South Africa, it took several decades of political organisation before the blacks began to resist in the 1950s (above all, through the Defiance Campaign of 1952), and resistance was constructed in a political culture where it was viewed as shameful to be imprisoned.[91] For many decades, the African National Congress (ANC) had chosen only moderate claims-making, defensive appeals and protest declarations against the discrimination against blacks in the country. But in the 1950s, the ANC was radicalised and began to organise very influential nonviolent resistance, with civil disobedience, general strikes and boycotts. The change occurred when a culture of resistance was established and therefore new generations grew up with a self-evident resistance rather than the accommodation their parents had known.[92] One factor was the fact that the view of prison changed in South Africa thanks to the Indian example of peaceful resistance.

Cultural change 'can be attained by constructing new action repertoires'.[93] And nonviolence is indeed a new, specific and unique oppositional action repertoire that creatively relates to mainstream culture.[94]

In order to form a *nonviolence culture*, a culture has to be created in which various nonviolent actions and values become a meaningful whole that is mirrored in the movement's desired future society.[95] This culture must eventually lead to a working system to survive as a society.

The concept of the prefigurative or enacted nonviolent community

A kind of *protest culture* was constructed within the global justice movement and at its manifestations in Seattle in 1999 and Genova in 2001.[96] Demonstrations involving a great number of people from various organisations and nations showed that they did not accept the market-oriented politics conducted throughout the world by the global regimes of the World Bank, the World Trade Organization and the International Monetary Fund. The movements tried to enact an oppositional world opinion by collecting representatives from religious groups, unions, farmers, indigenous people, students and other social categories. In their own words, taken from the protests against the richest countries' organisation, the G8, they tried to show that: 'You are G8, we are 6 billion.' This is probably a little optimistic, but the dramatisation of the political logic in an oppositional protest culture is clear. They want to achieve a physical enactment of the opinion polls. Their hope is that the political and economic decision makers will be affected by the quantity of the opposition. Global regimes are assumed, like national regimes, to be dependent on the majority for their legitimacy.

Another type of political culture is created by movements that enact or prefigure a nonviolent society.[97] This is not about protesting – in the sense of pleading or demanding that those in power listen or change their policies – but about socially constructing the institutions, roles, organisations, rituals and discourses that together can form the basis of a new society, and that either replace the prevailing one or are robust enough to comprise a parallel, alternative society for those who want to 'jump off'. It is therefore not a question of some finished alternative, but of a growing and emerging community, an experimental culture of resistance where a prototype is tested. The main components are *alternatives* (possibilities for replacing the dominant society's elements and functions) and *resistance* (undermining the reproduction of the prevailing societal pattern).

Enacting or prefigurative movements try, in a fundamental way, to displace common sense and the everyday routines by institutionalising new patterns of behaviour. It is entirely different to maintain resistance for a long period of time than to inspire strong protest action, since maintaining it requires a re-construction of the dominant culture's patterns. This enactment is different from the previously discussed utopian enactment in risk situations. This enactment is more long term, ambitious, multidimensional and proactive – and not limited to transform-ing enemy images in violent situations. The aim is to replace a whole set of institutions, values and practices in an entire society.

Constructing another kind of society within the movement also means forming a new emotional culture: that is, new rules for feelings and forms of expression. In this respect, rituals are important:

> a cultural mechanism through which challenging groups express and transform the emotions that arise from sub-ordination, redefine dominant feeling and expression rules to reflect more desirable identities or self-conceptions, and express group solidarity.[98]

When a nonviolent group, for example, begins its meeting by sharing personal feelings and experiences, and finishes with 'healing circles' in which the group's community is confirmed, they practise an emotionally enacted politics – a direct realisation of the movement's values.

The enacted nonviolent society is a movement culture[99] that works within and acts against a dominant society by upholding criticism, dialogue and nonviolent actions. The nonviolent society is a new kind of society that continuously contradicts the existing one at the same time as it (partially) finds itself within it. Building a 'rich' or 'developed' movement culture requires extensive labour.[100] The creation of everything from unique values to cultural objects – which to some extent are split, made distinct, adjusted according to the situation, refined, and multiplied – demands hard cultural work. In addition, the formation of a culture that has the capacity to replace the dominant society demands even more hard work. In the latter case, what is required is not just a well-defined movement of plausibly like-minded people acting together in response to a limited array of questions, at certain places and under certain conditions. This nonviolent culture – in the movement society – must also be able to handle conflicts better than the hegemonic society it competes with. In turn, a conflict-transforming movement culture needs to provide capacity training for the movement's members.[101]

The environmental activists who fought a large-scale dam construction in 1978–81 in Innerdalen in southern Norway are an example of the nonviolent society in action.[102] In contrast, in another, better known, nonviolent struggle against a dam construction in Alta in northern Norway, the activists focused on dramatic and sporadic actions whereby they tried to prevent the construction project from starting by chaining themselves to each other with steel chains and by carrying out blockades.[103] A very different approach was implemented in Innerdalen. Grønn Aksjon Innerdalen tried to maintain a permanent resistance by moving down into the valley of the planned dam to live, to cultivate the land and to build a village community. Their village therefore also became a way of blocking the dam. Innerdalen's new village-dwellers created an 'environmental university' during the summer months where the visitors were educated in old handicrafts and built alternative energy systems. The point is that they did not protest with a short-lived blockade in front of the television cameras or isolate themselves from the rest of society in a secluded eco-village. They practised their ideas and began building an alternative society within the dominant society. The alternative was the blockade of the dam construction itself, or, rather, perhaps, *the blockade's resistance expressed their alternative*. As long as they carried out their work and lived in the village, the dam could not be finished without evicting the enacted nonviolent society's villagers.

Unfortunately, the movement was not sufficiently persistent. The inhabitants of this alternative and resistant society did not move back each time they were driven off, the movement dissolved, and the dam was completed. But other movements have been more successful with the same strategy. In India, through the nonviolent Narmada Movement, the indigenous population has not only maintained their resistance for a few decades, and has remained when water flooded their villages, but they have successfully driven off several transnational companies and even the World Bank from the enormous dam project in Narmada.[104]

§

I am now going to illustrate how a full-blown enactment of the nonviolent society can appear through an analysis of a movement that has succeeded in maintaining its unarmed resistance for thirty years: the Movimento dos Trabalhadores Rurais Sem Terra in Brazil (the Landless Workers' Movement or MST).[105] MST is an enacted or prefigurative nonviolent society applying a combination and institutionalisation of several movement activities. Lennart Kjörling, who has worked with the movement for several years, calls its enactment 'organised utopia'.[106] This is also a movement that is distinguished by its investment in training activists.[107] Interestingly, this particular nonviolence training does not result in a vacuum in the form of weekend training for an interested public. It is for active members of the movement or those who live in MST camps. Like the approach of the Indian liberation movement, MST's 'culture of liberation' is an example of nonviolent resocialisation: a combination of nonviolent habitus modification and, as I will indicate, a nonviolent social field.[108] But first, I will set out a few of the distinctive features of MST's community construction.[109]

First, a movement culture needs to be able to transfer its culture to members through *self-managed socialising institutions*. Primary socialisation occurs in the family, group of peers and school, institutions that within MST are situated in the same social space – the land occupant's community. The first thing they build in their temporary tent villages are schools for the children. The children's education begins in plastic tents and continues, if and when they receive legal recognition of their land rights, in their own school buildings built using collective labour, government aid or the organisation of their mutual resources. When at last they can take over the land, they disseminate their own educational forms and content: for example, 'militants' travel around Brazil in order to organise new occupations, so that the movement's values and experiences are spread to both the next generation and those with a budding interest in it. Today, MST even has its own university. Through this strong development of self-managed education, it is uniquely able to create its own leadership, even as it grows. On long treks through Brazil, the children study the societies their itinerant school brings them into contact with.[110] In part, their pedagogy is inspired by the Brazilian educationalist Paolo Freire,[111] and in part, as we will see below, MST conducts its own rituals and social dramas that present the struggle's actions and that confirm human solidarity. This also contributes to the socialisation of new members in the community.

Second, there is a need for *institutions that effectively reproduce the movement's material resources in accordance with its values.* The occupations that eventually win their areas of land form cooperatives that both generate the new villages' subsistence and mobilise the movement's resources towards a more professional and more intense struggle. Through their own 'taxation' and allocation, the new resources for the political struggle are created as a side effect of the daily work. Each new piece of land and each new cooperative strengthens MST's ability to carry out a self-sufficient nonviolent struggle and furthers the socialisation of the movement's members.[112]

Third, *the movement reconstructs the dominant culture* by mixing and displacing meanings of established cultural elements.[113] The movement has its own 'uniform' – a red cap, used like its own 'national flag', featuring the movement's logo of a man and a woman raising an agricultural implement in front of a map of Brazil. When I visited a village in one of the first land occupations in the movement's history, I lived with a family that, on one of the living room walls, mixed images of the Virgin Mary with Che Guevara, the local football team and the courageous struggle of the landless farmers. In one of the early occupations, radical priests inspired activists to carry a large wooden cross at the front of their marches. The result was a special 'MST culture' that mixes parts of Brazil's cultural heritage with the movement's experiences, perspectives and needs in a Brazilian cultural hybrid of meaningful resistance.

Fourth, the movement enacts values, successes and suffering in the struggle against the prevailing system's cruelty by means of *the movement's everyday stories*, in which movement participants repeatedly tell narratives that articulate strong positive and negative emotions and experiences of their struggle.[114] The narration is part of the construction of the movement's history of iconic events and personalities. One such story is about the movement's birth. During my visit to the movement's first village, I was taken to a very large tree on a hill. I was told how, twenty years before, landless farmers had sat on the grass in the shade of the tree, looking out over a vast area of fertile land, which its owner did not bother to cultivate. On this spot, the pioneers of the movement decided as a group to carry out the first occupation, an occupation that, after many years of hard work and living in black plastic tents, led to the end of their suffering and to their success. All the land that surrounds the tree is now cultivated by freeholding farmers and various cooperatives. This story plays a key part in the construction of the movement's community and identity. It is one story among several that contain all the classic ingredients of great tales: protagonists and antagonists continuously driving the plot forward, the production of a subject with a point[115] – and even religious parallels in the Christian community's suffering and rebirth. Through this and many other widespread tales that are retold in daily life, MST constructs its own culture.[116]

Fifth, certain elements of the movement's culture have a

higher status or simply have a religious quality due to *rituals and ceremonies.* In the movement's '*mística*', movement actions are dramatised on stage. The *mística* constitutes the basic structure of MST's main ritual during large gatherings or on important dates and varies according to current topics.

In one state, several members of MST were murdered; then, when the meeting that chose the new leadership ended, a *mística* was performed. On the stage there was a wooden coffin for each person murdered, and dancers moved to the rhythm of sombre music. The music changed character and children appeared with flowers for the coffins, the lids of which were all opened and from the coffins the new leadership of MST arose.

In order to describe the *mística*, activists use religions or spiritual concepts and references. The *mística* is an example of the explicit ritualisation of the movement's activity. But even in communal actions, which are formed with reference to iconic events from the movement's history, rituals contribute to creating a new emotional culture. As soon as the activists arrive on their land and begin a new occupation, they gather in a circle and sing together in the silence of the night.[117] Sometimes, you can even see how the movement views certain places as holy by virtue of them having given rise to decisive events in the movement's birth and growth ('the Mecca of the movement').[118] It is interesting that MST's birthplace is claimed to be next to a tree. The symbolism is obvious and well suited for rituals. Like trees, the movement's farmworkers are deeply rooted in the earth, and from their own fertile land they are tied to the roots of the movement – individuals and families spread like flourishing branches. As long as they have sun and water, they will grow together, stretching up to the sky above.

Sixth, liberated zones or '*movement havens*' are constructed and sought out and make cultural renewal possible.[119] During acute social struggle, special social places for safe refuge, relatively free from domination, can serve as spatial and organisational tools for cultural transformation and social change. During the Algerian liberation struggle, the traditional and previously conservative family, the mosque and the market place served as bases for the ongoing cultural change and, eventually, a revolution, to the extent that the veil became a symbol of the strong, liberated and freedom-fighting woman.[120] In crises, certain parts of the periphery can become resistance centres or liberated zones thanks to their distance from the system's centre. I think that the landworkers' families and parts of the countryside's untilled land serve as this kind of movement haven for MST, just as the cities' shanty towns (favelas) have become a symbol for the new movement created by their poor inhabitants and MST activists in cooperation.[121] These places are permeated with a tradition of resistance or are excluded social areas in which Brazil's hegemonic global capitalist class has limited control. Moreover, the landless and slum-dwellers are neither profit-generating consumers nor workers, and therefore essentially not even proper citizens in the authoritarian state's eyes. They are 'negligible' to the structures of power, which give them (limited and temporary) space. Naturally, the landholders have private militia in the countryside, and criminal gangs are found in the slums, but the terror created by these power groups cannot reasonably be equated with the detailed discipline that prevails in state schools, in the capitalists' factories or in the country's military barracks. It is by acting in the shadow of the dominant power system that MST finds a sufficient space to form alternatives to the societal system it is fighting.

The last three elements that exemplify the nonviolent

movement culture are the creation of group boundaries (seven), interpretative frameworks (eight) and the politicisation of daily life (nine); these are central and connected processes in the creation of a movement identity that is formed through social interaction in the movement's communities.[122]

Without *group boundaries*, the experience of a collectively acting 'we' disappears, whereas borders that are too strong, and which new members must pass through to become part of the movement's community, reduce the possibilities of mobilising and involving the rest of society. Therefore, there is a complicated problem of balancing boundaries that are simultaneously sufficient but traversable. MST has solved this problem in a creative way. The decisive membership initiation into MST is the act of occupation. By occupying land, you show that you need land and that you are prepared to take risks in the fight against the injustices of land allocation. All those who participate in the movement's land occupations and accept the principles of resistance that MST has developed (for example, no firearms) can be included. Due to the collective benefits, most choose to stay within MST once the occupation is over and land entitlements have been obtained, although some opt to become independent farmers.

The *movement's interpretive framework* is a rich stew that the actors prepare strategically using various ingredients from the hegemonic culture and that feeds the movement's understanding of the world.[123] The movement researchers Gamson, Snow and Benford, who developed the concept of 'collective action frames', find that the interpretive framework has several functions: to identify and formulate perceptions of problems in order to bring a collective's 'unjust' situation to people's attention; to localise the 'causes' and parties responsible; and to suggest strategies, 'cures' and alternative visions in a way that mobilises consensus and fosters action – the emphasis is on the movement's active role in changing these circumstances. Thus, the elaboration and articulation of collective action frames also turn the movement activists' various individual experiences into a cohesive, collective viewpoint that benefits the movement's production of a 'we'. Collective action frames are interpretive perspectives that demand cultural work; they are not ready-made but are continuously constructed and reconstructed in complex and conflict-filled processes. And they are spread to others by 'bridging' previously separated elements or by 'amplifying', 'extending' or 'transforming' the meaning of concepts.[124] A collective action frame is formed in a discursive and material struggle where power relations are dramatised in ritual performances of action manuscripts. By organising peaceful occupations with cooperative and ecological farming, despite knowing that landowners and the police will attack the participants with excessive force and even with illegal violence, MST dramatises the unjust allocation of land in Brazil and, at the same time, its own power to change things. The struggle creates a community of 'landless' people who, together with other actors – opponents and potential adherents and constituents (including unorganised poor people who do not perceive themselves as 'landless workers') – become participants in the construction of the collective action frame. New communities are constantly drawn into the drama through local mobilisation and through contact with organisers sent out by MST.

Even if the construction of MST's interpretive framework is directed, it is interactive and has no real stability. Rather, it is negotiated internally between various tendencies in the movement, in conflicts and temporary unity, and it is affected by the actions of all the other actors (other movement organisations, counter-movements, state actors, the media, and so on). The difficulty for MST is to align its interpretations and perspectives with its interest groups: that is, the landless people and small farmers of Brazil along with slum inhabitants and other marginalised groups. It is one thing to adopt an interpretive perspective within the movement, and quite another to connect with or influence those groups that objectively share a common interest with the movement but who do not identify themselves with MST. Furthermore, these collective action frames also need to be understood by and be appealing to the urban middle-class professionals from the media, law and politics, in order to generate enough political leverage to affect political reforms and to win land rights.

The *politicisation of daily life* occurs if the eight elements described above are integrated in a community's daily way of life within the structure of MST. When you shop at a store, place your children in a school, work at a cooperative slaughter-house or relax at a café – which are all taken care of by fellow MST workers – daily life is bestowed with political meaning. It is precisely through people's own participation in their daily reconstruction of MST – through the hundreds of large and small actions – that individual activists incorporate and become co-creators of the movement's values, socio-material structure and political view of the surrounding world.

In sum, we can now state that there are nine descriptive concepts for the nonviolent society's cultural activity. And because these cultural activities express and embody the values of non-violence, a nonviolent society will emerge alongside them. The nine concepts are:

1   socialisation;
2   socio-material reproduction;

3 cultural reconstruction (of the dominant culture);

4 movement stories in daily life;

5 movement rituals and ceremonies;

6 the construction of free zones ('movement havens');

7 group boundaries (traversable boundaries);

8 movement-oriented interpretive frameworks; and

9 the politicisation of daily life.[125]

Taken together as a meaningful cohesive whole, they express a *nonviolent culture*. Nonviolent culture can be specialised and coordinated to various degrees – that is, it can express varying degrees of a complex whole (for example an activist community or an alternative society to the hegemonic culture the movement fights against).

This enactment of the culture of the nonviolent society is not limited to liberal forms of protest and claims-making but is about *enacting and living both the alternative and the resistance* by practising it, by living the social change or revolution and not just talking about it. This enactment of the alternative does not occur individually – or does not *only* occur individually – as a way of life or for personal (privileged) self-development, but is *coordinated collectively* like Gandhi's constructive programme, which was based on the community of the nonviolent groups (in ashrams or in *assentamentos* in Brazil) and on local village development. However, this movement culture is not only about a collective's alternative way of life either, but about creating an *alternative of resistance* that challenges power structures by living according to its own values and principles and positioning itself in such a way that it disrupts or prevents the dominant system's functions. Such a movement culture reconstructs traditional forms of criticism by institutionalising them as permanent parts of life instead of isolated events or spontaneous protests. In other words, they create the social and material basis for a new life and a new subjectivity in the struggle by integrating everything within one coherent, symbolic structure. This dynamic process is problematic and multidimensional. Many separate things must function and fit together as a whole if the nonviolent resistance is to survive and grow.

Now that the one-dimensional variations and the nonviolent culture in its entirety can be summarised conceptually, I would like to make four conceptual distinctions. There is a nonviolent *alternative culture* that does not intervene in relationships of domination but that aims to create an alternative way of living. Such an alternative culture focuses on *without violence* but ignores *against violence*, or the resistance dimension of nonviolence. As such, it is a one-dimensional variation of nonviolent culture. There is also a nonviolent *protest culture* that voices criticism and discontent directed at the existing violent way of living. This one-dimensional nonviolent culture focuses on the legal or tolerated symbolic gestures that show that the participants are against violence, but they do not engage in direct resistance. This is common in liberal democracies where there is a large public space for expressions of risk-free critique that is largely ignored, tolerated or even encouraged by a regime that gains legitimacy from a vibrant civil society. There is also a nonviolent *resistance culture* that focuses on interventions against domination and the violence of others but does not have much interest in developing alternatives or caring for its own culture of nonviolence. The only form that creates a meaningful whole out of the elements of nonviolence is therefore the *nonviolent society's culture of resistance alternatives* that combines the values and practices of both *without violence* and *against violence*.

8 | A THEORY OF NONVIOLENT ACTION

This concluding chapter brings together the conceptual descriptions expanded in the previous chapters. Based on this compilation, I develop a few additional steps in my reasoning with the aim of making the descriptions as complete as possible. In Chapter 3, I suggested that nonviolence can be described using Habermas's action typology, which I then utilised in Chapters 4 to 7. I levelled rigorous challenges at Habermas's ideal speech situations in what I call the *dystopian dialogue situation* of protracted violent conflicts. Throughout my analysis, I have developed key concepts that help us understand nonviolent action from a perspective of social science. If you combine the concepts that have been developed in this book, there emerges what we can call *an ideal nonviolence*, in which its social potential is realised. This is nonviolence when it works ideally.

But an ideal description is not sufficient. We need concepts that are as complete as possible and that describe the variations in the social manifestations of nonviolence. We need a conceptual framework to enable us to describe how these social practices fail, are only partially realised, or simply – and unintentionally – gain new meanings or functions. This examination of theoretical concepts relates to the *immanent* or inherent limitations in the concept of nonviolence. Only once we put together a conceptual description of ideal nonviolence and 'additional' nonviolence can we provide the basis for a complete sociological and conceptual scheme for this investigation. Let us begin by summarising the ideal typology of nonviolence.

The ideal practice of nonviolence: constructive resistance

The four connected action types of nonviolence are fundamental, ideal types that have been developed theoretically with the aim of differentiating the various dimensions of nonviolent action, which, in practice, is a multidimensional combination of rationalities (see Figure 8.1).

The four types of action have been extensively discussed in their own chapters, based on a critical examination of the obstacles to nonviolence's truth-seeking (Gandhi) and to the ideal speech situation (Habermas), thereby allowing for a nuanced conceptual development. Each of the four types of action provides ways of handling its own obstacles.

Note: The rationalities listed are those that Habermas claims are fundamental to human action. The terms in parentheses are the designations that Gandhi uses and that largely correspond to each of the action types. (*Tapasya*, the voluntary acceptance of bodily pain to achieve some higher aim in life, is outlined in Chapter 1.)

8.1 The rational action types of nonviolence as a social whole (satyagraha)

- The constructive work of *normative regulation*, nonviolence training and nonviolent ways of life all counteract society's socialisation of violence and build the foundations of a non-violent society's culture.
- The truth orientation of *dialogue facilitation*, through factual research, supported argumentation, negotiations with middle-level groups and formal treaties with top-level groups, democratic organisation and decision making, attempts to manage competing truth claims as well as disunity.
- The *utopian enactment*'s care for the opponent, refusal to injure or kill, exposure of both justice and injustice, inclusive identification, contrast effect and 'political ju-jitsu' (or 'backfire') all try to address hate and enemy images and foster human relationships and solidarity.
- *Power breaking*'s struggle over symbols and definitions, use of humour, competition, nonviolent non-cooperation with power relations and cooperation with people, as well as its avoidance and prevention of power, undermine oppressive power relationships.

Ideally, these nonviolent action types form a coordinated unity. I initially suggested that nonviolence's social practice could usefully be divided into two connected dimensions: *nonviolent resistance* and *nonviolent construction*. I would now like to show that this unity is indissoluble by elucidating the ways in which nonviolent resistance and nonviolent construction are woven together. In fact, the two main dimensions are so tightly connected that one can see that *every nonviolent type of action is itself a form of nonviolent resistance*:

- Normative regulation means building a culture of resistance to habitus and role socialisation characterised by violence hegemonies as well as society's cultural legitimisation of violence.

- Dialogue facilitation is a counter-structure and a way of producing resistance methods that undermine master suppression techniques and dominance in dialogue.
- Utopian enactment is a form of resistance that undermines hate and enemy images through consequent contradiction.
- Power breaking entails resistance against power by breaking relationships of subordination (by refusal and intervention, among other methods).

At the same time, each nonviolent action type *can be understood as nonviolent construction*:

- Normative regulation involves socially constructing (institutionalising) and following a legitimate nonviolent morality and normative ideal (the social construction of a new society and a new subjectivity).
- Dialogue facilitation is an experiment with egalitarian forms of dialogue and an attempt to develop the conditions that promote an ideal speech situation.
- Utopian enactment attempts to realise or practise utopian ideals of equality and friendship (even in hostile situations).
- Power breaking is the attempt to regain agency or self-control over one's actions (despite being in subordinate relationships) and is a form of individual and collective 'empowerment' in the sense that it increases one's capacity to act (based on one's own decisions and practical control).

Nonviolent resistance and nonviolent construction are analytical categories that can be differentiated. In social practice, these two dimensions are so intimately linked that they comprise two sides of the same coin. The point is that nonviolence is, in fact, a *union* of resistance and construction.

The actions of nonviolent movements crystallise the combination more clearly at some times than at others. When the boycott of certain products or services (for example, a brand of coffee or segregated cafés) is combined with support for alternatives (such as 'fair trade coffee' or integrated cafés), then resistance and construction intertwine. This occurred when the Sicilian nonviolent activist Danilo Dolci, 'Italy's Gandhi', and a movement of jobless people carried out a 'reverse strike'. They chose to construct a road that the region needed, despite the authorities denying that need. In the same way, MST's land occupations entail cultivating land that the organisation does not own and resisting by occupying that land while simultaneously constructing a new society through the occupation: that is, MST does not only 'occupy' in the sense of taking the land into its possession. Thus, nonviolence appears ideally as *constructive resistance*: the construction of social forms, practices and institutions that work as both alternatives and resistance to that which the struggle is against. Nonviolence combines building the new society with tearing down the old.

We therefore have a basic ideal structure for nonviolence in a rationality typology, and we have the ideal characteristics of constructive resistance. Based on this conceptual development, it is now possible to describe the basic sociological structure of nonviolence (see Figure 8.2).

The basic social structure of nonviolence The figure illustrates the basic sociological concepts that have been developed. A suggestion is presented of how the relationships between concepts may look. Since this conceptual development research has not

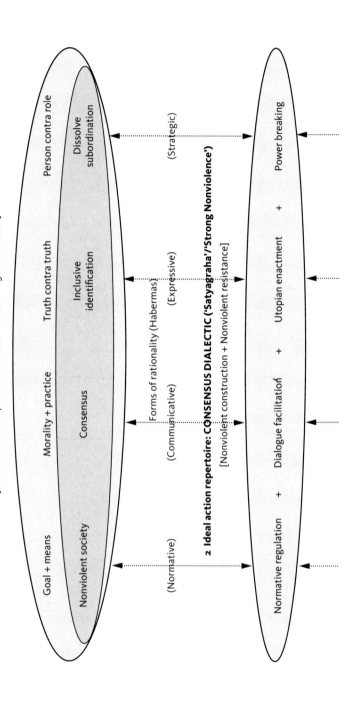

1 Utopian value system: MUTUAL TRUTH AND IDENTITY ('Satya/God')
[Nonviolence interpreted as *without violence* + *against violence*]

Goal + means	Morality + practice	Truth contra truth	Person contra role
Nonviolent society	Consensus	Inclusive identification	Dissolve subordination

(Normative)   (Communicative)   Forms of rationality (Habermas)   (Expressive)   (Strategic)

2 Ideal action repertoire: CONSENSUS DIALECTIC ('Satyagraha'/'Strong Nonviolence')
[Nonviolent construction + Nonviolent resistance]

Normative regulation	+	Dialogue facilitation	+	Utopian enactment	+	Power breaking

Common designations: 'non-', 'passive', 'civil', 'nonviolent resistance', 'nonviolent direct action'

| ('Constructive programme') | ('Truth-force') | ('Self-suffering') | ('Civil disobedience') |
| ('Community building') | ('Consensus') | ('Love force', 'Agape', 'Witness') | ('Non-cooperation') |

3 Pragmatic action repertoire: NONVIOLENT MOVEMENTS ('Weak Nonviolence')

Movements' empirical combinations of applied nonviolent discourse, organisation and action forms; necessarily articulate a pragmatic (i.e. a socially functioning) relationship of practical application to a given context, which fluctuates between two extremes:

Constructive resistance ⟷ Nonviolent paradox

Note: The figure summarises the main conceptual relationships that have been suggested to describe the social practice of non-violence. The sociological concepts of nonviolence are organised on three levels that mutually affect each other: 1) the higher values of nonviolent utopia; 2) the ideal action repertoire of nonviolence; and 3) the pragmatic action repertoire of nonviolent movements (which comprises empirically applicable versions of theoretically possible discourse, organisation and action forms). The practical expression of nonviolence involves functioning combinations of the ideals and values listed above. A 'constructive resistance' appears in those cases where practice articulates the values and ideals of nonviolence to a great extent. As practical (and unintentional) effects arise from inner tensions and contradictions, there ensues a 'paradox of nonviolence' (in various kinds of dominance relationships). '*Agape*' or selfless love is the highest term for love in Greek philosophy and is what Martin Luther King Jr uses for explaining nonviolence.

8.2 The basic social structure of nonviolence (conceptual scheme) explored empirical data, the suggested relationships between concepts are possibilities but are not established facts.

The utopian values that together describe the discursive structure of nonviolence are organised in three concrete value levels. On the first, more abstract, level, nonviolence (that is, *without violence* and *against violence*) can be described as common or universal truth and identity. This nonviolence can also be described in rather more concrete terms as a combination of nonviolent ends and means; of nonviolent morality and practice; of nonviolent (absolute) truth and (relative) truth; and as the difference between nonviolence's support for an (oppressive) individual and its resistance to the (oppressive) role. Finally, the values of nonviolence can be described even more concretely as an effort to realise both a nonviolent society and a consensus, including the identification and resolution of subordination.

Through a discussion of Habermas's ideal, typical rationality forms and the literature's previous designations of nonviolence (above all, by Gandhi and Sharp), we have arrived at four ideal types of rationality of nonviolent action (normative regulation, dialogue facilitation, utopian enactment and power breaking). As with the concepts on the other levels, these types of rationality are only analytical divisions of nonviolence, not empirical manifestations. Nonviolence must be understood as a whole made up of these four forms, even if in social practice they can be explored more or less one-dimensionally. A main conclusion of this study is that *an ideal combination of rationality types constitutes a possible sociological translation of Gandhi's nonviolent ideal: satyagraha.*

I have previously shown in an explicit historical survey of ideas how the meaning of nonviolence has varied extensively.[1] Throughout this investigation, we have seen how nonviolent methods and articulations vary in different movements. Thus, there is no reason to assume either that all nonviolent movements apply the entirety of this scheme or that some of the conceptual levels of nonviolence predominate over others.

With the aim of organising my concepts, I thus assume that nonviolence's utopian values, ideal action types and empirical repertoires affect each other reciprocally. Even if future empirical research can show otherwise, I tentatively assume that the interaction between levels means that the concrete higher values and the ideal action types that a movement discursively articulates have an effect on the organisational forms and forms of action that the movement applies, and vice versa. A movement's practical and social application of nonviolence forms experiences and interpretations which in turn reform the movement's utopian values and ideal action types.

A utopian nonviolent society in motion A concluding conceptual description of *nonviolence's ideal action repertoire* could be formulated as follows:

The action repertoire of nonviolence is designed for subordinate groups' liberation struggles that are active in conflicts characterised by organised violence or oppression.

Nonviolence is a creative combination of resistance and construction that attempts to unite ends and means, morality and practice. This is impossible to realise fully, but it is something that can be aimed and that can be achieved to the fullest extent possible.[2]

In accordance with the ideal of separating the person from what they do, all people involved (but especially 'opponents' or 'enemies') are included through constructive care, and basic needs, legitimate concerns and reasonable claims are respected at the same time as the central roles, behaviours and structures of violence or oppression are undermined.

Nonviolent resistance against oppression is achieved by the movement undermining the structures of power and depriving them of their resources, with the aim of creating a serious societal interest in dialogue among 'those in power' and to enable subordinate people to discover and develop their own capacity to act, individually and collectively, and thereby develop self-respect and empowerment.

Mistrust is counteracted by illustrating common utopian visions and ideals in practical action, despite the risk of suffering. Also enemy images and emotional distance are counteracted in order to facilitate dialogue and trust.

By fighting for sincere convictions, by being aware that truth is always relative and subjective, and especially by trying to understand and agree with those who have an opposing opinion when possible, the practice of nonviolence can try to contribute to the growth of knowledge or the construction of a mutual truth.

And, finally, through constructive work with social alternatives and normative regulation, there emerge the preconditions needed to create a legitimate and functioning order in a new society where nonviolence is socially integrated.

The action repertoire of nonviolence can thus be understood as a utopian nonviolent society in motion within – and in conflict with – a dominant and violent structure.[3]

If they are handled using nonviolent struggle, conflicts become not only necessary but even potentially positive: a means of developing society and of revealing or building truth. Thus, nonviolent activists treat conflicts as opportunities for necessary social change and learning.

§

Now we have a conceptual scheme that provides us with a tool to describe what nonviolence achieves when it works in accordance with its ideals. But we also need concepts for nonviolence when it deviates from those ideals. A critical examination of nonviolence's inbuilt contradictions, and thus its limited ability to create liberation, will provide us with several new concepts.

The ideal combinations and one-sidedness of nonviolence

One quality of nonviolence is both a strength and a weakness: *the diversity of its ambitions and articulations.* Nonviolence's inherent values, approaches, methods and rationalities comprise a diversity that can contribute to its creative dynamic but can also lead to paralysis and distortion. The strength of nonviolence is that it combines several complementary types of action, thereby increasing the possibility of handling the various dimensions of a conflict creatively. Its unique contribution is its multidimensional transformation of conflicts, attempting to achieve liberation from both violence and oppression. At the same time, the nonviolent struggle's multi-rational approach is also a problem. Nonviolence is initially difficult to grasp as the action repertoire may seem like an illogical, ineffectual and masochistic suicide strategy to the uninitiated. It is also, even for the initiated, difficult to master in practice and a complex unity with inbuilt tensions between various approaches and behaviours.

We have seen that an antagonism exists between goal-rational power breaking and the communicative facilitation of dialogue. On the one hand, a movement's activists aim to undermine the order of power on which their opponent depends; on the other, they do not want to force their opponent into an agreement but want to create a situation where both sides have an equal opportunity to argue their point, and make an understanding possible. Power breaking can be so ineffective that it does not lead to dialogue. It can also be so effective that dialogue is not needed. In a pure form, resistance and dialogue are incompatible.

However, to the extent that they are successful temporarily and in practice, and if they succeed in combining power breaking and the facilitation of dialogue, the preconditions can be created for increased dialogue and a genuine consensus between opposing parties. The strategic action in this case aims to achieve not a preconceived goal but an interest in dialogue and agreement. If a common truth is indeed the goal, then, of course, even the activists must be open to the opponent's arguments. However, this does not mean that the activists must be prepared to change their fundamental values or goals; rather, they need to be open to new ways of achieving their goals and to seek compromises on questions that are not matters of principle. If an ideal speech situation is the goal, no one should change their views without having heard an acceptable or convincing reason to do so.

The strategic action of nonviolent civil disobedience is thus not only goal rational but also (potentially) understanding-oriented. But that will only be the case if the activists try to manage the difficult combined work of dialogue facilitation and power breaking.

If the various rationality forms are combined skilfully, the action repertoire can work with creative and transformative force in a conflict. But if the combination does not work in the social context, it will be dominated by one of the action types at the expense of the others, and there will be a risk that nonviolence will lose its unique, distinctive character and will appear to be incomprehensible or (seriously) contradictory. The temptation to dedicate oneself to just one of the rationality forms is reasonably strong, as suitable combinations require extensive practical and theoretical knowledge about nonviolence, experience of previous struggles, a good analysis of the conflict and its context, and the ability to discern the (at times invisible) results of this type of social experiment. It is not at all unusual for action repertoires of nonviolence to spread to other movements in a fragmentary form. It is also not surprising that these watered-down versions have created prejudice about nonviolence.

Table 8.1 overleaf shows how nonviolence ideally utilises all the dimensions of rational action.

Every nonviolent action type unites traits of *against violence* and *without violence*. For example, the normative regulation entails struggling against the norms that support violence and oppression (for example, by breaking 'unjust' laws) and at the same time constructing norms based on *without violence* and alternatives (for example, by creating a new 'defence education' where 'soldiers' are trained in nonviolent methods). Similarly, this 'two-sidedness' characterises the other action types in the table.

The typology also helps us understand how nonviolence sometimes might be articulated one-dimensionally. Certainly, the point is that the rationalities can be applied as a measured, creatively combined whole in which each rationality is given its role in cooperation (i.e. ideal nonviolence). At the same time, this division means that the rationalities are likely to be applied in such a way that some types dominate the others. Nonviolent movements can be thought, in practice, to apply the nonviolence whole in a one-dimensional way in the sense that they highlight one of these ideal types but neglect the others. The typology provides us with at least five basic possibilities for the articulation of nonviolence. Moreover, the types of nonviolence (1–4) can be viewed as having an orientation that is either *without violence* or *against violence*, which gives us a total of nine types:

TABLE 8.1 The ideal combinations of activities of nonviolence

RATIONALITY	Normative action	Communicative action	Expressive action	Strategic action
TYPE OF NONVIOLENCE	Normative regulation	Dialogue facilitation	Utopian enactment	Power breaking
Against violence	1a. Breach of norms and deconstruction of the cultural legitimisation of violence	2a. Methods and structure against oppression in dialogue; respectful critique of the ideology of violence	3a. Exposure of injustice, oppression and falsehood	4a. Undermining of oppressive subordination and hierarchy
Without violence	1b. Further new roles and institutions' norms of without violence	2b. Development of nonviolent forms of dialogue and self-reflexive critique	3b. Exposure of justice, truth and mutually attractive visions	4b. Development of a working system without oppression

Note: The activities are analytically divided based on *against violence* and *without violence*, which in practice must be combined.

1   Normative nonviolent movements: oriented *against violence* (1a) or *without violence* (1b).

2   Dialogue-oriented nonviolent movements (2a or 2b).

3   Utopian enacting nonviolent movements (3a or 3b).

4   Power-breaking nonviolent movements (4a or 4b).

5   Consensus-oriented nonviolent movements (a combination of all types, from 1a to 4b).

Theoretical orientations and implicit values given to preferred forms of 'nonviolent action' show that Gene Sharp and his followers within the 'technique approach' limit their interest to movements of the 4a type: 'power-breaking nonviolent movements' with an *against violence* orientation. The technique approach has portrayed the field of nonviolent action studies as consisting of a conflict between its own preferred 4a type and the 'soft' pacifism of various religious, moral or spiritual versions (types 1b and 2b). My discussion has shown that the Gandhian version of nonviolent action is of a different kind altogether (type 5), one that tries to combine all the elements of the others and that seeks consensus by engaging creatively in violent conflicts. A classification of concrete nonviolent movements requires empirical investigation, something we do not have room for here. But the Civil Rights Movement was probably a consensus-oriented nonviolent movement, while Gandhi's heir, Vinoba Bhave, organised a dialogue-oriented movement. Vinoba's Bhoodhan Movement carried out no resistance against rich landowners, instead appealing to them for land for the poor.[4] They achieved a certain amount of success in the division of land but they did not resist the unjust property structure that created poverty. Thus they allowed the dialogue of mutual understanding to dominate the movement and, unlike Gandhi, they did not let resistance actions create the conditions for that understanding.

Antagonisms between the action types It is crucial to understand that there are decisive and unavoidable contradictions between the rationalities of the action types, which makes creative combinations difficult and puts them at risk of veering towards a one-sided position.[5] These contradictions can be expressed in six relational pairs, since there are separate tension between all four types of action (Figure 8.3). They all approach a conflict based on partially contradictory principles, approaches and methods.

- First, there is a tension between, on one side, power breaking's high-handed attempt to *prevent the other's* activity and to maintain *one's own truth* regardless of the reactions of

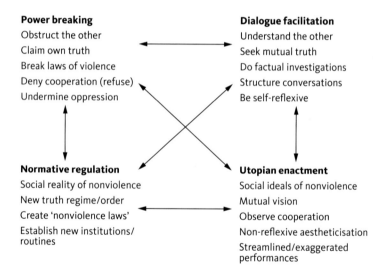

Power breaking
Obstruct the other
Claim own truth
Break laws of violence
Deny cooperation (refuse)
Undermine oppression

Dialogue facilitation
Understand the other
Seek mutual truth
Do factual investigations
Structure conversations
Be self-reflexive

Normative regulation
Social reality of nonviolence
New truth regime/order
Create 'nonviolence laws'
Establish new institutions/routines

Utopian enactment
Social ideals of nonviolence
Mutual vision
Observe cooperation
Non-reflexive aestheticisation
Streamlined/exaggerated performances

Note: There are tensions between the four action types since power breaking, dialogue facilitation and utopian enactment all have contradictory methods and activities. It is not clear whether any antagonisms are stronger than others. Overall, there is a conflict configuration with six antagonistic relational pairs. The definition of each type includes a few examples for clarification but is not exhaustive.

8.3 Antagonisms between nonviolent action types

others, and, on the other side, dialogue's attempt to find *common understanding* and *cooperation* with others. When a larger group or a key group resists in a society, by breaking laws, striking, boycotting or in other ways, the purely physical or economic influence can be so strong that even minorities with undemocratic ambitions can force a government to compromise. For example, soldiers, pilots and the police have a much greater chance of getting their demands heard by those in power if they decide to go on strike or carry out (nonviolent) resistance, due to their key position in the power system. This problem is probably also present in less extreme cases. It is difficult to know whether an agreement that is reached as a result of an encompassing nonviolent resistance is indeed a genuine agreement that expresses understanding and truth, or rather an effect of power.

- Second, there is a tension between power breaking's *undermining* of existing laws and normative regulation's *construction* of new laws and rules. Certainly, resistance occurs with reference to (the dominant) law's legitimisation of violence and oppression and construction with reference to the (new) law's protection of nonviolent ways of life. However, there is no definite way to determine whether a law or norm is securing nonviolence or not.

- Third, there is a tension between power breaking's *refusal to cooperate* with the other and the utopian representation's *vision of future cooperation and coexistence*. A nonviolent movement should specifically show the activities to which non-cooperation applies and why, but, like much else, the border becomes difficult to define and actions may appear contradictory to some people. In an occupation situation, a simple thing like a single kind conversation with the enemy can seem like treason against one's own side. So this could also be the case if selective cooperation is developed with the enemy, even if it is combined with nonviolent non-cooperation in other areas.

- Fourth, there is a tension between dialogue facilitation's *reflexive, critical and mutual examination* of truth claims and normative regulation's *assertion, institutionalisation and sanctioned protection* of a specific ('nonviolent') truth regime.

- Fifth, there is a tension between dialogue facilitation's *argumentative reflexivity of all truth claims* and the utopian enactment's *imaginary aestheticisation of a certain truth perspective* (irrespective of whether that truth/vision is mutually attractive to the parties involved).

- Finally, there is a tension between the normative regulation's practical construction of *the social reality of nonviolence* (a nonviolent society) and the utopian enactment's *idealisation of the future of nonviolence* (a nonviolent utopia). Thus the nonviolent society's realisation is necessarily incomplete while the nonviolent utopia can be depicted as complete. In the best case, the utopian vision can spur society to completely re-evaluate and develop the nonviolence it practises; in the worst case, the contrast between the two becomes a threat to be suppressed.

If we suppose that my suggested analysis and description of the sociality of nonviolence are sustainable, this means that nonviolence's action repertoire includes insoluble internal conflicts, which leads to an unintended repertoire, a kind of *paradox of nonviolence* (see Figure 8.2). Against this background, the risk of establishing a new, serious, illegitimate order of power in a nonviolent society cannot be excluded. The dilemma can be either neglected and thereby reinforced, or handled openly and thereby counteracted. But even when these antagonisms are recognised, only temporary solutions are likely. Several of the antagonisms are of a type that cannot be solved permanently; this is particularly true of the impossibility of realising the utopian values of nonviolence. These values are guiding ideals, and not realisable. At the same time, several antagonisms seem capable of being managed temporarily, to some extent and in certain situations, if the activists are sufficiently creative. For example, power breaking and dialogue facilitation can work together when a people's peaceful resistance to a dictator leads to more inclusive dialogue and democratisation through negotiated agreements.

These antagonisms do not result from an incorrect or deficient application of nonviolence. On the contrary, *the application of the values of nonviolence, in accordance with the discourse on which it is founded, leads to a range of problems*. It is when activists take the creation of the nonviolent society seriously that discipline, the truth regime and other antagonisms become acute problems that have to be resolved. Thus, if we accept the conceptual structures described thus far, yet another concept is required, something that describes how the antagonisms manage to unite – at least partially and temporarily.

Nonviolence: a consensus-dialectical interaction

If it is correct that nonviolence is comprised of the four types of rationality (temporarily) in a coordinated whole, the question is: what is capable of coordinating this whole? In other words: what makes nonviolent action possible? Even if the four types refer to separate worlds and have separate forms of rationality, this division of activity also means that any coordination must

318 | EIGHT

tackle borders, internal conflicts and tensions: quite simply, it must manage, at least temporarily, to bridge the type of contradictions that, as we have stated, characterise the rationalities of nonviolence. They cannot all be equal when deciding the activity in its entirety. *In order for nonviolence to work, an encompassing rationality must be assumed.* Some kind of guiding rationality that facilitates the coordination and management of contradictions is needed. Consensus through dialogue is the most reasonable alternative.

I propose that every nonviolent action type primarily aims to create the conditions for high-quality dialogue. Dialogue facilitation must be understood as the coordinating force, just as mutual rationality or truth (*satya*) lies at the core of nonviolence. According to our use of concepts, the promotion of understanding and consensus between conflicting parties is what (ideally) steers the application of other types of nonviolent action.

As we have seen, in Habermas, communicative rationality is similarly given a superior role as coordinator of the other rationalities. Thus, communicative rationality is the overarching rationality for both Habermas and Gandhi.

I have analysed nonviolent action under the conditions of the dystopian dialogue situation, where Habermas's ideal speech situation is challenged by violence, hatred, domination and fundamentalism.

Nonviolence makes Habermas's attempt to liberate dialogue believable, even in conflicts. Communicative rationality (mutual reason) is facilitated by the conversation's inherent *understanding orientation being freed*: freed from power (through power breaking), from lies and violence (through utopian enactment and normative regulation), from exclusion (through resistance's facilitation of dialogue), and from indifference (by holding on to the truth, furthering an interest in dialogue and not giving up – that is, 'satyagraha').

The action types of nonviolence are developed conceptually based on Habermas's action typology, while the discussion of action types is based on the conditions that prevent the ideal speech situation occurring. One should therefore be able to object that it is natural for Gandhi's 'satyagraha' to fulfil Habermas's 'ideal speech situation'. But it would be circular reasoning if one therefore believed that we have 'proven' what nonviolence 'is'.

However, it is striking how *well* Gandhi's and Habermas's concepts and reasoning fit together, a theoretical fact that gives the conceptual combination a credibility that transcends both variants of problematic idealism. Gandhi's spiritual terminology is translated with the help of contemporary sociology into a *socially practical language*, and Habermas's narrow consensus in a (Western) 'bourgeoisie public sphere' is filtered through violence's and oppression's anti-dialogue to become a *conflict language*. Together, possibilities arise for describing a social practice in conflicts that furthers (more inclusive) consensus: nonviolence.

Since my project is a conceptual and theoretical one, I have not proven anything in an empirical sense, but I have offered a new conceptual toolbox for describing and analysing what nonviolent action is all about and what nonviolent movements are doing. If this conceptual framework helps us to understand what nonviolent action is and what it does in conflicts in a more comprehensive way, it might also open up new practical and political possibilities. My conclusion is that it is entirely possible to conceptually describe nonviolence as *communicative liberation*. Nonviolence is communicatively liberating because it transforms conflicts' violence, oppression, falsehood and hate in a consensus-rational way. The goal is an ideal dialogue situation and a mutual establishment of what should be and what is true and valuable or good.

In this respect, it is important to be clear about how this communicative liberation is only the *aim* of nonviolence, its primary rationality. To aim for something and to succeed are two different things.

Nonviolence is fundamentally ambivalent. The objective of mutual truth is an ideal. The contradictions are not eradicated just because we suppose that the primary aim is to create the preconditions for an ideal dialogue. This ambivalence may, in fact, have its origin in the enforced conditions that nonviolent movements end up in when they attempt to transform all the dimensions of conflict and establish a *mutual moral truth.* The assertion of morality is in itself ambivalent:

> [There is an] *ambiguous nature of normative validity.* While there is an unequivocal relation between existing states of affairs and true propositions about them, the 'existence' or social currency of norms says nothing about whether the norms are valid.[6]

We must differentiate between *the fact* that norms exist and the question of their *justification*; however, a norm cannot exist in the long term without at least partially being legitimate (both in the specific context and in the opinion of those affected).[7] Thus, it is not surprising that the nonviolent struggle, which both breaks established norms and constructs new norms in hate-filled and power-permeated conflicts, involves conflicting actions and an ambivalent approach.

The creation of a nonviolent society reveals its contradictions. For Richard Fox, it is the combination of utopian revolution and concrete reform that creates the uniqueness of Gandhi's societal project.[8] Fox is right, but at the same time he does not follow his reasoning to its ultimate consequence. It is neither the unusual combination of radical individualism and collectivism nor the combination of utopia and reform that makes it unique. Since Gandhi tries to transgress the established dichotomies, this societal project has been described quite differently by different authors. It has been called revolutionary, progressive (gradual), populist, anarchist, socialist and totalitarian.[9] The societal project is (potentially) all these things at once, depending on how the contradictory elements *are combined and practised* by a concrete movement. What to me appears as the truly unique characteristics are precisely *the inbuilt inner contradictions*, not the fact that they are utopian or anything else. Gandhi is anti-dichotomous, to a much greater degree than commonly recognised, and seeks to transcend contradicting conceptions both in his philosophy and in his practical treatment of conflicts. It seems to be this ambition to transcend that cultivates contradictions.

The tension caused by antagonisms within nonviolence is not to be understood as something wrong, incomplete or failed in the action repertoire. Based on this perspective, one must reasonably interpret it as if the contradictions are (at least temporarily and partially) soluble, otherwise nonviolence's sociality would not be possible; rather, only certain isolated parts of the activities would be possible. Based on the same conceptual logic, one should instead interpret the contradictions as a creative tension, a dynamic that gives nonviolence its social 'force'.

Gandhi's most original contribution to political conflict theory is perhaps the claim that the means used in conflicts decide which ends can be achieved, that *ends and means are tied together* in an irresolvable way, and in practice cannot be separated.

Put succinctly, violence and oppression cannot give us peace, freedom or equality; the only way to achieve peace is through peace. This continuous whole of nonviolence as both means and ends together comprises satyagraha: that is, 'truth force', 'soul force' or 'love force'.[10] By combining the different stages at which nonviolence encompasses both means and ends, the whole comprises a 'goal-revealing' form of struggle.[11]

According to Bondurant, the main ingredients in the satyagraha struggle – nonviolence, suffering and truth-seeking – are parts of a dynamic whole. They are not additional pieces of the puzzle, but should rather be described as self-multiplying powers. Generally, one can say that the basic theoretical idea is that the combination of nonviolence and the readiness to suffer for one's truth-seeking eventually leads to success in the form of a higher degree of truth-infused agreement between parties, as well as nonviolent relationships and therefore also a reduction in suffering. This occurs (in theory) not through one's own party winning the struggle, but through the victory of mutual truth and nonviolence. The conflict is transformed into a reciprocal consensus. The agreement is based on reciprocal understanding and convincing arguments, and does not overstep the parties' partisan convictions. Thus, consensus does not comprise a compromise, but a new conviction or synthesis.

It is important to note that you *cannot separate the various attempts at managing the different dimensions of a conflict*, which is what sometimes occurs in conflict resolution theory.[12] The aspects can certainly be distinguished analytically, but they are indissolubly tied into Gandhi's conflict philosophy and practical conflict transformation in such a way that they are cooperating parts of a whole.

Since ends and means are tied together, the handling of each dimension of the conflict must also be tied together. This not only means that utopia, nonviolence and truth must be part of conflict transformation in all positions, situations and phases of that conflict; it also, and above all, means that the different approaches must be united, despite the contradictions.

According to Bondurant, satyagraha comprises *a dialectic treatment of conflicts.*[13] This nonviolent dialectic differs from Hegel's or Marx's dialectic because it does not focus on history or material relationships.

> The Gandhian dialectic, which lies in the heart of Satyagraha, is a process to be made explicit by human action, not to be found as implicit either in the nature of things or the process of time.[14]

Gandhi's dialectic should be described as an interaction of different kinds of acts where opposites temporarily unite in synthesis at higher qualitative levels. The dialectic of action affects both how social changes occur through collective action and how dialogues (speech acts) create understanding. At least a few of the immanent tensions of nonviolence essentially seem impossible to resolve, but it is assumed that it is possible to unite them in a number of temporary syntheses.

What people do in a specific situation is decisive in Gandhi's dialectic. In contrast, in Marx's or Hegel's dialectical theories, the historical development and societal relationships dictate what people can and should do. Gandhi's dialectic corresponds more closely to the Socratic dialogue, where people, through dialogue, can reach a new understanding by allowing opposing theses to meet. Thus, Gandhi's dialectic is more a question of the possibility of social construction than of something that is inherent in the regularities of history's spiritual or material development.

Marx examines the material conditions for human action while Gandhi examines the conditions for social interaction. However, they are both interested in the conditions required for human liberation.

A competing explanatory model might be that nonviolence, in a way that conforms to some kind of universal 'law' (of history, God or the universe), produces consensus between conflicting parties (if the nonviolence is implemented knowledgeably). The question is whether or not Gandhi himself would claim that. Bondurant does not ignore Gandhi's statements about non-violence's 'conformity to law'.[15] Gandhi claims the existence of a universal law that makes the actors' nonviolent actions not only morally correct but also effective in creating peace and equality.[16] In this respect, there is a certain incompatibility between predictable conformity to law and dialectical renewal. A constructive possibility of action is contradicted by the certainty of the struggle's result. Gandhi claims that: 'All society is held together by non-violence, even as the earth is held in her position by gravitation ... What is happening today is disregard of the law of non-violence.'[17] If nonviolence is a power that leads to peaceful change by automatically conforming to the universal law, then how others choose to act plays no decisive role. In other words, if only one party's (nonviolent) action matters, then the opposing party is reduced to a chess piece or an object. The conflict is therefore not a dialectic, and not even an interaction, and 'agreement' becomes purely an effect of the nonviolent method. This is a problem if the goal is *mutual* truth.

The dialectical synthesis of nonviolence is necessarily only a *possibility*, driven by a desire for mutual truth or by the orientation towards consensus that is built into a full combination of the repertoire of nonviolence. What the nonviolent struggle leads to is *an uncertain result*, even when the nonviolent action is characterised by a high degree of knowledge and skill. The other's (opponent's) will, decisions and opinion must be given space. Without the other's freedom to say no, the idea of mutual truth fails. 'Without the individual's uninfringeable freedom to respond with a "yes" or "no" to criticisable validity claims, consent is merely factual rather than truly universal.'[18]

But if, in contrast to Bondurant, we discuss how nonviolence can be described regardless of what Gandhi thought of it, there is a stronger reason why nonviolence should be described as dialectical and not (automatically) bound by law. The undeniable fact that nonviolent activism arises empirically in one form or another – combined with our lengthy theoretical exposure of a number of inherent contradictions that characterise nonviolence – motivates us to describe the action repertoire as a *temporary transgression of permanent contradictions*: that is, a dialectic.

The dialectic of nonviolence seeks synthesis between a thesis and its antithesis. The synthesis is temporary since it does not completely abolish the contradiction but instead pushes it to a new level, thereby giving it a new form. Thus the goal of the satyagraha struggle is not to defeat or persuade the opponent, but to find a synthesis between the two separate views, an agreement. On the other hand, it is about defeating the locked and violence-permeated situation together. In order to hold on to the truth, '[n]on-violent resistance must continue until persuasion has carried the conflict into mutually agreeable adjustment'.[19]

For that reason, the satyagraha struggle should be understood as *an attempt to reach agreements in conflicts through dialectical interaction*. The emphasis is on social action, new understanding, liberation from communicatively obstructive situations, and creative conflict solutions. The nonviolent dialectic is an 'intersubjective' process that can lead to mutual understanding between parties. The understanding of what is true is certainly limited to those people who are involved and who agree; however, as it transcends previous disagreements, it goes beyond borders and conflicting parties. Overstepping the bounds of what is permissible is a sign of the social validity of the conflicting partners' mutual truth. The more democratically inclusive and power-free agreements there are, and the more divided positions are transcended, the more the agreements that arise in conflicts will form a temporary guide for what (in a utopian sense) is mutually truthful.

The conceptualisation of truth as *always limited and emerging* enables new understandings at a qualitatively higher level, which come closer to the controversial ideas of 'absolute' and 'universal' truth (to the extent that we, like Habermas, are able to view truth as universally intersubjective, an agreement between all those people affected).[20] The idea of *mutual understanding* is an abolishment (albeit a temporary one) of the conflict between thesis and antithesis where a synthesis or a consensus emerges.

But the fundamental problem – for both Gandhi and Habermas – is the existential impossibility of reaching the absolute truth, and this impossibility has not been eradicated, since mutual understanding is always limited. The mutual understanding of 7 billion people is indeed an impossible utopia. When conflicts are eliminated, it is only temporary. The disunity and uncertainty arise again, in new questions or with new people, wherever fundamental thesis–antithesis positions reappear. Each time these new conflicts are transformed, the thesis–antithesis relation assumes new forms and content, and on a new level of greater inclusivity (where even more questions or even more people are included in the consensus).

The dialectic of action can be given new expression in several ways, not just in the nonviolent activists' conflicts with other parties but also within the nonviolent movement itself, through its handling of internal conflicts. In the southern states of the USA, black culture was characterised by resignation, subordination and anger at the white overlords until the period after the Second World War. A new form of action was facilitated by the Civil Rights Movement bringing about a synthesis of two conflicting traditions in the culture: the feelings of bitterness and hate against the whites because of oppression, and the learned disciplining of these aggressive impulses. Wrath against the oppressors was turned into a disciplined, holy struggle against the system of oppression through an open (and peaceful) defiance of its rules. The hate was both legitimised and made into a Christian duty, but it was aimed only at the system of rules. The whites themselves were instead the object of the Christian message of love. This combination founded a morally justified anger that became decisive in strengthening the sense of self among a people who traditionally suffered from an inferiority complex after the experience of degradation that had endured for generations.[21] A possibility and feeling of power to overcome the fear and to resist opened up.[22] Nonviolent confrontational behaviour was a unique role combination of the 'contented negro' and the 'violent negro'.[23]

The creative tension that arises from contradictions in the nonviolent action repertoire is likely to drive out both the syntheses of the consensus dialectic and the unintentional repertoire (where, for example, manipulation seems unavoidable). From a descriptive perspective, *the paradox of nonviolence* (the unintended action repertoire) becomes a logical expression for *the failure to creatively develop syntheses.*

Nonviolence, as presented here, can be summarised as *a multi-rational action repertoire's whole, and a consensus orientation that creates an interaction dialectic in conflict processes, which in turn creates opportunities for transformation and new mutual agreements.* The different rationalities of action are assumed to exist in a creative tension that cannot be completely harmonised and that merges with the aim of reaching a higher level of mutual truth. Dialogue's orientation towards understanding is liberated with the help of the gradual escalation of resistance, a readiness to negotiate and the dialectic of the other action types. Habermas's ideal speech situation is progressively approached through a nonviolent struggle that gradually tries to create the conditions for dialogue, by means of further negotiations, progressively transgressing the conflict boundaries between groups.

Of the four fundamental types of action, it is dialogue facilitation's communicative rationality that ensures that there is coordination of the others, since nonviolence's repertoire should be described as consensus-oriented and action-dialectical. Thus satyagraha or nonviolent action, in this conceptual context, is *a consensus–dialectical interaction in violent and repressive conflict situations.*

APPENDIX: THE PHILOSOPHY OF GANDHI

Arne Næss has systematised the philosophy of Gandhi in a set of norms and hypotheses (Næss 1974: 151–2), as reproduced below.

Norms and hypotheses: a survey

First-level norm

N1   Act in group struggle and act, moreover, as an autonomous person in a way conducive to long-term, universal, maximal reduction of violence.

Second-level hypotheses

H1   The character of the means used in a group struggle determines the character of the results.

H2   In a group struggle you can keep the goal-directed motivation and the ability to work effectively for the realization of the goal stronger than the destructive, violent tendencies, and the tendencies to passiveness, despondency or destruction, only by making a constructive programme part of your total campaign and by giving all phases of your struggle, as far as possible, a positive character.

H3   Short-term violence counteracts long-term universal reduction of violence.

Second-level norms

N2   Make a constructive programme part of your campaign.

N3   Never resort to violence against your opponent.

N4a Choose that personal action or attitude which most probably reduces the tendency towards violence of all parties in a struggle.

N4b Never act as a mere functionary, a representative of an institution or an underling, but always as an autonomous, fully responsible person.

Third-level hypotheses

H4   You can give a struggle a constructive character only if you
     conceive of it and carry it through as a struggle in favour of
     human beings and certain values, thus eventually fighting
     antagonisms, but not antagonists (Positive struggle).

H5   It increases your understanding of the conflict, of the parti-
     cipants, and of your own motivation, to live together with the
     participants, especially with those for whom you primarily
     fight. The most adequate form for living together is that of
     jointly doing constructive work.

H6   If you live together with those for whom you primarily struggle
     and do constructive work with them, this will create a natural
     basis for trust and confidence in you.

H7   All human beings have long-term interests in common.

H8   Cooperation on common goals reduces the chance that the
     actions and attitude of the participants in the conflict will
     become violent.

H9   You invite violence from your opponent by humiliating or
     provoking him.

H10 Thorough understanding of the relevant facts and factors
     increases the chance of a nonviolent realization of the goal of
     your campaign.

H11a Incompleteness and distortion in your description of your case
     and the plans for your struggle reduce the chance of a non-
     violent realization of the goal, and also that of future struggles.

H11b Secrecy reduces the chance of a nonviolent realization of the
     goal of your campaign.

H12 You are less likely to take a violent attitude, the better you make
     clear to yourself what are the essential points in your cause and
     your struggle.

H13 Your opponent is less likely to use violent means, the better he
     understands your conduct and your case.

H14 There is a disposition in every opponent such that whole-
     hearted, intelligent, strong, and persistent appeal in favour
     of a good cause is able ultimately to convince him (General
     convincibility).

H15 Mistrust stems from misjudgement, especially of the disposition of your opponent to answer trust with trust, mistrust with mistrust.

H16 The tendency to misjudge and misunderstand our opponent and his case in an unfavourable direction increases his and our tendency to resort to violence.

H17 You win conclusively when you turn your opponent into a believer in and active supporter of your case.

Third-level norms

N5 Fight antagonisms, not antagonists: conceive of your struggle and carry it through as a (positive) struggle in favour of human beings and certain values.

N6 Live together with those for whom you struggle and do constructive work for them.

N7 Try to formulate the essential interests which you and your opponent have in common and try to establish a cooperation with your opponent on this basis.

N8 Do not humiliate or provoke your opponent.

N9 Acquire the best possible understanding of the facts and factors relevant to the nonviolent realization of the goal of your cause.

N10 Do your utmost in order to be in full accordance with the truth in your description of individuals, groups, institutions, and circumstances relevant to the struggle (Unbiased description).

N11a Do not use secret plans or moves or keep objectives secret.

N11b Withdraw the intended victim from the wrongdoer.

N12 Announce your case and the goal of your campaign explicitly and clearly, distinguishing essentials from nonessentials.

N13 Seek personal contact with your opponent and be available to him. Bring conflicting groups into personal contact.

N14 Do not judge your opponent harder than yourself.

N15 Trust your opponent.

N16 Turn your opponent into a believer in and supporter of your case, but do not coerce him.

Fourth-level hypotheses

H18 You provoke your opponent if you deliberately or carelessly destroy his property.

H19 Adequate understanding of your opponent presupposes personal empathy.

H20 Avoidance of misjudgement and misunderstanding of your opponent and his case requires understanding him and his case.

H21 If you keep in mind your own fallibility and failures, you are less likely to exaggerate those of your opponent. Opponents are then less likely to be misjudged in an unfavourable way, and their case underestimated intellectually or morally.

H22 Every political action, your own included, is likely to be based, in part, on mistaken views, and to be carried out in an imperfect way (Universal imperfection).

H23 You make it difficult for your opponent to turn to support of your case if you are unwilling to compromise on nonessentials.

H24 It furthers the conversion of your opponent if he understands that you are sincere.

H25 The best way of convincing your opponent of your sincerity is to make sacrifices for your cause.

H26 During a campaign, change of its declared objective makes it difficult for opponents to trust your sincerity.

Fourth-level norms

N17 Do not destroy property belonging to your opponent.

N18 Cultivate personal *Einfühlung* with your opponent.

N19 Do not formulate your case and the goal of your campaign and that of your opponent in a biased way.

N20 Try to correct bias in your opponent only in so far as it is necessary for the campaign.

N21 Keep in mind and admit your own factual and normative mistakes, and look for opportunities to correct your judgements.

N22 Be always willing to compromise on nonessentials.

N23 Do not exploit a weakness in the position of your opponent.

N24 Be willing to make sacrifices and suffer for your cause.

N25 During a campaign, do not change its objective by making its goal wider or narrower.

NOTES

Introduction

1 Eyerman and Jamison (*Social Movements: A cognitive approach*, 1996: 160–6).

2 Karatnycky and Ackerman (*How Freedom is Won: From civic resistance to durable democracy*, 2005).

3 There is no data available for nonviolent action that is continuous or global in scope, when compared with similar data on, for example, non-governmental organisations. Today, however, databases are constructed using a large number of cases that will then make statistical analysis possible in the future. Specifically, there is the comprehensive database Erica Chenoweth is creating (the Nonviolent and Violent Campaigns and Outcomes (NAVCO) Data Project at the University of Denver) as well as George Lakey's Global Nonviolent Action Database at Swarthmore University in Pennsylvania. See also Vogele and Bond ('Nonviolent struggle: the contemporary practice of nonviolent action', 1997: 365 ff.); Swamy and Singh (*Against Consensus: Three years of public resistance to structural adjustment programme*, 1994). In addition, documentation exists of the historical (Sharp, *The Politics of Nonviolent Action*, 1973: Volume II) and geographical spread of nonviolence (Zunes et al., *Nonviolent Social Movements: A geographical perspective*, 1999).

4 Swamy and Singh (1994).

5 *The Nuclear Resister*, 132–3, www.serve.com/nukeresister/nr133/index.html (accessed 15 July 2005).

6 One of the best studies was made by Charles Tilly (*Social Movements 1768–2004*, 2004: in particular 58, 142–3), but Tilly does not use the term 'nonviolence'. Some research has been conducted on the society-changing role of nonviolent movements: see, in particular, Chenoweth and Stephan (*Why Civil Resistance Works*, 2011); Karatnycky and Ackerman (2005); Johansen ('Gewaltfreie erfolgreicher als bewaffneter Kampf. Neue Bedingungen für zivilen Widerstand', 2004); Schock (*Unarmed Insurrections: People power movements in nondemocracies*, 2005); Sharp (*Waging Nonviolent Struggle: 20th century practice and 21st century potential*, 2004); Zunes et al. (1999). However, it is a more complex matter to assess the degree of 'success' of nonviolent struggle: see Wehr et al. (*Justice without Violence*, 1994).

7 For general overviews, see Sharp (2004); Ackerman and Du Vall (*A Force More Powerful: A century of nonviolent conflict*, 2000).

8 Vinthagen ('Motståndets globalisering', 2002; 'Motståndet mot den nya världsordningen', 2003a).

9 Dejke (*Trädkramare inför rätta*, 1989).

10 See, for example, Chabot ('Crossing the great divide: the Gandhian repertoire's transnational diffusion to the American Civil Rights

Movement', 2003: 27–8) in reference to other authors' descriptions.

11 Bouillier ('The violence of the non-violent', 2003: 49) quoting 'the Hindu revivalist' Lajpat Raj in a statement from 1925.

12 Peterson (*Neo-Sectarianism and Rainbow Coalitions: Youth and the drama of immigration in contemporary Sweden*, 1997; *Contemporary Political Protest: Essays on political militancy*, 2001).

13 Churchill (*Pacifism as Pathology: Reflections on the role of armed struggle in North America*, 1999).

14 For a criticism of common stereotypes, see Schock ('Nonviolent action and its misconceptions: insights for social scientists', 2003).

15 Gandhi (*The Collected Works of Mahatma Gandhi*, 1999: Volume 70: 261).

16 Goss and Goss-Mayr (*The Gospel and the Struggle for Justice and Peace: Training seminar in evangelical nonviolence and methods of engaging in it*, 1990: 33), who are proponents of principled nonviolence, write that: 'Nonviolent methods are not used for pragmatic and tactical reasons, but as the consequence of a fundamental ethical attitude.' Nhat Hanh writes: 'Out of love ... techniques for a non-violent struggle arise naturally' (*Love in Action: Writings on nonviolent social change*, 1993: 39).

17 The nonviolence of the strong relates to whether they are strong in their faith, resolution and 'soul' – those who have 'stout hearts', not physical strength (Gandhi, *Gandhi for 21st Century*, 1998: Volume 4: 24, 29).

18 Burrowes (*The Strategy of Nonviolent Defense: A Gandhian approach*, 1996: 98 ff.). Burrowes describes this 'pragmatic-principled dimension' together with a 'reformist-

revolutionary dimension' as 'the Matrix of Nonviolence'. This makes him situate various nonviolence moments along axes: for example, the Palestinian Intifada during the 1980s as revolutionary pragmatism; the bus boycott in Montgomery as principled reformism; Gandhi's Salt Satyagraha as principally revolutionary, and so on.

19 Satha-Anand ('Overcoming illusory division: between nonviolence as a pragmatic strategy and a way of life', 1996).

20 Sharp (1973: 5). In *Gandhi as a Political Strategist* (Sharp 1979), he presents and analyses the strategist Gandhi in detail.

21 Satha-Anand (1996) claims that the normativity of nonviolence and its practical strategy are mixed in a form of principled pragmatism.

22 Like most concepts, pragmatism has competing definitions. Sharp uses 'pragmatic' in the sense of (amorally) technique-oriented or (instrumentally) effective. Here, 'pragmatism' refers to language and other social acts as well as its *practical use* or *consequences*. My use of concepts is inspired by the pragmatic perspective on collective learning and social change that Myles Horton and Highlander Folk School have represented since 1932. Highlander was developed based on Horton's studies of American pragmatism (John Dewey and William James) and Danish folk high schools and served as a place of retreat and an educational centre for nonviolent movements and in particular for the development of the Civil Rights Movement in the 1950s (Chabot 2003: 161 ff., 183). The principles behind Highlander's pragmatism accentuate liberal education and the social transformation of

the participants' *practical experience* and *concrete reality*, the *local traditions* of communities, *resources and self-organisation* (Morris, *The Origins of the Civil Rights Movement: Black communities organizing for change*, 1984: 143).

23 An external morality is different to a lived social morality. Social morality or ethics is both a representation inherited historically from previous generations and an accommodation to a contemporary collective's societal situation. There is no morality 'from below' without a historically sedimented morality arising from complex layers of power groups' inflicted discipline, the experience of daily life and the competing representations of the traditions of resistance.

24 Sharp (1973: 64). This definition still applies, see Sharp (2004: 547) and has even been given status in encyclopaedias. See, for example, Sharp ('Nonviolent action', 1999).

25 Vinthagen ('Ickevåldsaktion: En social praktik av motstånd och konstruktion', 2005).

26 This interpretation and conceptual analysis is distinct from but inspired by Gandhi's texts (1998: Volume 4: 40–1); see also Norenius (*Vägra leva på knä: Civilmotstånd för frigörelse och som försvar*, 1983: 62–3); Ebert (*Gewaltfreier Aufstand: Alternative Zum Bürgerkrieg*, 1983: 37). Mathai interprets Gandhi's nonviolence as 'resistance and reconstruction' (*Mahatma Gandhi's World-View*, 2000: 237). My division of nonviolence is above all a development of the one introduced by Herngren (*Handbok i Civil Olydnad*, 1990: 32–3). Similarly, Norenius argues for nonviolence *against* and *for* something (1983: 62 ff.).

27 Mathiesen (*Den dolda disciplineringen*, 1978; *Makt och motmakt*, 1982).

28 Gandhi notes the opposition's progressive reactions of ignorance, ridicule and finally punishment that then turns into victory if the movement perseveres (1999: Volume 35: 69).

29 Fox (*Gandhian Utopia: Experiments with culture*, 1989); Chabot (2003).

30 Fox (1989: 270).

31 McAdam et al. (*Dynamics of Contention*, 2001).

32 Chabot (2003); Fox (1989).

1 Nonviolent action studies

1 Chabot (2003: 152); Markovits (*The Un-Gandhian Gandhi: The life and afterlife of the Mahatma*, 2003).

2 Fox (1989); Chabot (2003).

3 Gandhi (*Non-Violence in Peace and War*, 1942: Volume 1: 107, 262, note 17); Næss (*Gandhi and Group Conflict*, 1974: 109–15, 117–20).

4 Juergensmeyer (*Gandhi's Way*, 2003); Vinthagen ('Makt och Motstånd', 2001).

5 Erik Erikson calls Gandhi a 'religious actualist' who highlights the practical realisation of the divine (*Gandhi's Truth*, 1969: 396–9). Gandhi called himself a 'practical idealist' (*För pacifister*, 1983: 25–6).

6 Gandhi (1999: Volume 32: 373).

7 Næss (*Gandhi*, 2002: 80 ff.).

8 Næss (1974: especially 151–3); Bondurant (*Conquest of Violence*, 1988 [1958]). Gandhi never tried to systematise his various theses into a cohesive theory. Both Bondurant's and Næss' work comprise valuable attempts at systematising Gandhi's reflections from his practical work with nonviolence.

9 Bondurant (1988: 32–3).

10 Gandhi (1999: Volume 49: 408–9).

11 See, for example, Holm ('Teknisk moralisme i teori for ik-kevoldsaksjon og "civilian defence"', 1978: 28). Truth is epistemological, ontological and axiological (ethical) for Gandhi (Mathai 2000: 66–7). According to Næss, it is not only epistemological and ontological, but also 'personological', 'pragmatic' and 'religious' (1974: 27–34).

12 Gandhi (1998: Volume 1: 25, 44–5; 1999: Volume 8: 120).

13 Gandhi (1998: Volume 1: 46).

14 The illusion only has an exist-ence as an illusion, not as truth about reality.

15 Næss (1974: 15, 19, 21.)

16 Næss (1974: 28, 32–3); Gandhi (*Essential Writings*, 1970: 29).

17 'In the application of satya-graha, I discovered in the earliest stages that pursuit of truth did not admit of violence being inflicted on one's opponent but that he must be weaned from error by patience and sympathy. For what appears to be truth to the one may appear to be error to the other' (Gandhi 1999: Volume 19: 206).

18 Næss (1974: 27–30, 34–5).

19 Næss (1974: 40–1).

20 Næss (2002: 61 ff., 76). Here, 'collective' is not something that is only social, but the ultimate foundation of existence, 'cosmos' or *Brahman*.

21 Næss (1974: 44–7, 53).

22 Næss (1974: 48).

23 Gandhi (1942: 258).

24 Gandhi thought humanity was a whole, indivisible (*advaita*) (Mathai 2000: 267).

25 Næss (1974: 93–6); also see Bondurant (1988: 23–4).

26 Gandhi (1999: Volume 21: 135).

27 Bondurant (1988: 38–41). Gandhi himself uses the concept 'satyagraha campaign' (see 1999: Volume 8: *passim*).

28 The formulation comes from Shridharani, according to Bondurant (1988: 34).

29 Gandhi (1970: 29, 38).

30 Bondurant (1988: 42–3).

31 Ostergaard ('Liberation and development: Gandhian and pacifist perspectives', 1986: 149).

32 Næss (2002: 91).

33 Gandhi (*Constructive Pro-gramme: Its meaning and place*, 1945).

34 Previously the anti-colonial struggle had been formulated by the educated, urban classes, which led to the movement being based on a small elite without a footing among the people.

35 See, for example, Karn (*Science of Satyagraha*, 1994: 162, 241).

36 Martin ('Assessing the Gulf peace team', 1991).

37 This is accomplished through risk-filled 'utopian enactment', whereby activists deliberately contra-dict the enemy's image of them (see Chapter 6).

38 The steps proceed in this order: 1) negotiation and arbitration, where you begin by trying to solve the conflict through established channels; 2) preparations for civil disobedience; 3) agitation (mass meetings, demonstrations, etc.); 4) giving ultimatums (with explana-tions of the issue and campaign strategy, constructive suggestions for a solution, and efforts to prevent the opponent from being humiliated); 5) economic boycott and strike; 6) non-cooperation; 7) civil disobedi-ence; 8) taking over the regime's functions by establishing new competing institutions; and 9) parallel

government (which develops from stage 8).

39 Fox (1989); Chabot (2003).

40 Martin Luther King Jr instead speaks in terms of aspects of non-violent struggle: 'somebodyness', 'group identity', 'full and constructive use of the freedom we already have', 'powerful action programs', 'a continuing job of organization', and 'giving society a new sense of values' (Moses, *Revolution of Conscience*, 1997: 168 ff.).

41 Hardiman (*Gandhi in His Time and Ours*, 2003).

42 'Act in group struggle and act, moreover, as an autonomous person in a way conducive to long-term, universal, maximal reduction of violence' (Næss 1974: 60). The starting point is in itself a conclusion from the previous systematisation of Gandhi's metaphysics (1974: 52–3) but it can be treated as the only norm that the above system of action is based upon. Thus, N1 can be seen as a kind of 'axiom'.

43 'Gandhian thought corpus is constructed as a *weltanschauung*, a world-view, and not a systematic or scientific philosophy' (Mathai 2000: 266). Additionally, he changed his viewpoint several times during his life. The majority of what he wrote is composed of letters and articles that, based on concrete cases, discuss the principles of nonviolence. The complete material totals about 50,000 pages.

44 Gandhi (1983: 23–4).

45 Coy ('Whither nonviolent studies', 2013); Martin ('Researching nonviolent action', 2005); Schock ('The practice and study of civil resistance', 2013).

46 Ostergaard (1986: 154).

47 According to Bergfeldt ('Expe-riences of civilian resistance: the case of Denmark 1940–1945', 1993: 29).

48 Gregg (1935: 68–102).

49 Hare and Blumberg (*Non-violent Direct Action*, 1968) and Sharp (*Exploring Nonviolent Alternatives*, 1971) are representative examples for their time.

50 Sharp (*Gandhi Wields the Weapon of Moral Power*, 1960; 1973; 1979; *Social Power and Political Freedom*, 1980). The designation 'The Machiavelli of nonviolence' has been given by William B. Watson from MIT (Massachusetts Institute of Techno-logy) and is reproduced on the cover of Sharp (1973: Volume 1).

51 Sharp (1973: 7–8).

52 Sharp (1973: 7 ff.).

53 Sharp (1973: 9).

54 Sharp (1973: 8); Liddell-Hart (*Deterrence or Defence*, 1960).

55 Sharp (1973: 25 ff.).

56 Sharp (1973: 28).

57 This is why it is unfortunate that the ability to endure the 'suffer-ing' of the punishment is emphasised by Gandhi and many of his followers. I instead focus on risk taking in the representation of appealing utopias in Chapter 6, where the risk of pun-ishment strengthens the dramatisa-tion of the utopia.

58 Ajangiz ('Conscientious objec-tion in Spain', 1997).

59 At that point the movement, over seven years, had mobilised 12,000 total resisters and 330,000 conscientious objectors and the non-combatant services were practically non-existent due to the organisation's boycotts. The minister of defence claimed that the activists 'are pushing the Armed Forces into a dead end street' (Ajangiz, 'Conscientious objec-tion as manifestation of the conflict between society and (the military

dimension) of the state', n.d.). Spain distinguishes itself from France, for example, where compulsory military service was abolished because of the government's own interests (Ajangiz, 'Empowerment for demilitarisation: civil disobedience gets rid of conscription (Spain 1985–2000)', 2001; 'The European farewell to conscription', 2002). Interestingly, the mobilisation of nonviolent actions collapsed when compulsory military service (and thereby the punishment) were abolished.

60 Arendt (*Crisis of the Republic*, 1972: 141).

61 Sharp (1980: 158).

62 Sharp (1980: 190).

63 Sharp (1980: 23–4).

64 Sharp (1973: 10).

65 Burrowes (1996: 83–96). Bergfeldt even shows that conflict based on 'territorial control, especially of sparsely inhabited areas, is much less dependent on popular cooperation' (1993: 358).

66 Burrowes (1996: 96).

67 Sharp (1973: 11–12).

68 This perspective deviates from Max Weber's classical analysis in which the charismatic personality's authority depends on their own 'personal strength' (*From Max Weber: Essays in sociology*, 1974: 248–9).

69 Sharp (1973: 109–445).

70 Ackerman and Kruegler (*Strategic Nonviolent Conflict: The dynamics of people power in the twentieth century*, 1994); Helvey (*On Strategic Nonviolent Conflict: Thinking about the fundamentals*, 2004).

71 McCarthy and Sharp (*Nonviolent Action: A research guide*, 1997). They distinguish between 'nonviolence' and 'nonviolent action', where nonviolence entails morals or principles about violence being

wrong, while their stress on action involves using nonviolence for 'pragmatic' reasons and highlights its effectiveness in a power struggle (Helvey 2004: especially 25 ff., 148).

72 Helvey (2004: 93).

73 Sometimes research that arises from the technique approach has more nuance. One of the most sophisticated attempts at measuring effectiveness in the technique approach can be found in Wehr et al. (1994).

74 For the entire list, see www. peacemagazine.org/198.htm.

75 Helvey (2004: 77).

76 Helvey (2004: 77 ff.).

77 Sharp (1973: II).

78 Even for adherents of the technique approach, the list is difficult to use in certain contexts (see Bergfeldt 1993: 348–9).

79 See Bergfeldt (1993: 350) for an interpretation that merges Sharp and Boserup and Mack (*War without Weapons*, 1974).

80 See also Sommer ('Bringing nonviolence back into the study of contentious politics', 2000) and the more encompassing studies of Chabot (2003) and Schock (2005). The same situation applies in revolution studies, with a few exceptions, such as Chenoweth and Stephan (2011) and Erickson-Nepstad (*Nonviolent Revolutions: Civil resistance in the late 20th century*, 2011). However, the 'Arab Spring' will probably stimulate more nonviolence perspectives on revolutionary processes in the future.

81 Schock (2005: xviii).

82 See, for example, the cultural anthropologist Fox (1989) or the movement sociologist Chabot (2003).

83 Shah (*Social Movements in India: A review of the literature*, 2004: 148–9). Gandhi gained decisive im-

portance by legitimising the women's movement after liberation. Also see Kapadia ('A tribute to Mahatma Gandhi: his views on women and social change', 1995).

84 Meyerding ('Women and nonviolent action in the United States since 1950', 1997: 569 ff.); Woehrle ('Feminism', 1997: 180 ff.).

85 Steger (*Gandhi's Dilemma: Nonviolent principles and nationalist power*, 2000).

86 Crowell (*The SEWA Movement and Rural Development: The Banaskantha and Kutch experience*, 2003: 3, 189 ff.); Meyerding ('Reclaiming nonviolence: some thoughts for feminist womyn who used to be nonviolent, and vice versa', 1982: 10–11).

87 McAllister (*Reweaving the Web of Life: Feminism and nonviolence*, 1982; *You Can't Kill the Spirit*, 1988; *This River of Courage: Generations of women's resistance and action*, 1991).

88 Feminism and Nonviolence Study Group (*Piecing It Together: Feminism and nonviolence*, 1983: 26, italics added).

89 Feminism and Nonviolence Study Group (1983: 26); also see Cook and Kirk (*Greenham Women Everywhere: Dreams, ideas, and actions from the women's peace movement*, 1983, especially 163–79); Jones (*Keeping the Peace: Women's peace handbook 1*, 1983).

90 Feminism and Nonviolence Study Group (1983: 27).

91 McAllister (1982: iii).

92 Rigby (*Living the Intifada*, 1991).

93 McAllister (1982: Introduction).

94 Meyerding (1982: 10).

95 See McAllister in Women's Encampment for a Future of Peace & Justice (*Seneca Army Depot, NY: Resource handbook*, 1983: 34–5).

96 Summers-Effler ('The micro potential for social change: emotion, consciousness, and social movement formation', 2002).

97 Feminism and Nonviolence Study Group (1983); McAllister (1982).

98 Bala ('Why performance studies should be interested in nonviolent action', 2004).

99 Martin (2005: Part 2).

100 The deciding criterion for finding relevant examples of nonviolent action among the many movements and collective actions that exist is that the movement conducts actions of resistance of some kind and acts peacefully (regardless of the concepts underpinning their peaceful action) and has an explicit motivation for its action (see Chapter 3). Even if movements use violence on certain occasions, they are not automatically excluded if their strategy is based on nonviolence. The classic example of a nonviolent movement, the Indian liberation movement, encompassed repeated and serious incidents of violence, for instance when police stations were burned down. There is a problematic idealisation that ignores both the nationalists' violence in the Indian struggle (see Sahmat, *Indian People in the Struggle for Freedom: Five essays*, 1998) and the actual use of nonviolent methods in movements that do not identify themselves as 'nonviolent' (for example, the MST or the first Palestinian Intifada). When nonviolence is identified, the method of selection is historical, thematic and geographical, with the aim of securing a sufficient variation of cases to make a general conceptual development possible. The choice of movements is consciously both focused on and open to the existing variations of the meaning of 'nonviolence'.

101 King (*Vi kan inte vänta*, 1964).

102 'Black Power' grew directly out of the Civil Rights Movement. Stokely Carmichael, who launched the concept in 1966, became one of the founders of the Black Power movement and originally came – like many others – from the Civil Rights Movement's student organisation, the SNCC (Chabot 2003: 217–18).

103 On the struggle for independence, see Chandra (*India's Struggle for Independence*, 1989).

104 Description taken from the Swedish National Encyclopaedia ('Kongresspartiet' in *Nationalencyklopedin*).

105 The campaign was interrupted by Gandhi as incidents of violence broke out that were not in accordance with the campaign's guidelines.

106 Gandhi participated in a number of other lesser campaigns, for example with farmers in Kheda (who wanted fee reductions after crop failures) and in Champaran (against exploitation by landowners) and with textile labourers in Ahmedabad (Chabot 2003: 47).

107 Branford and Rocha (*Cutting the Wire: The story of the landless movement in Brazil*, 2002) and www.mstbrazil.org.

108 Stedile ('Landless battalions: the Sem Terra Movement of Brazil', 2002).

109 Catholic liberation theologists, among others, have characterised the peaceful methods of resistance as peaceable politics (Branford and Rocha 2002: 3 ff.). But, like other liberation theology in Latin America, it is not strictly nonviolent; however, even an armed struggle for liberation can be motivated by the theology. Thus, it is reasonable to interpret MST as pragmatically nonviolent. Principles and practical benefit are mixed in what theoretically may not be an entirely consistent way. The movement as a whole is classified as nonviolent as the activists, as shown by experience, view nonviolence as more meaningful, effective and suitable for their situation.

110 Awad and Scott Kennedy (*Nonviolent Struggle in the Middle East*, 1985); Zunes et al. (1999).

111 Dajani ('Nonviolent resistance in the occupied territories: a critical re-evaluation', 1999: 63).

112 Anderson and Larmore (*Nonviolent Struggle and Social Defence*, 1991: 30 ff.); Zunes et al. (1999: 47).

113 Anderson and Larmore (1991: 33).

114 However, the Intifada can be seen as a 'failure for nonviolence' (Rigby, 'The possibilities and limitations of nonviolence: the Palestinian Intifada 1987–1991', 2002).

115 Dajani (1999).

116 DAC worked in a similar way for the Committee of 100 as the Congress of Racial Equality (CORE) did for the Civil Rights Movement in the USA: a small group of nonviolent activists and trainers who, through long experience, studies and small-scale experiments with methods and techniques, could offer the necessary competence when a people's movement took off (Chabot 2003; Taylor, *Against the Bomb: The British Peace Movement 1958–1965*, 1988).

117 Wittner (*The Struggle Against the Bomb. Volume 2: Resisting the bomb: a history of the world nuclear disarmament movement 1945–1970*, 1997: 187).

118 Wittner (1997: 188–9).

119 Kuper (*Passive Resistance in South Africa*, 1960).

120 Holland (*The Struggle: A history of the African National Congress*, 1989: 81).

121 During the 1980s, the South African and international anti-apartheid movement mainly adopted peaceful demonstrations (see, for example, Holland 1989).

122 Meli (*A History of the ANC: South Africa belongs to us*, 1988: Chapter 5). In 1952, 8,000 activists were arrested and, together with boycotts, strikes and other actions, the campaign's civil disobedience constituted a radicalisation of the anti-apartheid struggle (Mbeki, *The Struggle for Liberation in South Africa: A short history*, 1992: Chapter 7).

123 Gandhi and the South African Indians influenced the ANC from 1906 by launching nonviolent disobedience. Women, who initially were not welcomed by the ANC, became influential from 1913 and 1918 as a result of the anti-pass campaign. As of 1921, the communists influenced the ANC through their radical politics, cooperation with 'races' and the unionised struggle.

124 This is according to a member of the Augsburg group, which is still active in the Graswurzelrevolution (Hertle, '... und sie bewegt sich doch!', 1974: 1–2).

125 Text from the information folder about Graswurzelrevolution that the office Graswurzel Werkstatt GWW sent out during the 1990s (Vinthagen, 'En direktdemokratisk organisations historia: En undersökningsrapport utifrån en studie av tyska Graswurzelrörelsen och dess organisation Graswurzelrevolution, Föderation Gewaltfreier Aktionsgruppen (FöGA)', 1997b).

126 During the 1980s and 1990s, the cooperation worked through a federation (FöGA) that introduced both formalised membership criteria and rules for arbitration (Vinthagen,

'Direktdemokratins svårigheter: En studie av den tyska Graswurzelrörelsen och dess organisation Graswurzelrevolution, Föderation Gewaltfreier Aktionsgruppen (FöGA)', 1997a; 1997b).

127 Vinthagen (1997b: Chapters on 'Graswurzelrevolution – starten' and 'Organisationens politiska aktiviteter').

128 Nick et al. (*Mutlangen 1983–1987: Die Stationierung der Pershing II und die Kampagne Ziviler Ungehorsam bis zur Abrüstung*, 1993); Olsen (*Wir Treten in den Un-Ruhestand: Dokumentation der 1 Seniorenblockade Mutlangen 8 bis 10 Mai 1986*, 1986).

2 The concept of nonviolence

1 Vinthagen (2005).

2 Logically, this includes the forerunners of the nonviolent movement (Buddhism, Anabaptism, Quakers, Diggers, Thoreau, Tolstoy and others) and representatives (Ballou and Gandhi) of the tradition of 'utopian movements' (Hollis, *The ABC-CLIO World History Companion to Utopian Movements*, 1998).

3 Nhat Hanh (*Creating True Peace: Ending violence in yourself, your family, your community, and the world*, 2003: 65).

4 For comparison, see the movement researcher Håkan Thörn's 'future-oriented action' as characteristic for a utopian movement (*Rörelser i det moderna: Politik, Modernitet och kollektiv identitet i Europa 1789–1989*, 1997b: 48).

5 Several concepts seem to be relevant: non-resistance, passive resistance, *ahimsa*, direct action, civil disobedience and satyagraha, among others.

6 The centre founded by Marshall Rosenberg tries to monopolise

'nonviolent communication' as part of its 'service mark' of CNVC (the Center for Nonviolent Communication): see www.cnvc.org. CNVC is against violence to such a degree that it even disregards criticism or condemnations of violence. As a conglomeration of nation states, the UN can, with difficulty, recommend resistance that breaks national laws. Despite that, the UN has declared 2001–10 to be the International Decade for a Culture of Peace and Non-violence for the Children of the World: see www3.unesco.org/iycp/.

7 See Næss (1974: 115). It cannot, as some believe, be nonviolent to kill just because the intention is nonviolent (cf. Nagler, 'Nonviolence', 1986: 74).

8 Different movements naturally have different understandings of the essential meaning of violence and oppression and they direct their resistance at different things. Nonviolent resistance is characterised by breaking *power relations* (see Chapter 5) and need not break norms or laws – it is not the same thing as civil disobedience, even if resistance against hegemonic violence and oppression systems is usually illegal. Methods for undermining power can even, at least partially and theoretically, be legal, since *not all moments* in the organisation of acts of resistance need be illegal and since the resistance to violence and oppression is *a form of resistance regardless of what the law says*, even if there is no legislative regime or if the organisation of those in power is illegal (for example, in a collapsed state characterised by rival, private armies or a 'liberated' area where another organisation 'writes revolutionary laws').

9 Women's Encampment for a Future of Peace & Justice (1983: 34) instead suggests 'radical and uncompromising action' or 'truth force'.

10 Herngren (1990: 32).

11 See, for example, Goss and Goss-Mayr (1990: 22–3).

12 Johan Galtung ('Violence, peace and peace research', 1969) launched the concept of 'structural violence', inspired by Gandhi's argument that 'exploitation' was the essence of violence. This has been expounded with the help of the concept of 'cultural violence' and other means ('Cultural violence', 1990), which in itself is not really violence but cultural *legitimation* of (direct or structural) violence (*Peace by Peaceful Means: Peace and conflict, development and civilization*, 1996: 196).

13 Mabee (*Black Freedom: The nonviolent abolitionists from 1830 through the Civil War*, 1970: 67).

14 Galtung (*On the Meaning of Nonviolence*, 1965; 1996) applies 'nonviolence' and 'violence' based on their resultant type of positive or negative *influence*, and describes an endless domain of varied influence. In a similar way as in Gandhi's '*himsa*' (to *hinder* self-realisation or to injure), all negative influence constitutes violence. In a corresponding manner, I have a type categorisation based on what is carried out (*without violence* or *against violence*) and an endless *social* domain (Figure 2.3).

15 If nonviolent activists include animals in their commitment, as several known proponents of nonviolence have claimed (such as Tolstoy and Gandhi), the moral requirements then become more dizzying.

16 As I focus on the sociality of nonviolence, only the social domain is relevant, despite Gandhi and other advocates of nonviolence seeing

nonviolence in relation to 'the universe' or all living beings (animals and plants, or simply 'Mother Earth').

17 The question remains about *which* domain of violence is to be counted. Even if you see humanity as a whole, as belonging to the 'we', you can view the various forms of violence in quite a limited way – as only about killing, for example.

18 In order to talk of 'maximal nonviolence', we could also argue for the need for a dimension of time. In a simple model of time, violence can be placed as *history* (violence already carried out), *present* (violence occurring now) and *future* (violence that might arise). In this case, maximal nonviolence would try to manage violence in all three timeframes. Historical violence cannot be undone, but through healthcare, therapy, organisational work and reconciliation, the effects of violence that has already occurred can be minimised after the fact. Violence of the present – and to some extent the future – is my focus in this context.

19 But to be counted as nonviolence, both *without violence* and *against violence* must be included in some kind of meaningful combination.

20 If a nonviolent movement sees 'the enemy' as a part of the social domain ('we'), it does not necessarily mean that you feel friendship, love or unity. However, it does mean that the nonviolent struggle's *without violence* and *against violence* encompass all these people, and that the violence occurring in the social domain comprises a common problem to be dealt with.

21 Other boundaries may be suitable in other contexts: for example, other definitions of 'nonviolence',

'violence' and 'we' could be necessary if one were to research various types of Gandhian nonviolent movements.

22 Giddens (*Sociologi*, 1994: 162–3). 'The essence of nonviolent resistance is unaccustomed non-conformity' (Seifert, *Conquest by Suffering: The process and prospects of nonviolent resistance*, 1965: 184).

23 It is important to understand that actions are not independent units of events with a clear end or beginning (naïve realism's perception of action), but rather are a flow of unceasing actions that transition into analytically inseparable phases in which 'non-action' in an absolute sense is impossible as long as one still lives (see Chapter 3; Mortensen, 'Den amerikanska pragmatismen', 2003). 'Passivity' – i.e. choosing to *not* act in a given situation – is a behaviour on the same level as 'activity'. Both phenomena express different variations of a behavioural pattern that can, in different groups and situations, be normatively sanctioned or not.

24 A different and common definition is 'to intentionally break the law to protest against injustices' (Hugo Adam Bedau's chapter 'Civil disobedience' in Powers and Vogele, *Protest, Power, and Change: An encyclopedia of nonviolent action from ACT-UP to women's suffrage*, 1997: 83). Compare with other definitions in Herngren (*Civil Olydnad: En dialog*, 1999); Rawls (*A Theory of Justice*, 1971). Sharp (1973); Smith and Deutsch (*Political Obligation and Civil Disobedience: Readings*, 1972). See also the appendix in Månsson (*Olydnad: Civil olydnad som demokratiskt problem*, 2004), in which a number of different definitions from the literature are provided. Note that here civil disobedience is used according to

a Gandhian tradition in which personal (public) responsibility and nonviolence are incorporated: 'We must,
therefore, give its full, and therefore,
greater value to the adjective "civil"
than to "disobedience". Disobedience
without civility, discipline, discrimination, non-violence, is certain destruction. Disobedience combined with
love is the living water of life' (Gandhi
1998: Volume 4: 52–3).

25 It is unusual for activists to be
acquitted in court but it happens regularly. See, for example Angie Zelter
(*Trident on Trial: The case for people's
disarmament*, 2001), who was acquitted in both England and Scotland, or
Peace News 2463–4, July–August 2005,
p. 3, which reports on two acquitted
environmental activists in Australia.

26 Rigby ('Be practical, do the
impossible: the politics of everyday
life', 1986: 94).

27 Rigby (*Alternative Realities: A
study of communes and their members*,
1974; 1986) and Gugel (*Gewaltfreiheit:
Ein Lebensprinzip: Materialen 6*, 1983)
discuss nonviolent ways of life in relation to several aspects and describe
different way-of-life projects within
the movement. See above all Rigby
(1974: 21–2, 32–3) and the criticism
of the escape from responsibility in
alternative ways of life: that is, people
living in an alternative way but not acting nonviolently and in solidarity with
the rest of society (Rigby 1974: 39–42).

28 Rigby (1986: 90–1).

29 Goss-Mayr et al. (*De fattigas
gåva till de rika: Om ickevåldskamp i
Latinamerika*, 1979); Mathai (2000:
120 ff.) on vows; O'Gorman (*Base
Communities in Brazil: Dynamics of a
journey*, 1983) on 'community'; Rigby
(1974; 1986); Rawlinson (*Communities
of Resistance: Nuclear and chemical
pollution cross frontiers and so did the

protesters of the Upper Rhine*, 1986)
on 'communities of resistance'; Tracy
(*Direct Action: Radical pacifism from the
Union Eight to the Chicago Seven*, 1996:
76–81) on 'intentional community'.

30 Goss and Goss-Mayr (1990: 33).

31 Goals, means, morality and
practice typically tend to meld
together in nonviolence. Næss
describes Gandhi's conflict theory as
both pragmatic and moral (1974: particularly 15, 19, 21). See also Bondurant
(1988: 34).

32 Sit-ins were popularised in
1936–37 when 200,000 workers, first
at Goodyear Tire in Akron, Ohio, and
then later in several General Motors
factories, were organised by the nonviolent and labour movement activist
A. J. Muste (Cooney and Michalowski,
The Power of the People, 1977: 69–70,
138–9).

33 McKay (*Training for Nonviolent
Action for High School Students: A
handbook*, 1971: 12).

34 Violence from whites during
the Freedom Summer of 1964 was
a contributing factor in several
students deciding to recommend
violence and their organisation, the
SNCC, abandoning the discipline of
nonviolence (see McAdam, *Freedom
Summer*, 1988: 122–3).

35 Sharp (1973: 559–60).

36 Næss (1974: especially 151–3).
The argument can be compared with
the difference in classic social psychological theory between individuals
and their roles in structured contexts.
Even recent theorisation is relevant.
Both Goffman (for example) and
post-structural theory criticise the
belief that there is something 'true'
behind the mask of roles or socially
constructed identities. The notion of
the autonomous and unified 'subject'
has been powerfully criticised and

many have instead argued for a frag-
mented, multiple and shifting subject.
This perspective questions nonviolent
movements in new ways but also
reveals new openings. No one – not
the nonviolent activist nor the 'oppressor' – is unified or unambiguous.
Many incongruous aspects of the
same person can be engaged, and
therefore there are also possibilities
of meeting across group borders and
enemy lines.

37 Klaus Bögniel (now Engell-
Nielsen), Per Herngren and Stellan
Vinthagen coined and developed the
term 'Power-breaking and dialogue-
facilitation conflict management' in
1997.

38 This is a selection from
Bondurant (1988), Gandhi (1970),
Næss (1974) and Sharp (1979). See the
Appendix.

39 Pelton (*The Psychology of
Nonviolence*, 1974: 212).

40 Pelton (1974: 212–19). See also
Juergensmeyer (2003: 38–9). It is a
matter of putting one's immediate
fate partially in the hands of the
opponent. If this act is to create faith,
even in a relationship characterised
by distrust, risk taking is required.
See the 'GRIT' method discussed by
Osgood (*An Alternative to War or Surrender*, 1962); this involves a gradual
reduction in tension using step-by-
step de-escalation, in which you have
to act first as a good example and
to show trust in the disarmament
negotiations.

41 Winther Jörgensen and Phillips
(*Diskursanalys som teori och metod*,
1999: 7).

42 Foucault (*The Archaeology
of Knowledge & The Discourse on
Language*, 1972: 31 ff.). Foucault claims
that discursive formations are practical rules that can make 'statements'

relate *within* a discourse and *with*
'non-discursive' behaviour. See also
Jaworski and Coupland (*The Discourse
Reader*, 1999: 3).

43 Gandhi (1999: Volume 37: 228,
300, 324, referring to Hindu texts). In
a fundamental sense we are *already*
one with *Brahman*, but the haze of
the illusion stops us from seeing
that. Through our self-realisation, we
individually or collectively become
aware of this and live in harmony
with God. For Gandhi, the path to this
realisation came through karma yoga
and correct action – and therefore
nonviolence.

44 The discourse's degree of orientation towards consensus or power
is discussed in relation to the action
repertoire in its totality in Chapter 8.

3 The rationality of nonviolent action

1 Here, Sharp reasons in accordance with authors writing about
nonviolence (see, for example, Moyer,
*The Practical Strategist: Movement
action plan (MAP) strategic theories
for evaluating, planning, and conducting social movements*, 1990) and the
previously dominant movement
theory in North America, the resource
mobilisation school that emphasises
strategy, rational self-interest and the
economic use of resources (see, for
example, Zald and McCarthy, *Social
Movements in an Organizational Society: Collected essays*, 1994; McCarthy
and Zald, 'Social movement industries:
competition and cooperation among
movement organizations', 1980). For
criticism of this theory of movements,
see Melucci (*Nomads of the Present*,
1989: *Challenging codes: Collective
action in the information age*, 1996a).

2 Habermas (*Kommunikativt
handlande*, 1988: 176, italics added).

3 Alexander and Wiley, 'Situated activity and identity formation', in Rosenberg and Turner (*Social Psychology: Sociological perspectives*, 1990: 272–6).

4 Österberg (*Metasociologisk essä*, 1986).

5 This view of the meaning of actions is inspired by Paul Ricoeur's hermeneutics (*Från text till handling*, 1993: 78–89, 179–81) and Habermas's theory of communication (1988: 175–7, 189, 200), as well as Blumer's symbolic interactionism (*Symbolic Interactionism: Perspective and method*, 1969: 101–13).

6 I mean that this condition applies to disobedience in the same way as it applies to power. In a corresponding manner, power must tie into traditions (Machiavelli, *Fursten*, 2003: 10–11) or people's expectations (Bloch, *Prey into Hunter: The politics of religious experience*, 1992: 79 ff.).

7 Klandermans and Tarrow ('Mobilization into social movements: synthesizing European and American approaches', 1988).

8 Habermas (*The Theory of Communicative Action: Reason and the rationalization of society*, 1984).

9 The foremost source illustrating this example is Nick et al. (1993).

10 Nick et al. (1993: 130, translated from the German).

11 Ricoeur (*The Conflict of Interpretations: Essays in hermeneutics*, 1974: 12).

12 Herngren (1999: 135 ff.).

13 Michael A. Hogg states: 'Social identity theory maintains that social identity phenomena (i.e., group and intergroup phenomena) cannot be reduced to or explained in terms of personal identity' (in Manstead and Hewstone, *The Blackwell Encyclopedia of Social Psychology*, 1999: 555).

14 Johansson ('La mujer sufrida: the suffering woman', 1999: 74). The opposite perspective is founded on 'essence' and uses references to static images of culture, kinship, race and historical origin.

15 '*Value-rationally* – through conscious belief in the (ethical, aesthetic, religious or however interpreted) unconditional, *intrinsic* value of a certain mode of behaviour, purely as such and independently of success' (Habermas 1984: 281).

16 Ricoeur (1993: 77, 59).

17 The identity concept risks reducing everything the movement claims in a communication to a question of 'Who are we?' (see, for example, Melucci, *The Playing Self: Person and meaning in the planetary society*, 1996b: 51–2, 100). For a critique of Melucci's reductionism of communication to identity, see Vinthagen (*Symboler i rörelse: Om sociala rörelser som tilltal*, 1997c).

18 Ricoeur ('The model of the text: meaningful action considered as a text', 1981). Naturally, even the acting agent can become a reader of 'their' action, but as one reader among others, not as a 'prime agent' with a privileged right of interpretation.

19 Blumer (1969: 8).

20 Smelser (*Sociology*, 1995: 86–8).

21 Blumer (1969: 12, 111); Giddens (1994: 219).

22 Stryker (*Symbolic Interactionism: A social structural version*, 1980: 65–7). Also see Maines ('In search of mesostructure: studies in the negotiated order', 1982: 267–79).

23 According to symbolic interactionism, society is a web of communication (see Manstead and Hewstone, 1999: 648).

24 Habermas (1988: 77 ff.).

25 Understanding is *weak* while consensus or agreement is a *strong* form of communicative action (Habermas 1998: Chapter 7). This is similar to Gandhi's discussion about strong and weak nonviolence.

26 Life worlds provide the *context* for the process of understanding and the *resources* – in terms of 'a storehouse of unquestioned cultural givens' – which make understanding possible (Habermas, *Moral Consciousness and Communicative Action*, 1996: 135; 1998: 335).

27 Habermas (1984: 319–28; 1988: 175–203; *The Theory of Communicative Action: Lifeworld and the system: a critique of functionalist reason*, 1989: 62–76; *On the Pragmatics of Communication*, 1998: 7–8, 122). The pure 'speech act' is an 'illocutionary act' where real consequences arise through speech: 'making statements, asking questions, issuing commands, giving reports, greeting, and warning' (Searle, 'What is a speech act?', 1996: 263).

28 See Habermas (1988: 177 ff.).

29 Habermas (*Moral Consciousness and Communicative Action*, 1990: 43 ff.). See also Apel (*Etik och kommunikation*, 1990).

30 Vinthagen (1997c).

31 The four basic types of action are summarised in Habermas (1988: 168) and communicative action is developed (1988: 175–203). For Habermas's discussion of Weber's theory of social action, see Habermas (1984: 279–86; 1988: 149–74). Habermas claims that Weber adopts the goal-rational action as a reference point in his analysis and misses the communicative action. Weber distinguishes between goal-rational, value-rational, affectual and traditional actions,

which are rational on a decreasing scale (based on goal-rational actions as the norm for 'rationality'). Interestingly, Foucault uses a similar categorisation of four human 'technologies' ('Technologies of the self', 1998: 18).

32 Habermas (1984: 22–3). Bodily movements are included in actions but are not actions in themselves (1984: 96–8).

33 Burger (*Max Weber's Theory of Concept Formation: History, laws, and ideal types*, 1976: 115–40, 154–67).

34 Habermas (1988: 166).

35 See Sharp (1973: 705–76; 2004: 415–21).

36 The method was used early in the Civil Rights Movement and during the 1960s to a great degree in the southern states, when thousands of activists were arrested (see Sharp 1973: 373–4). For an analysis of how sit-in actions spread, see Oberschall (*Social Movements: Ideologies, interests, and identities*, 1993: 213–37).

37 Chabot (2003: 134–5, 143 ff.).

38 Powell Bell (*CORE and the Strategy of Non-violence*, 1968). They were strongly politicised by the prison experience that many activists went through during the Second World War (see Cooney and Michalowski, 1977: 88 ff., 99–100). In 1943, the sit-ins and strikes in prisons succeeded after a 143-day strike to give Danbury federal prison the first desegregated mess hall (Tracy 1996: 18, 37–8).

39 The seven steps are: '1. Investigation of the injustices, 2. Negotiation of the difficulty with those who seem to be primarily responsible, 3. Education of the public on the issue through speeches, pamphlets, etc., 4. Organization of public pressure through letter-writing campaigns, petitioning, organizing

Citizens Committees to protest, etc., 5. More direct demonstration through picketing or leafletting, 6. Direct action through civil disobedience and non-cooperation with injustice, 7. Non-retaliation in case violence enters into the picture' (Chabot 2003: 135). CORE even had 'Rules for action': thirteen rules for members including behaviours allowed in the name of the organisation (Powell Bell 1968).

40 Chabot (2003: 145).

41 Chabot (2003: 133).

42 Sit-ins in other places in the country during the following two years also led to successful desegregation, even if success was not always as easy to achieve as in the first attempt in Chicago (Chabot 2003: 147).

43 Carson et al. (*The Eyes on the Prize Civil Rights Reader: Documents, speeches and firsthand accounts from the black freedom struggle 1954–1990*, 1991: 115).

44 Marable (*Race, Reform and Rebellion: The second reconstruction in black America 1945–1990*, 1991: 61–2); Sharp (1973: 373).

45 Ackerman and Du Vall (2000).

46 Sharp (1973: 694).

47 Marable (1991: 62).

48 Habermas (1984: 15–17, 85–6; 1988: 157, 182–3).

49 Habermas (1988: 182).

50 Habermas (1984: 89).

51 For example, 'codes of discipline' were used that the participants were to follow. This ensured that the activists did not use violence when they were provoked (see Sharp 1973: 632).

52 Those who break social rules can sometimes live according to high normative requirements. Pelton claims that a central aspect of non-violence is making promises (the act of promising is intimately tied to

social norms) by the way in which you act as a role model and as a good example in conflicts (1974: 153, 157–62).

53 Turner (*The Ritual Process: Structure and anti-structure*, 1969) calls it a 'rite of affliction', a kind of healing through a number of phases. Rituals are of special importance for social crises and to treat social conflicts.

54 Marable (1991: 65). In a similar way, it is common that Israeli 'refuseniks' – military servicemen or officers who refuse to take part in military operations in occupied territories (the West Bank and Gaza) – justify their refusal based on Israel's safety and the nation's interest in peace and stability. The refuseniks start from the same values held by those who punish their refusal, but reach another conclusion as they claim that the occupation of Palestine threatens Israel.

55 It was often a matter of the movement breaking state laws or ordinances but following federal laws.

56 Habermas (1988: 182–3).

57 Habermas (1988: 183).

58 Goffman (*Jaget och maskerna: En studie i vardagslivets dramatik*, 1974).

59 Smelser (1995: 90–1). 'Stigma' refers to the deviant, the non-normal, the other (see Goffman, *Stigma: Notes on the management of spoiled identity*, 1963: 1–19). In accordance with the theory of stigma, the group's judgement of what is seen as deviant is so powerful that there is a risk that the person labelled 'criminal' or 'evil' eventually accepts their label and begins to identify with it (Giddens 1994: 175–6).

60 Goffman writes that a person's self is constituted by performance, not that the self causes the perfor-

mance (Lemert and Branaman, *The Goffman Reader*, 1997: lxvii).

61 Lemert and Branaman (1997: lxxiii, xlvi, lii). When people act dramaturgically, they are not actors as in a theatre but are honestly dramaturgical. In contrast, it is the actors who try to represent reality's social drama.

62 The social movement scholars Benford and Hunt have described this 'framing' aspect of collective action in a persuasive manner (see Lyman, *Social Movements: Critiques, concepts, case-studies*, 1995: 84–109 – 'Dramaturgy and social movements: the social construction and communication of power').

63 See, for example, the training manual produced by Trainingskollektive Graswurzelbewegung (*Methodensammlung Training für Gewaltfreie Aktion*, 1984), published by Graswurzelrevolution/FöGA, Cologne.

64 One of the central organisers of the strategy was the Ruckus Society, which was composed of conscious drama actors (www.ruckus.org). See also Students for a Free Tibet (SFT, *Students for a Free Tibet: SFT worldwide action for Tibet, organizer's guide, 1999–2000*, 2000: 45 ff.) as an example of an organisation that has been educated in dramaturgical nonviolent actions.

65 Here, 'justice' and 'injustice' cover the actors' own understanding of these concepts but also the activists' attempt to prove, communicate and agree about what the concepts should mean.

66 McAdam ('The framing function of movement tactics: strategic dramaturgy in the American civil rights movement', 1996: 348–9).

67 McAdam (1996: 353).

68 Pelton (1974) has argued that nonviolent resistance in the Civil Rights Movement gave the activists a strong sense of self, more self-respect and pride. One can see that the Civil Rights Movement in some ways paved the way for its own militant reaction, the Black Power movement.

69 Carson et al. (1991: 115).

70 King ('Martin Luther King, Jr., and the meaning of freedom: a political interpretation', 1993: 140).

71 The Civil Rights Movement began during the 1950s. During the mid-1960s, identity groups that talked about 'black pride' and 'black power' grew even stronger.

72 In this respect, 'the others' are not a social group but a non-desirable role that anyone can adopt. Even the activists might have played that role previously, before they became activists. Of course, in practice this focus on unity and community is a complicated process that (in other contexts) can hide the dominance of the powerful (Orjuela, 'Civil society in civil war: peace work and identity politics in Sri Lanka', 2004: 250–1). The possibility of transgressing identity borders is developed in terms of *inclusive identification* in Chapter 6.

73 A *we* and *them* without communication means that we cannot see ourselves from outside, from the perspective of other people, which means that we would then be unable to comprehend our own identity. Without a *you* (singular), there is no *I*. Without a *you* (plural), there is no *we*.

74 Georg Simmel claims that even the struggle between people is a social and communicative interplay (*Kamp!*, 1970 [1908]).

75 Habermas (1984: 8–9, 87–8). Goal-rational action has been emphasised in economic theory and game theory, among other fields.

76 Habermas (1988: 179–81).

77 Habermas (1988: 181).

78 See norm 9 in the Appendix.

79 Oppenheimer and Lakey (*A Manual for Direct Action: Strategy and tactics for civil rights and all other nonviolent protest movements*, 1965: 16 ff.).

80 Sharp (1973: 503). In some places this was of importance (Sharp 1973: 737–8). See also Seifert (1965: 74).

81 Sharp (1973: 526).

82 Sharp (1973: 689).

83 Under the pressure of massive disobedience, social order itself can become politically impossible and lead, eventually, to 'disintegration' of the regime if no solution is negotiated (see Sharp 2004).

84 Habermas (1984: 101; 1996: 58).

85 Habermas (1998: 334).

86 Habermas (1984: 86, 94–101; 1996: 134–5). Communicative actions have previously been emphasised by the symbolic interactionists Mead and Garfinkel.

87 Habermas (1984: 99; 1988: 189).

88 Habermas (1988: 200).

89 Habermas (1984: 295; 1988: 175–7).

90 According to Habermas (1996: 202–3), agreements are built on all parties having the right to say yes or no to suggestions. My interpretation is that those who are denied their right to *say* no on a decisive issue (such as the segregation order in the USA) can 'say' no through the *act* of blocking the execution of the decision. The action becomes a way of creating a conversation from which they were previously excluded.

91 To the extent that the strategy is hidden, it is, according to Habermas, the opposite of communicative rationality: that is, ideological production or manipulation.

92 Berrigan (*Fighting the Lamb's War: Skirmishes with the American empire; the autobiography of Philip Berrigan*, 1996); Dear (*Disarming the Heart: Toward a vow of nonviolence*, 1993); Douglass ('We cannot stop the white train by being the white train', 1984); Laffin and Montgomery (*Swords into Plowshares: Nonviolent direct action for disarmament*, 1987); VanEtten Casey (*The Berrigans*, 1971).

93 Douglass (1984).

94 Habermas (1988: 200).

95 See Habermas on 'distortion' (1984: 333), system colonisation (1989: 318–31) and structural violence (1989: 187). See also Habermas (1988: 346–7), which addresses this criticism.

96 Young (2000: 148–70) writes that diversity is denied from the start. Deliberative democracy theorists, including Habermas, propose *conversational competitions* and indirectly suggest an *exclusion* of diversity and deviant perspectives by presupposing a unified harmony of interests, by appealing to 'the common good', and by claiming a group-specific style of discourse to be universal.

97 Chambers ('Feminist discourse/practical discourse', 1995: 176, italics added).

4 Nonviolent 'dialogue facilitation'

1 Gandhi (1999: Volume 27: 338).

2 Some find that 'conscience' is a sufficient justification for nonviolent civil disobedience or non-cooperation, but this is not so for Gandhi. Instead, he demands tolerance and a (non-violent) attempt to convince other people (Gandhi 1999: Volume 36: 344).

3 On the whole, Sharp does not discuss 'truth', 'dialogue' or 'con-

sensus', while only sparingly talking about 'conversion' and 'persuasion' (1973: 841–93). 'Conversion' is mentioned as a form of 'mechanism of change' whereby 'the opponent reacts to the actions of the nonviolent actionists by finally coming around to a new point of view in which he *positively accepts their aims*' (1973: 69, italics added). 'Persuasion' is mentioned as an influence technique whereby 'mild' methods are used 'to produce a stronger action by someone else' (1973: 118).

4 Galtung and Næss (*Gandhis politiske etikk*, 1990: 94 ff.).

5 Juergensmeyer (2003: 18–19, 147).

6 Gandhi (1999: Volume 8: 31, 80).

7 Bondurant (1988: 197).

8 Chilton ('Comparing satyagraha and the US Peace and Justice Movement in the light of discourse ethics', 2005).

9 Bondurant (1988: 46 ff.).

10 See King (*Gandhian Nonviolent Struggle and Untouchability in South India: The 1924–25 Vykom satyagraha and mechanisms of change*, 2014), who refutes much in the earlier accounts of the campaign, especially the suggestion that high caste individuals were convinced, not coerced.

11 Juergensmeyer (2003: 61).

12 Bondurant (1988: 49).

13 Habermas (1988: 303–70). See also Næss (2002: 57–8) on 'Gandhian dialogue'.

14 Pantham ('Thinking with Mahatma Gandhi: beyond liberal democracy', 1983).

15 Criteria 1 and 2 are taken from Habermas (1988: 189; 1996: 136–7), while 3 and 4 are regularly mentioned by him. Criterion 5 is my interpretation of Habermas's demand placed on democratic institutions and 6 to 9

also come from him (1996: 58–9, 122, 202–3). I also use other general texts by Habermas (1984; 1988: 137–47, 188–9, 282–99; 1998: 87–8).

16 Habermas (1998: 367–8). See Habermas (1984: 36, 42) on the difference between conventional and universal statements.

17 *Every* comprehensible utterance must implicitly claim validity in *all three* world perspectives at the same time (Habermas 1988: 189), but explicitly only a limited part of a world's relations are thematised (1996: 136–7).

18 Andersen ('Jürgen Habermas', 2003: 439).

19 Habermas (1996: 42 ff., 89).

20 Andersen (2003: 440). The quotation within brackets is from p. 439 (my translation from Swedish).

21 Habermas (1988: Chapter 4).

22 Sharp (1979: 273–85); Gandhi (1970: 18, 146; 1942: 108).

23 Habermas (1996).

24 Habermas (1996: 65), or, as a practical rule of argumentation: 'For a norm to be valid, the consequences and side effects of its general observance for the satisfaction of each person's particular interests must be acceptable to all' (1996: 197). Like Rawls ('original position') and Mead ('ideal role taking'), Habermas finds that universal demands require non-partisanship, but, in contrast to them, and to Kant, he argues that individual parties cannot justify norms on their own (Habermas 1996: 66, 198). Justification can only *be practised*. It requires actual dialogues and approval among those who are affected: that is, deliberative democracy.

25 Habermas (1996: 65).

26 Andersen (2003: 438–9); Habermas (1988: 283–4). 'Universalist' means that something applies

in general, regardless of culture or epoch.

27 Andersen (2003: 440).

28 Habermas (1996: 122).

29 Habermas (1984: 99–101).

30 The Quakers have used consensus since the seventeenth century in their societies and in peace work. There, it involves someone in a position of trust interpreting the will of the meeting (Sheeran, *Beyond Majority Rule: Voteless decisions in the Religious Society of Friends*, 1983). In other cases, instead of voting rights, groups use the right of veto ('veto' means 'I forbid', and a veto ends the possibility of reaching a decision); this is thought to apply only when a suggested decision conflicts with the participants' *principled* perception of justice. Certain groups use group vetoes instead of individual vetoes, something that also denotes the fact that consensus does not need to mean agreement.

31 Young (2000: 159–60).

32 Hardiman (2003: 52).

33 According to Pantham ('Habermas' practical discourse and Gandhi's satyagraha', 1986). However, Rajan ('Gandhi and Habermas: irreconcilable differences', 1991) claims the opposite: that Habermas 'emphasises rationality and self-reflection [and] ethics as a collective, intersubject quest', in contrast to Gandhi who promotes 'mystical, irrational forms, and stressed the private quest for ethics'. My investigation is a fundamental critique of Rajan's conclusion.

34 Pantham (1983). Their respective views of democracy are summarised in *Legitimation Crisis* (Habermas 1975) and *Hind Swaraj: And other writings* (Gandhi 1997). Nonviolent and liberation struggle were, for Gandhi, simultaneously a project of democratisation. '[Gandhi] therefore proposed and experimented with an action project, namely satyagraha, for superseding the modernist, amoral, elitist paradigm of government' (Pantham 1983: 175). 'Democracy and violence can ill go together. The States that are today nominally democratic have either to become frankly totalitarian [*sic*] or, if they are to become truly democratic, they must become courageously non-violent' (Gandhi 1999: Volume 74: 194).

35 Pantham (1983: 176).

36 Pantham (1983: 165–6).

37 Gandhi (1999: Volume 30: 159).

38 Karn (1994: especially 93 ff., 219).

39 Compare the Appendix and the list of dialogue-facilitation methods.

40 Gandhi (1970: 25).

41 Galtung and Næss (1990: 114–15).

42 Burrowes (1996: 106 ff.).

43 Bondurant (1988: 189 ff.).

44 Unlike Gandhi, Habermas is not a radical nonviolent protagonist, but his theory allows for a more radical interpretation than the one at which he arrives (deliberate democracy, social democracy, EU, etc.).

45 If more affected people are included and power has less influence, then more of the decisive disagreements will be transformed into understanding and agreement and we will come closer to *Satya* or ideal dialogue – which serves as both a utopian ideal and a measure for evaluating the quality of the truth or dialogue.

46 Moyer's list is included in most action manuals in the USA (see, for example, War Resisters' League, *Handbook for Nonviolent Action*, 1989). It lists a number of concrete oppressive behaviours, such as 'hogging the

show', 'speaking in capital letters', 'negativism', 'self-listening' and 'speaking for others'.

47 Ås ('Hersketeknikker', 1978).

48 ENSU suggests *counter-strategies* – taking up space, questioning, cards on the table, altering patterns and intellectualisation – as well as *confirmation techniques* such as visibilising, respecting, informing, double rewarding and setting reasonable standards (see Amnéus et al., 'Validation techniques and counter strategies: methods for dealing with power structures and changing social climates', 2004).

49 Goss and Goss-Mayr (1990: 38–9).

50 Habermas (1988: 175 ff.).

51 Clamshell Alliance (We Can Stop the Seabrook Nuclear Plant: Occupier's handbook. Join us: April 30, 1977); Herngren (1990); Livermore Action Group (*International Day of Nuclear Disarmament*, 1983).

52 Clark (*Preparing for Non-Violent Direct Action*, 1984); Coover et al. (*A Resource Manual for a Living Revolution*, 1977); Herngren (1990); Justice and Reconciliation Division (*Minutes of the Workshop: Training of trainers in effective nonviolent action*, 1989).

53 See, for example, Gugel and Furtner (*Gewaltfreie Aktion*, 1983: 54–5). With the aim of promoting listening, they train 'controlled dialogue': during the dialogue each statement is retold in one's own words by the person listening before moving on to the next contribution.

54 Coover et al. (1977); Herngren (1999: 185 ff.).

55 Herngren (1999: 185 ff.); Livermore Action Group (1983: 29); War Resisters' League (1989: 10–11). See also www.trainingforchange.org.

56 Coover et al. (1977).

57 Even evaluation procedures are developed and learned through exercises (see Trainingskollektive Graswurzelbewegung, 1984: Chapter 11).

58 Groups can have a pre-agreed solution: for example, to wait and have further discussions, or to adopt the decision of a qualified majority or division (see Herngren 1990; Livermore Action Group 1983; Sheeran 1983).

59 The thinking behind this is that 'the private is political' and that it is good for the group's sense of community and effectiveness to be *informed* by what is happening in people's private lives. However, the group does not take it upon itself to solve any private problems and participants divulge only as much as they want to.

60 The participants in a workshop or training session sit at small tables and have a few minutes to discuss each subject, which increases participation in the dialogue process considerably.

61 Falk and Olsson (*Överens: En bok om demokratiska mötesformer*, 2000: 27–31, 52–3).

62 MPD ('Workshop on marshalling & peacekeeping', 1994: 25–6).

63 MPD (1994: 27). This is also called 'structured dialogue' or 'restatement technique' (see Coover et al. 1977: 84–5; Gugel and Furtner 1983: 55).

64 Herngren and Vinthagen (*Handbok för Avrustningslägret i Linköping*, 1992).

65 Chambers (1995: 165).

66 Chambers (1995: 167–8).

67 See, for example, April Mobilization (*Nonviolent Civil Disobedience at CIA Headquarters, Langley, Virginia,*

Monday April 27, 1987, 1987); Livermore Action Group (1983: 12).

68 The testable proposition is
that the quality of communication
possible with a higher level depends
on the leverage mobilised by the
nonviolent resistance movement.

69 Italics added. Available at www.
sas.upenn.edu/African_Studies/Ar-
ticles_Gen/Letter_Birmingham.html.

70 Quoted from 'An open letter
to the government of the Federal
Republic of Germany, for the atten-
tion of the Chancellor', signed by
Christoph Then and Volker Nick,
Tübingen, May 1984.

71 Quoted from Uwe Painke's
unpublished English translation of
his own text 'Diaserie zur Kampagne
Ziviler Ungehorsam bis zur Abrüstung: Wir müssen uns entscheiden ...'

72 Bondurant (1988); Næss (1974:
76).

73 Kuper (1960: 73).

74 Martin and Varney ('Nonviolence and communication', 2003)
find that nonviolent resistance creates 'the preconditions' for dialogue.

75 Rigby (*Justice and Reconciliation: After the violence*, 2001: 123–45).

76 Long and Brecke (*War and
Reconciliation: Reason and emotion
in conflict resolution*, 2003: 29–32,
36, 69–70) describe how an enemy
image can go through a 'redefinition'
through a process of 'truth-telling'.

77 Gandhi (1942: 237).

78 Næss (1974: 89–90).

79 Harvey Seifert states that:
'an opponent has been coerced if he
continues to hold a contrary conviction, but nevertheless acts favourably'
(1965: 103).

80 Gandhi (1970: 43).

81 Juergensmeyer (2003: 37).

82 Gandhi (1999: Volume 48:
365–6).

83 Sharp (2004: 415 ff.).

84 Sharp (1973: 705–76, especially
745 on how nonviolent coercion is
derived from resistance).

85 Each level encompasses a few
different meanings of consensus, but
each participant has to at least follow
the rules that are created by the
interaction (Vinthagen 1997c).

86 Næss (1974: 90–3).

87 See Chapter 6.

88 Over 30,000 people participated in the occupation (see Coalition
for Direct Action at Seabrook, *Let's
Shut Down Seabrook! Handbook for
Oct. 6, 1979: Direct action occupation*,
1979: 6; Rasch, *Whyl finns överallt: Ett
exempel på kärnkraftsmotstånd*, 1979;
Sternstein, *Überall ist Whyl: Bürgerinitiativen gegen Atomanlagen aus der
Arbeit eines Aktionsforschers*, 1978).

89 Rigby (1986: 92).

90 Hirdman (*Vi bygger landet: Den
svenska arbetarrörelsens historia från
Per Götrek till Olof Palme*, 1990: 59).

91 Holland (1989: 88–100); Mbeki
(1992: 82); quotation from Meli (1988:
123–4).

92 Luthuli (*Släpp mitt folk!*, 1962:
175).

93 Ackerman and Du Vall (2000:
Chapter 9); Zunes et al. (1999: Chapter 11).

5 Nonviolent 'power breaking'

1 A preliminary version of this
chapter appeared in *Gandhi Marg* 22
(2): July–September 2000, published in
New Delhi. I am grateful for comments
given by the IPRA Nonviolence Commission, Sean Chabot and Senthil Ram.

2 Max Weber in Sharp (1980: 212).

3 Gandhi (1945: 7).

4 See, above all, Sharp (1973:
Part One; 1979: 43–59; 1980: 21–67,
309–78).

5 See also Ackerman and Kruegler

(1994); Randle (*Civil Resistance*, 1994); Sharp (1973; 2004); Zunes et al. (1999). Martin (*Uprooting War*, 1984; 'Gene Sharp's theory of power', 1989) is an exception in his approach, but he does not use Foucault.

6 Holloway (*Change the World without Taking Power: The meaning of revolution today*, 2002).

7 See also Waters (*Modern Sociological Theory*, 1994).

8 Sharp (1973: 7–62).

9 Sharp (1973: 28).

10 Sharp (1973: 6); Zunes et al. (1999: 2); Ackerman and Kruegler (1994).

11 Martin (1989: 213); Sharp (1973; 1979; 1980; 2004, among others).

12 Sharp (1973: 7–8).

13 Gandhi (1970).

14 Arendt (1972: 141).

15 Sharp (1980: 158).

16 Sharp (1980: 190).

17 Sharp (1980: 23–4).

18 Sharp (1973: 7–10).

19 Sharp (1973: 9).

20 Sharp (1980: 23–4).

21 Sharp (1973: 10).

22 Sharp (1973: 12).

23 Sharp (1973: 16).

24 Sharp (1973: 11–12).

25 In this text I call the leader 'he' as men have traditionally been in power over subjugated 'others': women, slaves, children, etc.

26 This suggests that the more extensive and detailed the power of a leader and his control, the more dependent he is on the cooperation of his subordinates. Accordingly, a late modern, complexly organised and highly technological society is in some respects more dependent on cooperation and obedience from different groups to continue to function. Power relations may be more diffuse and mobile: that is, power resources can be replaced if necessary and networks of linked power relations may be difficult to detect. At the same time, this should mean that resistance in key nodes of a power system encompasses more possibilities for obstruction than ever before. Today, a single individual may seriously affect the computerised world economy by unleashing a virus that disrupts the IT network on which global cooperation is built.

27 Burrowes (1996: 11–12).

28 Burrowes (1996: 96).

29 Sharp (1973: 25–30).

30 Sharp (1973: 28).

31 Vinthagen (2005).

32 Sharp (1973: Part Two).

33 Vinthagen (2005: Chapter 2).

34 Holm (1978); McGuinness ('Some thoughts on power and change', 1994); Burrowes (1996: 83–96).

35 Vinthagen (2005).

36 See, for example, Lukes (*Power*, 1974); Foucault (*Övervakning och straff*, 1974).

37 See also Ackerman and Kruegler (1994); McCarthy and Sharp (1997); Sharp (2004).

38 Burrowes (1996); Martin (1989: note 3).

39 Sharp (1973: 25–32).

40 Sharp (1980: 98, 212, 341).

41 Sharp (1980: 20).

42 McGuinness (1994).

43 Foucault (*Power/Knowledge: Selected interviews and other writings 1972–1977*, 1980: 180).

44 Foucault (1980: 89).

45 Foucault (1980: 200).

46 Beronius (*Den disciplinära maktens organisering: Om makt och arbetsorganisation*, 1986: 25).

47 Foucault (1974: 36–7).

48 Foucault (1980: 117).

49 Cheater (*The Anthropology of Power: Empowerment and disempower-*

ment in changing structures, 1999: Chapter 1).

50 Foucault ('Critical theory/ intellectual history', 1994: 133).

51 Foucault (1980: 142).

52 Foucault (1980: 137–8).

53 Lilja and Vinthagen ('Sovereign power, disciplinary power and biopower: resisting what power with what resistance?', 2014).

54 Vinthagen ('Power and non-violent movements', 1998; 2001).

55 Foucault (1994: 128–9).

56 Foucault (*Society Must be Defended: Lectures at the Collège de France 1975–1976*, 2003: 45).

57 Holloway (2002).

58 Vinthagen (2005).

59 The quotes are edited to indicate just the message of this scene in *Life of Brian*. The complete script exists at http://montypython.50webs.com/scripts/Life_of_Brian/20.htm.

60 Waters (1994: Chapter 7); Foucault (1994: 30).

61 Every society needs some kind of order, although one should not assume that it has to be hierarchical and marked by patterns of superiority and subordination. Whether power is a political problem or not is something that needs to be judged on more specific grounds, and not at this general theoretical level. Still, understanding what power is will facilitate the relevant judgement. This text, however, is about how to understand nonviolent activists' resistance to repressive kinds of subordination and power.

62 Lukes (1974: 21, 25).

63 Bourdieu (*The Logic of Practice*, 1995).

64 Broady (*Sociologi och Epistemologi: Om Pierre Bourdieus författarskap och den historiska epistemologin*, 1991: 225–33).

65 Foucault (1980: 141–2).

66 Dahl according to Lukes (1974: 11–15).

67 Bourdieu and Wacquant (*An Invitation to Reflexive Sociology*, 1992); Broady (1991).

68 Lukes (1974: 65).

69 Sharp (1979: 44–6, 54).

70 Foucault (1974).

71 Foucault (1974).

72 Foucault (1980: 120); Haugaard (*The Constitution of Power: A theoretical analysis of power, knowledge and structure*, 1997: 65, 87–92).

73 Goffman (*Asylums: Essays on the social situation of mental patients and other inmates*, 1961).

74 Johansen ('Humor as a political force', 1991).

75 Kaldor (*New and Old Wars: Organized violence in a global era*, 2012).

76 Foucault (1980: 109–33).

77 Vinthagen (2005).

78 Vinthagen (2005).

79 Sharp (1973: 27).

80 Coady (The idea of violence', 1999: 23–38).

81 Thoreau (*Om civilt motstånd*, 1977).

82 Cox ('Gramsci, hegemony and international relations: an essay in method', 1993: 52); Arendt (1972).

83 See, for example, Arad ('The Jewish fighting underground in the ghettos of Eastern Europe – ideology and reality', 1996); Marrus ('Jewish resistance to the Holocaust', 1995).

84 See Sartre's preface in Fanon (*The Wretched of the Earth*, 1963: xliii–lxii).

85 Holloway (2002).

86 Cohen and Arato (*Civil Society and Political Theory*, 1994: 294).

87 Foucault according to Beronius (1986: 25, 28).

88 Gandhi (1999).

89 Foucault (1980: 142).

90 Bondurant (1988); Gandhi (1970); Næss (1974); Sharp (1973).

91 Sharp (1979: 81).

92 Burrowes (1996: 108); Galtung and Næss (1990: 147–53, 199 ff., 243); Goss-Mayr (1979: 130).

93 Hardt and Negri (*Empire*, 2000: 212).

94 Cheater (1999: 5).

95 Foucault (1980: 138).

96 For more on 'critical communities' and 'free spaces' and their decisive role in the development of a Gandhian movement repertoire in the American Civil Rights Movement, see Chabot (2003: especially 181–218).

97 Dielemans and Quistbergh (*Motstånd*, 2000: 138 ff.).

98 Johansen (1991).

99 Lucas (*OutRage! An oral history*, 1998).

100 Rosenberg (*Qeerfeministisk agenda*, 2002).

101 The list's six methods of resistance comprise a development of Sharp's classic list of three nonviolent methods: protest, non-cooperation and intervention. In addition, 198 variations of these three method types are provided: see www.peacemagazine.org/198.htm or the Albert Einstein Institution website at www.aeinstein.org. Note that the list does not aim to be complete: creative experimentation with nonviolence has probably developed many more variations.

6 Nonviolent 'utopian enactment'

1 Fanon (*Les Damnés de la Terre*, 1961).

2 Sartre ('Förord', 1971).

3 In this respect, we are not talking about individuals committing violent crimes, but organised and (often) legal campaigns of violence by groups that aspire for legitimacy and power. Nonviolent methods against individuals, especially the mentally ill or those under the influence of drugs, comprise an entirely different challenge and lie outside this study (cf. Yoder, *En beväpnad man anfaller din familj: Vad gör du då?*, 1990).

4 Glasl (*Konfliktmanagement: Ein Handbuch zur Diagnose und Behandlung von Konflikten für Organisationen und ihre Berater*, 1994: Part 2); Wallensteen (*Understanding Conflict Resolution: War, peace and the global system*, 2002: 34–5). Bergfeldt (1993: 358) shows that nonviolence tends to balance such polarisation.

5 Izard and Ackerman ('Motivational, organizational, and regulatory functions of discrete emotions', 2000: 262).

6 See Keen (*Faces of the Enemy: Reflections of the hostile imagination: the psychology of enmity*, 1988); Satha-Anand ('The nonviolence prince', 1981: 20); Stangor ('Stereotyping', 1999: 629–30); Tester (*Sociologi och moral*, 2000: 118–19).

7 Gandhi (1999: Volume 54: 48).

8 See above all Goffman (*Interaction Ritual: Essays on face-to-face behaviour*, 1967; 1974; also *Strategic Interaction*, 1970). Enactment means that the physical form or an organised whole comes to the fore.

9 Breines ('Community and organization: the new left and Michels' "iron law"',1980); Maeckelbergh ('The road to democracy: the political legacy of "1968"', 2011a; 'Doing is believing: prefiguration as strategic practice in the Alterglobalization Movement', 2011b).

10 Thörn (1997b: 48, Chapter 5, 271).

11 Thörn (1997b: 49 ff.).

12 Thörn (1997b: 52).

13 Gandhi (1983: 27).

14 Trainingskollektive Graswurzelbewegung (1984: Chapter 8). See also 'Gelenkte Phantasie', which envisions a non-sexist society (1984: Chapter 5: 3).

15 Trainingskollektive Graswurzelbewegung (1984: Chapter 1, Introduction).

16 Quoted in Dear (1993: 55). Original quotation in Scott King (*The Words of Martin Luther King, Jr.*, 1983: 73). A shorter version is found in Ansbro (*Martin Luther King, Jr.: Nonviolent strategies and tactics for social change*, 2000: 9).

17 Gandhi (1970: 41–3; 1998: 10 ff.). Bergfeldt states that 'internal unity' is decisive for the dynamics of the nonviolent campaign (1993: 357).

18 This is a sober and practical recommendation for any soldier, even a nonviolent soldier. War and the military often comprise a comparative model of thinking in nonviolence literature (for example, Gregg 1935; Sharp 1973).

19 Gandhi (1970: 142–7).

20 'And as a *Satyagrahi* never injures his opponent and always appeals, either to his reason by gentle argument or to his heart by the sacrifice of self, *Satyagraha* is twice blessed; it blesses him [*sic*] who practises it, and him against whom it is practised' (Gandhi 1998: Volume 4: 30).

21 Gandhi (1970: 142–7). Gandhi even claims that the 'purer' the suffering, the greater the result will be. 'Purity' supposes that the suffering does not occur for egotistical reasons, such as a desire for acclaim or admiration or as a declaration of holiness or martyrdom.

22 Gandhi (1998: Volume 4: 17).

23 Galtung and Næss (1990: 178–85, 259–60).

24 Gandhi (1970: 143).

25 Gandhi (1998: Volume 4: 74).

26 See, for example, Hoeber Rudolph and Rudolph (*Gandhi: The traditional roots of charisma*, 1983: especially 42, 46 ff., 56).

27 Here, the starting point accords with the sociology of emotions, that feelings are constructed through social interaction, normative order and moral judgement (Johansson 1999: 64–8, 386–91). See also Lewis and Haviland-Jones (*Handbook of Emotions*, 2000), and especially Kemper ('Social models in the exploration of emotions', 2000).

28 See Næss (2002: 77 ff.) and 'the psychology of trust' in Gandhi. Nancy Eisenberg finds that having a perspective entails understanding but not necessarily feeling like the other (in Manstead and Hewstone 1999: 203).

29 Gregg (1935: 198–202).

30 Gregg (1935: 199).

31 See, for example, Burrowes (1996: 111); Galtung and Næss (1990: 181–5).

32 See, for example, McAllister (1982).

33 Meyerding (1982: 10).

34 Quoted from Kriesberg (*Constructive Conflicts: From escalation to resolution*, 1998: 113–14).

35 Biggs also writes that internal 'credibility' for the movement's leader occurs through sacrifices and the risk of suffering ('When costs are beneficial: protest as communicative suffering', 2003: 18).

36 See, for example, the Cambodian movement Dhammayietra in Moser-Puangsuwan and Weber (*Nonviolent Intervention Across Borders: A recurrent vision*, 2000: 262).

37 See, for example, Continental Walk (*The Continental Walk for Disarmament and Social Justice: Organizers manual*, 1975); A Day without the Pentagon (*A Day without the Pentagon: Tactical manual*, 1998).

38 National Lesbian and Gay Civil Disobedience Action (*Out & Outraged: Non-violent civil disobedience at the U.S. Supreme Court – for love, life & liberation, October 13, 1987, C.D. handbook*, 1987: 10).

39 Livermore Action Group (1983: 41).

40 Livermore Action Group (1983: 41).

41 There arose several conflicts between Gandhi (who emphasised good social relations with the English in the future) and others (who emphasised India's formal, legal independence).

42 'Individuals would be expected to change their beliefs about outgroups through contact with outgroup members if the encountered individuals are perceived to engage in *behaviors that contradict the stereotypical beliefs*' (Stangor 1999: 631, italics added).

43 'Even if the opponent plays him false twenty times, the *Satyagrahi* is ready to trust him the twenty-first time; for, an implicit trust in human nature is the very essence of his creed' (Gandhi 1998: Volume 4: 74).

44 Næss finds that two more preconditions exist: that there are always common interests and that the activists are capable of carrying out the action (2002: 86).

45 Here, it is necessary to understand that the nonviolent struggle does not presuppose that *all* individuals are convinced or emotionally affected – the vast majority is sufficient. As a result of the

utopian enactment being combined with resistance, certain individuals (those in power, for example) are forced to accept the fact. When the activists' power breaking becomes so extensive and powerful that the power base shifts (through strikes, boycotts, massive civil disobedience and non-cooperation, among other actions), those in power and regimes fall whether they are convinced or not (Chenoweth and Stephan 2011; Sharp 1973; 2004).

46 Sharp (1973: 711–17); Christie et al. (*Peace, Conflict, and Violence: Peace psychology for the 21st century*, 2001: 41–2, 78).

47 See especially 'emotional distance' in Grossman (*On Killing: The psychological cost of learning to kill in war and society*, 1996). Sharp talks about 'the barrier of social distance' (1973: 711).

48 Burrowes (1996: 111).

49 Lakey ('Mechanisms of non-violent action', 1968: 386–93).

50 The conscious *risk taking for utopia* differentiates the nonviolent movement from the broader trend since the 1960s of 'new social movements' that can be said to be characterised by action in their new, lived utopia in the here and now (Melucci 1989).

51 One's belief and views are tested by the truth content of the action. Gandhi found that you cannot even know if your own 'inner voice' belongs to God or the devil, 'for both are wrestling in the human breast. Acts determine the nature of the Voice' (Gandhi 1998: Volume 1: 35). See also Gandhi (1998: Volume 4: 42).

52 Mason (*Beaches, Blood, and Ballots: A black doctor's civil right struggle*, 2000). Sharp (1973: 378) calls the action technique 'wade-in'.

53 Mohl ('Civil rights movements', 2003).

54 Sharp (1973: 554).

55 Sharp expands upon Gregg (1935) but understands ju-jitsu as mainly working politically and socially, not morally or individually. Rigby calls it 'shame power' (2002: 5 ff.). Brian Martin has developed this as 'backfire': see his texts online at www.bmartin.cc/pubs/peace.html.

56 Sharp (1973: 657–98).

57 Holm (1978: 102–4); Sharp (1973: 657 ff.).

58 See, for example, Wirmark (*Kamp mot kriget: Buddisterna i Vietnam*, 1974: 47–8).

59 Gandhi (1983: 57).

60 Goss and Goss-Mayr categorise three types of fasts: fasting for purification, the political fast, and fast as blackmail (1990: 48). They find that the third type 'is not part of nonviolent liberation'.

61 Brad Bennet builds upon Sharp (1973), claiming that there is a difference between fasting for moral pressures, hunger strikes and 'satyagrahic fast' (see 'Fasting' in Powers and Vogele 1997: 177–8).

62 Juergensmeyer (2003: 56).

63 Erikson (1969: 242–3).

64 Gandhi (*An Autobiography or The Story of My Experiments with Truth*, 1927: 230).

65 Burrowes (1996: 112).

66 Blumer (1969: 108).

67 Blumer (1969: 109).

68 Lemert and Branaman (1997: 40–1, 229–61); Montiel ('Toward a psychology of structural peacebuilding', 2001); Sheldon Stryker in Manstead and Hewstone (1999: 486–7).

69 Lemert and Branaman (1997: xlv–lxxxii, 3–25, 35–41, 95–107).

70 Goffman (1974: 97 ff.).

71 Lemert and Branaman (1997: 25). The established definition of a social interaction masters the interaction, not the reverse (1997: 40). This means that it is difficult for the role action to undermine the definition, and it will be met with other participants' corrections. For that reason, the nonviolent movement needs to conduct internal role training behind the stage of the conflict or a 're-socialisation' of the movement (in a context where the deviant definition is accepted and becomes the dominant norm) in order to then be able to go out and act with trustworthiness and perseverance.

72 The exception is when one acts with 'role distance', which is when a person's 'personal style' is formed (see Lemert and Branaman 1997: 35–41, especially 36).

73 Lemert and Branaman (1997: 16).

74 See, for example, Hare and Blumberg (1968).

75 Benford and Hunt ('Dramaturgy and social movements: the social construction and communication of power', 1995: 86).

76 Goffman (1974: 185–99).

77 Johnston and Klandermans (*Social Movements and Culture*, 1995).

78 Bala (2004).

79 'In sum, movement performances incongruent with audience interpretations of their empirical, experiential and cultural realities may fail to resonate or move them to participate actively in the collective drama' (Benford and Hunt 1995: 100).

80 Lemert and Branaman (1997: lxiv–lxvi).

81 In Goffman (1974: 39–51), the social drama of actors' 'idealisation' is described as power-conforming, and therefore as profoundly different

to the idealisation of the nonviolent movement, which tries to perform the ideal of its own collective norms in resistance to existing power relations.

82 Montiel (2001).

83 War Resisters' League (1989: 5); the handbook's authors took the advice from an article by Markley Morris.

84 For other lists of recommendations, see MPD (1994: 33); Yoder (1990); Painke ('Selbstbestimmtes Handeln in Situationen personaler Gewalt', 1991).

85 In Tübingen, nonviolence trainers called this a 'paradox intervention'.

86 Branagan ('The art(s) of nonviolent activism', 2002).

87 See Dejke (1989) about the tree-huggers.

88 Moser-Puangsuwan and Weber (2000: 345).

89 The work was the beginning of 'Engaged Buddhism' and organised from 1964 by the School of Youth for Social Service (see Nhat Hanh 2003: 94 ff.).

90 Queen ('The peace wheel: nonviolent activism in the Buddhist tradition', 1998: 39).

91 Potorti (*September 11th Families for Peaceful Tomorrows: Turning our grief into action for peace*, 2003).

92 Martin (1984: Chapter 10).

93 Bläsi claims that nonviolence initially creates *role insecurity* ('*rollenverunsicherung*') in the opponent, then *role weakening, role breaching and role exchanging* (*Konflikttransformation durch Gütekraft: Interpersonale Veränderungsprozesse*, 2001: 58).

94 Rasmussen (*Solvognen: Fortællinger fra vores ungdom*, 2004: especially 212–13). It was a street theatre group, Solvognen, based in the autonomous neighbourhood of

Christiania in Copenhagen, that acted as the Father Christmas army.

95 Seifert (1965: 55).

96 Stangor (1999: 632).

97 Noresson (*Kynnet som försätter berg*, 1985).

98 Dielemans and Quistbergh (2000: 148 ff.).

99 Waterhouse (*Design Improv: An investigation into creating a design method for interaction design that is based on the ideas of improvisational theatre*, 2005).

100 Stangor (1999: 630).

101 The movement culture needs to provide support and each activist must find ways of handling frustrations. See Robert Coles, who worked as a psychologist in the Civil Rights Movement in the USA ('Social struggle and weariness', 1969).

102 Bläsi (2001: 72–3).

103 Gandhi (1998: Volume 4: 75).

104 See also Laclau (*The Making of Political Identities*, 1994).

105 Johansson (1999: 74).

106 Berg ('Främlingen i jaget: en interaktionistisk tolkning av främlingskapet', 1996: 37).

107 On 'anti-identity', see Holloway (2002).

108 Holland (1989: 80).

109 Keen (1988).

110 Igra (*Den tunna hinnan*, 2001: 110).

111 Young (2000: 80–1) discusses W. E. B. Du Bois's expression 'double consciousness'.

112 Habermas (1984: 41).

113 Gandhi (1970: 49). Gandhi writes that satyagraha teaches us both the art of living and the art of dying, to live and to die with honour.

114 Grossman (1996); Keen (1988).

115 Eisenberg ('Empathy and sympathy', 2000: especially 683).

116 The previously popular

'contact hypothesis' has proved to be insufficient: contact between the 'in-group' and the 'outgroup' is not enough. According to Rupert Brown and Miles Hewstone, what is needed is for people to be seen as belonging to the same group: 'the contact situation should be so structured that previous outgroup members can be recategorised as members of the ingroup' (in Manstead and Hewstone 1999: 124).

117 Nancy Eisenberg claims that 'people who experience another's pain or distress are likely to refrain from aggression or cease their aggression' (in Manstead and Hewstone 1999: 203).

118 Eisenberg (2000: 678).

119 Ofstad (*Vårt förakt för svaghet*, 1987: 164 ff.).

120 Ofstad (1987: 166–7).

121 See, for example, Vander Zanden ('The non-violent resistance movement against segregation', 1969: 58–9). But, as Horsburgh writes, it is contradictory: 'if pain is welcomed by non-violent resisters, why should one expect it to soften the hearts of one's opponents?' (*Non-violence and Aggression: A study of Gandhi's moral equivalent of war*, 1968: 169).

122 Contempt for weakness is in itself a contradiction to nonviolence (see Ofstad 1987).

123 The ANC's acts of reconciliation with apartheid supporters and Inkatha after the great victory in the first election in 1994 are an excellent example. Another example is the Zapatistas. The fact that the Chiapas Indians' Zapatista guerrillas are unusually well respected as a serious, democratic actor at a time when very few people retain a romantic view of guerrilla fighters probably results from the (militarily) paradoxical fact

that the Zapatista guerrillas have not fought violently for several years, although they have refused to lay down their arms. Instead, they organise peaceful demonstrations, alternative social structures and international conferences.

124 Gandhi meant that provocations were the decisive test for the nonviolent activist (see Gandhi 1970: 153).

125 See Chapter 5.

126 Kuper (1960: 89).

127 Gregg (1935: 74).

128 Næss (1974).

129 A common thesis is that nonviolence works by 'dramatising injustice' (Harris, 'Nonviolence in urban areas: conversations with practitioners of nonviolence in the Milwaukee area, 1989 to 1994', 1998), violence or oppression, which is thereby exposed to the opposition and the audience. This is something that Sharp (1973) developed in his theory of 'political ju-jitsu' and that Brian Martin discusses as 'backfire'.

130 McAllister (1982: iii).

7 Nonviolent 'normative regulation'

1 Satha-Anand (1981; 'From violent to nonviolent discourse', 1991).

2 Bauman (*Auschwitz och det moderna samhället*, 1989); Millgram (*Lydnad och auktoritet: Experimentsituationer, resultat och utvärdering*, 1975).

3 Gandhi (1945: 3–4).

4 Gandhi (1945: 21).

5 Gandhi (1945: 21).

6 Gandhi (1945: 25–6).

7 Chabot (2003: 55).

8 Chabot (2003: 201).

9 McAdam (1988: 122–3).

10 Chabot (2003: 198–9).

11 Shoben Jr, Werdell and Long ('Radical student organizations', 1970:

218). See also Tracy (1996), who finds that the 'radical pacifism' in the 1940s played a decisive role for the radicalism of the 1960s in the USA.

12 Ebert (1983). Norenius (1983) develops a similar argument.

13 Ebert (1983: 36–45). My translation from German, here and in all subsequent quotes from Ebert.

14 The concept of 'civil usurpation' is Ebert's own, and is formulated in reaction to Sharp's 'nonviolent intervention', which does not discern the constructive dimension of action (see Ebert 1983: 208).

15 Ebert (1983: 42).

16 Ebert (1983: 43, 231).

17 Ebert (1983: 233).

18 In an empirical and historical study of several nonviolent movements, especially actions in Nevada against test detonations of nuclear weapons, Futrell and Brents ('Protest as terrorism?: The potential for violent anti-nuclear activism', 2003) have shown that, precisely because of 'normalising relations between authorities and protesters', violence by the activists is 'highly unlikely', even at the centre of the conflict.

19 Maeckelbergh (2011: 302).

20 Van de Sande ('The prefigurative politics of Tahrir Square: an alternative perspective on the 2011 revolutions', 2013: 230, 232).

21 Springer ('Human geography without hierarchy', 2014: 408, 412).

22 Even if prefigurative politics corresponds directly to what is done within normative regulation, the concept – *prefigurative* – does not position itself within a social theory of action. So, what I am referring to is what is discussed in relation to normative rationality in order to continue applying Habermas's theoretical social action framework.

23 Gandhi (1945: 4).

24 See, for example, Gregg (1935: 224 ff., 239 ff.). For modern approaches to the preparation for nonviolence based on Gandhi's perspective, see Desai (*Handbook for Satyagrahis*, 1985) or Nhat Hanh (2003).

25 Foucault (1998: 35); Horsburgh (1968: 65–9).

26 Merritt ('One dent at a time: a sociological perspective of the Plowshares Movement', 1992: 93) thinks that the nonviolent community's 'nonconformity to dominant norms' prepares activists for prison.

27 Gregg (1935: 293, note 5).

28 Mohammad Raqib in Sharp (2004: Chapter 8).

29 Mohammad Raqib in Sharp (2004: 120).

30 Zietlow (*A Reflective History of Training for Nonviolent Action in the Civil Rights and Peace Movements 1942–1972, USA*, 1977).

31 Gregg (1935) describes nonviolence as 'remoralising'. For a critical analysis of how nonviolence training handbooks also express a new and problematic use of power, and not just training in nonviolence, see Vinthagen (2005: Chapter 8).

32 McKay (*Training for Nonviolent Action for High School Students: A handbook*, 1971: Chapter 15).

33 Coover et al. (1977: xi).

34 Heiss ('Social roles', 1990: 97–9).

35 See Bourdieu and Wacquant (1992); Bourdieu (1995; *Practical Reason: On the theory of action*, 1998).

36 Bourdieu alternates between describing habitus as a 'disposition', 'style/taste', 'feeling for the game', practical knowledge, embodied habit and so on.

37 Bourdieu (1998: 4–5, especially Figure 1, p. 5).

38 Bourdieu (1995: 12).

39 Bourdieu (1995: 13–14). 'Practical sense' is similar to the way in which dancers 'know' through their bodies what should be done, but they cannot completely explain it to others. The practice's patterns of interaction are taught through their application.

40 Bourdieu (1995: 19–20, 91–2, 122).

41 Bourdieu (1995: 53).

42 Bourdieu (1995: 54–5).

43 Bourdieu (1995: 56).

44 Tilly (2004).

45 Giddens (*Contemporary Social Theory*, 1982).

46 Bourdieu (*Den manliga dominansen*, 1999: Chapter 1).

47 Bourdieu (1995: 56).

48 Bourdieu (1995: 61).

49 Burkitt ('Technologies of the self: habitus and capacities', 2002: 225).

50 Bourdieu and Wacquant (1992: 133 ff.).

51 Burkitt (2002: 225).

52 Bourdieu (1995: 64–5).

53 Pileggi and Patton ('Introduction: Bourdieu and cultural studies', 2003: 323).

54 'Habitus is ... an *open system of dispositions* that is constantly subjected to experiences ... and, depending upon the stimuli and structure of the field, the very same habitus will generate different, even opposite, outcomes' (Bourdieu and Wacquant 1992: 133, 135). See also Broady (1991).

55 Burkitt (2002: 226–7).

56 Bourdieu and Wacquant (1992: 133, 137).

57 Burkitt (2002); Pileggi and Patton (2003).

58 Bourdieu (1999: Chapter 1).

59 In a strict sense, it is not a 'habit' (in the sense of everyday language) that needs to be changed, but the *habitus* in which the practical rationality is built in (Burkitt 2002: 225). Habitus goes deeper than 'habit' and is more difficult to change.

60 Stokke ('Habitus, capital and fields: conceptualizing the capacity of actors in local politics', 2002: 6) finds that a modification is complicated: 'dispositions are durable in the sense that they are embodied in individuals and operate at the sub-conscious level. This means that they are not *readily* available to conscious reflection and modification' (italics added).

61 Social experimentation is a central part of the training (see Coover et al., 1977: 153).

62 See, for example, McKay (1971: 9, 46). Drama exercises in which the participants play animals or machines are to facilitate the 'loosening up of a group'.

63 Vinthagen (1997a). See Held (*Demokratimodeller: Från klassisk demokrati till demokratisk autonomi*, 1995: 95–110) on the concept of 'radical democratic'.

64 Logically, it follows that the more the practical skill required by the nonviolent activists deviates from the culture in which the participants have been formed, the more difficult it is for an individual to maintain this new nonviolent culture. As a result, both support and pressure are required to an even greater extent from the surrounding nonviolent social field in which the individual finds him- or herself so that they can maintain that practice.

65 However, the question is: how long do the normalising effects of training last? This is an empirical question that lies outside the scope of this inquiry.

66 The sociologists and activists

Martin Oppenheimer and George Lakey (1965: 64–5) find that there are five reasons for using forms of role playing in training: to practise skills, to understand the opponent, to build up morale, to release tensions and to create more democracy within the movement.

67 Zietlow (1977: Chapter 2, 'Action and training').

68 Zietlow (1977: Chapter 2, 'Action and training').

69 Walker (*Training for Nonviolent Action: Some history, analysis, reports of surveys*, 1973: 8, in 'Trainers and organizers').

70 Gandhi (1983: 56). But Gandhi thinks that a collective must experience its own nonviolent strength and that this strength cannot come from strong and highly developed individuals solving the group's problems.

71 Sharp (1979: 273–85); Gandhi (1970: 18, 146). Gandhi thought that even he was very far from perfection.

72 Sharp (1979: 285); Gandhi (1942: 108). Gandhi certainly argued often against cowardice and weakness (see, for example, 1942: 82, 254), but, from what I can gather, this was in polemics against those who claimed that nonviolent struggle was an expression of the weak person's alternative within the struggle.

73 Vinthagen (2005: Chapter 3).

74 Gandhi (1942: 108).

75 See Gandhi's text about the constructive programme (1945). Ebert makes a basic classification of nonviolent actions based on whether they are mainly forms of *subversion* or *construction* (1983: 37). Even spiritual development was seen by Gandhi as a creation of the ability to act nonviolently.

76 Several of Gandhi's most dedicated collaborators had a background in ashrams (see Pandya, *Gandhiji and his Disciples*, 1994).

77 Weber (*On the Salt March*, 1997).

78 Ostergaard (*Nonviolent Revolution in India*, 1985).

79 Toh and Floresca-Cawagas ('Institutionalization of nonviolence', 1999).

80 Gandhi (1999: Volume 79: 65).

81 Fox (1989: Chapter 3).

82 Berrigan (1996: 163 ff.); Coover et al. (1977); O'Gorman (1983).

83 Shepard (*The Community of the Ark*, 1990).

84 Quoted from Chabot (2003: 188).

85 O'Gorman (1983: 42–3).

86 Fox (1989); Vinthagen and Chabot ('The relational and constructionist dynamics of nonviolent action', 2002).

87 McAdam et al. (2001).

88 Habermas (1988: 200).

89 Thomson (*Gandhi and His Ashrams*, 1993).

90 Rigby (1974). 'Resistance communities' or other intentional communities are found in certain current nonviolent movements, for example the Catholic Worker Movement in the USA.

91 Kuper (1960).

92 According to Walter Sisulu, in an interview with the author, summer 1994. He was one of the main organisers of the disobedience campaign. See also Holland (1989: 80–1).

93 Taylor and Whittier ('Analytical approaches to social movement culture: the culture of the women's movement', 1995: 186).

94 Sörensen and Vinthagen ('Nonviolent resistance and culture', 2012: 444–70).

95 Concerning the concept of culture, see McLaren ('On ideology

and education: critical pedagogy and the politics of education', 1988: 171); Kreisberg (*Transforming Power: Domination, empowerment, and education*, 1992: 13).

96 Vinthagen (2001).

97 Enacting means that *the physical form appears* as an organised whole. Turner and Killian (*Collective Behavior*, 1987) prefer 'prefigurative culture' and Epstein ('The politics of prefigurative community: the non-violent direct action movement', 2002) uses 'prefigurative community' when discussing nonviolent movements.

98 Taylor and Whittier (1995: 178–9).

99 Thörn (*Modernitet, sociologi och sociala rörelser*, 1997a; 1997b).

100 Lofland (*Polite Protesters: The American peace movement of the 1980s*, 1993: Chapter 3).

101 Lederach (*Building Peace: Sustainable reconciliation in divided societies*, 1997: especially Chapter 9).

102 Miljöko (*La Innerdalen leve!*, 1981); Ringen ('Innerdalen: Norge ved skilleveien', 1980).

103 Næss (2002: 96–7).

104 Sangvai (*The River and Life: People's struggle in the Narmada Valley*, 2002).

105 The details about MST are primarily based on about ten interviews with the movement's organisers, mainly conducted during a month's visit to southern Brazil in 2002, but also draw on secondary literature: see Kjörling (*Så länge det finns hunger: De jordlösas rörelse i Brasilien*, 2004); Plummer and Ranum ('Brazil's Landless Workers Movement: Movimiento de Trabajadores Rurales Sem Terra: MST', 2002); Veltmeyer and Petras ('The social dynamics of Brazil's Rural Landless Workers' Movement: Ten

hypotheses on successful leadership', 2002); Branford and Rocha (2002). A previous version of this cultural analysis has been presented in a conference paper: Vinthagen (*A Movement Culture of Nonviolent Action*, 2003b). See also Chabot and Vinthagen ('Rethinking nonviolent action and contentious politics: political cultures of nonviolent opposition in the Indian independence movement and Brazil's Landless Workers Movement', 2007).

106 Kjörling (2004: Chapter 8).

107 Branford and Rocha (2002: 121).

108 Branford and Rocha think that MST is transformed from a 'culture of resistance' to a 'culture of liberation' in the process of community building (2002: Chapter 13).

109 The selection of elements is inspired by Johnston and Klandermans (1995).

110 Branford and Rocha (2002: 117–18).

111 See, for example, Frazer Evans et al. (*Pedagogies for the Non-Poor*, 1987).

112 Lucas ('And the meek shall occupy the earth', 2001: 2).

113 Sörensen and Vinthagen (2012).

114 Lofland ('Charting degrees of movement culture: tasks of the cultural cartographer', 1995: 192); Fine ('Public narration and group culture: discerning discourse in social movements', 1995).

115 Johansson (*Narrativ teori och metod*, 2005: 121 ff.).

116 Johansson (2005).

117 Kjörling (2004).

118 Lofland (1995: 203).

119 Fantasia and Hirsch ('Culture in rebellion: the appropriation and transformation of the veil in the Algerian revolution', 1995).

120 Fantasia and Hirsch (1995); Fanon (1963: Chapter 4).

121 The movement of the shanty towns is called Movimento dos Trabalhadores Sem Teto (MTST), the Homeless Workers' Movement.

122 Taylor and Whittier (1995).

123 The concept of the 'frame' comes from Goffman (*An Essay on the Organization of Experience: Frame analysis*, 1986).

124 Snow et al. ('Frame align-ment processes, micromobilization, and movement participation', 1986); Melucci (1996a).

125 Nonviolent culture comes about through a complex combination of cultural activities, for example these nine used by MST. The concepts express the organisation of central values, practices and perceptions for nonviolence (cf. Johnston and Klandermans 1995). Put together, they organise a nonviolent society.

8 A theory of nonviolent action

1 Vinthagen (2005: Chapter 3).

2 'This applies to nonviolence ... that it *can never completely be realised*' (Goss-Mayr 1979: 55).

3 Erikson (1969: 445) uses the term 'ashram-in-motion' to describe the Indian Salt March participants' wandering, while, as ashram members, they maintained the essential routines that applied in their everyday life in the ashrams during the march.

4 Ostergaard (1985) and Shepard (*Gandhi Today: A report on Mahatma Gandhi's successors*, 1987). Vinoba focused on 'positive satyagraha', which then met with Jayaprakash Narayan's (JP) 'negative satyagraha' (Ostergaard 1985: 348). A division oc-curred in the nonviolent construction as it related to nonviolent resistance.

Both movements were large and partially successful but suffered from not effectively combining the various elements (see ibid.: 348 ff.): Vinoba did not disrupt the unjust division of land and JP's resistance movement for 'Total Revolution' did not work sufficiently on building alternative institutions. Ultimately, the 'Total Revolution' failed to disrupt the elite-controlled democracy; instead, it led to Prime Minister Indira Gandhi intro-ducing a state of emergency in 1975 (she was the daughter of Nehru and not related to Gandhi – they merely shared a name that is common in India). See also Bhattacharjea (*Unfin-ished Revolution: A political biography of Jayaprakash Narayan*, 2004).

5 Moreover, there are inherent tensions or contradictions *inside* each of the action types, something I have discussed in other contexts (Vinthagen 2005).

6 Habermas (1996: 61).

7 'There is a connection between the "existence" of norms and the anticipated justifiability of the corresponding "ought" statements, a connection for which there is no parallel' (Habermas 1996: 62).

8 Fox (1989: 60).

9 Fox (1989: 59).

10 Gandhi (1970: 17, 22).

11 Næss (1974: 121) discusses nonviolence as 'goal revealing'.

12 Vinthagen (2005: 427, note 2).

13 Bondurant (1988: 189–99).

14 Bondurant (1988: 190).

15 Karn (1994) emphasises conformity to law, but he creates a mathematical model of nonviolence.

16 See Gandhi (1970: 142–7) on 'the law of suffering' and nonviolence as 'conscious suffering'. Gandhi viewed himself as a Hindu karmic yogi, and Hinduism is sometimes

called the Eternal Law (*sanatana dharma*). Karma expresses conformity to law (*dharma*) and a yogi is a person who follows the religious law in an attempt to reach perfection.

17 Gandhi (1999: Volume 75: 47).

18 Habermas (1996: 202). At the same time, the other side of the coin is that all participants (even the other) must be empathetically sensitive enough towards each other in order to reach a solution.

19 Bondurant (1988: 197). However, Bondurant's choice of the concept of 'adjustment' indicates that compromise rather than consensus is a (realistic) goal.

20 One difference is that Habermas sees the moral truth as only social, while for Gandhi it is part of life itself, an actual truth about reality. For Habermas, rationality relates to three different worlds – the objective, the social and the subjective – while for Gandhi there is just one world and it is rational in itself, not because people describe it rationally.

21 See Sharp (1973: 716–17, 787–8) on self-esteem and happiness among activists in the fight against oppressors.

22 Sharp (1973: 783–4) claims that there was an 'increased fearlessness' among the civil rights activists.

23 Vander Zanden (1969: 58). 'Negro' was the common self-designation within the Civil Rights Movement at the time (on the designations used here, see Sharp 1973: 717). Vander Zanden ('The non-violent resistance movement against segregation', 1963), however, uses the designations 'accommodating negro' and 'the new militant negro'. See Fox (1989) on the way in which Gandhi implemented a corresponding culture combination in India.

BIBLIOGRAPHY

A Day Without the Pentagon (1998) *A Day without the Pentagon: Tactical manual*. New York NY: War Resisters' League.

Ackerman, Peter and Jack DuVall (2000) *A Force More Powerful: A century of nonviolent conflict*. New York NY: St Martin's Press.

Ackerman, Peter and Christopher Kruegler (1994) *Strategic Nonviolent Conflict: The dynamics of people power in the twentieth century*. Westport CT: Praeger Publishers.

Ajangiz, Rafael (1997) 'Conscientious objection in Spain'. Paper presented at the conference Conscientious Objection in Europe, Georgsmarienhütte, Germany, 18 October.

— (2001) 'Empowerment for demilitarisation: civil disobedience gets rid of conscription (Spain 1985–2000)'. Case study for War Resisters' International, Nonviolence and Social Empowerment Project. Presented at the conference in Puri, Orissa, India, 18–24 February. Available at www.wri-irg.org/archive/nvse2001/nvse/nvsecase-en.htm#insumiso (accessed 12 August 2005).

— (2002) 'The European farewell to conscription' in Lars Mjøset and Stephen Van Holde (eds) *The Comparative Study of Conscription in the Armed Forces*. Oxford: Elsevier Science, pp. 307–33.

— (n.d.) 'Conscientious objection as manifestation of the conflict between society and (the military dimension) of the state'. Workshop handout (copy with author).

Amnéus, Diana, Ditte Eile, Ulrika Flock, Pernilla Rosell Steuer and Gunnel Testad (2004) *Validation Techniques and Counter Strategies: Methods for dealing with power structures and changing social climates*. Stockholm: University of Stockholm.

Andersen, Heine (2003) 'Jürgen Habermas' in Heine Andersen and Bo Kaspersen (eds) *Klassisk och modern samhällsteori*. Lund: Studentlitteratur, pp. 427–47.

Anderson, Shelley and Janet Larmore (eds) (1991) *Nonviolent Struggle and Social Defence*. London: War Resisters' International.

Ansbro, John J. (2000) *Martin Luther King, Jr.: Nonviolent strategies and tactics for social change*. Lanham MD: Madison Books.

Apel, Karl-Otto (1990) *Etik och kommunikation*. Gothenburg: Daidalos.

April Mobilization (1987) *Nonviolent Civil Disobedience at CIA Headquarters, Langley, Virginia, Monday April 27, 1987*. Washington DC: April Mobilization.

Arad, Yitzhak (1996) 'The Jewish fighting underground in the ghettos of Eastern Europe – ideology and reality' in Yisrael Gutman and Avital Saf (eds) *Major Changes* within the Jewish People in the Wake of the Holocaust: Proceedings of the Ninth Yad Vashem International Historical Conference. Jerusalem: Yad Vashem, pp. 337–57.

Arendt, Hannah (1972) Crisis of the Republic. San Diego CA: Harcourt Brace & Company.

Ås, Berit (1978) 'Hersketeknikker'. Kjerringråd 3: 17–21.

Awad, Mubarak E. and R. Scott Kennedy (1985) Nonviolent Struggle in the Middle East. Philadelphia PA: New Society Publishers.

Bala, Sruti (2004) 'Why performance studies should be interested in nonviolent action' in Christopher B. Balme and Meike Wagner (eds) Beyond Aesthetics: Studies in performance and media. Trier: Wissenschaftlicher Verlag, pp. 101–10.

Bauman, Zygmunt (1989) Auschwitz och det moderna samhället. Gothenburg: Daidalos.

Bedau, Hugo Adam (ed.) (1996) Civil Disobedience in Focus. London: Routledge.

Benford, Robert D. and Scott A. Hunt (1995) 'Dramaturgy and social movements: the social construction and communication of power' in Stanford M. Lyman (ed.) Social Movements: Critiques, concepts and case-studies. London: Macmillan.

Berg, Lars Eric (1996) 'Främlingen i jaget: en interaktionistisk tolkning av främlingskapet' in Gunilla Hallerstedt and Thomas Johansson (eds) Främlingskapets anatomi. Stockholm: Carlssons, pp. 29–58.

Bergfeldt, Lennart (1993) 'Experiences of civilian resistance: the case of Denmark 1940–1945'. Dissertation, Uppsala University.

Beronius, Mats (1986) Den disciplinära maktens organisering: Om makt

och arbetsorganisation. Lund: Studentlitteratur.

Berrigan, Philip (with Fred A. Wilcox) (1996) Fighting the Lamb's War: Skirmishes with the American empire. The autobiography of Philip Berrigan. Monroe ME: Common Courage Press.

Bhattacharjea, Ajit (2004) Unfinished Revolution: A political biography of Jayaprakash Narayan. New Delhi: Rupa and Co.

Biggs, Michael (2003) 'When costs are beneficial: protest as communicative suffering'. Paper presented at the Comparative Politics Workshop, University of Chicago, May.

Bläsi, Burkhard (2001) Konflikttransformation durch Gütekraft: Interpersonale Veränderungsprozesse. Münster: Lit Verlag.

Bloch, Maurice (1992) Prey into Hunter: The politics of religious experience. Cambridge: Cambridge University Press.

Blumer, Herbert (1969) Symbolic Interactionism: Perspective and method. Englewood Cliffs NJ: Prentice Hall.

Bondurant, Joan V. (1988 [1958]) Conquest of Violence: The Gandhian philosophy of conflict. Princeton NJ: Princeton University Press.

Boserup, Anders and Andrew Mack (1974) War without Weapons. London: Frances Pinter.

Bouillier, Véronique (2003) 'The violence of the non-violent' in Denis Vidal, Gilles Tarabout and Eric Meyer (eds) Violence/Nonviolence: Some Hindu perspectives. New Delhi: Manohar Publishers & Distributors, pp. 27–63.

Bourdieu, Pierre (1995) The Logic of Practice. Oxford: Blackwell Publishers.

— (1998) Practical Reason: On the

theory of action. Oxford: Polity Press.

— (1999) *Den manliga dominansen*. Gothenburg: Daidalos.

— and Loïc J. D.Wacquant (1992) *An Invitation to Reflexive Sociology*. Cambridge: Polity Press.

Branagan, Marty (2002) 'The art(s) of nonviolent activism'. Paper presented at the conference Arts of Dissent, Melbourne, 21 October.

Branford, S. and J. Rocha (2002) *Cutting the Wire: The story of the landless movement in Brazil*. London: Latin American Bureau.

Breines, Wini (1980) 'Community and organization: the new left and Michels' "iron law"'. *Social Problems* 27(4): 419–29.

Broady, Donald (1991) *Sociologi och Epistemologi: Om Pierre Bourdieus författarskap och den historiska epistemologin*. Stockholm: HLS Förlag.

Burger, Thomas (1976) *Max Weber's Theory of Concept Formation: History, laws, and ideal types*. Durham NC: Duke University Press.

Burkitt, Ian (2002) 'Technologies of the self: habitus and capacities'. *Journal for Theory of Social Behaviour* 32(2): 219–37.

Burrowes, Robert J. (1996) *The Strategy of Nonviolent Defense: A Gandhian approach*. Albany NY: State University of New York Press.

Carson, Clayborne, David J. Garrow, Gerald Gill, Vincent Harding and Darlene Clark Hine (eds) (1991) *The Eyes on the Prize Civil Rights Reader: Documents, speeches and firsthand accounts from the black freedom struggle 1954–1990*. New York NY: Penguin.

Case, Clarence Marsh (1923) *Nonvio-*

lent Coercion, New York: Century Meredith Press.

Chabot, Sean Taudin (2003) 'Crossing the great divide: the Gandhian repertoire's transnational diffusion to the American Civil Rights Movement'. Dissertation, University of Amsterdam.

— and Stellan Vinthagen (2007) 'Rethinking nonviolent action and contentious politics: political cultures of nonviolent opposition in the Indian independence movement and Brazil's Landless Workers Movement'. *Research in Social Movements, Conflicts and Change* 27: 91–122.

Chambers, Simone (1995) 'Feminist discourse/practical discourse' in Johanna Meehan (ed.) *Feminists Read Habermas: Gendering the subject of discourse*. New York NY: Routledge, pp. 163–79.

Chandra, Bipan (1989) *India's Struggle for Independence*. New Delhi: Penguin Books.

Cheater, Angela (1999) *The Anthropology of Power: Empowerment and disempowerment in changing structures*. London: Routledge.

Chenoweth, Erica and Maria J. Stephan (2011) *Why Civil Resistance Works*. New York NY: Columbia University Press.

Chilton, Stephen (2005) 'Comparing satyagraha and the US Peace and Justice Movement in the light of discourse ethics'. Paper in progress. Available at www.d.umn.edu/~schilton/Articles/TMDEsatyagraha.article.html (accessed 16 September 2012).

Christie, Daniel J., Richard Wagner and Deborah DuNann Winter (2001) *Peace, Conflict, and Violence: Peace psychology for the 21st century*. Upper Saddle River NJ: Prentice Hall.

Churchill, Ward (1999) *Pacifism as Pathology: Reflections on the role of armed struggle in North America.* Edinburgh: AK Press.

Clamshell Alliance (1977) *We Can Stop the Seabrook Nuclear Plant: Occupier's handbook. Join us: April 30.* Seabrook NH: Clamshell Alliance.

Clark, Howard (1984) *Preparing for Non-violent Direct Action.* London: Peace News and CND.

Coady, C. A. J. (1999) 'The idea of violence' in Manfred B. Steger and Nancy S. Lind (eds) *Violence and Its Alternatives: An interdisciplinary reader.* London: Palgrave Macmillan.

Coalition for Direct Action at Seabrook (1979) *Let's Shut Down Seabrook! Handbook for Oct. 6, 1979: Direct action occupation.* Cambridge MA: Boston Clamshell.

Cohen, Jean L. and Andrew Arato (1994) *Civil Society and Political Theory.* Cambridge MA: MIT Press.

Coles, Robert (1969) 'Social struggle and weariness' in Barry McLaughlin (ed.) *Studies in Social Movements: A social psychological perspective.* New York NY: Free Press.

Continental Walk (1975) *The Continental Walk for Disarmament and Social Justice: Organizers manual.* New York NY: The Continental Walk.

Cook, Alice and Gwyn Kirk (1983) *Greenham Women Everywhere: Dreams, ideas, and actions from the women's peace movement.* London: Pluto Press.

Cooney, Robert and Helen Michalowski (eds) (1977) *The Power of the People.* Culver City CA: Peace Press.

Coover, Virginia, Charles Esser, Ellen Deacon and Christopher Moore (1977) *A Resource Manual for a Living Revolution.* Philadelphia PA: New Society Publishers.

Cox, Robert W. (1993) 'Gramsci, hegemony and international relations: an essay in method' in Stephen Gill (ed.) *Gramsci, Historical Materialism and International Relations.* Cambridge: Cambridge University Press.

Coy, Patrick G. (2013) 'Whither nonviolent studies'. *Peace Review: A Journal of Social Justice* 25(2): 257–65.

Crowell, Daniel W. (2003) *The SEWA Movement and Rural Development: The Banaskantha and Kutch experience.* New Delhi: Sage Publications India.

Dajani, Souad (1999) 'Nonviolent resistance in the occupied territories: a critical re-evaluation' in Stephen Zunes, Lester R. Kurtz and Sarah Beth Asher (eds) *Nonviolent Social Movements: A geographical perspective.* Malden MA: Blackwell Publishers.

Dear, John (1993) *Disarming the Heart: Toward a vow of nonviolence.* Scottdale PA: Herald Press.

Dejke, Anders (ed.) (1989) *Trädkramare inför rätta.* Gothenburg: Bokskogen.

Desai, Narayan (1985) *Handbook for Satyagrahis.* New Delhi: Gandhi Peace Foundation.

Dielemans, Jennie and Fredrik Quistbergh (2000) *Motstånd.* Stockholm: Bokförlaget DN.

Douglass, Jim (1984) 'We cannot stop the white train by being the white train'. Poulsbo WA: Ground

Zero Center for Non-Violent Action.

Ebert, Theodor (1983) *Gewaltfreier Aufstand: Alternative Zum Bürgerkrieg*. Waldkirch: Waldkircher Verlagsgesellschaft.

Eisenberg, Nancy (2000) 'Empathy and sympathy' in Michael Lewis and Jeanette M. Haviland-Jones (eds) *Handbook of Emotions*. New York NY: Guilford Press, pp. 677–91.

Epstein, Barbara (2002) 'The politics of prefigurative community: the non-violent direct action movement' in Stephen Duncombe (ed.) *Cultural Resistance Reader*. New York NY: W. W. Norton and Co., pp. 333–46.

Erickson-Nepstad, Sharon (2005) *Prophetic Provocation: War resistance in the Plowshares Movement*. No publisher details (copy of the manuscript with author).

— (2011) *Nonviolent Revolutions: Civil resistance in the late 20th century*. Oxford: Oxford University Press.

Erikson, Erik (1969) *Gandhi's Truth: On the origins of militant nonviolence*. New York NY: W. W. Norton & Company.

Eyerman, Ron and Andrew Jamison (1996) *Social Movements: A cognitive approach*. University Park PA: Penn State University Press.

Falk, Tomas and Igge Olsson (2000) *Överens: En bok om demokratiska mötesformer*. Uppsala: Fria Förlaget.

Fanon, Frantz (1961) *Les Damnés de la Terre*. Paris: F. Maspero.

— (1963) *The Wretched of the Earth*. New York NY: Grove Press.

Fantasia, Rick and Eric L. Hirsch (1995) 'Culture in rebellion: the appropriation and transformation of the veil in the Algerian revolution' in Hank Johnston and Bert Klandermans (eds) *Social Movements and Culture*. Minneapolis MN: University of Minnesota Press, pp. 144–59.

Feminism and Nonviolence Study Group and War Resisters' International (1983) *Piecing It Together: Feminism and nonviolence*. Westward Ho!, Devon: Feminism and Nonviolence Study Group in co-operation with the War Resisters' International.

Fine, Gary Alan (1995) 'Public narration and group culture: discerning discourse in social movements' in Hank Johnston and Bert Klandermans (eds) *Social Movements and Culture*. Minneapolis MN: University of Minnesota Press, pp. 127–43.

Foucault, Michel (1972) *The Archaeology of Knowledge & The Discourse on Language*. New York NY: Tavistock Publications and Pantheon Books.

— (1974) *Övervakning och straff*. Lund: Studentlitteratur.

— (1980) *Power/Knowledge: Selected interviews and other writings 1972–1977*, edited by Colin Gordon. New York NY: Pantheon Books.

— (1988) 'Politics and reason' in L. D. Kritzman (ed.) *Politics, Philosophy, Culture, Interviews and other Writings 1977–1984*. New York NY: Routledge.

— (1994) 'Critical theory/intellectual history' in Michael Kelly (ed.) *Critique and Power: Recasting the Foucault/Habermas debate*. Cambridge MA: MIT Press.

— (1998) 'Technologies of the self' in L. H. Martin, H. Gutman and P. H. Hutton (eds) *Technologies of the Self: A seminar with Michel Foucault*. Cambridge MA: MIT Press, pp. 16–49.

— (2002) *Sexualitetens historia: Viljan att veta*, Volume 1. Gothenburg: Daidalos.

— (2003) *Society Must be Defended: Lectures at the Collège de France 1975–1976*. New York NY: Picador.

Fox, Richard G. (1989) *Gandhian Utopia: Experiments with culture*. Boston MA: Beacon Press.

Frazer Evans, Alice, Robert A. Evans and William Bean Kennedy (1987) *Pedagogies for the Non-poor*. New York NY: Orbis Books.

Futrell, Robert and Barbara G. Brents (2003) 'Protest as terrorism? The potential for violent anti-nuclear activism'. *American Behavioral Scientist* 46(6): 745–65.

Galtung, Johan (1965) *On the Meaning of Nonviolence*. PRIO Publication 20–2. Oslo: Peace Research Institute Oslo (PRIO).

— (1969) 'Violence, peace and peace research'. *Journal of Peace Research* 6(3): 167–91.

— (1990) 'Cultural violence'. *Journal of Peace Research* 27(3): 291–305.

— (1996) *Peace by Peaceful Means: Peace and conflict, development and civilization*. London: Sage Publications.

— and Arne Næss (1990) *Gandhis politiske etikk*. Oslo: Pax Forlag A/S.

Gandhi, M. K. (1927) *An Autobiography or The Story of My Experiments with Truth*. Translated by Mahadev Desai. Ahmedabad: Navajivan Publishing House.

— (1942) *Non-Violence in Peace and War*, Volume 1. Ahmedabad: Navajivan Publishing House.

— (1945) *Constructive Programme: Its meaning and place*. Ahmedabad:

Navajivan Trust (edited version of 1941 original).

— (1970) *Essential Writings*. Ahmedabad: Navajivan Publishing House.

— (1983) *För pacifister*. Gothenburg: Haga Bokförlag (extracts from Gandhi's writings, originally published in 1949).

— (1997 [1910]) *Hind Swaraj: And other writings*. Edited by Anthony J. Parel. New Delhi: Foundation Books.

— (1998) *Gandhi for 21st Century: 1–24*, edited by S. Ramakrishnan and A. T. Hingorani (eds). Mumbai: Manibhavan Gandhi Sangrahalaya.

— (1999) *The Collected Works of Mahatma Gandhi*. New Delhi: Ministry of Information and Broadcasting Publications Division.

Giddens, Anthony (1982) *Contemporary Social Theory*. London: Macmillan.

— (1994) *Sociologi*. Lund: Studentlitteratur.

— (1995) *Modernity and Self-Identity: Self and society in the late modern age*. Cambridge: Polity Press.

Glasl, Friedrich (1994) *Konfliktmanagement: Ein Handbuch zur Diagnose und Behandlung von Konflikten für Organisationen und ihre Berater*. Stuttgart: Verlag Freies Geistesleben.

Goffman, Erving (1961) *Asylums: Essays on the social situation of mental patients and other inmates*. New York NY: Anchor Books.

— (1963) *Stigma: Notes on the management of spoiled identity*. Englewood Cliffs NJ: Prentice Hall.

— (1967) *Interaction Ritual: Essays on face-to-face behaviour*. New York NY: Pantheon Books.

— (1970) *Strategic Interaction:*

Conduct and communication No. 1. Philadelphia PA: University of Pennsylvania Press.

— (1974) *Jaget och maskerna: En studie i vardagslivets dramatik*. Stockholm: Nordstedts Akademiska Förlag.

— (1986) *An Essay on the Organization of Experience: Frame analysis*. Boston MA: Northeastern University Press.

Goss, Jean and Hildegard Goss-Mayr (1990) *The Gospel and the Struggle for Justice and Peace: Training seminar in evangelical nonviolence and methods of engaging in it*. Stockholm: Swedish Ecumenical Council and International Fellowship of Reconciliation.

Goss-Mayr, Hildegard et al. (1979) *De fattigas gåva till de rika: Om ickevåldskamp i Latinamerika*. Falköping: Gummessons.

Gregg, Richard B. (1935) *The Power of Non-Violence*. London: George Routledge & Sons.

Grossman, Dave (1996) *On Killing: The psychological cost of learning to kill in war and society*. Boston MA: Little, Brown & Co.

Gugel, Günther (1983) *Gewaltfreiheit: Ein Lebensprinzip: Materialen 6*. Tübingen: Verein für Friedenspädagogik.

— and Horst Furtner (1983) *Gewaltfreie Aktion: Materialen 7*. Tübingen: Verein für Friedenspädagogik.

Habermas, Jürgen (1975) *Legitimation Crisis*. Boston MA: Beacon Press.

— (1984) *The Theory of Communicative Action: Reason and the rationalization of society*, Volume 1. Oxford: Polity Press.

— (1988) *Kommunikativt handlande*. Gothenburg: Daidalos.

— (1989) *The Theory of Communicative Action: Lifeworld and the system: a critique of functionalist reason*. Volume 2. Oxford: Polity Press.

— (1990) *Moral Consciousness and Communicative Action*. Cambridge MA: MIT Press.

— (1996) *Moral Consciousness and Communicative Action*. Cambridge MA: MIT Press.

— (1998) *On the Pragmatics of Communication*. Edited by Maeve Cooke. Cambridge MA: MIT Press.

Hardiman, David (2003) *Gandhi in His Time and Ours*. Delhi: Permanent Black.

Hardt, Michael and Antonio Negri (2000) *Empire*. Cambridge MA: Harvard University Press.

Hare, A. Paul and Herbert H. Blumberg (eds) (1968) *Nonviolent Direct Action: American cases: social-psychological analyses*. Washington DC: Corpus Books.

Harris, Ian (1998) 'Nonviolence in urban areas: conversations with practitioners of nonviolence in the Milwaukee area, 1989 to 1994'. *Research and Opinion* 12(1) (January).

Haugaard, Mark (1997) *The Constitution of Power: A theoretical analysis of power, knowledge and structure*. Manchester: Manchester University Press.

Heidegren, Carl-Göran (2004) 'Livsstil och livsföring i Simmels och Webers klassiska sociologi'. *Sociologisk Forskning* 4–2004: 39–62.

Heiss, Jerhold (1990) 'Social roles' in Morris Rosenberg and Ralph H. Turner (eds) *Social Psychology: Sociological perspectives*. New Brunswick NJ: Transaction Publishers.

Held, David (1995) *Demokratimodeller: Från klassisk demokrati till demokratisk autonomi*. Gothenburg: Daidalos.

Helvey, Robert L. (2004) *On Strategic Nonviolent Conflict: Thinking about the fundamentals*. Boston MA: Albert Einstein Foundation.

Herngren, Per (1990) *Handbok i Civil Olydnad*. Stockholm: Bonniers.

— (1999) *Civil Olydnad: En dialog*. Gothenburg: Lindelöws Bokförlag.

— and Stellan Vinthagen (1992) *Handbok för Avrustningslägret i Linköping: Tidskriften Omega nr 2*. Åseda: Omega och Avrustningslägret.

Hertle, Wolfgang (1974) '... und sie bewegt sich doch!' (article with author).

Hirdman, Yvonne (1990) *Vi bygger landet: Den svenska arbetarrörelsens historia från Per Götrek till Olof Palme*. Stockholm: Tiden.

Hoeber Rudolph, Susanne and Lloyd I. Rudolph (1983) *Gandhi: The traditional roots of charisma*. 2nd edition. Chicago IL: University of Chicago Press.

Holland, Heidi (1989) *The Struggle: A history of the African National Congress*. London: Grafton Books.

Hollis, Daniel (1998) *The ABC-CLIO World History Companion to Utopian Movements*. Santa Barbara CA: ABC-CLIO.

Holloway, John (2002) *Change the World without Taking Power: The meaning of revolution today*. London: Pluto Press.

Holm, Berit G. (1978) 'Teknisk moralisme i teori for ikkevoldsaksjon og "civilian defence": kritisk analyse av Gene Sharps ikkevoldsteori'. Dissertation, Institute of Philosophy, Oslo University.

Horsburgh, H. J. N. (1968) *Nonviolence and Aggression: A study of Gandhi's moral equivalent of war*. Oxford: Oxford University Press.

Igra, Ludvig (2001) *Den tunna hinnan*. Stockholm: Natur och Kultur.

Izard, Carroll and Brian P. Ackerman (2000) 'Motivational, organizational, and regulatory functions of discrete emotions' in Michael Lewis and Jeanette M. Haviland-Jones (eds) *Handbook of Emotions*. New York NY: Guilford Press, pp. 253–64.

Jaworski, Adam and Nikolas Coupland (eds) (1999) *The Discourse Reader*. London: Routledge.

Johannisson, Karin (2002) 'Modern askes blandar njutning och neuros'. *Axess* 6 (October). Available at www.axess.se (accessed 18 August 2005).

Johansen, Jørgen (1991) 'Humor as a political force'. *Philosophy and Social Action* 17(3–4): 23–7.

— (2004) 'Gewaltfreie erfolgreicher als bewaffneter Kampf. Neue Bedingungen für zivilen Widerstand'. *Wissenschaft und Frieden* 3(22): 12–16.

Johansson, Anna (1999) '*La mujer sufrida*: the suffering woman'. Monograph No. 70. Dissertation, Department of Sociology, University of Gothenburg.

— (2005) *Narrativ teori och metod*. Lund: Studentlitteratur.

Johnston, Hank and Bert Klandermans (eds) (1995) *Social Movements and Culture*. Minneapolis MN: University of Minnesota Press.

Jones, Lynne (ed.) (1983) *Keeping the Peace: Women's peace handbook 1*. London: The Women's Press.

Juergensmeyer, Mark (2003) *Gandhi's Way: A handbook of conflict resolution*. New Delhi: Oxford University Press.

Justice and Reconciliation Division (1989) *Minutes of the Workshop:*

Training of trainers in effective nonviolent action. Johannesburg: Justice and Reconciliation Division, Church of the Province of South Africa.

Kaldor, Mary (2012) *New and Old Wars: Organized violence in a global era*. Cambridge: Polity Press.

Kapadia, Sita (1995) 'A tribute to Mahatma Gandhi: his views on women and social change'. *Journal of South Asia Women Studies* 1(1) (November).

Karatnycky, Adrian and Peter Ackerman (2005) *How Freedom is Won: From civic resistance to durable democracy*. New York NY: Freedom House.

Karlsson, Svante (2004) *Freds- och konfliktkunskap*. Lund: Studentlitteratur.

Karn, Anil (1994) *Science of Satyagraha*. New Delhi: Calyx Publications.

Keen, Sam (1988) *Faces of the Enemy: Reflections of the hostile imagination: The psychology of enmity*. London: Harper & Row.

Kemper, Theodore D. (2000) 'Social models in the exploration of emotions' in Michael Lewis and Jeanette M. Haviland-Jones (eds) *Handbook of Emotions*. New York NY: Guilford Press, pp. 45–58.

King, Martin Luther (1964) *Vi kan inte vänta*. Stockholm: Gummessons Bokförlag.

King, Mary Elizabeth (2014) *Gandhian Nonviolent Struggle and Untouchability in South India: The 1924–25 Vykom satyagraha and mechanisms of change*. Oxford: Oxford University Press.

King, Richard H. (1993) 'Martin Luther King, Jr. and the meaning of freedom: a political interpretation' in Peter J. Albert and Ronald

Hoffman (eds) *We Shall Overcome: Martin Luther King Jr. and the Black Freedom Struggle*. New York NY: Da Capo Press, pp. 130–52.

Kjörling, Lennart (2004) *Så länge det finns hunger: De jordlösas rörelse i Brasilien*. Stockholm: Ordfront.

Klandermans, Bert and Sidney Tarrow (1988) 'Mobilization into social movements: synthesizing European and American approaches' in Bert Klandermans, Hanspeter Kriesi and Sidney Tarrow (eds) *From Structure to Action: Comparing social movement research across cultures*. Greenwich CT: JAI Press, pp. 1–38.

Kriesberg, Louis (1998) *Constructive Conflicts: From escalation to resolution*. Lanham MD: Rowan & Littlefield Publishers.

Kreisberg, Seth (1992) *Transforming Power: Domination, empowerment, and education*. Albany NY: State University of New York Press.

Kuper, Leo (1960) *Passive Resistance in South Africa*. New Haven CT: Yale University Press.

Laclau, Ernesto (ed.) (1994) *The Making of Political Identities*. London: Verso.

Laffin, Arthur J. and Anne Montgomery (eds) (1987) *Swords into Plowshares: Nonviolent direct action for disarmament*. San Francisco CA: Harper & Row.

Lakey, George (1968) 'Mechanisms of nonviolent action' in A. Paul Hare and Herbert H. Blumberg (eds) *Nonviolent Direct Action: American cases: social-psychological analyses*. Washington DC: Corpus Books.

Lederach, John (1997) *Building Peace: Sustainable reconciliation in divided societies*. Washington DC: United States Institute of Peace Press.

Lemert, Charles and Ann Branaman (eds) (1997) *The Goffman Reader*. Oxford: Blackwell Publishers.

Lewis, Michael and Jeanette M. Haviland-Jones (eds) (2000) *Handbook of Emotions*. New York NY: Guilford Press.

Liddell-Hart, B. H. (1960) *Deterrence or Defence*. London: Stevens.

Lilja, Mona and Stellan Vinthagen (2014) 'Sovereign power, disciplinary power and biopower: resisting what power with what resistance?' *Journal of Political Power* 7(1): 107–26.

Livermore Action Group (1983) *International Day of Nuclear Disarmament*. Berkeley CA: Livermore Action Group.

Lofland, John (1993) *Polite Protesters: The American peace movement of the 1980s*. New York NY: Syracuse University Press.

— (1995) 'Charting degrees of movement culture: tasks of the cultural cartographer' in Hank Johnston and Bert Klandermans (eds) *Social Movements and Culture*. Minneapolis MN: University of Minnesota Press, pp. 188–216.

Long, William J. and Peter Brecke (2003) *War and Reconciliation: Reason and emotion in conflict resolution*. Cambridge MA: MIT Press.

Lucas, Ian (1998) *OutRage! An oral history*. London: Cassell.

Lucas, Kintto (2001) 'And the meek shall occupy the earth'. *The Courier* (Unesco), January, pp. 24–6. Available at http://unesdoc.unesco.org/images/0012/001215/121514e.pdf (accessed 6 August 2015).

Lukes, Steven (1974) *Power*. London: Macmillan.

Luthuli, Albert (1962) *Släpp mitt folk!*

Stockholm: Diakonistyrelsens Bokförlag.

Lyman, M. Stanford (ed.) (1995) *Social Movements: Critiques, concepts, case-studies*. London: Macmillan.

Mabee, Carleton (1970) *Black Freedom: The nonviolent abolitionists from 1830 through the Civil War*. London: Collier-Macmillan.

Machiavelli, Niccolò (2003 [1513]) *Fursten*. Stockholm: Bokförlaget Natur och Kultur.

Maeckelbergh, Marianne (2011a) 'The road to democracy: the political legacy of "1968"'. *International Review of Social History* 56(2): 301–32.

— (2011b) 'Doing is believing: prefiguration as strategic practice in the Alterglobalization Movement'. *Social Movement Studies: Journal of Social, Cultural and Political Protest* 10(1): 1–20.

Maines, David. R. (1982) 'In search of mesostructure: studies in the negotiated order'. *Urban Life* 11(3): 267–79.

Månsson, Tomas (2004) *Olydnad: Civil olydnad som demokratiskt problem*. Stockholm: Thales.

Manstead, A. S. R. and M. Hewstone (eds) (1999) *The Blackwell Encyclopedia of Social Psychology*. Oxford: Blackwell Publishers.

Marable, Manning (1991) *Race, Reform and Rebellion: The second reconstruction in black America 1945–1990*. Jackson MS: University of Mississippi.

Markovits, Claude (2003) *The Un-Gandhian Gandhi: The life and afterlife of the Mahatma*. Delhi: Permanent Black.

Marrus, Michael (1995) 'Jewish resistance to the Holocaust'. *Journal of Contemporary History* 30(1): 83–110.

Martin, Brian (1984) *Uprooting War.* London: Freedom Press. Available at www.bmartin.cc/pubs/90uw/ (accessed 6 August 2015).

— (1989) 'Gene Sharp's theory of power'. *Journal of Peace Research* 26(2): 213–22.

— (1991) 'Assessing the Gulf peace team'. *Nonviolence Today* 22 (August–September): 6–7.

— (2005) 'Researching nonviolent action: past themes and future possibilities'. *Peace & Change* 30(2): 247–70.

— and Wendy Varney (2003) 'Nonviolence and communication'. *Journal of Peace Research* 40(2): 213–32.

Mason, Gilbert (2000) *Beaches, Blood, and Ballots: A black doctor's civil right struggle.* Jackson MS: University Press of Mississippi.

Mathai, M. P. (2000) *Mahatma Gandhi's World-View.* New Delhi: Gandhi Peace Foundation.

Mathiesen, Thomas (1978) *Den dolda disciplineringen.* Gothenburg: Korpen.

— (1982) *Makt och motmakt.* Gothenburg: Korpen.

Mbeki, Govan (1992) *The Struggle for Liberation in South Africa: A short history.* Cape Town: David Philip Publishers.

McAdam, Doug (1988) *Freedom Summer.* New York NY: Oxford University Press.

— (1996) 'The framing function of movement tactics: strategic dramaturgy in the American civil rights movement' in Doug McAdam, John D. McCarthy and N. Zald Mayer (eds) *Comparative Perspectives on Social Movements: Political opportunities, mobilizing structures, and cultural framings.*

Cambridge: Cambridge University Press.

— and Sidney Tarrow (2000) 'Nonviolence as contentious interaction'. *PS Political Science and Politics,* June. Available at www.apsanet.org (accessed 17 December 2003).

— — and Charles Tilly (2001) *Dynamics of Contention.* Cambridge: The Press Syndicate of the University of Cambridge.

McAllister, Pam (1982) *Reweaving the Web of Life: Feminism and nonviolence.* Philadelphia PA: New Society Publishers.

— (1988) *You Can't Kill the Spirit.* Philadelphia PA: New Society Publishers.

— (1991) *This River of Courage: Generations of women's resistance and action.* Philadelphia PA: New Society Publishers.

McCarthy, John D. and Mayer N. Zald (1980) 'Social movement industries: competition and cooperation among movement organizations'. *Research in Social Movements* 3: 1–20.

McCarthy, Ronald M. and Gene Sharp (1997) *Nonviolent Action: A research guide.* New York NY: Garland Publishing.

McGuinness, Kate (1994) 'Some thoughts on power and change'. Seminar synopsis, Program on Nonviolent Sanctions and Cultural Survival, Harvard University. Available at www.data.fas.harvard.edu/cfia/pnscs/DOCS/s94mcgui.htm (accessed 24 July 2000).

McKay, Bridge (1971) *Training for Nonviolent Action for High School Students: A handbook.* Philadelphia PA: Friends Peace Committee.

McLaren, P. (1988) 'On ideology and education: critical pedagogy

and the politics of education'.
Social Text 19–20: 153–85.

Meli, Francis (1988) *A History of the ANC: South Africa belongs to us.* Harare: Zimbabwe Publishing House.

Melucci, Alberto (1989) *Nomads of the Present.* London: Hutchinson Radius.

— (1996a) *Challenging Codes: Collective action in the information age.* Cambridge: Press Syndicate, University of Cambridge.

— (1996b) *The Playing Self: Person and meaning in the planetary society.* Cambridge: Press Syndicate, University of Cambridge.

Merritt, Karl Smith (1992) 'One dent at a time: a sociological perspective of the Plowshares Movement'. Master's thesis, Department of Sociology, University of Colorado.

Meyerding, Jane (1997) 'Women and nonviolent action in the United States since 1950' in Roger S. Powers and William B. Vogele (eds) *Protest, Power, and Change: An encyclopedia of nonviolent action from ACT-UP to women's suffrage.* New York NY: Garland Publishing.

— (1982) 'Reclaiming nonviolence: some thoughts for feminist womyn who used to be nonviolent, and vice versa' in Pam McAllister, *Reweaving the Web of Life: Feminism and nonviolence.* Philadelphia PA: New Society Publishers, pp. 5–15.

Miljöko (1981) *La Innerdalen leve!* Oslo: Miljöko.

Millgram, Stanley (1975) *Lydnad och auktoritet: Experimentsituationer, resultat och utvärdering.* Stockholm: Wahlström & Widstrand.

Mohl, Raymond A. (2003) 'Civil rights movements'. H-Net Book Review, Reconstruction Period Research Forum, 18 December. Available at www.afrigeneas.com/forum-reconstruction/index.cgi?noframes;read=70 (accessed 16 September 2012).

Montiel, Cristina Jayme (2001) 'Toward a psychology of structural peacebuilding' in Daniel J. Christie, Richard V. Wagner and Deborah DuNann Winter (eds) *Peace, Conflict, and Violence: Peace psychology for the 21st century.* Upper Saddle River NJ: Prentice Hall.

Morris, Aldon D. (1984) *The Origins of the Civil Rights Movement: Black communities organizing for change.* New York NY: Free Press.

Mortensen, Nils (2003) 'Den amerikanska pragmatismen' in Heine Andersen and Bo Kaspersen (eds) *Klassisk och modern samhällsteori.* Lund: Studentlitteratur, pp. 147–61.

Moser-Puangsuwan, Yeshua and Thomas Weber (2000) *Nonviolent Intervention Across Borders: A recurrent vision.* Honolulu: University of Hawai'i Press.

Moses, Greg (1997) *Revolution of Conscience: Martin Luther King, Jr., and the philosophy of nonviolence.* New York NY: Guilford Press.

Moyer, Bill (1990) *The Practical Strategist: Movement action plan (MAP) strategic theories for evaluating, planning, and conducting social movements.* San Francisco CA: Social Movement Empowerment Project.

MPD (1994) 'Workshop on marshalling & peacekeeping'. Cape Town: Institute for Multi-Party Democracy (MPD), 23–26 March.

Næss, Arne (1974) *Gandhi and Group Conflict.* Oslo: Universitetsforlaget.

— (2002) *Gandhi*. Stockholm: Natur och Kultur.

Nagler, Michael N. (1986) 'Non-violence' in Linus Pauling, Ervin Laszlo and Jong Youl Yoo (eds) *World Encyclopedia of Peace*, Volume 2. Oxford: Pergamon Press and Institute of International Peace Studies, pp. 72–8.

National Lesbian and Gay Civil Disobedience Action (1987) *Out & Outraged: Non-violent civil disobedience at the U.S. Supreme Court – for love, life & liberation, October 13, 1987, C.D. handbook*. Washington DC: National March on Washington for Lesbian and Gay Rights.

Nhat Hanh, Thich (1993) *Love in Action: Writings on nonviolent social change*. Berkeley CA: Parallax Press.

— (2003) *Creating True Peace: Ending violence in yourself, your family, your community, and the world*. New York NY: Free Press.

Nick, Volker, Volker Scheub and Christof Then (1993) *Mutlangen 1983–1987: Die Stationierung der Pershing II und die Kampagne Ziviler Ungehorsam bis zur Abrüstung*. Schorndorf: Windhueter.

Norenius, Ulf (1983) *Vägra leva på knä: Civilmotstånd för frigörelse och som försvar*. Gothenburg: Bokskogen and Haga Bokförlag.

Noresson, Jan-Åke (1985) *Kynnet som försätter berg*. Gothenburg: Bokskogen and Vinga Press.

O'Gorman, Frances (1983) *Base Communities in Brazil: Dynamics of a journey*. Rio de Janeiro: Base-Nuclar.

Oberschall, Anthony (1993) *Social Movements: Ideologies, interests, and identities*. New Brunswick NJ: Transaction Publishers.

Ofstad, Harald (1987) *Vårt förakt för svaghet*. Stockholm: Bokförlaget Prisma Magnum.

Olsen, Hinrich (ed.) (1986) *Wir Treten in den Un-Ruhestand: Dokumentation der 1 Seniorenblockade Mutlangen 8 bis 10 Mai 1986*. Mutlangen: Hinrich Olsen.

Oppenheimer, Martin and George Lakey (1965) *A Manual for Direct Action: Strategy and tactics for civil rights and all other nonviolent protest movements*. Chicago IL: Quadrangle Books.

Orjuela, Camilla (2004) 'Civil society in civil war: peace work and identity politics in Sri Lanka'. Thesis, Peace and Development Research Institute (Padrigu), University of Gothenburg.

Osgood, Charles E. (1962) *An Alternative to War or Surrender*. Urban IL: University of Illinois Press.

Österberg, Dag (1986) *Metasociologisk essä*. Gothenburg: Bokförlaget Korpen.

Ostergaard, Geoffrey (1985) *Nonviolent Revolution in India*. New Delhi: Gandhi Peace Foundation.

— (1986) 'Liberation and development: Gandhian and pacifist perspectives' in Gail Chester and Andrew Rigby (eds) *Articles of Peace: Celebrating fifty years of Peace News*. Bridport, Dorset: Prism Press, pp. 142–68.

Painke, Uwe (1991) 'Selbstbestimmtes Handeln in Situationen personaler Gewalt'. Degree coursework, Institute of Education, Tübingen University.

Pandya, Jayant (1994) *Gandhiji and his Disciples*. New Delhi: National Book Trust India.

Pantham, Thomas (1983) 'Thinking with Mahatma Gandhi: beyond liberal democracy'. *Political Theory* 11(2): 165–88.

— (1986) 'Habermas' practical discourse and Gandhi's satyagraha'. *Praxis-International* 6(2): 190–205.

Pelton, Leroy H. (1974) *The Psychology of Nonviolence*. Pergamon General Psychology Series Volume 48. New York NY: Pergamon Press.

Peterson, Abby (1997) *Neo-Sectarianism and Rainbow Coalitions: Youth and the drama of immigration in contemporary Sweden*. Aldershot: Ashgate Publishing.

— (2001) *Contemporary Political Protest: Essays on political militancy*. Aldershot: Ashgate.

Pileggi, Mary S. and Cindy Patton (2003) 'Introduction: Bourdieu and cultural studies'. *Cultural Studies* 17(3/4): 313–25.

Plummer, Dawn and Betsy Ranum (2002) 'Brazil's Landless Workers Movement – Movimiento de Trabajadores Rurales Sem Terra: MST'. *Social Policy* 33(1): 18–22.

Potorti, David (2003) *September 11th Families for Peaceful Tomorrows: Turning our grief into action for peace*. New York NY: RDV Books and Akashic Books.

Powell Bell, Inge (1968) *CORE and the Strategy of Non-violence*. New York NY: Random House.

Powers, Roger S. and William B. Vogele (eds) (1997) *Protest, Power, and Change: An encyclopedia of nonviolent action from ACT-UP to women's suffrage*. New York NY: Garland Publishing.

Queen, Christopher S. (1998) 'The peace wheel: nonviolent activism in the Buddhist tradition' in Daniel L. Smith-Christopher (ed.) *Subverting Hatred: The challenge of nonviolence in religious tradi-*

tions. Maryknoll NY: Orbis Books, pp. 25–47.

Rajan, Nalini (1991) 'Gandhi and Habermas: irreconcilable differences'. *Indian Journal of Social Science* 4(3): 415–23.

Randle, Michael (1994) *Civil Resistance*. London: Fontana Movements and Ideas.

Rasch, Olov (ed.) (1979) *Whyl finns överallt: Ett exempel på kärnkraftsmotstånd, skriven av 17 lärare och elever vid Marieborgs Folkhögskola*. Norrköping: Marieborgs Folkhögskola.

Rasmussen, Nina (2004) *Solvognen: Fortællinger fra vores ungdom*. Copenhagen: Rosinante.

Rawlinson, Roger (1986) *Communities of Resistance: Nuclear and chemical pollution cross frontiers and so did the protesters of the Upper Rhine*. Nonviolence in Action Series. London: Quaker Peace and Service.

Rawls, John (1971) *A Theory of Justice*. Cambridge MA: Belknap Press, Harvard University Press.

Ricoeur, Paul (1974) *The Conflict of Interpretations: Essays in hermeneutics*. Evanston IL: Northwestern University Press.

— (1981) 'The model of the text: meaningful action considered as a text' in Paul Ricoeur and John B. Thompson (eds) *Hermeneutics and the Human Sciences*. Cambridge: Cambridge University Press, pp. 197–221.

— (1993) *Från text till handling*. Stockholm: Brutus Östlings Bokförlag Symposium AB.

Rigby, Andrew (1974) *Alternative Realities: A study of communes and their members*. London: Routledge & Kegan Paul.

— (1986) 'Be practical, do the impossible: the politics of everyday life' in Gail Chester and Andrew Rigby (eds) *Articles of Peace: Celebrating fifty years of Peace News*. Bridport, Dorset: Prism Press, pp. 90–105.

— (1991) *Living the Intifada*. London: Zed Books.

— (2001) *Justice and Reconciliation: After the violence*. Boulder CO: Lynne Rienner Publishers.

— (2002) 'The possibilities and limitations of nonviolence: the Palestinian Intifada 1987–1991'. Paper presented at the seminar 'The Possibilities of Nonviolence', University of Gothenburg and Swedish Peace and Arbitration Society, April.

Ringen (1980) 'Innerdalen: Norge ved skilleveien'. *Ringen* 8/9.

Rosenberg, Morris and Ralph H. Turner (eds) (1990) *Social Psychology: Sociological perspectives*. New Brunswick NJ: Transaction Publishers.

Rosenberg, Tiina (2002) *Qeerfeministisk agenda*. Stockholm: Atlas.

Sahmat (1998) *Indian People in the Struggle for Freedom: Five essays*. New Delhi: Safdar Hashmi Memorial Trust (Sahmat).

Sangvai, Sanjay (2002) *The River and Life: People's struggle in the Narmada Valley*. Mumbai: Earthcare Books.

Sartre, Jean-Paul (1971) 'Förord' in Frantz Fanon, *Jordens Fördömda*. Stockholm: Rabén & Sjörgren.

Satha-Anand, Chaiwat (1981) 'The nonviolence prince'. Part of dissertation, University of Hawaii.

— (1991) 'From violent to nonviolent discourse' in Elise Boulding, Clovis Brigagao and Kevin Clements (eds) *Peace Culture and Society: Transnational research and*

dialogue. Boulder CO: Westview Press, pp. 124–32.

— (1996) 'Overcoming illusory division: between nonviolence as a pragmatic strategy and a way of life'. Paper presented at International University of Peoples' Institutions for Peace (IUPIP), Rovereto, Italy.

Schock, Kurt (2003) 'Nonviolent action and its misconceptions: insights for social scientists'. *Political Science and Politics* 4 (October): 705–12.

— (2005) *Unarmed Insurrections: People power movements in nondemocracies*. Minneapolis MN: University of Minnesota Press.

— (2013) 'The practice and study of civil resistance'. *Journal of Peace Research* 50(3): 277–90.

Scott King, Coretta (1983) *The Words of Martin Luther King, Jr*. New York NY: Newmarket Press.

Searle, John (1996) 'What is a speech act?' in Paul Cobley (ed.) *The Communication Theory Reader*. London: Routledge, pp. 263–81.

Seifert, Harvey (1965) *Conquest by Suffering: The process and prospects of nonviolent resistance*. Philadelphia PA: Westminster Press.

SFT (2000) *Students for a Free Tibet: SFT worldwide action for Tibet, organizer's guide, 1999–2000*. New York NY: Students for a Free Tibet (SFT).

Shah, Ghanshyam (2004) *Social Movements in India: A review of the literature*. New Delhi: Sage Publications India.

Sharp, Gene (1960) *Gandhi Wields the Weapon of Moral Power: Three case stories*. Ahmedabad: Navajivan Publishing House.

— (1971) *Exploring Nonviolent Alterna-*

tives. Second edition. Boston MA: Porter Sargent Publishers.

— (1973) *The Politics of Nonviolent Action: Parts One, Two and Three.* Boston MA: Porter Sargent Publishers and Extending Horizons Books.

— (1979) *Gandhi as a Political Strategist.* Boston MA: Porter Sargent Publishers and Extending Horizons Books.

— (1980) *Social Power and Political Freedom.* Boston MA: Porter Sargent Publishers and Extending Horizons Books.

— (1999) 'Nonviolent action' in Lester Kurtz (ed.) *Encyclopedia of Violence, Peace, & Conflict*, Volume 2. San Diego CA: Academic Press, pp. 567–74.

— (2004) *Waging Nonviolent Struggle: 20th century practice and 21st century potential.* Boston MA: Porter Sargent Publishers.

Sheeran, Michael J. (1983) *Beyond Majority Rule: Voteless decisions in the Religious Society of Friends.* Pennsylvania PA: Graphics Standard.

Shepard, Mark (1987) *Gandhi Today: A report on Mahatma Gandhi's successors.* Arcata CA: Simple Productions.

— (1990) *The Community of the Ark.* Arcata CA: Simple Productions.

Shoben Jr, E. Joseph, Philip Werdell and Durward Long (1970) 'Radical student organizations' in Julian Foster and Durward Long (eds) *Protest! Student activism in America.* New York NY: William Morrow & Company, pp. 202–22.

Shridharani, Krishnalal (2003 [1939]) *War without Violence.* Canton ME: Greenleaf Books.

Simmel, Georg (1970 [1908]) *Kamp!* Uppsala: Argos Förlags AB.

Smelser, Neil. J. (1995) *Sociology.* Englewood Cliffs NJ: Prentice Hall.

Smith, Michael P. and Kenneth L. Deutsch (eds) (1972) *Political Obligation and Civil Disobedience: Readings.* New York NY: Thomas Y. Crowell Company.

Snow, David A., R. Burke Rochford Jr., Steven K. Worden and Robert D. Benford (1986) 'Frame alignment processes, micromobilization, and movement participation'. *American Sociological Review* 51: 464–81.

Sommer, Henrik (2000) 'Bringing nonviolence back into the study of contentious politics'. *Politikon* 27(2): 255–75.

Sörensen, Majken and Stellan Vinthagen (2012) 'Nonviolent resistance and culture'. *Peace & Change* 37(3) (July): 444–70.

Springer, Simon (2014) 'Human geography without hierarchy'. *Progress in Human Geography* 38(3): 402–19.

Stangor, Charles G. (1999) 'Stereotyping' in A. S. R. Manstead and M. Hewstone (eds) *The Blackwell Encyclopedia of Social Psychology.* Oxford: Blackwell Publishers.

Stedile, João (2002) 'Landless battalions: the Sem Terra Movement of Brazil'. *New Left Review* 15 (May/June). Available at http://newleftreview.org/II/15/joao-pedro-stedile-landless-battalions (accessed 6 August 2015).

Steger, Manfred B. (2000) *Gandhi's Dilemma: Nonviolent principles and nationalist power.* New York NY: St Martin's Press.

Sternstein, Wolfgang (1978) *Überall ist Whyl: Bürgerinitiativen gegen Atomanlagen aus der Arbeit eines Aktionsforschers.* Frankfurt am Main: Des Umweltwissenschaftlichen Instituts and Haag Herchen Verlag.

Stokke, Kristian (2002) 'Habitus, capital and fields: conceptualizing the capacity of actors in local politics'. Paper presented to the colloquium on Local Politics and Democratisation in Developing Countries, University of Oslo, 12 March.

Stryker, Sheldon (1980) *Symbolic Interactionism: A social structural version*. Menlo Park CA: Benjamin/ Cummings Publishing Company.

Summers-Effler, Erika (2002) 'The micro potential for social change: emotion, consciousness, and social movement formation'. *Sociological Theory* 20(1) (March): 41–60.

Swamy, Dalip S. and Kavaljit Singh (1994) *Against Consensus: Three years of public resistance to structural adjustment programme*. Delhi: Public Interest Research Group.

Taylor, Richard (1988) *Against the Bomb: The British Peace Movement 1958–1965*. Oxford: Clarendon Press, Oxford University Press.

Taylor, Verta and Nancy Whittier (1995) 'Analytical approaches to social movement culture: the culture of the women's movement' in Hank Johnston and Bert Klandermans (eds) (1995) *Social Movements and Culture*. Minneapolis MN: University of Minnesota Press, pp. 163–87.

Tester, Keith (2000) *Sociologi och moral*. Lund: Studentlitteratur.

Thomson, Mark (1993) *Gandhi and His Ashrams*. Bombay: Popular Prakashan.

Thoreau, Henry David (1977 [1849]) *Om civil motstånd*. Stockholm: Arkturus Förlag.

Thörn, Håkan (1997a) 'Modernitet, sociologi och sociala rörelser', Monograph No. 62. Part 1(2) of a dissertation, Department of Sociology, University of Gothenburg.

— (1997b) *Rörelser i det moderna: Politik, Modernitet och kollektiv identitet i Europa 1789–1989*. Stockholm: Tiden Atena. Originally Part 2(2) of a dissertation, Department of Sociology, University of Gothenburg.

Tilly, Charles (2004) *Social Movements 1768–2004*. Boulder CO: Paradigm Publishers.

Toh, Swee-Hin and Virginia Floresca-Cawagas (1999) 'Institutionalization of nonviolence' in Lester Kurtz and Jennifer Turpin (eds) *Encyclopedia of Violence, Peace, and Conflict*. Volume 2. San Diego CA: Academic Press, pp. 211–29.

Tracy, James (1996) *Direct Action: Radical pacifism from the Union Eight to the Chicago Seven*. Chicago IL: University of Chicago Press.

Trainingskollektive Graswurzel-bewegung (1984) *Methodensammlung Training für Gewaltfreie Aktion*. Updated version of the 1980 original. Cologne: Training-skollektive Graswurzelbewegung. Loose pages collected in a folder (copy with author).

Turner, Ralph and Lewis Killian (1987) *Collective Behavior*. 3rd edition. Englewood Cliffs NJ: Prentice Hall.

Turner, Victor (1969) *The Ritual Process: Structure and anti-structure*. London: Routledge and Kegan Paul.

Van de Sande, Mathijs (2013) 'The prefigurative politics of Tahrir Square: an alternative perspective on the 2011 revolutions'. *Res Publica* 19: 223–39. doi 10.1007/ s11158-013-9215-9.

Vander Zanden, James W. (1963) 'The non-violent resistance movement against segregation'. *American Journal of Sociology* 68(5): 544–50.

— (1969) 'The non-violent resistance movement against segregation' in Barry McLaughlin (ed.) *Studies in Social Movements: A social psychological perspective*. New York NY: Free Press.

VanEtten Casey, William S. J. (ed.) (1971) *The Berrigans*. New York NY: Avon Books.

Veltmeyer, Henry and James Petras (2002) 'The social dynamics of Brazil's Rural Landless Workers' Movement: ten hypotheses on successful leadership'. *Canadian Review of Sociology and Anthropology* 39(1): 79–96.

Vidal, Denis, Gilles Tarabout and Eric Meyer (eds) (2003) *Violence/Nonviolence: Some Hindu perspectives*. New Delhi: Manohar Publishers & Distributors.

Vinthagen, Stellan (1997a) 'Direktdemokratins svårigheter: En studie av den tyska Graswurzelrörelsen och dess organisation Graswurzelrevolution, Föderation Gewaltfreier Aktionsgruppen (FöGA)'. BA thesis in sociology, Department of Sociology, University of Gothenburg.

— (1997b) 'En direktdemokratisk organisations historia: En undersökningsrapport utifrån en studie av tyska Graswurzelrörelsen och dess organisation Graswurzelrevolution, Föderation Gewaltfreier Aktionsgruppen (FöGA)'. Empirical appendix to the BA thesis in sociology, Department of Sociology, University of Gothenburg.

— (1997c) 'Symboler i rörelse: Om sociala rörelser som tilltal'. BA thesis in international relations, Peace and Development Research Institute (Padrigu), University of Gothenburg.

— (1998) 'Power and nonviolent movements'. Research paper, Peace and Development Research Institute (Padrigu), University of Gothenburg.

— (2001) 'Makt och Motstånd' in Leif Eriksson and Björn Hettne (eds) *Makt och Internationella relationer*. Lund: Studentlitteratur.

— (2002) 'Motståndets globalisering' in Mikael Löfgren and Masoud Vatankhah (eds) *Vad hände med Sverige i Göteborg?* Stockholm: Ordfront Förlag.

— (2003a) 'Motståndet mot den nya världsordningen' in Janne Flyghed and Magnus Hörnqvist (eds) *Laglöst land*. Stockholm: Ordfront Förlag, pp. 232–64.

— (2003b) 'A movement culture of nonviolent action'. Paper presented at the conference 'Fattiga & Rika', Lund University, January.

— (2005) 'Ickevåldsaktion: En social praktik av motstånd och konstruktion'. Dissertation, Department of Peace and Development Research (Padrigu), University of Gothenburg.

— and Sean Taudin Chabot (2002) 'The relational and constructionist dynamics of nonviolent action'. Paper presented at a conference, Tromsö University, November.

Vogele, William B. and Doug Bond (1997) 'Nonviolent struggle: the contemporary practice of nonviolent action' in Roger S. Powers and William B. Vogele (eds) *Protest, Power, and Change: An* encyclopedia of nonviolent action from ACT-UP to women's suffrage. New York NY: Garland Publishing.

Walker, Charles (1973) *Training for Nonviolent Action: Some history, analysis, reports of surveys.* Haverford PA: Nonviolent Action Research Project, Center for Nonviolent Conflict Resolution, Haverford College.

Wallensteen, Peter (2002) *Understanding Conflict Resolution: War, peace and the global system.* London: Sage Publications.

War Resisters' League (1989) *Handbook for Nonviolent Action.* New York NY: War Resisters' League.

Waterhouse, Nathan (2005) *Design Improv: An investigation into creating a design method for interaction design that is based on the ideas of improvisational theatre.* Ivrea: Interaction Design Institute Ivrea. Available at http://people. interaction-ivrea.it/n.waterhouse/ thesis/ (accessed 18 August 2005).

Waters, Malcolm (1994) *Modern Sociological Theory.* London: Sage Publications.

Weber, Max (1974) *From Max Weber: Essays in sociology*, edited by H. H. Gerth and C. Wright Mills (eds). London: Routledge & Kegan Paul.

Weber, Thomas (1997) *On the Salt March.* New Delhi: HarperCollins Publishers India.

Wehr, Paul, Heidi Burgess and Guy Burgess (1994) *Justice without Violence.* Boulder CO: Lynne Rienner Publishers.

Winther Jörgensen, Marianne and Louise Phillips (1999) *Diskursanalys som teori och metod.* Lund: Studentlitteratur.

Wirmark, Bo (1974) *Kamp mot kriget:*

Buddisterna i Vietnam. Falköping: Gummessons Boktryckeri AB.

Wittner, Lawrence S. (1997) *The Struggle Against the Bomb. Volume 2: Resisting the bomb: a history of the world nuclear disarmament movement 1945–1970.* Stanford CA: Stanford University Press.

Woehrle, Lynne M. (1997) 'Feminism' in Roger S. Powers and William B. Vogele (eds) *Protest, Power, and Change: An encyclopedia of nonviolent action from ACT-UP to women's suffrage.* New York NY: Garland Publishing.

Women's Encampment for a Future of Peace & Justice (1983) *Seneca Army Depot, NY: Resource handbook.* Romulus NY: Women's Encampment for a Future of Peace & Justice.

Yoder, John H. (ed.) (1990) *En beväpnad man anfaller din familj: Vad gör du då?* Örebro: Bokförlaget Libris.

Young, Iris Marion (2000) *Att kasta tjejkast: Texter om feminism och rättvisa.* Stockholm: Atlas.

Zald, Mayer N. and John D. McCarthy (1994) *Social Movements in an Organizational Society: Collected essays.* New Brunswick NJ: Transaction Publishers.

Zelter, Angie (ed.) (2001) *Trident on Trial: The case for people's disarmament.* Edinburgh: Luath Press.

Zietlow, Carl P. (1977) *A Reflective History of Training for Nonviolent Action in the Civil Rights and Peace Movements 1942–1972, USA.* Grand Rapids MI: Ammon Hennacy House.

Zunes, Stephen, Lester R. Kurtz and Sarah Beth Asher (eds) (1999) *Nonviolent Social Movements: A geographical perspective.* Malden MA: Blackwell Publishers.

INDEX

of suffering, 215–49; withdrawal to ashram, 280 see also dialectic, Ghandian; and fasting, by Gandhi
Gandhi studies, 48, 52
Gandhian techniques, 24–37, 104
gender, power hierarchy of, 255
general strikes, 284
Genova, protest movement in, 285
Germany: anti-nuclear campaigning in, 4, 89–92; civil disobedience movement in, 82–4; peace movement in, 52–3
goal-rationality, 88–93
God, as truth, 28
Goffman, Erving, 110, 209, 226–7, 229–30; drama model of, 22
good will, perennial possibility of, 219
Goss, Jean, 145
Goss-Mayr, Hildegard, 145
graha (holding onto), 134
Graswurzelbewegung (West Germany), 58–9, 95–6, 111
Graswurzelrevolution: Föderation Gewaltfreier Aktionsgruppen (FÖGA), 58, 272
Greenham Common peace camp, 5
Gregg, Richard, 213; The Power of Non-Violence, 37–8, 101
Grønn Aksjon Innerdalen, 288
group boundaries, 297; creation of, 294
guerrilla warfare, 40

Habermas, Jürgen, 72, 98–9, 106, 110, 120, 134, 135–42, 150, 155, 159, 166, 261, 283, 300, 318, 326, 328; consensus theory, 128; ideal speech situation, 22; theory of communication, 22, 209; typology of action, 82, 100–1, 126–31, 299, 306, 319
habitus, 182, 265–70; definition of, 265; internalisation of, 271; modification of, 270–3, 289; production of, 266–7; training in, 275–7; various views of, 268

handbooks see training, in nonviolence, handbooks
Hardiman, David, 35
hartal form of resistance, 54
Harvard University, 44
hassle lines, 262–3
hatred, 131
healing circles, 287
Hegel, G. W. F., 323
Helvey, Robert, 45
hermeneutics, 93, 95
himsa, 30 see also ahimsa
Hinduism, 24, 26, 29, 239
homosexuality: defined as illness, 202–3; outing of, 203
honesty of statements, 137
hunger strikes, 223
hypotheses, system of, 35–7

ideal speech situation, 99, 135, 136, 144, 159, 299, 300, 318, 319, 320, 328
identity: borders of, transgression of, 239; construction of, 91–2, 116; negotiation of, 92
imperfection, universal, 332
imprisonment, 27, 54, 58, 60, 105, 108, 113, 118, 154, 171, 221, 251, 262, 284; exemplary behaviour during, 32; fear of, 241
improvisation, 225–6; mutual, 236–7
inclusive identification, 238–49
India, 24, 25–6, 288; liberation movement in, 2, 33–4, 52, 54, 158, 202, 207, 218, 280, 283; liberation of, 184–5; resistance to structural adjustment in, 4; under colonialism, 215
Indian National Congress, 54
influence, effect of, 121
initiative, spaces for, creation of, 202
injustice, exposing of, 218, 253
Innerdalen (Norway), dams resistance movement in, 287
instrumental action see action, instrumental

with, 209; seen as blessing, 143; softening of, 212; supporting of, 133; trusting of, 332; view of, 130 *see also* enemy; othering of the opponent, 254; *and* taking the other into consideration
othering of the opponent, 254
Outrage, kiss-in campaign, 203

pacifism, 25
Painke, Uwe, 154
Palestine, liberation struggle in, 52, 56
Palestine Liberation Organisation (PLO), 56
Pan Africanist Congress (PAC), 240
parallel institutions, construction of, 35, 200, 258, 277, 286
paraphrasing, 149
paraskeuaz, 262
parliament, 170; as locus of power, 181
Parsons, Talcott, 105
participation, equal, creating possibility of, 146–7
Pashtuns, 262
patriarchy, 255
peace, achieved through peace, 322
perfection in nonviolence, 277–8
performative contradiction, 138
personal sharing, 148, 149
Persson, Lars-Eric, 232
plebs, 177–8
Plowshares Movement, 123
polarisation, 51, 113, 207; of identities, 238
police, 134–5, 162, 165, 202, 204, 231–2, 241, 295; choir sing at protest, 236; intervention of, 102–3, 104; strikes of, 315
Portillo-Barrow, Adiana, 1
power, 137, 191–5; as a relationship of struggle, 183; as consent, 168–95; as participatory subordination, 167; as productive discipline, 175–8; as relinquishing of responsibility, 189; as special case of interaction, 195; as subordination, 176, 178–80,

180–1, 195, 196, 199, 205; breaking of, 150–1, 151–61, 163, 255, 277, 301, 302, 309–10, 313, 314, 315, 317, 318 (nonviolent, 165–205); counteracting influence of, 146; created in relationships, 214; critical research into, 166; definition of, 176; dissolving of, 205; expressed through the individual, 176; given away, 186; given to those in power, 43; hindrance of, 204; in dialogue, 147; mythologised as self-acting techniques and discursive structures, 177; pluralistic view of, 40; political, 39–40, 169 (controlled at origin, 170–1); production of, 167; refusal of, 184; relations of, transformation of, 269; reproduction of, 190; social sources of, 42; symbols of, 181, 190; theories of, 167; total, 196; undermining structures of, 308, 309; understood as monolith, 198
power breaking *see* power, breaking of
power 'over', 168
power relations, addressing of, 22
powerlessness, 192, 198
practical knowledge, 11
practical skills, new, learning of, 274
pragmatic, use of term, 8
praying in protests, 2
pre-logical logic of practice, 266
prefigurative politics, 162, 209, 260–1, 272; concept of, 285–98
press releases, use of, 90
preventing the other's activity, 314
prison, 187; breaking into, 202–3; changing views of, 284; hunger strikes in, 223 *see also* imprisonment
privileges, threat to, 165
professions, engaged in pursuit of campaigns, 83
property, destruction of, 217, 332, 333
protest culture, 298